AF323423

Stocks, Bonds, and the Investment Horizon

Decision-Making for the Long Run

Stocks, Bonds, and the Investment Horizon

Decision-Making for the Long Run

Haim Levy

The Hebrew University of Jerusalem, Israel

World Scientific

NEW JERSEY · LONDON · SINGAPORE · BEIJING · SHANGHAI · HONG KONG · TAIPEI · CHENNAI · TOKYO

Published by

World Scientific Publishing Co. Pte. Ltd.

5 Toh Tuck Link, Singapore 596224

USA office: 27 Warren Street, Suite 401-402, Hackensack, NJ 07601

UK office: 57 Shelton Street, Covent Garden, London WC2H 9HE

Library of Congress Cataloging-in-Publication Data
Names: Levy, Haim, author.
Title: Stocks, bonds, and the investment horizon : decision-making for the long run /
    Haim Levy, The Hebrew University of Jerusalem, Israel.
Description: Hackensack, NJ : World Scientific, [2022] |
    Includes bibliographical references and index.
Identifiers: LCCN 2021055873 | ISBN 9789811250149 (hardcover) |
    ISBN 9789811250156 (ebook) | ISBN 9789811250163 (ebook other)
Subjects: LCSH: Investments. | Stocks. | Bonds. | Portfolio management.
Classification: LCC HG4521 .L6326 2022 | DDC 658.15/54--dc23/eng/20211213
LC record available at https://lccn.loc.gov/2021055873

British Library Cataloguing-in-Publication Data
A catalogue record for this book is available from the British Library.

For any available supplementary material, please visit
https://www.worldscientific.com/worldscibooks/10.1142/12665#t=suppl

Desk Editor: Lai Ann

Typeset by Stallion Press
Email: enquiries@stallionpress.com

To My Family

Contents

Chapter 6.   Risk and the Horizon: The Discounting Cash-Flows Approach with Rothschild and Stiglitz's Definition of Risk   285

Chapter 7.   Stock Risk: Do Historical Crashes Tell the Whole Story? The Black Swan Hypothesis   325

Chapter 8.   Discrete and Continuous Returns and the Investment Horizon   359

Preface

Most theoretical and empirical models in economics, and particularly in finance, assume a given predetermined investment horizon, typically without an elaborate discussion and justification for the selected investment horizon. For example, the Markowitz mean–variance analysis and the Sharpe capital asset pricing model (CAPM), two pillars of modern finance, simply assume a "one-period" model with no discussion regarding the selected period, which could be a decade, one year, one month, or even one day. These models remain silent regarding the scenario with heterogeneous horizons, where for example some investors invest for one year and others invest for one month. By the same token, empirical studies which apply these theoretical models, test their validity, or measure the individual asset's risk in the equilibrium context, namely the CAPM's beta, employ various horizons. The majority of the empirical studies assume a horizon of one month, hence employ monthly rates of return in the empirical tests. Presumably, the empirical motivation for the employing of monthly rather than annual returns is to increase the number of available observations.

Practitioners take two approaches: those reporting the *ex-post* performance of various funds, namely the performance measures suggested by Sharpe, Jensen, and Treynor, typically employ monthly rates of return, implicitly assuming that the investors' horizon is one-month. On the other hand, the mangers of life-cycle mutual funds believe that the investment horizon is important, and also that stocks become more attractive than bonds for longer horizons, hence they decrease the stocks' weight in the portfolio as savers age and the horizon until retirement decreases. Thus, the mangers of life-cycle mutual funds pay attention to the investment horizon as they distinguish between short and long investment horizon.

Does the assumed investment horizon matter? Surprisingly, even if the returns follow the identical independent distribution (*i.i.d.*) process, the theoretical as well as the empirical results are not invariant to the assumed investment horizon. For example, employing the same *ex-post* data, say of the last 10 years, we may find that fund A outperforms fund B with monthly rates of return but the opposite holds if the annual rates of return are employed. Thus, the way one "slices" the available data into pieces affects the result even with *i.i.d.*, let alone when the returns are serially correlated. Conducting empirical studies with monthly rates of returns to validate a theoretical model or to explain stocks price behavior may be inadequate if investors make investment decisions with a different planned horizon.

This book is devoted to the effect of the investment horizon on the main issues in finance. This is done once by assuming *i.i.d.*, and once by relying on actual historical data, which may be serially correlated. We do not always provide the ultimate correct answer to the various issues analyzed in this book, but rather pinpoint the possible changes of the results with changes in the assumed investment horizon. We believe that it is important that academics and investors are aware of the effect of the employed horizon on the obtained results. Particularly, investors should first determine the desired investment horizon, and only then select the portfolio which is optimal for their specific horizon. Thus, investors may hold different optimal portfolios even in the case that they have homogenous expectations.

I would like to thank the students of the University of Illinois, University of California, Berkeley, Wharton School of Business, University of Florida, and Hebrew University for their role in the development of many ideas presented in this book. Preparing the teaching material for these students has motivated my research in this area and led to the development of this book.

I would like to thank my coauthors of papers related to the topic of this book, from whom I have learnt a lot:

Harry Markowitz, Paul Samuelson, Giora Hanoch, David Levhari, Fred Arditti, Gideon Schwarz, Moshe Leshno, Marshall Sarnat, Jacob Paroush, Azriel Levy, Yitzhak Venezia, Allon Cohen, Ilan Guttman, Avner Wolf, Turan Bali, Benzion Barlev, Isabel Tkatch, Ran Duchin, Yoram Kroll, and Moshe Levy.

I owe special thanks to Matan Gibson who provided excellent research assistance, and went above and beyond.

Finally, I would like to thank Roberto Spindel and Lai Ann from World Scientific for working with me, and making this book happen.

Introduction

Most theoretical and empirical studies in finance assume, explicitly or implicitly, a one-period investment model — typically a period of one month or one year. For example, Markowitz's[1] portfolio selection model and Sharpe[2] and Lintner's[3] equilibrium capital asset pricing model (CAPM) use one-period models. Testing empirically the CAPM and other theoretical models is also generally done by employing monthly or annual rates of return, e.g., see Fama and French,[4] and Sharpe.[5] However, some investors plan to invest for a relatively long time period, certainly for more than one month or one year. Thus, the mismatch between monthly rates of return employed and the longer actual horizon may induce an economic distortion.

To the best of our knowledge, Tobin[6] was the first to analyze the effect of the assumed investment horizon on the mean–variance (M–V) efficient set of risky assets. He shows that, under the independent and identically distributed assumption (*i.i.d.*) on the return, an

---

[1]Markowitz, H. (1952). Portfolio selection. *The Journal of Finance* 7(1), 77–91.

[2]Sharpe, W. F. (1964). Capital asset prices: A theory of market equilibrium under conditions of risk. *The Journal of Finance* 425–442.

[3]Lintner, J. (1965). Security prices, risk and the maximal gains from diversification. *The Journal of Finance* 20(4), 587–615.

[4]Fama, E. F. and K. R. French (1992). The cross-section of expected stock returns. *The Journal of Finance* 47(2), 427–465.

[5]Sharpe, W. F. (1966). Mutual fund performance. *The Journal of Business* 39(1), 119–138.

[6]Tobin, J. (1965). The theory of portfolio selection. In Hann, F. U. and F. P. Brechling (Eds.), *The Theory of Interest Rates,* London.

asset (or a portfolio) which is M–V inefficient for a short investment horizon may be M–V efficient for a long investment horizon. However, any asset which is M–V multi-period inefficient must be also one-period M–V inefficient. Thus, the assumed investment horizon plays an important role in selecting the optimal investment from the efficient set by investors with different investment horizons.

It is important to emphasize that assuming a relatively long investment horizon does not mean that investors cannot revise their portfolio periodically. For example, suppose that an investor plans to invest for retirement, say for 30 years. Given the current estimated distribution of return (which may be objective or subjective) of various assets, say stocks and bonds, corresponding to a date 30 years in the future, a decision may be made to allocate 70% to stocks and 30% to bonds. After one year has elapsed, due to changes in the economy, this investor may revise the estimated distribution of the return (corresponding to a date 29 years ahead) and may change their portfolio to allocate say 50% to stocks and 50% to bonds. Thus, having a long-planned investment horizon does not imply that revisions are not allowed. Notwithstanding, faced with the same assets, and even with the same profitability and risk estimates, a 70-year-old investor with a relatively short investment horizon may have a completely different optimal investment than a 30-year-old investor who plans to invest for 40 years. Thus, the planned investment horizon plays a crucial role in selecting the optimal investment.[7]

The importance of the assumed investment horizon for choosing the optimal investment (particularly of stocks and bonds) has

---

[7]In the financial literature, the continuous time model is also employed, namely the investor is assumed to revise their portfolio instantaneously. Despite the theoretical importance of this model, in practice, even a negligible transaction cost would ruin these models, as the expected net return, including the transaction costs, would be negative. For the continuous time models, see Merton, R. C. (1990). *Continuous-Time Finance*, Cambridge, MA: Basil Blackwell Inc. Another methodology for multi-period investment is the dynamic programming suggested by Mossin. This methodology assumes knowledge of the individual preferences and, in addition, it is practically very difficult to employ. For more details, see Mossin, J. (1968). Optimal multi-period portfolio choices. *Journal of Business* 41(2), 215–229.

increased rapidly in the last few decades due to two main factors: a continuous increase in life expectancy, and very low prevailing interest rates. Realizing the increase in life expectancy and the need for long-term investments, life cycle mutual funds have grown rapidly, suggesting different investment recipes to investors with different investment horizons. Let us elaborate on these two important factors.

A century ago, with life expectancy at about 40 years (see Figure 1), saving for pension was unnecessary, but nowadays, with a life expectancy of 80 years or even more in many Western countries, one should plan investment–consumption behavior such that there are enough savings for retirement, which could last for 2–3 decades. The second issue is related to the available savings vehicle. In previous decades, the risk-free interest rate was high enough to allow investors to accumulate some wealth in bonds for retirement. However, in the last two decades, the risk-free interest rate, as well as the interest rate on bonds with moderate risk, in most Western countries has been very low, and in certain countries, it is even negative in real terms, implying that the relative attractiveness of bonds has decreased relative to the 1980s when the interest rate was relatively high. Let us discuss each of these two factors affecting the investment strategy for the long run.

Figure 1(a) presents the life expectancy in a sample of countries for the period 1543 to 2019 and Figure 1(b) focuses on the more relatively recent years of 1950–2019.

As we can see from Figure 1(a), life expectancy was less than 40 years in some countries even after the year 1900 (let alone before this year), and since then, life expectancy has tended to increase, albeit with some fluctuations. This is true for countries like Ethiopia and India with relatively low life expectancy, as well as Japan, South Korea, the United Kingdom, and the United States with relatively high life expectancy. As can be seen from both Figures 1(a) and 1(b), both the United Kingdom and the United States started with relatively high life expectancies compared to the rest of the world. Due to a declining increase rate in life expectancy in these two countries, together with a rising increase rate in the rest of the world, this gap has been shrinking over the past few decades. In

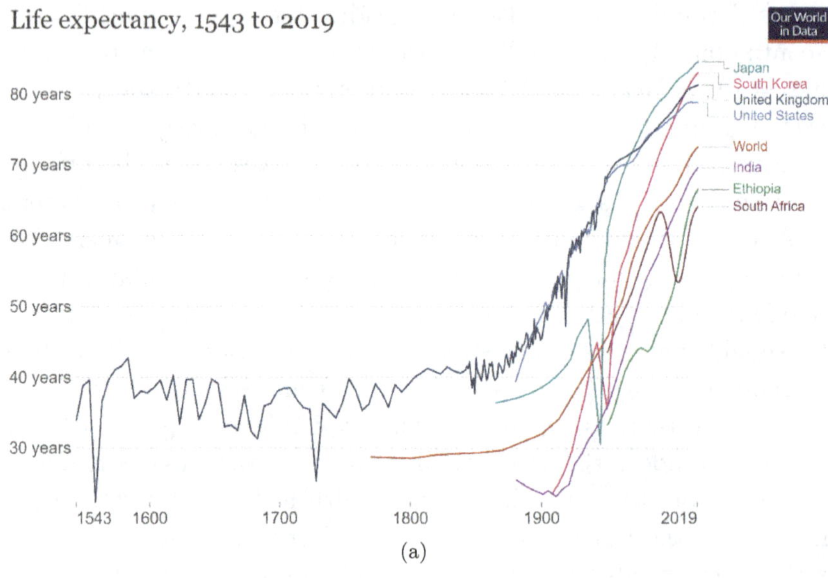

(a)

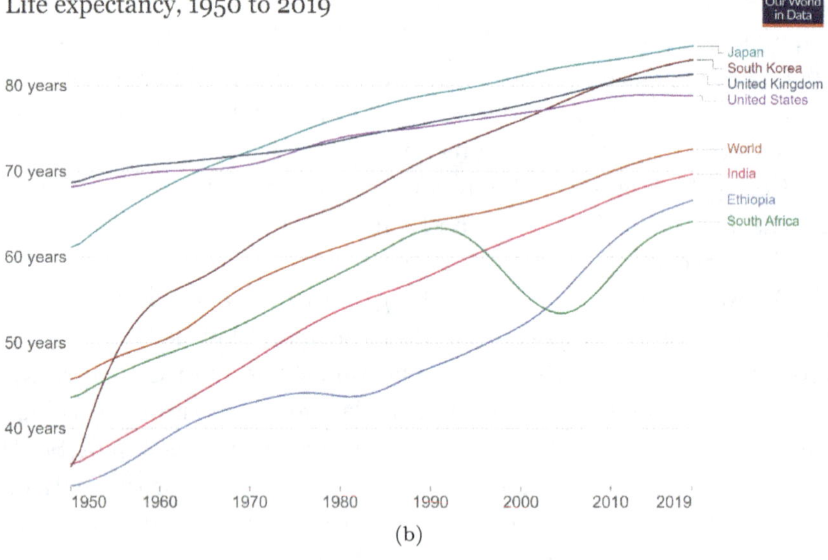

(b)

Figure 1: Life expectancy trends of selected countries: (a) Life expectancy 1543 to 2019; (b) Life expectancy 1950 to 2019.

Source: Rily, J. C. (2005). Estimates of regional and global life expectancy, 1800–2001. *Population and Development Review* 31(3), 537–543; Infra, C.L.I.O. (2015). Clio Infra Data Project; and UN Population Division (2019), OurWorldIn-Data.org.

fact, demographic research suggests that at the beginning of the 19th century, no country in the world had a life expectancy greater than 40 years, whereas today, a life expectancy of 80 years is quite common.

Figure 1(b) focuses on the more recent period, the years 1950–2019. During this period, life expectancy increased rapidly due to substantial health improvements. In this figure, it is shown that the life expectancy in Ethiopia, South Africa, and India increased from less than 40 years to 60–70 years in less than seven decades. Worldwide, the increase in life expectancy, on average, has risen from less than 50 years to more than 70 years. Thus, roughly every year, 0.39 years have been added to the life expectancy. In the richest countries, life expectancy in 2019 was over 80 years. For example, in Spain, Switzerland, Italy, and Australia, life expectancy was over 83 years, and in Japan, it was close to 85 years. Thus, even under the realistic assumption that this trend in the increase in life expectancy will not continue in the future, with the existing life expectancy in many countries, people are living for a long time after retirement; hence, funds should be saved for this period — savings which were not needed about 100 years ago. For example, in 2020, the retirement age in Japan was raised to 65. This means that in Japan, one needs to save for about 20 years of consumption after the retirement age.

The second issue, which is related to the previous one, is the low prevailing interest rate, particularly over the last two decades. Figure 2 presents the nominal one-year interest rate on United States Treasury bonds, the inflation rate, and the implied real interest rate. As we can see from this figure, in recent years, the real interest rate was in the negative territory. The low interest rate also characterized longer-term treasury bonds.

This negative real interest rate that has prevailed in the past may change in the future and may even become positive; hence, uncertainty about the future return on bonds plays a central role for investors. However, more relevant and more interesting for investors are the forward-looking real interest rates which are relevant for savers who are beginning to save for pensions in 2021. Treasury Inflation-Protected Securities (TIPS) provide the yield to maturity

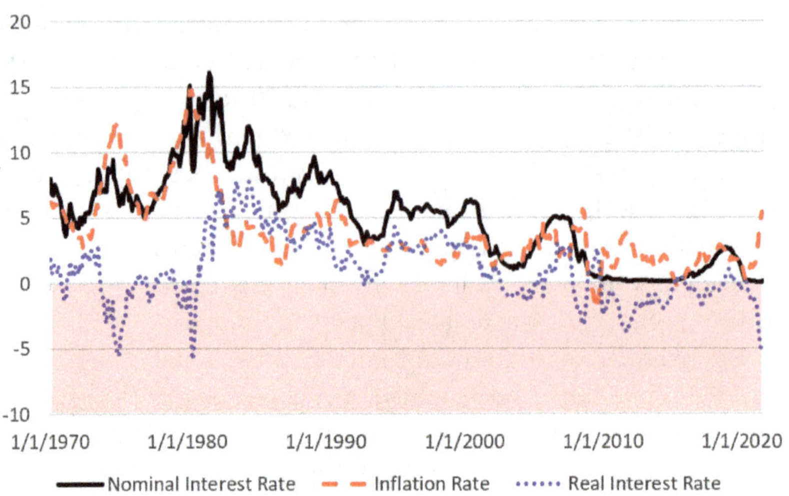

Figure 2: The real interest rate from January 1970 to July 2021.

Interpretation: The real interest rate is calculated as the difference between the **nominal interest rate** and the inflation rate. The chart above displays the nominal interest rate of a 1-year United States Treasury bond, the United States **inflation rate**, and the resulting one-year **real interest rate**. Inflation is defined as the yearly percentage change in the consumer price index (CPI). When inflation is high, prices for goods and services rise, and thus the purchasing power per unit of currency decreases. The chart shows that, adjusted for inflation, the yields on United States Treasury bonds (blue dotted line) have often been negative.

Source: longtermtrends.net.

in real terms. On August 9, 2021, the real yield on 10-year TIPS was -1.049% and on 30-year TIPS, which mature 30 years from the year 2021, it was -0.291%.[8] These figures are relevant for investors who wish to buy these bonds in 2021 and hold them for 10 years, and alternatively 30 years. This is terrible economic news for young people who are starting to save in 2021: For those who invest in 30-year TIPS, a yield to maturity of -0.291% implies that for each \$100 invested in 2021, after 30 years they will receive, in real terms, only about \$92. For older people who invest in year 2021 for 10 years, for each \$100 invested after 10 years, in real terms, they will receive, in real terms, only about \$90. Of course, one can obtain a larger

---

[8]https://www.wsj.com/market-data/bonds/tips.

expected yield by investing in risky long-term corporate bonds, but at the cost of being exposed to a larger risk.

The combination of increasing longevity and low interest rates spell economic disasters for current and future retirees. This phenomenon is not new, and is well known to economists and politicians. For example, Poterba[9] warned in his 2014 study of serious economic consequences of the increase in life expectancy accompanied with a decrease in the yield on TIPS. The situation is much more severe in 2021 than it was in 2013, the year to which he relates his study. In 2013, the yield on 20-year TIPS was 0.75%, while in 2021 it was negative, –0.0486%. Thus, for each \$100 invested in 2013 after 20 years, in real terms, one would have about \$116, while the corresponding figure for investors who began investing in the year 2021 is only about \$90; hence, the economic situation of retirees continues to deteriorate. While many investors may dislike low certain returns, they certainly do not tolerate a negative certain rate of return, which presumably is a factor affecting the boom in stock markets around the world during these negative interest rate years.

While the increase in life expectancy, particularly if one is in good health, presumably increases the individual's general welfare, from a purely economic point of view, the low interest rates and the increase in life expectancy are bad news for retirees. In this book, we try to explore alternative investment strategies that may mitigate the economic challenge posed by the two factors discussed previously. We focus on the investment in stocks and risky bonds for various investment horizons. It is well known that the expected return of an investment in stocks is larger than that of bonds. Moreover, based on the past returns of about a century, the probability of ending up with larger wealth by investing in stocks, rather than in bonds, increases with the horizon. Therefore, these facts tempt one to conclude that the longer the horizon, the larger the investment weight allocated to stocks should be. Generally, this is a hasty conclusion

---

[9]Poterba, J. M. (2014). Retirement security in an aging population. *American Economic Review* 104(5), 1–30.

because the most negative return on stocks is more negative than the most negative return on risky bonds, and this gap in favor of bonds increases with the horizon. Thus, the choice of stocks or bonds, or a mix of these two types of assets, may change with the horizon, but the desired direction of these changes is ambiguous as it depends on the individual's tolerance to this risk located in the left tails of the distributions of the returns on stocks and bonds.

In most of this book, we do not provide an investment recipe for the individual investor; hence, there is no need for information on individual investor risk tolerance (that is, there is no need for information on the utility function). Rather, we analyze the changes in the general investment rules with the horizon, like the M–V and stochastic dominance (SD) rules. These rules rely only on partial information on preferences, e.g., risk aversion. We also analyze, theoretically and empirically, how the optimal investment weights in stocks and bonds as recommended by these two general rules change with the horizon. In the empirical parts, we rely on about one century of data on rates of return on stocks and bonds. Thus, we assume that the historical risks in the stock and bond market reflect the future risks well. Yet, to be on the conservative side, in some tests, we also consider possible appearances of black swan events,[10] hence incorporate additional future risk to the investment in stocks — risks which were not observed in the last century.

Yet, there are future major risks, not analyzed in this book, which may affect both the stock and the bond markets: global warming, cyber terrorism, potential nuclear war, and a virus pandemic are a few of these risks. The magnitude of the effect of these risks on the capital market is hard to predict. For example, with the coronavirus, one would expect a crash in the stock market. Instead, the stock market boomed: for example, the S&P 500 stock index adjusted price was about 3,380 on February 15, 2020 (a date when the pandemic

---

[10]See Nassim, N. T. (2007). *The Black Swan: The Impact of the Highly Improbable.* Random House, New York. For incorporating black swan events into the analysis, see Chapter 7.

started hitting most countries in the world), and it increased to 4,446 on August 12, 2021 — an increase of about 31.5% during this sub-period (as this is written, the coronavirus pandemic is not yet over). Thus, the effect of a disaster, which appears about once in a century, on the stock market is hard to predict, and sometimes, the effect is in the opposite direction of what virtually all economists predict. While it is true that monetary and fiscal policies adopted by governments of most countries may explain, *ex-post*, the stock market rise mentioned, it would have been hard to predict these policies and, particularly, their huge effect on the stock market in early 2020 when the pandemic had just begun to make its effect known.

This book contains 11 chapters, most of which analyze the effect of the increase of the horizon on the future return profiles of risky assets, with an emphasis on the change in the relative attractiveness of stocks (the S&P 500 stock index) and bonds (10-year Treasury bonds) with the horizon.

Chapter 1 is devoted to the ongoing dispute in the literature about whether stocks become riskier or safer with the horizon. Note that if the conclusion is that stocks become safer with the horizon, maybe even safer than risky bonds, as a consequence, they may also become more attractive than bonds with the horizon, supporting the "stocks for the long run" investment strategy advocated by practitioners and by life cycle mutual funds. In this chapter, we also discuss the dispute regarding whether investing in the asset with the largest geometric mean (stocks rather than bonds or a portfolio of stocks and bonds) is optimal in the long run. We show empirically that the probability of stocks ending up with higher terminal wealth than bonds increases with the horizon, which may be the motivation for the investment strategy employed by life cycle mutual funds, although this investment policy does not necessarily conform with the expected utility paradigm. Finally, we show that life cycle mutual funds, which decrease the investment weight in stocks as the horizon becomes shorter, would economically benefit from adopting a fixed allocation to stocks in all years for each horizon rather than decreasing the investment weight in stocks gradually. In other words, for a 2-year horizon, it is better to invest, say, in each of the two years 30% in stocks rather than investing 40% in the first year and 20% in the second year.

Chapter 2 empirically analyzes the goodness of fit of the distribution of return on stocks with the horizon. This is an important issue, as the optimal investment decision rules depend on the distribution of return. We find that, for relatively short horizons (roughly up to one year), the best fit distribution is the logistic distribution.[11] Hence, for this horizon, or shorter horizons, the M–V rule can be safely employed, but for longer horizons (roughly for three years or more), the best fit distribution is the lognormal distribution. We show theoretically and empirically that a positive skewness is built up with the horizon; hence, the M–V rule is inappropriate for relatively long horizons, as the skewness, which is not taken into consideration in the M–V framework, plays a key factor in choosing among risky prospects.

Chapter 3 contrasts the changes in the M–V and SD rules with the horizon.[12] We find that while the M–V efficient set of investments increases with the horizon, the second-degree stochastic dominance (SSD) efficient set decreases with it. As the M–V rule is invalid for long horizons (as the distributions are no longer normal, or, more specifically, no longer elliptical), only the SSD efficient set is economically relevant. Thus, the decreases in the efficient set with the horizon, as implied by the SSD rule, conform with the expected utility paradigm.

Performance indices, particularly of mutual funds, are widely published. Chapter 4 is devoted to changes in the Sharpe performance index, Treynor performance ratio, and Jensen's alpha with the

---

[11]The logistic distribution belongs to the elliptic family for which the M–V rule is an optimal investment rule for all risk averters.

[12]We focus in this book on two stochastic dominance rules. By the first-degree stochastic dominance rule (FSD), prospect F dominates prospect G for all non-decreasing utility functions if and only if $F(x) \leq G(x)$ for all returns x, and there is at least one strict inequality, where F and G stand for the cumulative distributions of the two prospects under consideration. By the second-degree stochastic dominance (SSD) rule, F dominates G for all investors with risk-averse utility functions if and only if $\int_{-\infty}^{x} [G(t) - F(t)]dt \geq 0$ for all values x, and there is at least one strict inequality.

horizon. We find that these performance indices change with the horizon. Moreover, fund A may outperform fund B with monthly rates of return, and the opposite may be intact with, say, annual rates of return. This is of crucial importance to investors who rely on these performance reports in their investment decision-making. Thus, the published performance indices employing commonly monthly rates of return may be misleading to investors of longer horizons, of say one year.

Chapter 5 reveals that the correlation between the return on two risky assets (say, two stocks or stocks and bonds) approaches zero as the horizon increases indefinitely. Thus, the correlation between the return on two assets may be 0.5 with monthly rates of return and, say, 0.3 with annual rates of return. This decrease in the correlation with the horizon has an implication on the M–V optimal choice, as well as any econometric study with multiplicative variables like rates of return, growth rate of the population, interest rates, growth rate of the gross national product, etc. We find that for relatively long horizons, the M–V optimal portfolio is much different than the expected utility optimal portfolio, and the deviations are due to the fact that the M–V rule is a misleading rule for investment horizons, which are typically longer than one year. For example, with the M–V portfolio, "small stocks" become less attractive than "large stocks" with the horizon, while just the opposite occurs with expected utility maximization.

In analyzing whether stocks become riskier or safer with the horizon, the financial literature suggests to compare the *annualized* volatility of *log-return*. In Chapter 6, we discuss this methodology, showing that it is economically incorrect, and offer the following methodology for a comparison of risks faced on different dates: to first bring all cash flows to a common date (by employing the riskless interest rate), and in the second stage, to employ Rothschild and Stiglitz's definition of risk to investigate whether stocks become riskier or safer with the horizon.[13]

---

[13]Rothschild, M. and J. E. Stiglitz (1970). Increasing risk: A definition. *Journal of Economic Theory* 2(3), 225–243.

Relying solely on *ex-post* rates of return, it is quite clear that stocks become more attractive than bonds with the horizon, supporting the "stocks for the long run" investment strategy. However, there is a school of thought asserting that there are hidden future risks of stocks (black swans, see footnote 10) not reflected in the historical data. In Chapter 7, we employ the historical rates of return to analyze the change in the attractiveness of stocks and bonds with the horizon, but to the past historical data we add some hypothetical crashes.

While the M–V analysis reveals "bonds for the long run" (with historical data and, *a fortiori,* with the added crashes in the stock market), with the expected utility framework, we find that even after adding several -70% annual crashes in the historical stock market data, we obtain that the optimal investment strategy for all relatively long horizons is close to the "constant stocks–bonds" strategy.

Chapter 8 contrasts the continuous and discrete rates of return. While when there is certainty regarding future returns, one can employ the continuous and discrete rates of return interchangeably; when there is uncertainty, only the discrete calculation of the return is correct. Notwithstanding, some studies employ the continuous rates of return, and some employ the discrete rate of return even when uncertainty prevails. In this chapter, we show that with uncertainty, only the discrete rate of return calculation conforms with the expected utility, and that the economic distortion induced by employing the continuous rates of return rather than the discrete rates of return increases with the horizon. We show that even prospect-ranking by these two calculation methods may differ, inducing a loss to the decision-makers who rely on the continuous method for prospect-ranking.

In Chapter 9, we examine the change in the attractiveness of stocks and bonds by the almost stochastic dominance (ASD) rules,[14]

---

[14]The ASD rules are similar to the SD rules, but relate only to a sub-group of utility functions called non-pathological preferences. For more details, see Leshno, M. and H. Levy (2002). Preferred by "all" and preferred by "most"

which refer only to non-pathological preferences. We show that even after eliminating the pathological utility functions, by the ASD rules we cannot rationalize the "stocks for the long run" investment strategy that is advocated by practitioners.

One of the competing theories to the expected utility paradigm is prospect theory (PT).[15] In Chapter 10, we focus on the change in asset allocation with the horizon with PT. We find that with PT, stocks dominate bonds in the stock–bond portfolio, and for a horizon of three years or longer, allocating 100% to stocks is optimal. Thus, PT that does not conform with the expected utility paradigm does rationalize the "stocks for the long run" investment strategy.

While expected utility (SD rules) as well as the ASD rules do not support the "stocks for the long run" investment policy, one should wonder why practitioners and those investing in mutual funds not only believe in this policy, but also invest in practice according to it. The rationalization for such behavior may be by PT or by the probability dominance (PD) rule. Thus, practitioners may adhere to PT or PD rules, although these two rules do not conform with the expected utility paradigm. In Chapter 11, we suggest a rationalization to practitioners' actual investment behavior that conforms with the expected utility paradigm. We allow investors to borrow or lend the riskless asset (as done by shifting from Markowitz's M–V model to the Sharpe ratio). Thus, by adding the riskless asset, we shift from the first-degree stochastic dominance (FSD) rule to the FSDR rule (where R stands for the availability of the riskless asset). We find that with the FSDR rule, there is rationalization for the "stocks for the long run" in the expected utility framework. For a horizon of $N \geq 3$ years, stocks dominate bonds by the FSDR rule, that is, by all investors with non-decreasing utility functions, as long as the riskless asset is available.

---

decision makers: Almost stochastic dominance. *Management Science*, 48(8), 1074–1085.

[15]See Kahneman, D. and A. Tversky (1979). Prospect theory: An analysis of decision under risk. *Econometrica* 47(2), 263–291.

In sum, most expected utility models do not support the "stocks for the long run" investment strategy. However, there are three investment criteria which can rationalize it: the PD criterion and PT, which do not conform with expected utility, and the FSDR rule which conforms with expected utility, once borrowing and lending at the riskless interest rate is allowed.

Chapter 1

Asset Allocation and the Horizon: The Ongoing Disputes

Anyone seeking investment advice from professional investment consultants has probably faced the following first question: "For how long do you wish to invest?" This question indicates that the length of the investment horizon, at least from the practitioners' point of view, is an important ingredient needed in order to give the best investment advice to clients. Thus, the investment horizon is considered by practitioners as necessary information to establish the optimal asset allocation between risky and less risky assets, generally classified as stocks and bonds, respectively. Moreover, it seems that most investment consultants, albeit not all of them, believe that there is a connection between the length of the planned investment horizon and the desired asset allocation.[1] Specifically, the usual investment advice is that the longer the planned investment horizon, the larger the investment weight that should be allocated to risky assets (stocks) — not because investors like risk, but because they expect to obtain a reward, namely to realize a relatively large rate of return on the

---

[1]Of course, some investment consultants also recommend a list of preferable assets, or even suggest a short-term optimal asset allocation, believing that they have the ability to predict the market. As it is well documented in the literature that predicting the stock market is generally considered an impossible mission, the various index funds are flourishing, which implicitly assumes that the market is efficient, and that there is no ability to predict future rates of returns.

investment in stocks. Thus, the common view among practitioners is that by investing in stocks rather than in bonds, the advantage of a relatively large reward outweighs the disadvantage of a relatively large risk, as long as the investment horizon is relatively long. The common rule of thumb, which is consistent with the "stocks for the long run" investment strategy, is that investors should allocate 100% less their age to stocks.

Notwithstanding, there is empirical evidence that allegedly contradicts the "stocks for the long run" strategy. Specifically, although the planned investment horizon may be very long, say, saving for retirement, it is empirically observed that, in practice, the investor typically changes their portfolio mix or the mutual funds held after a relatively short period, typically one year. Thus, there is a gap between the "planned" investment horizon, that may be very long, and the "actual" investment horizon, that is typically about one year. The difference between these two horizon concepts is discussed in the next section.

1.1. The "Planned" and the "Actual" Investment Horizons

As the investment horizon is the central issue discussed in this book, we first elaborate on the difference between the planned investment horizon and the actual investment horizon. It is important to contrast these horizons, as they are relevant for investment decision-making. The optimal asset allocation, the performance indices, and the asset's risk measures, among other things, are all a function of the investment horizon. Thus, the important question is: what is the relevant horizon, the planned or the actual horizon, to be employed in measuring and analyzing all the above economic issues, particularly the optimal asset allocation that is of crucial importance for virtually all investment decisions?

To illustrate these two horizon concepts, suppose that a young person at age 25 wishes to invest for retirement for 40 years. If all economic and personal factors remain unchanged, the planned investment horizon may be equal to the actual investment horizon, that is, the investor will not change the portfolio with time. However, in reality, many things change economically (a recession, economic prosperity, the interest rate, inflation, a pandemic, and so forth) or in specific personal conditions (being fired versus getting another and more rewarding job). Hence, the investor who plans to invest for 40 years may change the investment strategy after a short period, say, one year, as a consequence of changes in the above conditions. The horizon where changes in the investment policy take place as a result of changes in the above-mentioned conditions is the actual investment horizon, which is generally much shorter than the planned investment horizon. Thus, we may find empirically that while the planned investment horizon is 40 years, as economic and personal conditions change, the actual investment horizon may be closer to one year.

However, what is relevant for investment decision-making is the planned investment horizon. Suppose that based on the present economic conditions, the initial planned horizon is 40 years. Yet, assume that after one year, the interest rate dramatically goes up. In this case, the investor may adjust the investment portfolio and, based on the new economic conditions, now make an investment decision for a planned investment horizon of 39 years. Thus, as future changes in the economy or in one's personal situation are unknown in advance, given the present conditions, 39 years is the new planned investment horizon in this example.

The difference between the planned investment horizon and the actual horizon is not confined to those saving for retirement. Suppose that a person invests for five years, aiming to buy a house at the end of the investment period. Another person saves for one year, aiming to use the money to travel around the world. These two people have different planned investment horizons; hence, they may adopt different investment strategies. For the five-year horizon investor, if nothing changes, say, after the first year has elapsed, the investor may adhere to the same initial investment strategy. In practice, however, because things generally do change over time, the actual investment horizon may be less than five years, and an investor may revise the held portfolio every year. Several factors may induce this investment revision after one year. However, even in the absence of changes in the above-mentioned factors, an investment revision may be desired because of a gap between the expected and actual performance of the selected investment. Let us elaborate.

Suppose that an investor has invested in a mutual fund, and based on historical performance, they expect to earn 10% a year. If the realized performance is less than expected, say, 2%, they may shift the money to another fund that has performed better in the past year. Indeed, Chevalier and Ellison show that investors (rationally or irrationally) commonly shift their investment from one investment vehicle to another based on the last period's performance.[2] Benartzi and Thaler show that the actual investment horizon is about one year even for those who have a very long planned investment horizon, such as for retirement.[3] Recall that investors receive annual reports detailing investment performance, and need to file annual tax reports, etc. Hence, there is an "evaluation period" of the investment strategy about once a year.

Even with this gap between the actual and planned investment periods, we would like to emphasize two important relevant factors regarding the importance of the investment horizon and the "stocks for the long run" investment strategy:

(a) An investor for a very long investment horizon may allocate a large proportion of the investment to stocks, and may replace the composition of stocks every year. This does not contradict the assertion of "stocks for the long run" despite the fact that the stock composition changes every year.

(b) Even if the average asset turnover is about one year, there are deviations from this average, and there is a whole distribution of actual investment horizons: some investors replace their assets every year, or even every quarter, and others replace their assets every longer period, say, every five or even 10 years.

---

[2]Chevalier, J. and G. Ellison (1997). Risk taking by mutual funds as a response to incentives. *Journal of Political Economy* 105(6), 1167–1200.

[3]Benartzi, S. and R. H. Thaler (1995). Myopic loss aversion and the equity risk premium. *The Quarterly Journal of Economics* 110(1), 73–92.

In sum, to make an optimal investment, one needs to know the planned investment horizon, realizing that with changes in the economic or personal situation, the actual horizon may be much shorter. Because, at any given moment, future changes are generally unknown, only the planned investment horizon is relevant for selecting the optimal investment strategy. Moreover, even if one advocates that the actual investment is relevant for investment decisions, recall that we have investors with different actual horizons, let alone with different planned horizons. Therefore, in this book, we stress the planned investment horizon, realizing that this horizon may change with economic circumstances.

Professional investors commonly believe that the longer the planned investment horizon, the larger the investment weight that should be allocated to stocks. While this recommendation to increase the investment weight in stocks with the horizon is common among practitioners, the issue regarding the horizon's effect is disputed mainly among academic researchers — even in the case where all agree that the planned investment horizon is relevant for investment. In contrast to the "stocks for the long run" investment strategy, some researchers argue that stocks become riskier with the horizon (hence less attractive with the horizon), and others believe that risk is invariant to the investment horizon.

The dispute regarding changes in stock risk with the horizon is not the only issue of controversy in the economic literature regarding the horizon's effect. This effect has been analyzed by numerous economic and financial researchers, revealing various disagreements. To mention only a few of the studies devoted to the horizon issue, see Fama and French,[4] Merton,[5] Samuelson,[6] Merton and Samuelson,[7]

---

[4]Fama, E. F. and K. R. French (2018). Long-horizon returns. *The Review of Asset Pricing Studies* 8(2), 232–252.

[5]Merton, R. C. (1969). Lifetime portfolio selection under uncertainty: The continuous-time case. *The Review of Economics and Statistics* 51(3), 247–257.

[6]Samuelson, P. A. (1969). Life time portfolio selection by dynamic stochastic programming. *The Review of Economics and Statistics* 51(3), 239–246.

[7]Merton, R. C. and P. A. Samuelson (1974). Fallacy of the log-normal approximation to portfolio decision-making over many periods. *Journal of Financial Economics* 1(1), 67–94.

Hakansson,[8] Barberis,[9] Campbell and Vicerira,[10] Levy,[11] Leshno and
Levy,[12] and Levy.[13] Some of these studies examine the effect of the
horizon on the changes in the attractiveness of stocks relative to
that of bonds, known in the literature as optimal asset allocation
corresponding to various investment horizons. Some researchers have
looked at the optimality of the geometric mean rule for investment
for the very long run, once again with ongoing disagreement. In this
chapter, we examine these important disputes and discuss empirically
how the distributions of returns on stocks and bonds change with the
horizon, with emphasis on the changes in the risk measure with the
horizon.[14]

---

[8]Hakansson, N. (1971). Multi-period mean–variance: Toward a general theory of
portfolio choice. *The Journal of Finance* 26(4), 857–884.

[9]Barberis, N. C. (2000). Investing for the long run when returns are predictable.
The Journal of Finance 55(1), 225–264.

[10]Campbell, J. Y. and L. M. Viceira (2002). *Strategic Asset Allocation: Portfolio
Choices for Long-Term Investors,* Oxford University Press, Oxford.

[11]Levy, H. (2015). Aging population, retirement, and risk taking. *Management
Science* 62(5), 1415–1430.

[12]Leshno, M. and H. Levy (2002). Preferred by "all" and preferred by "most"
decision-makers: Almost stochastic dominance. *Management Science* 48(8), 1074–
1085.

[13]Levy, M. (2009). Almost stochastic dominance and stocks for the long-run.
European Journal of Operation Research 194(1), 250–257.

[14]In virtually all studies regarding the "stocks for the long run" investment
strategy, it is assumed that one invests for N years, and the optimal diversification
strategy is determined today, with the possibility to change every year or every
several years, as done in practice by target-date funds (TDFs). There is another
branch of research regarding the optimal multi-period investment strategy —
employing dynamic programming to find the optimal diversification. By this
approach, the investor makes an optimal one-period decision at time $N-1$, namely
a decision regarding the last period. Then, based on the result obtained in the
last period, they know their new wealth (which is a random variable) and, based
on this result, make an optimal decision regarding period $N - 2$, and so forth.
This dynamic programming approach is very elegant theoretically, but one needs
to know the investor's utility function to obtain the optimal investment strategy.
There are numerous studies that employ dynamic programming. To mention only
one, probably one of the earliest studies employing this programming to study
multi-period optimal investment, see Mossin, J. (1968). Multiperiod portfolio
policies. *The Journal of Business* 41(2), 215–229.

We would like to stress at the outset that in measuring risk over different horizons, it is commonly assumed that the stock returns are drawn from identical and independent distributions (known as the *i.i.d.* assumption) over time, or that distributions are at least close to *i.i.d.*, but certainly there is no strong dependence of the returns over time. Otherwise, very little can be said about the change in risk with the horizon. If there is a pattern where, for example, a large positive return is followed by a relatively large negative return, and vice versa, we have a strong autocorrelation, and certainly the two-year return may be less volatile than the one-year return. Thus, such strong autocorrelation is ruled out in most investment horizon studies. However, some deviation from *i.i.d.* is commonly empirically observed (e.g., mean reversion), and, as we shall see in what follows, this is one of the arguments employed by one group of researchers, advocating that stocks become less risky with the horizon.

1.2. Dispute Number 1: Do Stocks Become Riskier or Safer with the Horizon?

Although most studies that analyze the connection between asset allocation and the horizon examine the entire distributions of the returns on stocks and on bonds, respectively, some studies focus on only one dimension: the change in the *riskiness* of stocks with the horizon. Some researchers advocate that stock risk increases with the horizon, while others argue just the opposite. There are mainly two approaches published in the literature to empirically measure the change in risk with the horizon. One approach is to employ the Black and Scholes option model to evaluate the price of put options on stocks, and the other approach is to directly measure the empirical volatility of stocks for various assumed investment horizons.

1.2.1. *Employing the Black and Scholes option model to evaluate stock risk*

The Black and Scholes[15] option model is mainly used to derive the equilibrium prices of put and call options. Having a put option

---

[15]Black, F. and M. Scholes (1973). The pricing of options and corporate liabilities. *Journal of Political Economy* 81(3), 637–654.

entitles holders to protect themselves against possible losses. For example, holding a stock with a market price of, say, $100, and holding also a put option with a strike price of, say, $90, protects investors from losses of more than $10 on the stocks. Therefore, if the price of the stock deteriorates to, say, $80, the put holders can sell it for $90 and protect themselves against losses of more than $10. Of course, the magnitude of this protection depends on the chosen strike price of the put option. If the strike price is $100, investors simply protect the principle, namely the $100. As there is no free lunch in the market, the larger the protection against losses (a larger strike price), the more expensive the cost of the protection against losses, that is, the larger the price of the put option that the investor buys.

To the best of our knowledge, Bodie[16] was the first to suggest the following original option method to evaluate whether stocks become safer or riskier with the horizon. According to his method, if the price of the put option increases with the horizon, it implies that stocks become riskier with the horizon (as one needs to pay more to get rid of the risk). And the opposite holds if the put option price decreases with the horizon. In short, looking at the distribution of stock returns for various horizons and calculating the put option corresponding to these distributions, one can empirically conclude whether stocks become riskier or safer with the horizon.

However, this methodology to evaluate changes of risk with the horizon, which seems to be very simple, implicitly contains one difficulty — the chosen strike price, in other words, the loss that is considered to be a disaster from the investor's point of view. Suppose that the current stock price is $100. Does the investor wish to protect the principle of $100 (to protect against any price drop), or to protect only $90 of the principle, that is, against losses of $10 or more?

If one finds that for a wide range of strike prices, that is, a wide range of the chosen loss protection, the price of the put option increases with the horizon, one can safely conclude that the riskiness

---

[16]Bodie, Z. (1991). On the risks of stocks in the long run. *Financial Analysts Journal* 51(3), 18–22.

of stocks increases with the horizon. Unfortunately, as we shall see in what follows, this is not the case, as for some strike prices, the put option price, as Bodie claims, indeed increases with the horizon, and for some other relevant strike prices, just the opposite holds. Therefore, we conclude that employing the option model does not provide a clear-cut answer whether stocks become riskier or safer with the horizon. Let us elaborate.

Bodie assumes that the strike price of the option is $S_0 e^{rN}$, where S_0 is the current stock price, r is the riskless interest rate, and N stands for the investment horizon. For example, suppose that one invests for $N = 5$ years, the interest rate is 5%, and the current stock price is \$100. By the strike price selected by Bodie, the investor protects not only the principle, but also the potential earning in the riskless asset, namely $S_0 e^{rN} = \$100 e^{.05 \times 5} \cong \$128.4$. With this strike price of the principle as well as the forgone profit in the riskless asset, Bodie's claim is that the price of the put option increases with the horizon; hence, one can safely conclude that with the existing empirical distribution of stock returns, the longer the investment horizon, the riskier stocks become. Obviously not all investors would adopt this insurance policy. What about investors who simply wish to protect the principle, in our example, the \$100? Of course the wider the protection, the better as long as this protection against losses is costless. However, recall that the larger the strike price (a larger protection cover), the higher the price of the put option that the investor has to buy to get the desired protection. Therefore, different investors would choose different levels of protection, that is, buying put options with different strike prices that reflect their subjective tradeoff between the level of protection and the cost of the put option.

Is it possible that for different strike prices, the stock riskiness (namely the price of the put option) decreases rather than increases with the horizon? Levy and Cohen[17] solve for the put option prices corresponding to various strike prices and for various assumed investment horizons. Like Bodie, they calculate how the put option price

---

[17]Levy, H. and A. Cohen (1998). On the risk of stocks in the long run: Revisited. *The Journal of Portfolio Management* 24(3), 60–69.

changes with the horizon for various strike prices. Their study, in this respect, is an extension of Bodie's study of various strike prices. The distribution of the stocks is assumed to be log-normal (which is necessary for the calculation of the option prices). Specifically, they selected the following alternative strike prices $S_0 e^{arN}$ for various values $a \geq 0$. For $a = 1$, we have the same strike price that Bodie uses. However, if investors choose $a = 0$, we have that $S_0 e^{arN} = S_0$. In this case, the investor wishes to protect only the principle and not larger values of future wealth. Generally, the investor may wish to protect more or less than the principle depending on their preference. Recall that the choice of the protection level depends on preference, as the higher the protection level, the larger the put price that one should pay to protect the investment. With the above formula, for the chosen strike price, if $a > 1$, the investor wishes to protect not only the principle and the forgone interest but even larger future wealth.

Figure 1.1 illustrates the changes in the put option prices with the horizon and with the chosen protection parameter a. For $a = 1$, as suggested by Bodie, the assumed strike price protects the principle as well as the forgone interest. Indeed, in this case, we obtain that the put option price increases with the horizon, and based on this strike price, we conclude that stock risk increases with the horizon (see the curve $a = 1$ in Figure 1.1). For a larger protection level, namely $a > 1$, the increase in the put option price with the horizon is even faster than in the case $a = 1$; hence, the increase in the riskiness of stocks with the horizon is enhanced. However, in the case where the investor wishes to protect only the principle, namely $a = 0$, the curve is declining, implying that the stock risk decreases with the horizon. Thus, for this protection level, the longer the horizon, the safer the stocks are (see curve $a = 0$ in Figure 1.1). For $a = 1/2$, that is, half of the forgone interest as well as the principle are protected, and the put price has a hump: it increases up to $N = 4$, and then declines with the horizon. This implies that stocks become riskier as the horizon increases, and beyond some horizon, they become less risky with it.

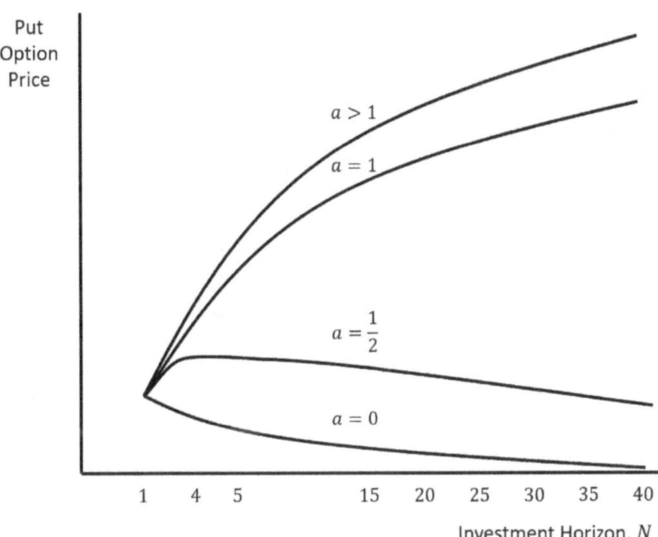

Figure 1.1: Put option prices for various strike prices and various horizons.

In sum, the selected shortfall level, which determines the critical level for defining a disastrous result from the investor's point of view, depends on the investor's preference. As the put option may increase or decrease with the horizon, depending on the subjective disastrous level as conceived by the investor, we cannot determine unequivocally by the put option prices whether stocks become riskier or safer with the horizon.

In analyzing riskiness with the put option price, only the left tail of the stocks' distribution of returns is considered. However, recall that by investing in stocks rather than bonds, we also have an upside: by investing in stocks, one may also enjoy a relatively large profit (the right tail of the distribution of returns) and not only exposure to potential loses (the left tail distribution of returns). Relying on this property of stock returns, Merrill and Thorley[18] consider both tails of the stock distribution returns. They suggest to use the call option and

---

[18]Merrill, C. and S. Thorley (1996). Time diversification: Perspectives from option pricing theory. *Financial Analysts Journal* 52(3), 13–19.

the riskless asset to construct *protected equity note* (PEN), through which the investor can partially sacrifice an upside return in exchange for insuring a minimum rate of return. Using this approach, which also relies on Black and Scholes' option model, they find that the relative amount of upside return that the investor has to sacrifice to protect from losses diminishes with the horizon. Hence, they conclude that, in contrast to Bodie, stocks become less risky with the horizon.

Thus, using the same Black and Scholes model and the same set of data, we have a conflicting result: in employing the put price for various horizons, stocks may be more or less risky with the horizon, depending on the chosen strike price. Relying on the call option as well as on the put option equilibrium pricing, stocks become safer with the horizon. This is the first dispute regarding the changes in the riskiness of stocks with the horizon.

A word of caution: Recall that these conflicting results regarding the changes in stocks' risk with the horizon relies on the Black and Scholes option valuation model, which in itself is far from being perfect. In particular, this model relies on several assumptions which do not hold in practice, e.g., to derive the equilibrium option price, one needs to conduct a portfolio rebalancing continuously, which is practically impossible as it induces enormous transaction costs. Without this continuous rebalancing process, the distribution of return is not log-normal, where log-normal distribution is employed in the derivation of the option model.[19]

1.2.2. *Measuring stock volatility for various horizons: Risk and stock/bond relative attractiveness*

Although we focus here on the changes of stocks' risk with the horizon, we also discuss the changes in the relative attractiveness of stocks and bonds with the horizon.

Another way to measure the changes in risk (or volatility) of stocks with the horizon is by calculating directly the variance of

---

[19]For the various shapes of the distributions of the return corresponding to various risky assets for various horizons, see Chapter 2.

returns corresponding to various investment horizons. However, the difficulty with this approach is that by comparing the volatility for various horizons, say the volatility of terminal wealth of a one-year investment horizon with the volatility corresponding to, say, a 10-year horizon, we are comparing apples with oranges, and it is almost certain that the 10-year horizon volatility will be larger than the one-year volatility. Therefore, it is suggested in the literature to compare the *annualized* volatility corresponding to various horizons.

However, even with this annualized volatility,[20] there is disagreement among academic researchers about whether stock volatility (which is identified with stock risk) increases or decreases with the horizon. Siegel[21] and Pástor and Stambaugh[22] represent two schools of thought regarding this issue with opposing views. Both analyze empirically the annualized variance of log-wealth and not the volatility of wealth itself. As we shall see in what follows, shifting from wealth to log-wealth greatly facilitates the mathematical analysis, as all relative formulas become additive.[23]

Investing for N periods the terminal wealth is given by W_N,

$$W_N = W_0 \prod_{i=1}^{N} (1 + R_i)$$

where W_0 stands for the initial invested wealth, and R_i stands for the rate of return in the ith period. For simplicity and without loss of generality, it is assumed that \$1 is invested and, therefore, this

---

[20]There is a concern about the comparison of risks obtained on various dates by the annualized method. Another method is to invest each outcome obtained in the short horizon case at the riskless asset up to the longer date and then calculate the variance of the two prospects. This method and the annualized method generally do not yield the same risk ranking.

[21]Siegel, J. (1994). *Stocks for the Long Run*, Chicago, Irwin.

[22]Pástor, L. and R. F. Stambaugh (2012). Are stocks really less volatile in the long run? *The Journal of Finance* 67(2), 431–478.

[23]Indeed, with log-return, the mathematical analysis is greatly facilitated. However, recall that expected utility is defined on wealth and not log-wealth, and there is no economic justification to employ log-return. However, in this chapter, we adhere to the methodologies employed in the literature, keeping in mind this reservation.

formula is reduced to

$$W_N = \prod_{i=1}^{N}(1 + R_i).$$

Shifting to log-wealth, we obtain the additive formula for the log-return,

$$\log(W_N) = \sum_{i=1}^{N} \log(1 + R_i)$$

and assuming *i.i.d.*, with this simple additivity of log-returns, we have

$$\text{Variance}\left[\log(W_N)\right] = N\left[\text{Variance}\left(\log(1 + R_i)\right]\right.$$

Denoting Variance$(\log(1 + R_i)$ by $\sigma^2_{i(log)}$, we finally obtain

$$\text{Variance}\left[\log(W_N)\right] = N\sigma^2_{i(log)}$$

where the subscript *log* reminds us that we employ the variance of log-return and not the variance of the return. It is clear from the above equations that under the *i.i.d.* assumption, the variance of the terminal wealth increases with N, but the *annualized* variance, $\sigma^2_{(log)}$, is unaffected by the horizon as

$$\text{Annualized variance} = N\sigma^2_{i(log)}/N = \sigma^2_{i(log)} = \sigma^2_{(log)}$$

where the subscript i is omitted, as under the *i.i.d.* assumption, the variance is identical for all periods. Employing the same formula, the average standard deviation decreases with the horizon with the square root of N as follows:

$$\text{Annualized standard deviation} = \sqrt{N}\sigma_{i(log)}/N = \sigma_{(log)}/\sqrt{N}$$

So far, there is a complete agreement between the two schools of thought regarding the changes in stock risk with the horizon. Indeed, according to Siegel, *"If asset returns follow a random walk, the standard deviation of each asset class will fall by the square root of the holding period"* (see footnote 21, p. 98).

Similarly, Pástor and Stambaugh conclude: *"Under the traditional random-walk assumption that returns are distributed independently and identical (i.i.d.) through time, return variance per period is equal at all investment horizons"* (see footnote 28, p. 1).

Thus, with *i.i.d.* assumption, there is agreement between the two views regarding the stock risk, concluding that the risk measured by the annualized variance of log-return is unaffected by the horizon. However, the disagreement is in regard to the *i.i.d.* assumption. Siegel believes that the stock risk decreases with the horizon due to the "mean reversion" observed empirically in the market. Conversely, Pástor and Stambaugh argue that history, as observed in the stock market, will not repeat itself, and due to possible changes in the return parameters, stock risk increases rather than decreases with the horizon. The two contrasting views regarding stock risk rely on empirical evidence. However, Pástor and Stambaugh employ sophisticated statistical tools advocating the *ex-ante* risk is much larger than the *ex-post* risk. Let us elaborate.

Siegel empirically analyzes the annualized variance of stocks for $N = 1$, $N = 10$, $N = 20$, and $N = 30$ years, where the long horizons are relevant for investment for retirement. He covers a long time period starting from 1882 and shows empirically that stocks are more profitable and less risky than bonds for long investment horizons. Based on historical data, he shows that if the investment horizon is 10 years, for any chosen 10-year-interval time period taken from the historical rates of return series, the worst performance of stocks and bonds are -4.1% and -5.4%, respectively. Hence, he concludes that not only does the risk of stocks decrease with the horizon, stocks also become safer than bonds. For any selected 20-year investment horizon taken from this long history, stocks yield positive returns, that is, they are not classified as a risky asset for a 20-year or longer horizon.

To strengthen his results, Siegel also examines the composition of stocks and bonds corresponding to the minimum-variance portfolio (of log-returns and not of the returns) located on the mean–variance efficient frontier. He finds that for $N = 1$ year, the minimum variance portfolio contains 13% stocks and for an $N = 30$-year horizon, the optimal weight of stocks in the portfolio increases to 68%. Based on this empirical evidence, Siegel argues that stock risk decreases with the horizon, and even is not risky at all for a horizon of $N = 20$ years or longer. The implication of these findings is that investors for the long run (e.g., for retirement) should allocate a relatively large investment weight to stocks, which for long horizons is more profitable and safer than bonds.

Pástor and Stambaugh advocate a contrasting view, arguing that even a very long historical rates of return series is insufficient to predict the future risk of stocks. Specifically, they show that once uncertainty concerning the stock return distribution is considered, particularly the uncertainty of the mean–return, stocks become riskier with the horizon. Considering this uncertainty (as well as other factors), they show that the $N = 30$ years annualized variance is 21–53% larger the one-year horizon variance. The two contrasting views regarding the changes in the stock risk with the horizon and the disagreement between the two approaches are summarized by Pástor and Stambaugh as follows:

> *Under the traditional random-walk assumption that returns are distributed independently and identically (i.i.d.) through time, return variance per-period is equal for all investment horizons.*
>
> *Explanation for the lower variance at long horizons commonly focus on "mean reversion" whereby negative shock to the current return is offset by positive shocks to future returns, and vice versa. Our conclusion that stocks are more volatile in the long run obtains despite the presence of mean reversion. We show that mean reversion is only one of five components of long-run variance:*
>
> > (i)   *i.i.d. uncertainty*
> > (ii)   *mean reversion*
> > (iii)   *uncertainty about future expected return*
> > (iv)   *uncertainty about current expected return*
> > (v)   *estimation risk*

> *Whereas the mean-reversion component is strongly negative, the other components are all positive, and their combined effect outweighs the mean reversion.*

Thus, relying either on the option model to measure risk of stocks or measuring risk directly by volatility, the issue of whether stocks become riskier or safer with the horizon is still in dispute. Abramov *et al.* show that the question of whether stock risk increases or decreases with the horizon depends on the investor's prior beliefs about the return dynamics.[24] However, it is worth mentioning that one approach (Siegel) solely relies on historical data, while the other approach (Pástor and Stambaugh), employing very sophisticated statistical tools, also considers possible deviations of the *ex-ante* distribution from the *ex-post* distribution.

The disagreement concerning the changes in the risk of stocks with the horizon has a direct implication on the relative attractiveness of stocks in the long run. We next turn to another dispute regarding the attractiveness of stocks in the unique case where the investment horizon increases indefinably.

1.3. Dispute Number 2: The Geometric Mean and Expected Utility Conflict for Investment for the Very Long Run

A major ongoing dispute is in regard to the optimal investment criterion in the specific case where the investment horizon increases indefinitely. One view is that, in this specific case, the geometric mean (GM) is the investment rule that should be employed in making choices, advocating that the prospect with the largest GM is the optimal choice for all investors regardless of their preferences, as long as the investment horizon is very long. Thus, for this opposing view, the maximum geometric mean rule, denoted by MGM, is an optimal rule for very long investment horizons. For example, if there are, say,

---

[24]Avramov, D., S. Cederburg and K. Lučivjanská (2018). Are stocks riskier in the long run? Taking cues from economic theory. *The Review of Financial Studies* 31(2), 556–594.

100 possible prospects to choose from, by the MGM rule, one needs to calculate the GM of each prospect, and the one with the largest GM is the best one for all investors regardless of their preferences, as long as the horizon is indefinitely long. However, it should be said at the outset that there is also an opposing view, asserting that for myopic utility function, the choice is independent of the length of the investment horizon and, therefore, the MGM rule is not optimal in this case. Thus, not for all expected utility (EU) maximizers, the prospect with the largest GM is optimal. We will elaborate on myopic preference in the next section.

1.3.1. *Definition of the GM*

Suppose that we have the distribution of returns given by $[(1 + R_i), p_i]$, $i = 1, 2, \ldots, k$, where p_i is the probability to obtain a return of $1 + R_i$ and there are k possible returns.

Then the GM is defined as $GM = \prod_{i=1}^{k} (1+R_i)^{p_i}$, where it is defined only for a non-negative return, namely $(1 + R_i) \geq 0$.

In contrast, the arithmetic mean (AM) is defined as $AM = \sum_{i=1}^{k} p_i (1 + R_i)$. We have that always $GM \leq AM$, and equality holds only in the case where there is no variability, that is, all returns are equal, a case where certainty prevails. The advocators of the MGM rely on the following theorem:

Theorem 1.1. *Suppose that there are two prospects, F and G, where the GM of F is larger than the GM of G. Then*

$$\text{Probability}\,(W_{F,N} > W_{G,N}) \to 1 \quad \text{as } N \to \infty \qquad (1.1)$$

where N is the number of investment periods, that is, the assumed investment horizon.

The proof provided by Latané[25] is according to the following argument: If the value of an asset that is initially priced at \$1 will change until the end of each year according to the probability distribution given by $[(1 + R_i), p_i]$, and one invests for N years,

---

[25]Latané, H. A. (1959). Criteria for choices among risky ventures. *Journal of Political Economy* 67(2), 144–155.

then the terminal wealth after N years' investment denoted by W_N "converges with probability" to

$$GM^N = (1 + R_1)^{p_1 N}(1 + R_2)^{p_1 N} \ldots (1 + R_k)^{p_k N} \qquad (1.2)$$

which is the GM raised to the power of N. To see this, recall that the realized terminal wealth, which is a random variable, after N investment periods is given by

$$W_N = (1 + R_1)^{n_1}(1 + R_2)^{n_2} \ldots (1 + R_k)^{n_k} \qquad (1.3)$$

which can also be rewritten as

$$W_N = (1 + R_1)^{(n_1/N)N}(1 + R_2)^{(n_2/N)N} \ldots (1 + R_k)^{(n_k/N)N} \qquad (1.4)$$

where n_i is the actual number of occurrences of the return $(1 + R_i)$

However, as we have

$$\lim(n_i/N) \to p_i, \quad \text{as } N \to \infty \qquad (1.5)$$

and from Eqs. (1.2), (1.4), and (1.5), we also have that

$$W_N \to GM^N, \quad \text{as } N \to \infty \qquad (1.6)$$

which is what is needed to prove the claim given in Theorem 1.1.

The result given in Eq. (1.6) is employed by the advocates of the MGM rule optimality. To see this, suppose that one has to choose between prospects F and H where GM(F) > GM(H). Then, with GM raised to the power of N, we still have this inequality; therefore, we conclude that $W_N(F) > W_N(H)$ with probability 1, as long as $N \to \infty$. As all investors prefer more than less wealth, it is concluded that the prospect with the largest GM is optimal for all investors with very long investment horizons. For further studies advocating the superiority of the MGM rule, see Latané, Kelly,[26] Breiman,[27] and Markowitz.[28]

---

[26]Kelly, J. L. (1956). A new interpretation of information rate. *Bell System Technical Journal* 35(4), 917–926.

[27]Breiman, L. (1960). Investment policies for expanding businesses optimal in the long-run sense. *Naval Research Logistic Quarterly* 7(4), 647–651.

[28]Markowitz, H. M. (1976). Investment for the long run: New evidence for an old rule. *The Journal of Finance* 31(5), 1273–1286.

1.3.2. *The MGM rule and diversification*

If one faces two prospects, F and H, and the GM of F is larger than the GM of H, one is tempted to believe that diversification between these two prospects reduces the GM, and hence is not optimal. However, this is not the case, as diversification may increase the GM. Thus, maximizing the GM does not rule out that diversification is optimal. To see this, let us first express the GM as a function of the arithmetic mean (AM) and of the variance of the return.

The GM is smaller than the AM, and generally the larger the variance of returns of the prospect under consideration, the larger the gap between the AM and also the GM. To see this claim, first recall that

$$GM = (1 + R_1)^{p_1}(1 + R_2)^{p_2} \dots .(1 + R_k)^{p_k}. \tag{1.7}$$

Therefore,

$$\log(GM) = \sum_{i=1}^{k} p_i \log(1 + R_i) \equiv E[\log(1 + R)] \tag{1.8}$$

where R is the random variable, the return of the asset under consideration.

Expanding $\log(1+R)$ to a Taylor series about the mean $[1+E(R)]$ yields

$$\log(1 + R) \cong \log[1 + E(R)] + [(1 + R) - (1 + E(R)]/(1 + (ER)$$
$$-[(1 + R) - (1 + E(R))]^2/2[1 + E(R)]^2$$

(where higher moments are ignored).

Taking the expected value of both sides, we obtain

$$E \log(1 + R) \cong \log(1 + ER) - \sigma_R^2/2[1 + E(R)]^2. \tag{1.9}$$

As $E \log(1 + R)$ is a monotonic increasing function of the GM (see Eq. 1.8), we obtain from this Taylor expansion that the higher the arithmetic mean, ER, and the smaller the variance σ_R^2, the larger the GM. Thus, in principle, we may have that prospect F with a larger AM than prospect G may have a smaller GM as long as it has a larger variance inducing a decrease in the GM. Another conclusion is that by the MGM rule, a diversification may be optimal. The reason is that by diversification, the portfolio variance decreases; therefore, the MGM may increase. We demonstrate this claim with the following example.

1.3.3. *Example: A case where the MGM implies diversification*

Suppose that in year 1 the return (namely 1+ rate of return) on asset F and asset G are 0.9 and 0.98, respectively, and in year 2, the return on F and G are 1.2 and 1.1, respectively. Table 1.1 provides the relevant parameters of these two assets.

As we can see from Table 1.1, the geometric mean of F is larger than that of G, but its standard deviation is also larger. Then, by diversification, one may decrease the portfolio variance, and may increase the GM. Indeed, this is the case with the example. Figure 1.2 depicts the GM of various diversified portfolios composed from these two assets. As we can see by the MGM rule, diversification is optimal. Investing about 0.625 in asset F and 0.375 in asset G maximizes the GM.

At this point, it is worth mentioning the difference between the mean–variance (M–V) investment rule and the MGM criterion. In this example, there is a perfect correlation between prospects F and G; hence, the M–V efficient set is a straight line and all points on this line represent efficient portfolios, namely there are many portfolios that are considered to be optimal, depending on the investor's preference. By the MGM criterion, there is only one optimal portfolio (see Figure 1.2) that can be diversified or specialized, where in our example, it is diversified.

We turn now to calculate the MGM of portfolios combined from stocks and bonds. Table 1.2 reveals that the mean rate of return

Table 1.1: The GM, AM, and standard deviations of assets F and G.

Asset	Geometric Mean	Arithmetic Mean	Standard Deviation
F	1.03923	1.05	0.212132
G	1.038268	1.04	0.084853

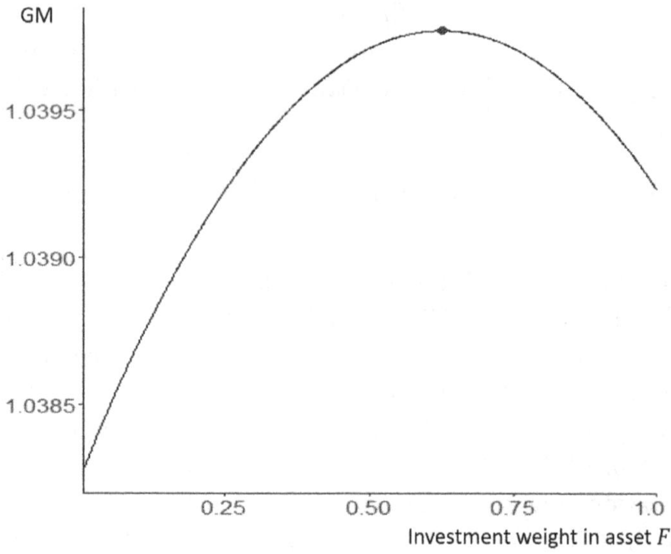

Figure 1.2: The GM of diversified portfolios of assets F and G.

Table 1.2: The GM, AM, and standard deviation of stocks and bonds.

	Geometric Mean	Arithmetic Mean	Standard Deviation
Bonds	1.048802	1.051464	0.076716
Stocks	1.097056	1.115723	0.195834

on bonds is about 5.1%, while the mean rate of return on stocks is much larger, about 11.6%. Hence, by increasing the weight allocated to stocks, the increase in the portfolio mean induces an increase in the portfolio GM, and the increase in the variance induces a decrease in the portfolio GM.

Figure 1.3 presents the MGM as a function of the proportion invested in stocks (the S&P 500 stock index) and bonds (10-year Treasury bonds). With this data corresponding to annual rates of return for the period 1928–2019,[29] we obtain a corner solution where in the MGM portfolio, 100% weight is allocated to stocks. Note that by increasing the investment weight in stocks, both the mean and

---

[29] *Source*: http://people.stern.nyu.edu/adamodar/pc/datasets/histretSP.xls.

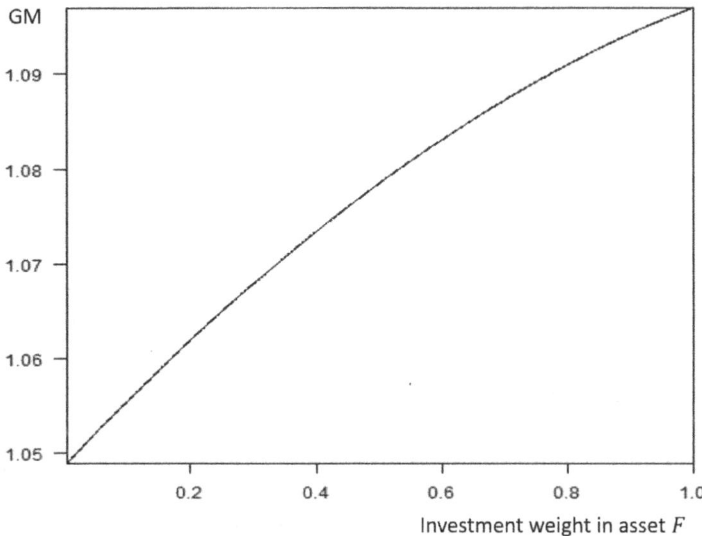

Figure 1.3: The GM of various portfolios of stocks and bonds.

the variance increase simultaneously. Hence, an interior solution is possible. However, with the actual parameters, the change in the portfolio mean is dominating, and the GM increases with the increase in the investment weight in stocks.

From this analysis, if the historical distributions of returns also well represent the future distributions, the MGM advocates would recommend investing 100% in stocks, as long as the investment horizon is indefinitely long.

Although Theorem 1.1 and the accompanying proof are mathematically correct, Merton and Samuelson (see footnote 7) argue that one cannot conclude that every risk averter who aims to maximize EU will choose the prospect with the larger GM. Specifically, they show that the choices of EU maximizers with a myopic utility function are unaffected by the assumed investment horizon, which refutes the optimality of the MGM criterion. Let us elaborate on this claim.

The myopic utility function is given by

$$U(W) = \frac{W^{1-\alpha}}{1-\alpha}$$

For all $\alpha \neq 1$, a conflict between the MGM rule and expected utility choice may arise.[30] For a \$1 investment, the utility of wealth accumulated for N-years investment is as follows:

$$U(W = 1) = \frac{[(1 + R_1)(1 + R_2) \cdots\cdots (1 + R_N)]^{1-\alpha}}{1 - \alpha}$$

and assuming independence over time, the EU is given by

$$EU(W) = \frac{[E(1 + R_1)E(1 + R_2) \cdots\cdots E(1 + R_N)]^{1-\alpha}}{1 - \alpha}$$

This can be rewritten as

$$EU(W) = [1/(1-\alpha)][E(1+R_1)^{1-\alpha}E(1+R_2)^{1-\alpha} \cdots\cdots E(1+R_N)^{1-\alpha}]$$

From this equation, one can conclude that maximizing the expected utility in each period also maximizes the expected utility corresponding to the N-period investment given by $EU(W)$. Thus, having a myopic utility, the investor should look at each period (say each year), choose the prospect which maximizes the expected one-period utility function, and by employing this procedure in each period, the optimization is also achieved for a long period horizon, regardless of the length of the assumed investment horizon. Thus, the length of the investment horizon does not affect the optimal choice as the investor maximizes expected utility in each period. This result is in strong contradiction to the MGM rule, asserting that the horizon affects the optimal choice and for an indefinitely long horizon, the MGM portfolio is optimal for all investors regardless of their preferences.

As Theorem 1.1 is mathematically correct, and the mathematical argument regarding the myopic utility functions is also correct, we conclude that for any two prospects, F and H, the following holds:

$$\text{Probability } (W_{F,N} > W_{H,N}) \rightarrow 1 \quad \text{as}$$

$$N \rightarrow \infty \nRightarrow EU(W_{F,N}) > EU(W_{H,N})$$

---

[30]In the case that $\alpha = 1$, the myopic preference reduces to the log-utility function, a case where EU maximization coincides with the MGM criterion.

for all monotonic non-decreasing risk-averse utility functions. The MGM rule may maximize the EU of most utility functions, but not all of them, as the EU of the myopic preference is not maximized by the MGM choice. For example, if $\alpha \neq 1$, the optimal choice for all myopic preferences is not necessarily the MGM portfolio. Therefore, by the EU paradigm, the MGM portfolio is not the optimal portfolio for all investors, even for an indefinitely long horizon.

In sum, for the myopic utility function with $\alpha = 1$, the myotonic utility function is reduced to the log-function, a specific case where there is no contradiction between Theorem 1.1 and the myopic choices. However, for $\alpha \neq 1$, a contradiction between these two approaches may arise.

As we shall see in the rest of this chapter, in practice, a large segment of investors and professional investment managers believe that the investment horizon does affect the optimal investment choice; hence, establishment of the life cycle mutual funds where the longer the horizon, the more is invested in risky but also more profitable assets. One way to reconcile the myopic argument with the statement given in Theorem 1.1, and particularly with the common belief by professional investors regarding the role that the investment horizon plays in choosing the optimal portfolio, is simply to rule out the myopic functions, arguing that they do not fit the preference of most investors. Another possibility is to assume a myopic utility function of the form $U(W + I)$, where $W + I$ is the total wealth of the investor under consideration, and in practice, only I is invested in the capital market. With this framework, W stands for all non-invested capital, e.g., houses, human capital, and so forth. In this case, the myopic argument for the independency of the optimal choice on the horizon does not hold.

Theorem 1.1 relates to the case where the horizon is indefinitely long. In practice, even investors for retirement who invest for long horizons do not invest for an indefinitely long horizon; hence, the statement given in Theorem 1.1 may be irrelevant for them. Thus, the probability that the MGM portfolio yields a larger terminal wealth than any other investment strategy for a finite long horizon is questionable. We next compare the cumulative distributions of stocks and bonds, and calculate the probability that stocks yield a larger terminal wealth than bonds also for finite, albeit long, investment horizons.

1.4. The Probability that a Stock's Terminal Wealth will be Larger than a Bond's Terminal Wealth for Various Finite Long Investment Horizons

We have seen that one group of economists believes that a long history, say, 100 years, is sufficient to predict the long-run investment future performance, while others believe that even 100 years' record of rates of returns is insufficient to predict the long-run performance in the future. In this section, we adopt an intermediate approach, as we assume that the historical distributions' parameters (e.g., the mean and standard deviation) remain the same also in the future; however, history does not precisely repeat itself, as many researchers advocate.

We observe empirically that on average, the return on stocks is larger than the return on bonds, yet the minimal annual rate of return on stocks is generally lower than that on bonds. Therefore, even for a very long investment horizon, there is always a small nagging probability that the investor will end up with less terminal wealth by investing in stocks than the terminal return obtained by investing in bonds. To see this claim, suppose that for a one-year investment in stocks, one faces a rate of return of either -10% or 40% with equal probability of 0.5, whereas investing in bonds yields either -1% or 6% with equal probability. Suppose that one invests for, say, 30 years. There is a relatively small probability that the investor will end up with a lower return with the stocks than with bonds, e.g., in the case where the -10% repeats itself for many years. In other words, history will not repeat itself, and in the extreme case, the -10% return will repeat itself for all 30 years in a row. It is true that the probability of such events is very small, but it always exists (unless the horizon is indefinitely large with $n \to \infty$ (see Theorem 1.1)). Indeed, this nagging small probability is the main obstacle for asserting unequivocally that the "stocks for the long run" strategy is the best investment strategy for all investors regardless of their preferences. To see why even a very small probability of the event where bonds outperform stocks may refute the assertion "stocks for the long run," recall that we may have an investor who assigns an extremely large utility weight to this range of returns, where with a small probability bonds outperform stocks in the long run. Even ruling out the myopic utility functions, for this investor, who invests for a long but finite horizon, we cannot safely assert that "stocks for the long run" is the best investment strategy. What we may be able to say, however, is that for most investors, the assertion "stocks for the long run," albeit not for all investors, is intact. Moreover, the longer the investment horizon, presumably, the smaller the set of investors for whom the above assertion does not hold. To shed more light on the relationship between all of these complex concepts, let us draw the cumulative distribution of the return of various assets and calculate the above-mentioned relatively small probability for which bonds outperform stocks, and show how this probability decreases with the horizon.

In order to estimate the cumulative distributions of the terminal wealth of investment in stocks (the S&P 500 stock index), and alternatively of the investment in bonds (10-year Treasury bonds), we employ the annual rates of return series for the period 1928–2019.[31] For a one-year horizon, we simply draw the cumulative distributions for annual returns given in this historical series. For a horizon of $N = 2$ years, we draw two observations (with replacement) at random from the historical return series and calculate the accumulated compounded returns corresponding to these two years. Then we repeat this simulation 100,000 times and draw the two-year horizon cumulative distribution. The same technique is employed in calculating the distributions of other assets, e.g., bonds. Having the cumulative distributions of two assets that are compared, we next calculate for various horizons the intersection point of the

---

[31] The return on bonds is calculated from New York University data that include data on both bonds and the S&P 500 stock index, see footnote 29.

two distributions under consideration. Of course, employing this bootstrapping technique, we assume that returns are identical and independent (*i.i.d.*) over time. We continue this procedure for other horizons $N = 1, 2, 5, 10, 15, 20, 25$, and 30 years, but as the trend of the changes in the intersection point of the two distributions are similar for all horizons, for brevity's sake, we report here only the results corresponding to horizons of $N = 1, 10$, and 30 years.

Note that by this simulation approach, we draw the observations from a given historical distribution, and do not change the characteristics of the distributions under consideration. However, we do not assume that history precisely repeats itself: for example, there is a small probability that, say, for the two-year horizon, the year 2008 will appear in the simulation many times, although in the historical data it appears only once. In this respect, the simulation approach is a mixture of the two approaches of predicting the future return distribution based on historical distributions. Of course, when the number of simulations grows indefinitely, we incline toward the historical distribution of returns.

Figure 1.4 provides the cumulative distributions corresponding to stocks (the S&P 500 stock index) and 10-year Treasury bonds for investment horizons of $N = 1$ year, $N = 10$ years, and $N = 30$ years. As we can see, indeed, the two distributions of bonds and stocks intersect for all horizons, implying that there is a nagging left tail to these two distributions, a range where bonds outperform stocks. This range of returns where this occurs is relatively large for the $N = 1$-year horizon, and it shrinks as the horizon increases, but never vanishes. Note that the intersection of the two distributions for $N = 10$ years is about a terminal wealth of 1.2, implying an annual rate of return of $1.2^{.1} \cong 1.018$. Thus, if the average annual rate of return on stocks is about 1.8% or lower, bonds outperform stocks. For a 30-year horizon, bonds outperform stocks for an average rate of return of about $1.75^{1/30} = 1.0188$ or lower, which is very similar to the result corresponding to a 10-year investment horizon.

Employing the simulated cumulative distributions of the returns on stocks and on bonds corresponding to various horizons, Table 1.3 provides the means and variances for various horizons, as well as the

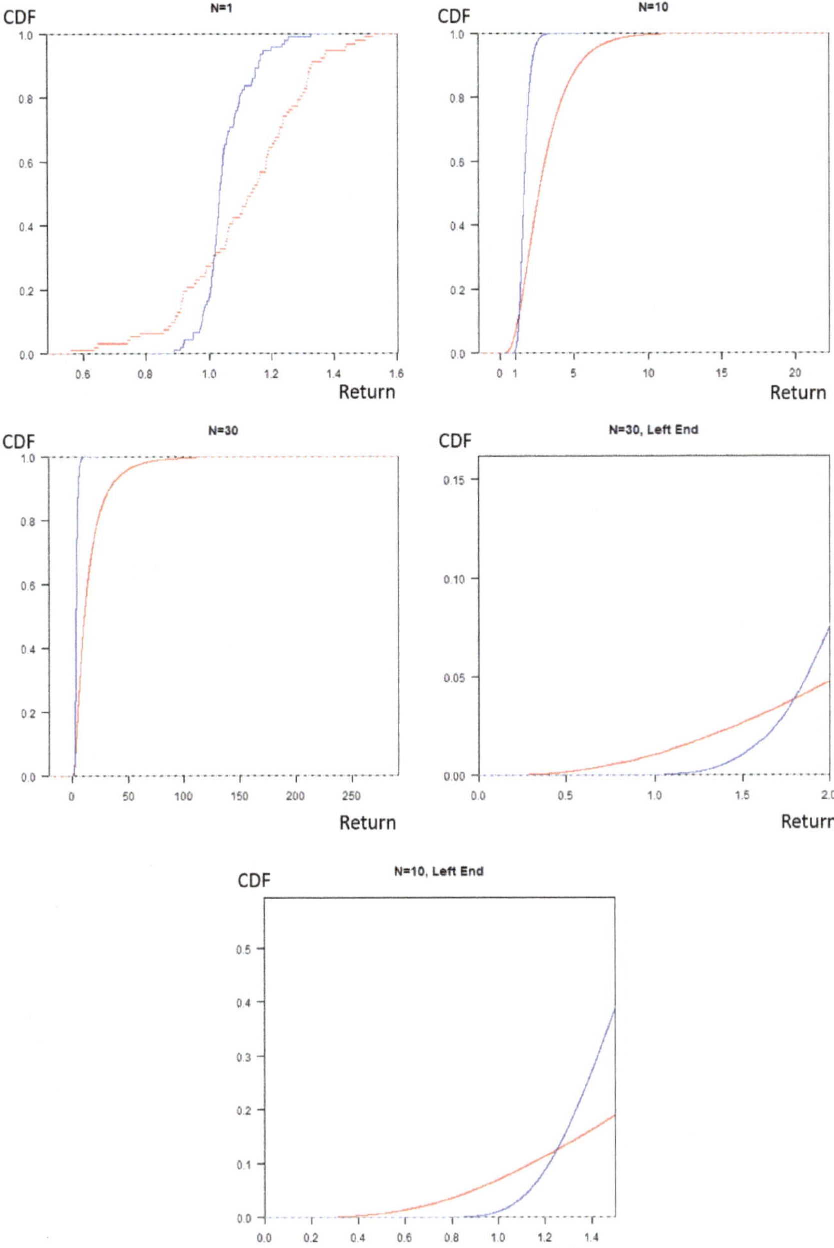

Figure 1.4: The cumulative distribution of returns on stocks (R_S) and on bonds (R_B) with *i.i.d.* assumption.

Table 1.3: The probability of the wealth invested in stocks (w_S) to be larger than the wealth invested in bonds (w_B) for various horizons (with *i.i.d.* assumption).

Years (N)	Mean		Standard Deviation		
	Stocks	Bonds	Stocks	Bonds	$Pr(w_S > w_B)$
1	1.1148	1.0513	0.1949	0.0761	0.6386
2	1.2439	1.1057	0.3094	0.1135	0.6612
3	1.3874	1.1619	0.4241	0.1458	0.6801
4	1.5484	1.2224	0.5533	0.1773	0.6939
5	1.7279	1.2848	0.6949	0.2090	0.7076
10	2.9838	1.6527	1.7752	0.3839	0.7650
15	5.1822	2.1204	3.9053	0.6039	0.8111
20	8.9126	2.7335	8.1409	0.9118	0.8376
25	15.4534	3.5096	16.2417	1.3199	0.8643
30	26.7006	4.5082	32.3596	1.8692	0.8874

probability that stocks yield a larger terminal wealth than bonds for various horizons. We can see from this table that the mean return and the standard deviation of the return on stocks grow with the horizon much faster with stocks than with bonds. However, when one looks at the probability of having a larger terminal wealth by investing in stocks rather than bonds, this probability increases with the horizon: from about 63% for a horizon of one year to about 89% for a horizon of 30 years, and this probability increases monotonically with the horizon. However, despite this relatively large advantage of stocks over bonds for the long run, we do not observe in Table 1.3 an absolute win of stocks which conforms with the findings that the two cumulative distributions intersect for all horizons.

Thus, the trend of the increasing probability of stocks outperforming bonds in the long run is consistent with Theorem 1.1; however, even for $N = 30$, we are not close to absolute dominance of stocks over bonds. Does this increased probability with the horizon matter? It seems that, in practice, investors assign a large weight to the probability of winning in the investment race, much more than expected by the expected utility paradigm.[32]

---

[32]Diecidue, Levy, and Levy report on an experiment's results showing that subjects assign a very large weight in their choices to this probability of winning in

From this finding, we tend to conclude that the typical investor would prefer stocks over bonds in the long run, resulting from the increasing probability to win in the investment race, despite the fact that the expected utility of stocks is not larger than that of bonds for all possible risk-averse utility functions. Thus, even if one accepts the theoretical argument objecting theoretically to the strategy of "stocks for the long run," this preference in practice for prospects with a larger probability of being ahead may explain the assertion of "stocks for the long run," as well as the observed demand for target-date mutual funds, which will be discussed in the next chapter.

1.5. Diversification Across Time — The Case for Target-Date Funds

While there is theoretical debate regarding the changes in the relative attractiveness of stocks with the horizon, examining the facts regarding investment in practice, it seems that practitioners, at least a large segment of them, have a more solid view, asserting that the longer the horizon, the more attractive the stocks become.

In this section, we report on investment vehicles suggested by practitioners for long-horizon investors, mainly those who save for retirement. We discuss the growing market value of funds traded in the market, suggesting to long-horizon investors to increase their investment weight of stocks with the length of the planned investment horizon. Thus, abstracting from the various theoretical arguments regarding the changes in the relative attractiveness of stocks with the horizon, we focus in this section on the actual investment strategies adopted by mutual funds as an investment for long-run investors. These mutual funds would not exist in the market without the demand for such vehicles by investors. Therefore, the presented facts

---

the race, or the probability of being ahead. They show that 73% of the risk-averse subjects aligned with the probability dominance (PD), as opposed to the optimal risk-averse investment rule that is consistent with expected utility. Thus, these subjects preferred to invest in a prospect that was inferior by the expected utility criterion, as long as it had a larger probability of being ahead. For more details see Diecidue, E., M. Levy, and J. Van de Ven (2015). No aspiration to win? An experimental test of the aspiration level model. *Journal of Risk and Uncertainty* 51(3), 245–266.

on the investment strategies of these funds must also reflect the investors' beliefs (which may be correct or erroneous) regarding the relation between the optimal asset allocation to stocks and bonds and the planned investment horizon. Otherwise, they would not invest in these funds, and the funds would simply vanish.

As we shall see below, the longer the planned investment horizon, say, in investing for retirement, the common strategies of target-date funds (TDFs) are to allocate a relatively larger proportion of the invested wealth to risky assets, say stocks, which on the one hand are admitted to be more volatile than bonds in the short run but, on the other hand, they are, on average, also much more profitable and less risky than bonds in the long run. This recommendation implicitly assumes that, in the long run, bad years in the stock market are offset by good years; hence, for relatively long-run investors, the risk of stocks is not as severe as for short-run investors. In essence, those advocating that stocks become relatively more attractive for the long run than in the short run think that long-run investors enjoy the relatively large reward but avoid a lion's share of the risk involved.

In the market, there are numerous traded funds like TDFs or Life Cycle Funds which adhere to this investment strategy: the longer the investment horizon, the larger the investment weight allocated to risky assets (generally, stocks) in the invested portfolio of these funds.[33] Thus, managers of TDFs presumably strongly believe that the planned investment horizon affects the desired optimal asset allocation and recommend investing a relatively large weight in stocks by long-horizon investors. In practice, these funds decrease the proportion of stocks, or any other risky assets, in the portfolio with the age of the investors, say, every five years.

---

[33] Note, however, that young investors have larger human capital than relatively old investors. Thus, it is possible that when decreasing the investment weight in stocks with age, the TDFs actually adopt a constant diversification between risky and riskless assets over time as the human capital, which is like a bond, also decreases with age.

Notwithstanding, at the moment, we do not take a stand whether this asset allocation approach is theoretically correct or wrong, but rather emphasize the fact that some theoretical researchers, and particularly professional investors, believe that this is the correct investment strategy. Moreover, in practice, as investors invest in these funds, this issue deserves our attention.

TDF market value has dramatically increased in the United States (US) from \$763 billion in 2015 to approximately \$1.9 trillion in 2020, an annual growth rate of about 19%. As we can see from Table 1.4, many investment companies that have traditionally offered mutual funds, in recent years, have developed a TDF branch aimed to consider the investment horizon as an important factor for investors for retirement.

As most TDFs have a similar investment strategy, we illustrate the strategy of Vanguard's TDF which is an investment company that has developed the "glide path" investment strategy. In an article discussing the Vanguard Capital Market Model, Donaldson *et al.*[34] describe the changes in the asset allocation of Vanguard's TDF with age. They show its asset allocation policy as a function of the planned investment horizon of the investors, or alternatively as a function of the number of years left to the planned retirement age. Figure 1.5 shows the asset allocation changes declared by Vanguard as a function of the investor's age.

Assuming investment for a retirement at age 65, the figure demonstrates the investment "glide path" of risky assets with age. At age 25, namely with an investment horizon of 40 years, the TDF of Vanguard allocates 50% to US stocks and 40% to international stocks; hence, 90% are invested in stocks that are considered to be risky for short-horizon investors, but presumably, at least as considered by Vanguard management, not very risky for long-run investors. At age 40, where there are 25 years to the retirement target date, the weights of these two risky assets gradually decrease; hence, the name "glide path," and at about age 72 (which is beyond

---

[34]See https://www.vanguard.com/pdf/s167.pdf

Table 1.4: TDFs in the US

*In the US, the use of TDFs accelerated from 2006 onward with the
   introduction of automatic-enrollment pension legislation, where the
   convenience of a single "fund for life" made them the most popular type of
   default strategy. Since that time, TDF assets under management have
   grown more than 10 times, reaching $763 billion at the end of 2015. As of
   March 2020, assets in target-date mutual funds and collective investment
   trusts totaled approximately $1.9 trillion.*

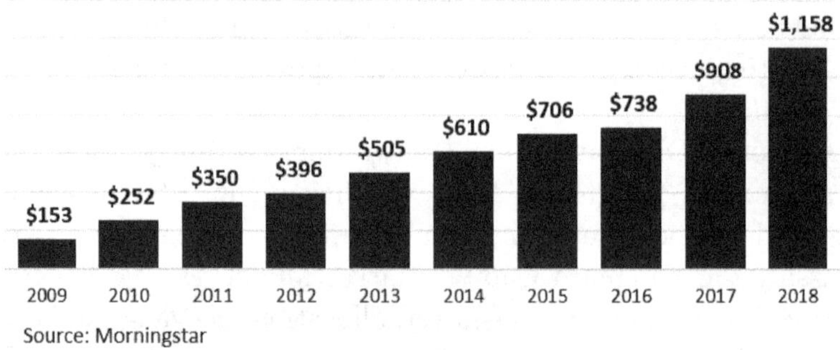

**Target-Date Mutual Fund Assets Under Management
(\$ Billions; As of Jan. 31 of Each Year Shown)**

Source: Morningstar

The main target-date benchmarks in the US are:
*S&P Target-Date Indices, Dow Jones Target-Date Indices, Morningstar
   Lifetime Allocation Indexes.*
*Major TDF managers in the US include Fidelity, Vanguard, T. Rowe Price,
   BlackRock (which manages the "Lifecycle Funds" — the target-date funds
   within the US Government Thrift Savings Plan), Principal Funds, Wells
   Fargo Advantage, American Century, and Northern Trust.*
*Note that the actual sizes of the books of different managers are difficult to
   estimate, as many hold assets in vehicles other than mutual funds.
   Northern Trust, for example, uses collective trust funds (CTFs), which
   typically do not figure in Morningstar or Bloomberg estimates of assets
   under management (AUM).*

Source: https://en.wikipedia.org/wiki/Target_date_fund.

the retirement age) only 20–30% is invested in risky assets, and
the lion's share of the investment is allocated to safer assets like
US bonds, international bonds, and Treasury inflation-protected
securities (TIPS). There are many other funds with different "glide
path" strategies; however, all have one common feature, albeit not

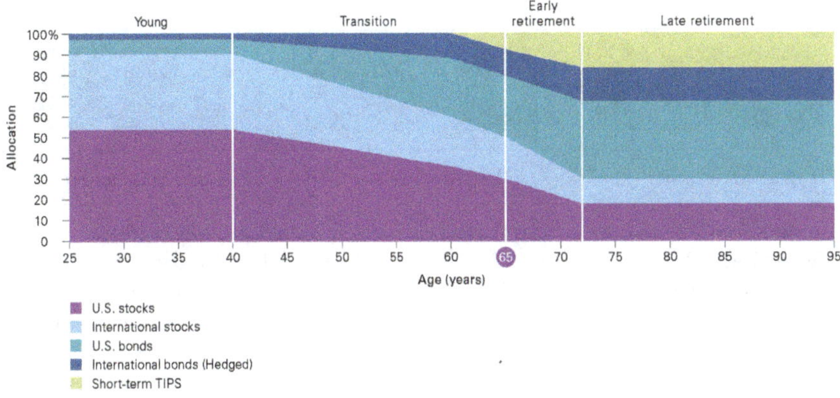

Figure 1.5: Glide path for Vanguard TDFs.

Notes: Figure assumes that a particular fund was selected based on a project target retirement age of 65.

Source: Vanguard.

at the same magnitude: the longer the investment horizon (young investors), the larger the investment weight allocated to risky assets, generally stocks.

Figure 1.5 relates to Vanguard's TDF. However, this investment strategy of decreasing the risky asset investment weight with age is quite common among practitioners and is not unique to Vanguard. Table 1.5, which conforms with Vanguard's investment strategy, provides the American Association of Individual Investors (AAII) allocation model, where the portfolio composition changes with age. Although this recommendation may change from one year to another, the basic idea of decreasing the weight in the risky asset in the portfolio with age is always intact. As can be seen from this table, at ages 18–35, it is recommended to invest 90% in stocks, while at age 55+, the recommended weight in stocks is reduced to 40%. It is estimated that investors whose age falls in the range of 18–25 may face a bad year with a loss of -37%, while a saver at age 55+ faces a potential bad year with a loss of only -12%. This difference is a direct result from the glide path strategy where young people invest a larger proportion of their wealth in stocks than older people.

Table 1.5: Asset allocation models to maximize your returns.

Aggressive Investor 90% Diversified Stock	Moderate Investor 60% Diversified Stock	Conservative Investor 40% Diversified Stock
Time Horizon	**Time Horizon**	**Time Horizon**
Age: often 18–35 **20+Years:** Long Investment Horizon	**Age:** often 35–55 **15+Years:** Mid-Term Investment Horizon	**Age:** often 55+ **10+Years:** Short-Term Investment Horizon
For investors who are very risk tolerant	*For investors who can tolerate some risk*	*For investors who are not risk tolerant*
Characteristics	**Characteristics**	**Characteristics**
Growth: Substantial **Income:** Very Low **Risk:** Substantial Year-to-Year Volatility of Portfolio Value **8%** Average Annual Growth in Value **−37%** Bad Year	**Growth:** Moderate **Income:** Low **Risk:** Moderate Year-to-Year Volatility of Portfolio Value **7%** Average Annual Growth in Value **−21%** Bad Year	**Growth:** Low **Income:** Moderate **Risk:** Low Year-to-Year Volatility of Portfolio Value **6%** Average Annual Growth in Value **−12%** Bad Year

Source: aaii.com.

At this point, we would like to emphasize that there are two relevant issues to consider with the TDF investment strategy, as well as with the AAII investing advice. There are two basic alternative ways to decrease risk with age, and considering these two alternative investment strategies is important, as the investor's welfare may increase by shifting from one investment strategy to another. We consider the following two ways to decrease risk with the horizon:

(a) The longer the investment horizon, the larger the average annual proportion of invested wealth in stocks.

(b) The "glide path" is a strategy employed to achieve the desired reduction of the weight allocated to stocks with age.

For example, for a two-year investment (we take the two-year case only to simplify the numerical example; however, the TDF investment policy actually corresponds to many years until retirement), and one can invest in 30% stocks in both years or employ the glide path policy by investing 40% in the first year and 20% in the second year. (Note that in both cases, the annual average investment in stocks is 30%; hence, by investing a constant percent, 30% in this case, we conform to the glide path strategy of investing 40% in the first year and 20% in the second year.)

Keeping this principle that the larger the investment horizon, the larger the average weight that is allocated to stocks, Levy and Levy[35] compare the two alternative ways given above to achieve the desired reduction in risk with the horizon. They investigate the economic efficiency of the glide path investment strategy by comparing it to the constant allocation to stocks, where this constant allocation is a function of the investment horizon. They show that the constant allocation to stocks in the whole period is optimal, and shifting from the glide path to the constant weight strategy can increase the terminal wealth of all risk-averse investors. Thus, for investors who invest for, say, 40 years, it is better to take all 40 years' annual weights allocated to stocks by the glide path strategy, calculate the average of all these weights, and instead of investing by the existing glide path strategy, simply allocate to stocks in each of the 40 years according to the obtained average weight. Note that by this constant investment strategy, for each investment horizon, we have a different constant investment weight. For example, an investor at age 25 will invest, say, 60% in stocks every year up to the retirement age, and an investor at age 40 may invest, say, 30% in stock every year up to the retirement age. By replacing the glide path investment strategy with the strategy of allocating a constant weight to stocks across all years, the risk is reduced and, as a result, welfare increases by 5–22% at the terminal date, depending on the case under consideration.

---

[35]Levy, H. and M. Levy (2021). The cost of diversification over time, and a simple way to improve target-date funds. *Journal of Banking & Finance.*

It is important to emphasize that Levy and Levy do not analyze the controversial issue whether the investment strategy known as "stocks for the long run" is theoretically justified. They adhere to the TDFs' strategy, asserting that the longer the horizon, the more should be allocated to stocks, but suggest replacing the "glide path" investment strategy with the "constant" annual investment strategy, where in both investment strategies, the longer the investment horizon, the larger the average weight allocated to stocks, which conforms with the school of thought advocating that the "stocks for the long run" investment strategy is optimal.

Notwithstanding, as is common in the literature, we employ the terms "glide path" and "stocks for the long run" interchangeably, as both refer to the belief that the longer the investment horizon, the larger the weight that should be allocated to stocks, and we keep in mind the fact that even those who believe in the investment strategy of "stocks for the long run" can increase their welfare by shifting from the "glide path" investment strategy to the "constant" allocation investment strategy suggested by Levy and Levy.

1.6. What is the Rationale for the Glide Path Investment Strategy?

What is the rationale of the "glide path" investment policy? Virtually all investors agree that short-run stocks are more profitable, but also riskier than bonds, as their volatility is much larger than the volatility of bonds. Covering a long historical number of years, the mean annual return on stocks is 11.57% with a volatility of $\sigma = 19.58\%$, while the corresponding figures for 10-year Treasury bonds are 5.14% and 7.67%, respectively, based on historical annual rates of return covering the period 1928–2019.[36] Thus, an investor for a one-year horizon faces the following classical investment dilemma: does the advantage of the extra average profit on stocks outweigh the additional risk involved? The common view in the financial literature is that each investor who invests for a relatively short horizon, say,

---

[36]Based on NYU data, see footnote 29.

one year, should make a choice in such a case depending on their preference that reflects its degree of tolerance to risk.

The investors in TDFs are well aware of the risk of investing in stocks, and do not ignore the relatively large volatility of stocks in the short run. However, they have invested for the long run, and as mentioned before, they implicitly or explicitly assume that bad as well as good years will occur in the stock market, and if the investment horizon is long enough, bad years and good years are offset. Therefore, the long-run investors' gain is approximately the average return on stocks which is larger than the average return on bonds, without experiencing a relatively large risk. Thus, investors in TDFs rely on reducing risk by diversification across time, but do not ignore the fact that good as well as bad years may occur during their long investment period.

Figure 1.6 demonstrates the diversification across time concept. It shows the historical risk premium measured for various investment horizons, emphasizing this diversification across time idea. It provides the average excess return (that is, the return on stocks less than the return on Treasury bonds) for the period 1926–2014, as well as the range of these excess returns, where the range actually provides an indication of the risk involved by investing in stocks. For example, if one invests for one year, the average annualized excess return is positive, but the realized return may fall in the range of approximately -40% to $+40\%$, that is, the risk of investing in stocks for one year is relatively large. However, as one increases the investment horizon, this range of rates of return decreases, and for a very long horizon of about 30–40 years, the excess return is always positive, as even the lower range is non-negative. This is the fundamental argument of those who advocate that the "stocks for the long run" investment strategy dominates the other competing strategies.

In essence, this is the foundation of TDF's "glide path" investment strategies, advocating that the longer the planned investment horizon, the larger the investment weight that should be allocated to stocks, where long-horizon investors enjoy the relatively large mean return of stocks, while the risk is reduced as the lower bound of the

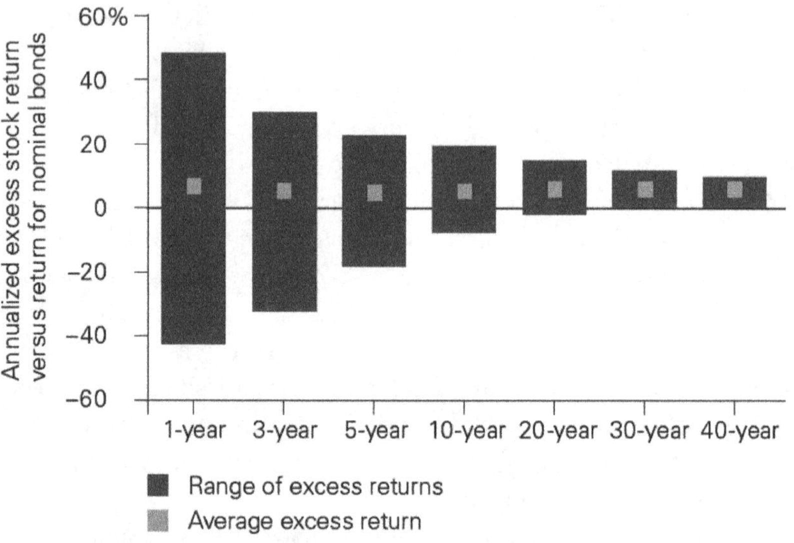

Figure 1.6: Historical equity risk premium over different periods, 1926–2014.

Notes: Past performance is no guarantee of future results. The performance of an index is not an exact representation of any particular investment, as you cannot invest directly in an index. US stock market returns are represented by the Standard & Poor's 90 from 1926 through March 3, 1957; the Standard & Poor's 500 Index from March 4, 1957 through 1974; the Wilshire 5000 Index from 1975 through April 22, 2005; the MSCI US Broad Market Index from April 23, 2005 through June 2, 2013; and the CRSP US Total Market Index thereafter. US bond market returns are represented by the Standard & Poor's High Grade Corporate Index from 1926 to 1968, the Citigroup High Grade Index from 1969 to 1972, the Lehman Brothers US Long Credit AA Index from 1973 to 1975, the Barclays Capital US Aggregate Bond Index from 1976 to 2009, and the Spliced Barclays U.S. Aggregate Float Adjusted Bond Index thereafter.

Sources: Vanguard calculations, based on data from Standard & Poor's, Wilshire, MSCI, CRSP, Citigroup, and Barclays.

return shifts upward with the horizon and even becomes non-negative for very long investment horizons. This explanation conforms with Siegel's (see footnote 21) assertion that for long horizons, stocks are actually riskless as the return is always non-negative.

Does stock risk indeed decrease with the investment horizon? Are stocks safer or riskier than bonds for relatively long horizons? One way to analyze the relation between the asset's risk and its long-run performance is to examine the wealth accumulation of a $1 investment in various assets (mainly stocks and bonds), as well as the volatility involved for various assumed investment horizons. Figure 1.7 presents the performance of stocks and bonds as a function of the horizon, a performance that is affected by both the average return as well as the volatility. As can be seen from this figure, for investment horizons of about 10–15 years, bonds, in most cases, outperform stocks. However, recall that the period covered (1928–2019) also includes the Great Depression, a period where investors in the stock market suffered from extremely large losses. Nevertheless, looking at longer investment horizons, stocks outperformed bonds by a wide margin: a $1 invested in stocks at the beginning of 1928 has grown to a terminal wealth of about $5,024 in 2019, while the parallel figure for investment in bonds is merely about $80 (see Figure 1.7). The results presented in Figure 1.7 conform with those presented in Figure 1.6, as both show risk reduction with the horizon or, more precisely, that the longer the horizon, the more attractive stocks become.

Figure 1.8 is similar to Figure 1.7 with the exception that, here, we compare the investment in Decile 1 of stocks, which are the 10% smallest stocks measured by their market value, with the 10% largest stocks, data taken from French's Website.[37] Note that the stocks included in each decile may shift to other deciles with time, as their market value increases or decreases with time. With the dataset employed here, the decile composition has been changed once a year according to the changes in the market values.

Once again, for relatively short investment horizons, small stock risk is very apparent, but as the horizon increases, the two curves do not intersect, revealing the clear advantage of small stocks for the long run. As we can see from Figure 1.8, $1 invested in 1927 in small stocks grew to about $40,000 by year 2019, in comparison to

---

[37] https://mba.tuck.dartmouth.edu/pages/faculty/ken.french/data_library.html. The portfolios are constructed at the end of each June using the June market equity and New York Stock Exchange (NYSE) breakpoints.

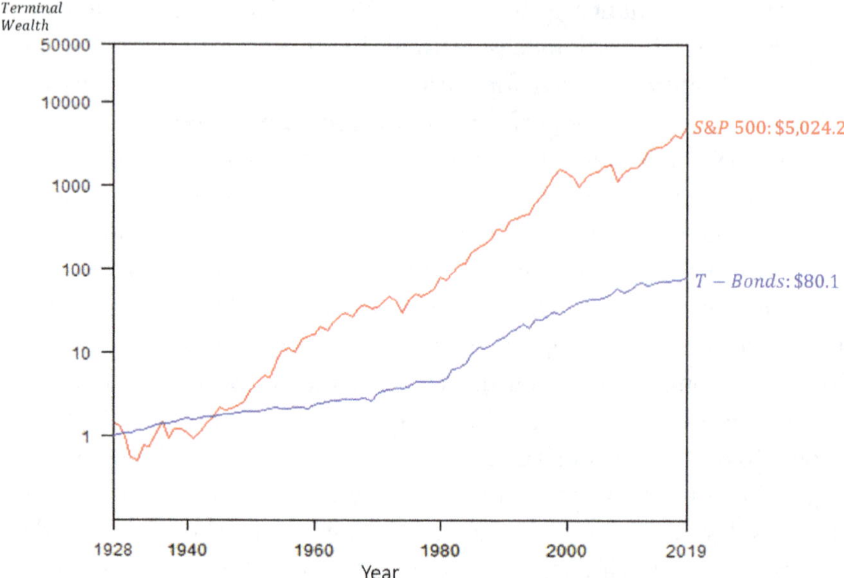

Figure 1.7: The terminal wealth of a $1 investment in January 1928 in the S&P 500 stock index and 10-year Treasury bonds.

Source: NYU, http://people.stern.nyu.edu/adamodar/pc/datasets/histretSP.xls.

only $7,953 and $5,665 invested in large stocks and the market,[38] respectively.

Those who disagree with the glide path investment strategy (but do not deny the empirical facts) have two reservations regarding the above empirical evidence:

(a) History may not repeat itself, and big losses in the stock market, even more than we experienced in the past, may occur in the future. More specifically, it is claimed that stocks become riskier rather than safer as the horizon increases. This claim conforms

---

[38]The monthly market return of month t is the value-weight return of all CRSP firms incorporated in the US and listed on the NYSE, American Stock Exchange (AMEX), or NASDAQ that have a CRSP share code of 10 or 11 at the beginning of month t, good shares and price data at the beginning of t, and good return data for t (from Ibbotson Associates).

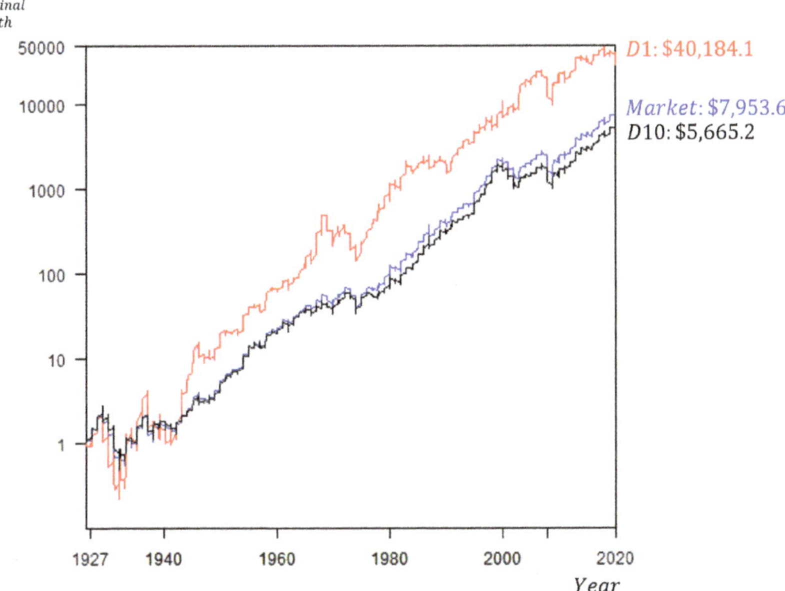

Figure 1.8: The terminal wealth of a $1 investment in January 1928 in the top decile, the bottom decile, and the S&P500 stock index.

Source: Kenneth French's website, https://mba.tuck.dartmouth.edu/pages/faculty/ken.french/data_library.html. The portfolios are constructed at the end of each June using the June market equity and NYSE breakpoints.

with Bodie's study and Pástor and Stambaugh's study discussed earlier in the chapter.

(b) Suppose that an investor's retirement date is in a year where a crisis in the stock market occurs, such as the crisis that we observed in the year 2008. In such a case, glide path investors may have insufficient funds for consumption after retirement.

While reservation (a) is intact, and it is hard either to confirm or to refute it, it will probably remain in dispute also in the future, whereas reservation (b) can be empirically examined.

Figure 1.9 reveals the terminal wealth of a $1 investment where it was assumed that the retirement date was at the end of 2008, which included the stock market crash. We have to read this figure as follows: on the horizontal axis, we have the number of years since

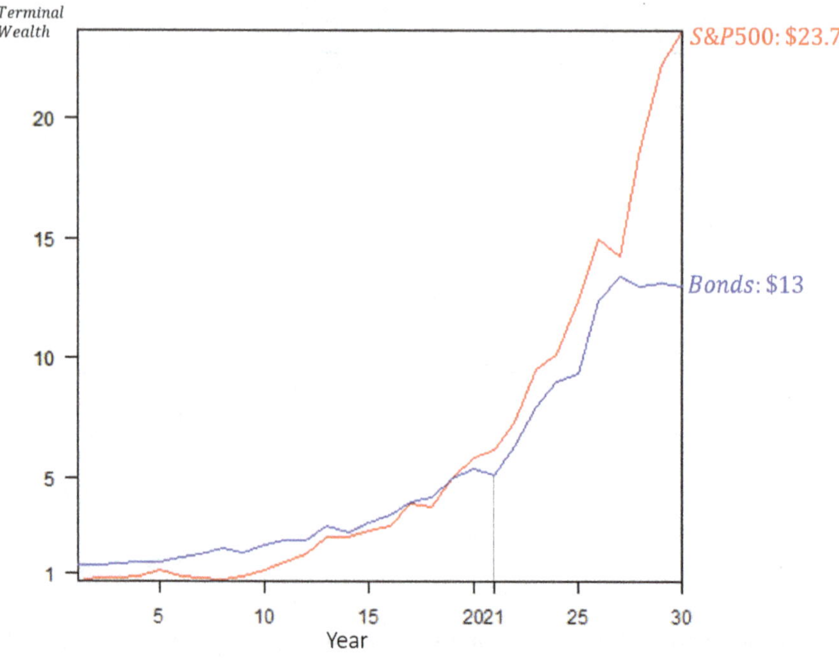

Figure 1.9: The terminal wealth as a function of the investment period of $1 prior to the 2008 financial crisis.

Source: NYU, http://people.stern.nyu.edu/adamodar/pc/datasets/histretSP.xls.

opening the investment for retirement to the retirement date that is assumed to be in 2008. Thus, $N = 5$ years, for example, indicates that the investor started the investment account for retirement five years before the 2008 crash, that is, in January 2004. As we can see from Figure 1.9, indeed, the 2008 stock market crash was devastating for stock investors. However, the more relevant question is: was it better to invest in bonds rather than in stocks when 2008 was indeed the retirement year? Well, it depends on the length of the investment period. Specifically, the main result revealed by Figure 1.9 is that up to about 20 years before 2008, the bonds curve is above the stock curve, meaning that if an investor started investing at age 45 and retired at age 65, it would be better to invest in bonds rather than in stocks, let alone for investors who start investing at an older age, say, at age 55, only 10 years before retirement.

However, there are two main points in defense of the "stocks for the long run" strategy which is adopted by TDFs, even in the case where the 2008 crash is considered. First, recall that TDFs are tailormade for long-horizon investors, generally for investments of 30–40 years and not for investors who start investing for retirement at age 45. Indeed, for a 30-year investment horizon, investing $1 in stocks grew to more than $23 in 2008 and investing in bonds grew only to $13, even when the 30-year horizon includes the 2008 stock market crash, which is assumed to be the retirement date. Second, even if one starts investing at age 45 for retirement, the investment weight in stocks is less than 100% (see Figure 1.5), which may moderate the damage of the 2008 stock market crash (relative to what we observe in Figure 1.9).

Thus, there are some academic studies that support the concept of "stocks for the long run" and others that cast doubt about the optimality of this investment policy.

Finally, it is important to emphasize that, in the empirical analysis, we are dealing with portfolios of risky assets (e.g., the S&P 500 stock index) and not individual stocks, as the investment in individual stocks may be riskier and also less profitable than investing in Treasury bills even in the very long run, as documented by Bessembinder.[39] Specifically, Bessembinder shows that less than 4% of the stocks account for the relatively good performance of stock portfolios, and most stocks underperform even Treasury bills. This 4% of stocks with relatively good performance has a very large positive skewness,[40] that is, they have some extreme large positive returns. The managers of TDFs are presumably aware of this issue, as they commonly invest in portfolio of stocks and not in individual stocks; hence, there is no contradiction between their investment policy and the empirical results of Bessembinder.

---

[39]Bessembinder, H. (2018). Do stocks outperform Treasury bills? *Journal of Financial Economics* 129(3), 440–457.

[40]The relation between the creation of skewness in the long run is discussed in detail in Chapter 2.

Despite the academic dispute regarding the desired changes in the relative attractiveness of stocks and bonds with the horizon, one fact is transparent and cannot be ignored: a substantial segment of investors and practitioners believe that stocks are more attractive than bonds in the long run; otherwise, we would not observe the flourishing and relatively fast-growing market value of the TDFs. It is possible that stocks do not dominate bonds even in the long run, but they provide a larger probability of being ahead, or winning the race, which may be the main motivation of investors to invest in TDFs.

1.7. Summary

Asset allocation, mainly between stocks and bonds as a function of the assumed investment horizon, is an ongoing debate where there is disagreement, mainly among academic researchers, regarding the following issues:

(a) The changes in the riskiness of stocks with the horizon.
(b) The changes in the attractiveness of stocks with the horizon, relative to the attractiveness of bonds.
(c) The superiority of the prospect with the largest GM over any other alternative investment strategy.

Unfortunately, all of these issues remain in dispute theoretically and empirically. The fact that there is no agreement makes the investment choice very difficult, but certainly intellectually more interesting, and we expect more research regarding the above three unsolved issues in the future.

One school of thought advocates that due to mean reversion, stocks become less risky with the horizon, and even argue that stocks become less risky than bonds for an investment horizon of 10 years or longer. Moreover, the claim is that for a 20-year horizon or more, stocks become riskless.

The opposing school of thought argues that history will not repeat itself, and due to possible changes in the future parameters of the distribution of stock returns, stocks become riskier with the horizon. Note, however, that this school of thought focuses solely on the risk, and does not rule out the possibility that stocks become more attractive than bonds as the horizon increases, when both risk and profitability are simultaneously considered.

The theoretical dispute concerning the attractiveness of stocks for the long run cannot overlook the observed investment in practice. Practitioners commonly claim that stocks become safer with the horizon; hence, they establish TDFs for savers for retirement, with an investment strategy that allocates about 90% to stocks for young investors (that is, a very long investment horizon) and only 20–30% in stocks for relatively old investors. While the academic dispute regarding this issue is still ongoing, in practice, these TDFs have increased rapidly in the past few years, indicating that the investors' view is that stocks become safer with the horizon, hence the common assertion of "stocks for the long run." The fact that the TDF industry has increased rapidly in recent years also indicates that investors believe in (or are at least persuaded by) the "stocks for the long run" investment strategy.

Chapter 2

The Distribution of Returns
and the Horizon

The investment criteria for optimal investment decision-making depends on the distribution of the returns characterizing the various risky prospects under consideration. For example, if the distributions of returns are normal (or more generally, the distribution belongs to the elliptic family distributions), one can safely employ the well-known Markowitz mean–variance (M–V) rule for choosing between prospects, as well as for finding efficient investment diversification strategies.[1] Moreover, if the riskless asset is also available, one can also find the optimal portfolio of risky assets, and under some additional assumptions, the capital asset pricing model (CAPM) suggested by Sharpe[2] can be derived.

While there is a lot of information on the distribution of returns calculated for relatively short horizons (mainly weekly and monthly distributions), less information is available on long-run distributions, say, 5- or 10-year distributions of returns — information that is required for investing for retirement. Knowing the shape of the distributions of returns corresponding to various investment horizons is important, as there are investors in the market who invest for various investment horizons, and for each horizon, a different

---

[1]For proof of this claim, see Chamberlain (1983). A characterization of the distributions that imply mean–variance utility functions. *Journal of Economic Theory* 29(1), 185–201

[2]Sharpe, W. F. (1964). Capital asset prices: A theory of market equilibrium. *The Journal of Finance* 19(3), 425–442.

distribution may emerge. Specifically, relatively short-run investors may apply the M–V rule for investment decisions (as the distributions are symmetrical, e.g., logistic or normal) and long-run investors need to employ different investment criteria as the distributions of returns are no longer elliptic. Thus, investors with different horizons need to employ different investment rules, ending up with different optimal investments.

Moreover, as the distributions of returns change with the horizon, investment consultants must know the length of the planned investment horizon of each customer, as the optimal investment decision that is relevant to the customer under consideration depends on the shape of the distribution of returns corresponding to the investor's planned investment horizon. Therefore, different investors may receive different advice concerning their optimal investment. The following quote from a recent study of Fama and French[3] regarding the horizon issue and the importance of the information regarding the distribution of returns for relatively long horizons sheds more light on the importance of the subject discussed in this chapter:

> *We also know a lot about the characteristics of short-horizon stock returns. Distribution of daily and monthly, for example, are leptokurtic relative to normal distribution (Fama 1965[4]). Because we have fewer observations, we know less about distributions of long-run returns. It seems likely, however, that the characteristics of long-horizon returns are of central interest to investors saving for distant payoffs. If so, it is likely that the characteristics of long-horizon returns affect asset pricing in ways missed by our models. Evidence on distribution of long-horizon returns is a logical first step in remedying this deficiency (Fama and French, 2018, p. 232).*

To overcome the shortage of observations when long-run distributions are analyzed, Fama and French suggest the bootstrap methodology. They find that the empirical distributions of long-term (30 years)

---

[3]Fama, E. F. and K. French (2018). Long-horizon returns. *The Review of Asset Pricing Studies* 8(2), 232–252.

[4]Fama, E. F. (1965). The behavior of stock-market prices. *The Journal of Business* 38(1), 34–105.

rates of return fit the log-normal distribution well. However, it is well known that the log-normal distribution is positively skewed; hence, one must take this property into account in the investment decision-making process. Specifically, one cannot safely employ the M–V rule, which assumes a symmetric distribution of returns, that is, it ignores the skewness.

In this chapter, we employ the Crystal Ball program to find out which of the theoretical distributions out of a set of a relatively large number of theoretical distributions best fits the empirical distributions of returns corresponding to various horizons. As we shall see, the distribution which best fits the data changes with the horizon, which causes major difficulty for the existing methodology of investment decision-making under risk, even if there is full information on the shape of the distribution corresponding to each given horizon. We find that for a relatively short horizon, say, less than about nine months (depending on the dataset), the distribution is symmetric, and the skewness can be safely ignored. However, for longer horizons, we get some instability in the shape of the empirical distributions, as the best fit theoretical distribution changes from one horizon to another. However, for a longer horizon of about one year (once again, this horizon also changes with the set of data), a positive skewness is built up, and the distribution tends to be log-normal. Thus, unless the horizon is relatively small, the popular M–V rule cannot be employed for investment choices without incurring an economic loss. In the log-normal case, the distribution's skewness should not be ignored as it also determines the investors' expected utility.

Three problems arise with changes in the distribution of returns with the horizon that make it difficult to establish optimal investment decision rules for all horizons, that is, for all investors:

(a) Suppose that the distributions of returns are neither normal nor log-normal. Specifically, we find that for intermediate horizons, the distribution that best fits the empirical distribution is found to be the gamma, beta, or extreme distribution. How can an optimal choice be made in these cases? To the best of my knowledge, for these distributions, there are no operational and optimal investment rules for all investors or to a subset of all investors (say, all risk averters) — rules which are consistent with an expected utility paradigm. The same is true for other well-known statistical distributions, with the exception of the normal (or elliptical) and log-normal distributions, for which we have optimal investment rules that conform to expected utility paradigms.

(b) Suppose that for important assets, say, stocks and risky bonds, the distributions of the one-period (say one month or one year) rates of returns are indeed normal (or logistic) or approximately normal (or approximately logistic); hence, the well-known M–V investment criterion can safely be employed by all risk averters. In such a case, all risk-averse investors with a one-period planned investment horizon can safely employ the M–V rule to select the optimal diversification investment. However, investors with a longer investment horizon, who even completely agree that the one-period distribution is normal, face a multi-period distribution that is not normal; hence, the M–V rule is no longer optimal for them. For example, it is possible that for a relatively long horizon, the distributions of returns are log-normal; hence, the M–V rule is not optimal in this case, and other optimal rules corresponding to log-normal distributions should be employed. Suppose that there are only two distributions that best fit all investors: the normal and the log-normal. Having these two distributions and having the optimal rule for each of them, we face the following problem related to asset pricing: By assumption, there are investors with both short and long planned investment horizons in the market, and therefore, both of these classes of investors determine equilibrium prices of risky assets. In this case, how can we figure out the appropriate risk index of an asset? What is the equilibrium price of a given risky asset in such a situation? We must admit at the outset that while we have some answers to some questions raised in this chapter, not all answers are available. In some cases, we discuss the problem, but, to the best of our knowledge, no answer is yet available to this question in the literature.

(c) A practical investment issue also arises with the horizon's effect on the shape of the distribution of returns: suppose that a mutual fund has many customers with various horizons. Suppose that there is an optimal investment rule for each horizon. By which investment criterion should the fund's management select its assets when there is information that various clients have different investment horizons, hence different optimal investment portfolios?

The purpose of this chapter is to investigate the changes in the rates of return distributions of various risky assets with changes in the horizon. Specifically, we show that for a short horizon, a symmetrical distribution (e.g., logistic, Student's t, or normal distribution) best fits the empirical distributions. However, as the horizon increases, asystematic positive skewness, theoretically and empirically, is built up. Therefore, we can no longer employ the M–V rule for investment choice, which is optimal only for symmetrical elliptic distributions, namely for distributions for which the skewness is equal to zero. We find that in the very long run, the distributions are approximately log-normal, which is positively skewed; hence, decision rules corresponding to log-normal distributions should be employed. For moderate horizons, the distribution should be neither normal nor log-normal; therefore, in such cases, one should employ distribution-free decision rules like stochastic dominance (SD) rules (see Chapter 3), which are consistent with the expected utility paradigm regardless of the shape of the distribution under consideration.

We analyze first theoretically, and then empirically, the changes in the shape of the distributions of returns of various risky assets with changes in the investment horizon. This information is important to investors who have different investment horizons as, in practice, some investors invest for a short term, and some invest for a long term. Particularly for those investing for retirement, the investment horizon is a crucial practical issue.

2.1. The Investment Horizon and Skewness: The Theory

In this section, we discuss the role of skewness in determining the expected utility and the buildup of skewness with the investment horizon.

2.1.1. *The importance of skewness for expected utility maximizers*

In this section, we show the importance of the distribution's skewness in determining risk-averters' expected utility for asymmetric distributions of returns.

The expected utility can be expended to a Taylor's series as follows:

$$EU(W + x) = U(E + E(x)) + U''(W + E(x))\sigma^2/2!$$

$$+ U'''(W + E(x))\frac{\mu_3(x)}{3!} + \cdots$$

where W is the initial wealth, x stands for the random return, σ^2 stands for the variance of the return x, and $\mu_3(x)$ is the skewness (the third moment) of the distribution of the random variable. The term of the form $U^i(W+E(x))$ indicates that the ith derivative is taken at the point $(W + E(x))$. Thus, in principle, the expected utility depends on all the central moments of the distribution. If the distribution of the rates of returns under consideration is symmetric, say, normal, all the odd central moments are equal to zero and all the even central moments are a direct function of the variance.[5] Therefore, with normal distribution, the expected utility depends only on the mean and variance, that is, $EU(W + x) = f(mean, variance)$, which is

---

[5]The nth central moment of normal distribution is given by M^n which is equal to zero for odd numbers n, and equal to $\sigma^n(n-1)!!$ for even numbers n, where the sign denotes a double factorial, that is, the product of all numbers from n to 1 that have the same parity as n. For example, $M^4 = 3\sigma^4$, $M^6 = 15\sigma^6$, and by this formula, it is clear that all central even moments are a function of the variance.

the economic justification for the employment of the M–V rule in the normal (or elliptic) case.

Generally, all of a distribution's moments should be considered in making choices under risk as, in principle, all moments determine the expected utility. However, the meaning of the distribution's higher moments, say, higher than the fourth moment, is questionable: even the information that the fourth moment provides on the shape of the distribution is vague.[6] As the effect of the fourth moment on the shape of the distribution is in dispute among statisticians, it is reasonable to assume that this moment is not useful to investors and, therefore, cannot help to improve the investment-making process. The statistical information and the economic meaning of the fifth moment and moments higher than the fifth one are economically meaningless. In contrast, the third moment has a clear statistical and economic interpretation: the higher the third moment, the longer the left tail of the distributions of returns. Other things being equal, the larger the skewness, the larger the risk-averter's expected utility. To see this, recall that the risk premium, $\pi(W)$, is given by

$$\pi(W) = -\frac{U''(W)}{U'(W)}(\sigma^2/2)$$

and Arrow[7] argues that investors are typically characterized by a decreasing absolute risk premium (DARA), implying that

$$\frac{\partial \pi(W)}{\partial W} = -(\sigma^2/2)\frac{U'(W)U'''(W) - [U''(W)]^2}{[U'(W)]^2} < 0.$$

Therefore,

$$\frac{\partial \pi(W)}{\partial W} < 0 \Rightarrow -[U'(W)U'''(W) - [U''(W)]^2] < 0$$

---

[6]See Kaplansky, I. (1945). A common error concerning kurtosis. *Journal of American Statistical Association* 40(230), 259.

[7]Arrow, K. J. (1971). *Essays in the Theory of Risk Bearing*, North-Holland, Amsterdam.

implying that

$$[U'(W)U'''(W) > [U''(W)]^2].$$

And this can occur only if $U'''(W) > 0$. Going back to the Taylor expansion of the expected utility, it implies that the larger the skewness, other things being held constant, the larger the expected utility. This means that risk-averse investors like positive skewness, which is one of among several explanations why investors purchase lottery tickets and insurance policies: by purchasing lottery tickets, they purchase a positive skewness, and by purchasing an insurance policy, they simply "sell" the undesired negative skewness exposure to the insurance company. For long-horizon investors, as we shall see in what follows, the rates of return distributions are positively skewed, a property that should be considered in investment decision-making.

2.1.2. *The multi-period skewness built up: The theoretical analyses*

In this chapter, we show that even when the one-period distribution (of a stock return or that of any other asset) is symmetric (unlike the distribution induced by buying a lottery ticket, which is positively skewed), the multi-period distribution has positive skewness and, therefore, the M–V rule which assumes a zero skewness distribution (symmetrical distributions) cannot be an optimal investment rule for long-horizon investors. We assume that returns are independent over time, as it is obvious that if autocorrelation prevails, this dependency certainly affects the changes in the distributions of returns with the horizon. Moreover, in the case of dependency, the horizon effects on the distributions of returns depends on the type of the assumed autocorrelation. Notwithstanding, in this chapter, we also discuss the horizon's impact on the distributions of returns when autocorrelations are considered.

Denoting the ith one-period return by $(1 + R_i)$, the first three central moments of the one-period distribution of returns are defined as follows:

$$\text{Mean: } E(1 + R_i) = (1 + \mu_i)$$

$$\text{Variance: } E[(1 + R_i) - (1 + \mu_i)]^2 = \sigma_i^2$$

$$\text{Skewness: } E[(1 + R_i) = (1 + \mu_i)]^3 = \mu_{3i}.$$

The N-period return is given by $\prod_{i=1}^{N}(1 + R_i)$. Employing the independence assumption, the mean, variance, and skewness of these multi-period returns are denoted by E, V, and M and are given by

$$(1 + E) = \prod_{i=1}^{N}(1 + \mu_i). \tag{2.1}$$

Employing the independence assumption and the one-period relationship,

$$\sigma_i^2 = E(1 + R_i)^2 - (1 + \mu_i)^2; \text{ hence, } E(1 + R_i)^2 = (1 + \mu_i)^2 + \sigma_i^2.$$

The multi-period variance can be rewritten as

$$V = \prod_{i=1}^{N}[(1 + \mu_i)^2 + \sigma_i^2] - \prod_{i=1}^{N}(1 + \mu_i)^2 \tag{2.2}$$

and the multi-period skewness is given by

$$M = E\left\{\left[\prod_{i=1}^{N}(1 + R_i) - \prod_{i=1}^{N}(1 + \mu_i)\right]^3\right\} \tag{2.3}$$

where $\prod_{i=1}^{N}[(1 + R_i)$ is the multi-period return (a random variable) whose mean is $\prod_{i=1}^{N}(1 + \mu_i)$. The goal is to formulate the multi-period skewness given in Eq. (2.3), as a function of the one-period skewness, showing that even with zero one-period skewness (e.g., normal distribution), a positive multi-period skewness emerges. In the first step, we show that even with zero one-period skewness, which characterizes the distributions of returns for one year or less than a one-year horizon, the multi-period skewness is no longer zero, and in the second more important step, we show that the multi-period skewness is positive, and the longer the horizon, the larger this positive skewness. Later, we present an empirical case where the multi-period skewness is positive despite the fact that the one-period distribution skewness is negative.

Expanding Eq. (2.3) yields

$$
M = E\left[\prod_{i=1}^{N}[(1+R_i)^3]\right] - 3E\left[\prod_{i=1}^{N}(1+R_i)^2\right]\left[\prod_{i=1}^{N}(1+\mu_i)\right]
$$

$$
+ 3E\left[\prod_{i=1}^{N}[(1+R_i)]\left[\prod_{i=1}^{N}(1+\mu_i)^2\right]\right] - \left[\prod_{i=1}^{N}(1+\mu_i)\right]^3 . \quad (2.4)
$$

Using the independence assumption, Eq. (2.4) can be simplified and rewritten as

$$
M = E\left[\prod_{i=1}^{N}(1+R_i)^3\right] - 3\left[\prod_{i=1}^{N}(1+\mu_i)\right]E\left[\prod_{i=1}^{N}(1+R_i)^2\right]
$$

$$
+ 2\left[\prod_{i=1}^{N}(1+\mu_i)\right]^3 . \quad (2.5)
$$

To obtain the multi-period skewness, we first need to express the terms $E[\prod_{i=1}^{N}(1+R_i)^3]$ and $E[\prod_{i=1}^{N}(1+R_i)]^2$ appearing in Eq. (2.5) in a different way.

(a) The term $E[\prod_{i=1}^{N}(1+R_i)^3]$: Employing the independence assumption, this term can be written as

$$
E\left[\prod_{i=1}^{N}(1+R_i)^3\right] = \prod_{i=1}^{N}[E(1+R_i)^3]
$$

$$
= \prod_{i=1}^{N}[(1^3 + 3 \times 1^2 \times E(R_i)
$$

$$
+ 3 \times 1 \times E(R_i^2) + E(R_i^3)]
$$

$$
= \prod_{i=1}^{N}[1 + 3\mu_i + 3(\sigma_i^2 + \mu_i^2) + E(R_i^3)]. \quad (2.6)
$$

However, as in the one-period case, we have[8] $E(R_i^3) = \mu_{3i} + \mu_i(3\sigma_i^2 + \mu_i^2)$.

Eq. (2.6) can be rewritten as

$$E\left[\prod_{i=1}^{N}(1 + R_i)^3\right]$$

$$= \prod_{i=1}^{N}[1 + 3\mu_i + 3(\sigma_i^2 + \mu_i^2) + \mu_{3i} + \mu_i(3\sigma_i^2 + \mu_i^2)]$$

$$= \prod_{i=1}^{N}[1 + 3\mu_i + 3\mu_i^2 + \mu_i^3 + 3\sigma_i^2 + 3\mu_i\sigma_i^2 + \mu_{3i}]$$

$$= \prod_{i=1}^{N}[(1 + \mu_i)^3 + 3(1 + \mu_i)\sigma_i^2 + \mu_{3i}]. \tag{2.7}$$

(b) The term $E[\prod_{i=1}^{N}(1 + R_i)]^2$: This term appearing in Eq. (2.5) can be rewritten as

$$E\left[\prod_{i=1}^{N}(1 + R_i)\right]^2 = \prod_{i=1}^{N}[(1 + \mu_i)^2 + \sigma_i^2]. \tag{2.8}$$

Plugging the terms in Eqs. (2.7) and (2.8) in Eq. (2.5) yields

$$M = E\left[\prod_{i=1}^{N}(1 + R_i)^3\right] - 3\left[\prod_{i=1}^{N}(1 + \mu_i)\right]$$

$$\times E\left[\prod_{i=1}^{N}(1 + R_i)^2\right] + 2\left[\prod_{i=1}^{N}(1 + \mu_i)\right]^3$$

---

[8]Note that $\mu_{3i} = E(R_i - \mu_i)^3 = E(R_i^3) + 3E(R_i)\mu_i^2 - 3E(R_i^2)\mu_i - \mu_i^3$; hence,

$$E(R_i^3) = \mu_{3i} - 2\mu_i^3 + 3\mu_i(\sigma_i^2 + \mu_i^2) = \mu_{3i} + \mu_i(3\sigma_i^2 + \mu_i^2).$$

$$= \prod_{i=1}^{N} [(1 + \mu_i)^3 + 3(1 + \mu_i)\,\sigma_i^2 + \mu_{3i}]$$

$$- 3\left[\prod_{i=1}^{N}(1 + \mu_i)\right]\prod_{i=1}^{N}[(1 + \mu_i)^2 + \sigma_i^2] + 2\left[\prod_{i=1}^{N}(1 + \mu_i)\right]^3.$$

$$(2.9)$$

Looking closely at Eq. (2.9), it is obvious that even if the one-period distribution is symmetric, namely $\mu_{3i} = 0$, the multi-period skewness, M, generally is different from zero, and it depends on all the other terms appearing in Eq. (2.9).

We turn next to show a few important features of the multi-period skewness M which holds under the *i.i.d.* assumption:

1. For $N = 1, M = \mu_{3i}$, and if the distribution for $N = 1$ is symmetric, then $M = 0$.
2. $\partial M/\partial \mu_i > 0$
3. $\partial M/\partial \sigma_i > 0$
4. $\partial M/\partial N > 0$

In other words, risky assets with a relatively large mean and large standard deviation, e.g., small stocks, will have larger multi-period skewness than less risky one-period assets, say, large stocks and bonds. Moreover, the larger the horizon, the larger the skewness, and it is theoretically well known that where $N \to \infty$, the distribution becomes log-normal, which is positively skewed, regardless of the skewness of the one-period distribution.

We turn now to prove the signs of these derivatives. Assuming that the one-period skewness is equal to zero (e.g., a one-period elliptic distribution) with the *i.i.d.* assumption, namely with $\mu_i = \mu$

and $\sigma_i^2 = \sigma^2$, the multi-period skewness, M, can be rewritten as

$$M = \prod_{i=1}^{N}[(1+\mu_i)^3 + 3(1+\mu_i)\,\sigma_i^2 + \mu_{3i}]$$

$$-3\left[\prod_{i=1}^{N}(1+\mu_i)\right]\prod_{i=1}^{N}[(1+\mu_i)^2 + \sigma_i^2] + 2\left[\prod_{i=1}^{N}(1+\mu_i)\right]^3.$$

Assuming *i.i.d.*, and that that the one-period distribution is symmetric (e.g., normal distribution), $\mu_{3i} = 0$, M can be rewritten as

$$M = [(1+\mu)^3 + 3(1+\mu)\sigma^2]^N$$

$$- 3(1+\mu)^N[(1+\mu)^2 + \sigma^2]^N + 2(1+\mu)^{3N}$$

where all the parameters determining M are the one-period parameters.

Dividing the first term inside the square bracket by $(1+\mu)$ and multiplying the first term by $(1+\mu)^N$, M can also be rewritten as

$$M = (1+\mu)^N\{[(1+\mu)^2 + 3\sigma^2]^N - 3[(1+\mu)^2 + \sigma^2]^N\} + 2(1+\mu)^{3N}.$$

$$(2.10)$$

It can be easily seen from Eq. (2.10) that for $N = 1$ and $M = 0$, it is assumed that the distribution under consideration is symmetric. We turn now to analyze the size and magnitude of M for $N > 1$.

Using the binomial expansion of the first two terms given in Eq. (2.10), we obtain

$$M = (1+\mu)^N\left\{\sum_{r=0}^{N}\binom{N}{r}[(1+\mu)^2]^{N-r}[3\sigma^2]^r\right.$$

$$\left. - 3\sum_{r=0}^{N}\binom{N}{r}[(1+\mu)^2]^{N-r}[\sigma^2]^r\right\} + 2(1+\mu)^{3N}.$$

For $r = 0$, the first term is equal to $(1 + \mu)^{3N} - 3(1 + \mu)^{3N} = -2(1 + \mu)^{3N}$, which cancels out with the last term on the right-hand side of the above equation.

Thus, M is given by (note that the range of r is now from 1 to N, and the term is canceled out)

$$M = (1 + \mu)^N \left\{ \sum_{r=1}^{N} \binom{N}{r} [(1 + \mu)^2]^{N-r} [\sigma^2]^r [3^r - 3]. \tag{2.11}$$

First note, once again, that for $N = 1$, $M = 0$, there is only one term, and $[3^r - 3] = [3^1 - 3] = 0$. As for $N > 1$ and $r > 1$, the term $[3^r - 1] > 0$, and all terms in Eq. (2.11), are positive; thus, M must be positive.

From this equation, it is simple to see (for a given N) that $\partial M / \partial \mu_i > 0$ and $\partial M / \partial \sigma_i > 0$. Thus, we expect the skewness of relatively risky assets, say, small stocks, to increase faster than the skewness of less risky assets, say, Treasury bonds. We will show later in this chapter that these theoretical results are indeed supported by empirical evidence.

We turn now to investigate the derivative $\partial M / \partial N$, which is even more interesting as it indicates the effect of the increase in the horizon on the deviation from symmetry, namely, a deviation from normality or from logistic distribution.

The proof that $\partial M / \partial N > 0$ is complicated. As N is discrete, we need to prove that $M(N + 1) > M(N)$. As the term $[3^r - 3]$ is larger for $N + 1$ than for N (as it includes more positive terms), and as $(1 + \mu)^{N+1} > (1 + \mu)^N$, it is clear from Eq. (2.10) that a sufficient condition for the inequality $M(N + 1) > M(N)$ to hold is that

$$\binom{N + 1}{r} [(1 + \mu)^2]^{N+1-r} [\sigma^2]^r > \binom{N}{r} [(1 + \mu)^2]^{N-r} [\sigma^2]^r. \tag{2.12}$$

Or by reducing the power by 1 of the terms on the left-hand side of this inequality, we need to prove that

$$(1 + \mu)^2 \binom{N + 1}{r} [(1 + \mu)^2]^{N-r} [\sigma^2]^r > \binom{N}{r} [(1 + \mu)^2]^{N-r} [\sigma^2]^r.$$

$$\tag{2.13}$$

As $(1+\mu)^2 > 1$ and always $\binom{N+1}{r} > \binom{N}{r}$, Eq. (2.13) holds, hence, so does Eq. (2.12). In addition, recall that with the $(N+1)$-period case, we have one more positive term than in the N-period case, this only enforces the claim that $M(N+1) > M(N)$.

Thus, we prove that even if the one-period distribution is symmetric, the multi-period distribution is positively skewed, and the larger the one-period mean, the larger the one-period variance, and the larger the N, the larger the skewness. We next demonstrate theoretically the magnitude of the changes in M as a function of the various parameters.

Table 2.1 reports the results corresponding to the multi-period skewness, M, where for $N = 1$-month, the skewness is assumed to be equal to zero. We employ Eq. (2.11) to calculate M for various horizons up to 120 months, that is, 10 years. This table is an extension of the table provided by Arditti and Levy up to $N = 10$ years.[9] A comparison of columns 2 and 3 of Table 2.1 reveals that increasing the standard deviation and holding the mean unchanged induces an increase in M, and a comparison of columns 3 and 4 also reveals that increasing the monthly mean return and holding the standard deviation unchanged induces an increase in M. However, the most important result refers to the change in M with the horizon

Table 2.1: The skewness, M, as a function of the monthly μ, monthly σ, and horizon N.

(1)	$\sigma = 0.05,\ \mu = 0.02$ (2)	$\sigma = 0.1,\ \mu = 0.02$ (3)	$\sigma = 0.1,\ \mu = 0.03$ (4)
1-month	0.0000	0.0000	0.0000
2-months	0.0000	0.0006	0.0006
10-months	0.0029	0.0501	0.0644
1-year	0.0048	0.0849	0.1157
20-months	0.0229	0.4369	0.7511
2-years	0.0427	0.8494	1.6396
5-years	2.6171	76.9664	421.5806
10-years	457.2058	28505.1622	884440.2713

---

[9]Arditti, F. and H. Levy (1975). Portfolio efficiency analysis in three moments: The multiperiod case. *The Journal of Finance* 30(3), 797–809.

N: Consistent with the theoretical results given previously, for a given mean and a given standard deviation, the skewness increases with the horizon, N: for example, with a monthly mean equal to 0.02 (that is, 2%) and a monthly standard deviation of 0.05, the skewness increases from zero for $N = 1$ month to 0.0427 for $N = 2$ years, and further increases dramatically to about 457 for $N = 10$ years.

Figure 2.1 illustrates the effect of changes in the standard deviation (for a given mean and given horizon of $N = 12$ months) on the multi-period skewness. Figure 2.2 illustrates the effects of changes in the monthly mean (for a given standard deviation and a given horizon) on the multi-period skewness. Both figures confirm the theoretical analysis asserting that the larger the mean and the larger the standard deviation, other things being held constant, the larger the skewness, M.

The most important result is illustrated by Figure 2.3. Figure 2.3(a) reveals that M increases from zero for $N = 1$ month to about 457 for a horizon of 120 months. Thus, investors who invest for one month face a symmetric distribution, but long-term investors, particularly those investing for retirement (10 years or more), face a

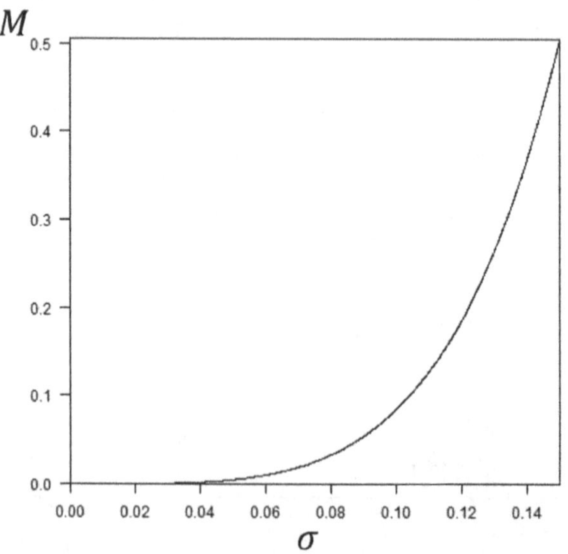

Figure 2.1: The multi-period skewness M as a function of σ (for $\mu = 0.02$ and $N = 12$ months).

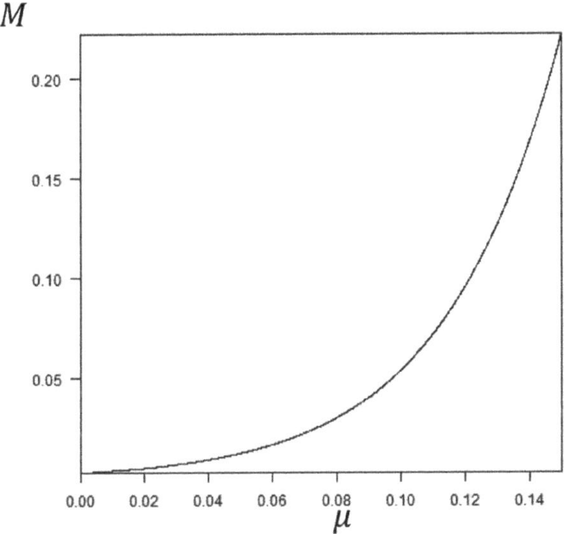

Figure 2.2: The multi-period skewness M as a function of μ (for $\sigma = 0.05$ and $N = 12$ months).

very large skewness that cannot be ignored in their investment choice decision-making process.

From Figure 2.3(a), one may get the impression that for a horizon up to about five years, skewness is negligible, and can therefore be ignored. This is certainly not the case. This is a graphical illusion induced by the large scale of the Y-axis given in this figure. Figure 2.3(b), which represents a zoom-in only on horizons up to 12 months, reveals that the skewness increases from zero for $N = 1$ month to 0.0048 for a 12-month horizon, and the increase is consistent. These figures are relatively small, but recall that also the mean and standard deviation for relatively short horizons are also very small; hence, the increase in the skewness for these short horizons cannot be ignored. Notwithstanding, as we shall see in the following, for short horizons (generally less than 6–9 months), the best fitting theoretical distributions to the empirical distributions are symmetric, implying that the empirical distributions of returns are approximately symmetric, albeit not perfectly symmetric. Therefore, for relatively short horizons, the economic damage induced by ignoring the skewness is presumably

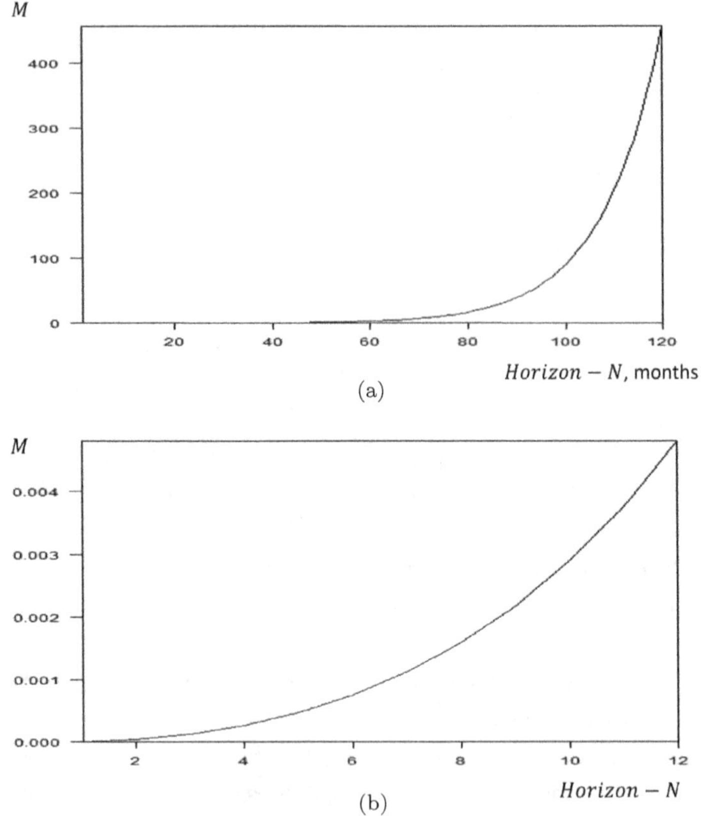

Figure 2.3: (a) The multi-period skewness M as a function of the horizon N (for $\sigma = 0.05$ and $\mu = 0.02$); (b) The multi-period skewness M as a function of the horizon $N \leq 12$ (for $\sigma = 0.05$ and $\mu = 0.02$).

not very large. However, the longer the investment horizon (even for a one-year horizon), ignoring the skewness and relying solely on the mean and the variance of returns may induce a substantial economic loss. Indeed, for relatively longer horizons, the best fitting theoretical distribution to the empirical distribution is positively skewed.

In the following section, we show empirically that for relatively short horizons, indeed, the distributions of returns are symmetrical, or approximately symmetrical, and as the horizon increases, a positive skewness is built up, and the riskier the asset under consideration, the larger the empirical observed positive skewness.

2.2. The Investment Horizon and Skewness: The Best Fit Theoretical Distribution

In this section, we report on the changes in the empirical distributions of various assets with the assumed changes in the investment horizons under the *i.i.d.* assumption. Later, we extend the analysis to also incorporate possible autocorrelations. The goal is to find out, for each horizon and for each asset, the theoretical distribution which best fits the empirical distribution, with particular emphasis on the speed of the skewness built up with the increase in the horizon. We particularly analyze for which horizons the empirical distributions are symmetrical and also elliptic (e.g., normal, logistic, etc.), a case where the M–V rule can be safely employed for investment choices; and for which horizon a substantial skewness exists; hence, the elliptic distribution is no longer the best fit and, therefore, the M–V can no-longer be employed. Thus, we examine empirically how the distributions of returns change with the assumed investment horizon and the speed with which the symmetrical characteristics of the distributions under consideration vanish. We also cover assets with different degrees of volatility; hence, we also indirectly examine empirically the effect of the mean and standard deviation on skewness built up corresponding to various horizons.

We conduct these analyses in two frameworks: one by assuming *i.i.d.*, and one by considering possible autocorrelations. The bootstrapping procedure, which assumes *i.i.d.*, is employed based on two sources of data: the first one is French's website,[10] which provides the monthly rates of returns corresponding to the period July 1927–October 2020, and the other is the Aswath Damodaran dataset,[11] providing annual rates of returns for the period 1928–2019. In the first source of data, we have monthly rates of returns for various classes of assets, particularly for 10 deciles of stocks classified by their market value. In the second source of data, we have only annual rates of returns for the S&P 500 stock index, 10-year Treasury bonds, and short-term Treasury bills.

---

[10]https://mba.tuck.dartmouth.edu/pages/faculty/ken.french/data_library.html.

[11]http://www.stern.nyu.edu/~adamodar/pc/datasets/histretSP.xls.

Deriving empirically the monthly distribution of returns of a given asset, we simply rely on the monthly historical empirical distribution, and no bootstrapping is required in the monthly case. However, for longer investment horizons, we employ the bootstrapping technique. For example, for an investment horizon of $N = 2$ months, we randomly draw two observations from the monthly returns distribution (with replacement), and multiply the two returns to obtain the two-month horizon returns. We repeat this procedure 100,000 times to obtain the two-month horizon distribution. We employ the same procedure up to a 360-month investment horizon. Thus, we cover also the investment horizon for investment for retirement, that is, 30 years. With the other source of data, since we have annual rates of returns, we employ the same procedure, but in this case, the shortest horizon is one year. With these two sets of data, we analyze the changes in the empirical distribution with the horizon for relatively risky assets (e.g., the first decile of the smallest firms traded in the United States (US) market) as well as for relatively less risky assets like the decile of the largest 10% stocks, Treasury bills (T-bills), and 10-year Treasury bonds.

For each horizon, for both datasets, we employ the Crystal Ball program for finding the theoretical distribution that best fits the empirical distribution of each asset for each horizon.

Tables 2.2–2.4 report the results corresponding to the monthly data taken from French's website which reports the monthly rates of returns. With monthly rates of returns corresponding to Decile 1 (the 10% smallest firms), Decile 10, (the 10% largest firms), and the market portfolio (which includes all firms), we observe a common feature: for a relatively short horizon (about 1–9 months, depending on the asset under consideration), the distributions of rates of returns are mostly symmetric, where the logistic distribution is dominant. For longer horizons, the dominant distribution is log-normal. Thus, for relatively short horizons, the distributions of rates of returns are leptokurtic, that is, a distribution of kurtosis larger than 3, which is the kurtosis of normal distribution. In general, leptokurtic distributions have heavier tails than normal distributions. The Student's t and logistic distributions are famous leptokurtic distributions.

Table 2.2: The change in the distribution with the horizon for the 10% smallest firms (Decile 1).

Horizon (Months)	Mean	Variance	Skewness	Density Function	Best Fit
1	1.01	0.01	0		Student's t
2	1.01	0.01	0	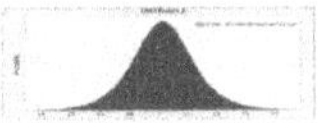	Logistic
3	1.02	0.02	0		Logistic
4	1.03	0.03	0		Logistic
5	1.04	0.04	0		Logistic
6	1.07	0.06	0.88		Log-normal
7	1.08	0.07	1.14		Max Extreme
8	1.09	0.08	1.14		Max Extreme
9	1.10	0.09	1.14	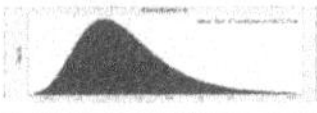	Max Extreme
10	1.11	0.11	1.14		Max Extreme
11	1.12	0.12	1.14		Max Extreme
12	1.13	0.13	1.14		Max Extreme
24	1.29	0.37	1.66		Log-normal
60	1.89	2.20	2.91		Log-normal
180	6.74	143.47	11.01		Log-normal
240	12.62	894.21	20.46		Log-normal
360	44.72	31090.33	73.13		Log-normal

Table 2.3: The change in the distribution with the horizon for the 10% largest firms (Decile 10).

Horizon (Months)	Mean	Variance	Skewness	Density Function	Best Fit
1	1.01	0.00	0		Logistic
2	1.01	0.01	0		Student's t
3	1.02	0.01	0		Student's t
4	1.03	0.01	0		Logistic
5	1.03	0.01	0	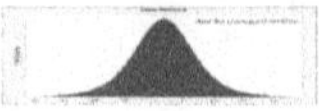	Logistic
6	1.04	0.02	0	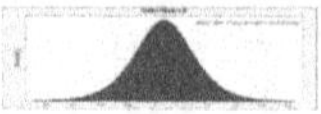	Logistic
7	1.04	0.02	0		Logistic
8	1.05	0.02	0		Logistic
9	1.05	0.03	0		Logistic
10	1.06	0.03	0.33		Log-normal
11	1.07	0.03	0.36		Log-normal
12	1.08	0.04	0.39		Log-normal
24	1.16	0.08	0.65		Log-normal
60	1.45	0.34	1.20		Log-normal
180	3.05	5.34	2.66		Log-normal
240	4.44	16.48	3.48		Log-normal
360	9.26	124.55	5.33		Log-normal

Table 2.4: The change in the distribution with the horizon for the stock market portfolio.

Horizon (Months)	Mean	Variance	Skewness	Density Function	Best Fit
1	1.01	0.00	0		Logistic
2	1.02	0.01	0		Logistic
3	1.03	0.01	0		Student's t
4	1.04	0.01	0		Student's t
5	1.05	0.02	0		Logistic
6	1.06	0.02	0		Logistic
7	1.06	0.02	0		Logistic
8	1.07	0.03	0		Logistic
9	1.08	0.03	0		Logistic
10	1.10	0.03	0.35		Log-normal
11	1.11	0.04	0.38		Log-normal
12	1.12	0.04	0.42		Log-normal
24	1.25	0.11	0.68		Log-normal
60	1.75	0.55	1.28		Log-normal
180	5.37	18.82	2.91		Log-normal
240	9.39	83.91	3.81		Log-normal
360	29.12	1500.92	6.33		Log-normal

The logistic distribution best fits the empirical distribution for relatively short horizons, as reported in the tables.

Note that there is a clear relationship between the horizon for which the symmetry vanishes and the volatility of the asset. For example, for the smallest 10% decile firms from month 6, the symmetry vanishes and the best fit distribution is one with a positive skewness, where for a two-year horizon or more, the dominant distribution is log-normal. As the table reports, the skewness is zero up to $N = 6$ months, and then it steadily increases up to about 73 for a horizon of 10 years (see the row corresponding to 360 months in Table 2.2).

Table 2.3 is similar to Table 2.2, but this time, we analyze the goodness of fit of the 10% largest firms. Here, as expected, the distribution is symmetrical up to $N = 9$ months and the dominant distribution is logistic. Then for $N > 9$ months, the log-normal distribution is the best fit. Note, however, that the skewness increases much slower with large firms than with small firms. For example, the skewness of 360 months for small firms is about 73, and the corresponding number for large firms is only about 5.3 (compare Tables 2.2 and 2.3).

Table 2.4 presents the results corresponding to the market portfolio. Obviously, as the large firms dominate the market portfolio, the results here are very similar to those corresponding to Decile 10. The distribution is symmetric up to $N = 9$ months, and the logistic distribution is the dominant one up to this horizon. Then for $N > 9$ months, the best fit distribution is log-normal.

Two main conclusions can be drawn from these tables. First, for relatively short horizons, the distribution skewness can be safely ignored, and secondly, for short horizons, one can employ the M–V rule for investment choices as the logistic distribution, which is the best fit in several cases, belongs to the elliptic distribution for which the M–V rule is optimal for all risk-averse expected utility maximizers. Note that the normal distribution is not the best fit for any horizon and for any asset reported in Tables 2.2–2.4. The logistic (leptokurtic) distribution rather than the normal distribution is the best fit in many cases.

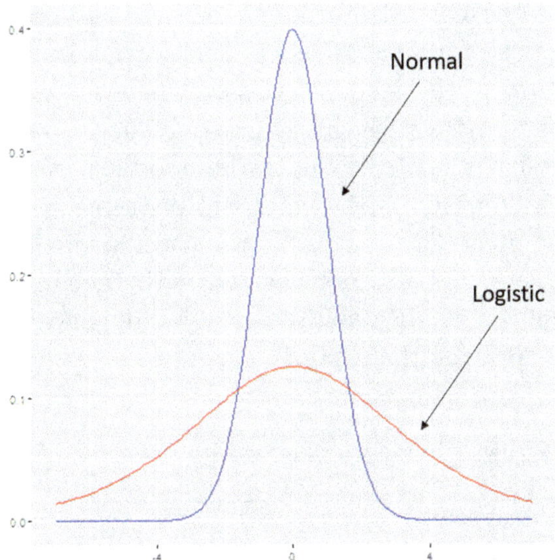

Figure 2.4: The logistic (mean 0 scale 2) and normal (mean 0 and $\sigma = 1$) density functions.

The density functions of the normal and logistic variables (with zero mean and standard deviation equal to 1) is illustrated in Figure 2.4. Despite the observed differences, both distribution functions are symmetric, namely with skewness equal to zero. Moreover, the fact that the logistic rather than the normal distribution best fits the empirical distributions for relatively short horizons does not constitute a deficiency of the M–V rule, as the logistic distribution belongs to the elliptic family with the following two properties (see footnote 1):

(1) Any combination of random elliptic variables also has an elliptic distribution.

(2) With a logistic distribution, we have

$$E_F(x) \geq E_F(x), \sigma_F(x) \leq \sigma_F(x) \Leftrightarrow E_F U(x) \geq E_G U(x)$$

for all risk-averse utility functions U.

Thus, for relatively short horizons, one can safely employ the M–V rule in investment choices, and if the other assumptions characterizing the CAPM are intact, one can also employ beta as a measure of risk of individual assets and portfolios alike.

We turn now to the other set of data where the smallest horizon is one year, as we have with this source only annual rates of returns. Therefore, we cover with this data the goodness of fit of the best theoretical distribution to the empirical distribution with horizons from one year up to 30 years. Also, we cover with the second data base three assets that are not covered with the first dataset: the S&P 500 stock index, 10-year Treasury bonds, and Treasury bills. Tables 2.5–2.7 provide the results.

Table 2.5: The change in the distribution with the horizon for the S&P 500 stock index.

Horizon (Years)	Mean	Variance	Skewness	Density Function	Best Fit
1	1.12	0.04	−0.41		Weibul
2	1.24	0.10	0.06		Beta
3	1.39	0.18	0.34		Beta
4	1.55	0.31	0.55		Beta
5	1.73	0.49	0.73		Beta
10	3.00	3.33	1.78		Log-normal
20	9.00	75.15	3.60		Log-normal
30	27.26	1312.40	6.19		Log-normal

Table 2.6: The change in the distribution with the horizon of 10-year Treasury bonds.

Horizon (Years)	Mean	Variance	Skewness	Density Function	Best Fit
1	1.05	0.01	1.14		Max Extreme
2	1.11	0.01	0.73		Log-normal
3	1.16	0.02	0.76		Log-normal
4	1.22	0.03	0.76		Log-normal
5	1.29	0.04	0.80		Log-normal
10	1.65	0.15	0.92		Log-normal
20	2.73	0.81	1.18		Log-normal
30	4.51	3.44	1.43		Log-normal

First, note that the skewness of the S&P 500 stock index is negative for $N = 1$ year, and it changes to a positive skewness for $N > 1$, reaching about 6.2 for an $N = 30$-year horizon (see Table 2.5). The dominating best distribution up to $N = 5$ years is the beta distribution, and for relatively long horizons, once again, the log-normal distribution has the best fit.

Table 2.6 provides the results corresponding to 10-year Treasury bonds. Here, we have a positive skewness for all horizons and the log-normal distribution is the best fit for all $N \geq 2$ years. Finally, Table 2.7 provides the results corresponding to Treasury bills. Here, the skewness is positive for all horizons, and the beta distribution is the best fit up to $N = 4$ years, gamma is the best fit for $N = 10$, and for longer horizons, once again, the log-normal distribution is the best fit.

Table 2.7: The change in the distribution with the horizon of T-bills.

Horizon (Years)	Mean	Variance	Skewness	Density Function	Best Fit
1	1.03	0.00	1.01		Beta
2	1.07	0.00	0.77		Beta
3	1.11	0.00	0.70		Beta
4	1.14	0.01	0.64		Beta
5	1.18	0.01	0.60		Beta
10	1.40	0.02	0.56		Gamma
20	1.95	0.07	0.61		Log-normal
30	2.72	0.19	0.66		Log-normal

Table 2.8 summarizes the results corresponding to all six assets covered in this study for the specific $N = 5$-year horizon.

Table 2.8 reveals that all five assets have positive skewness, with Decile 1 (the small stock decile) having the largest skewness reaching about 2.9. With this specific horizon, the beta distribution is the best for Treasury bills and the S&P 500 stock index, and the log-normal distribution is the best fit for the other three assets covered in this table.

The main conclusion, so far, is that for relatively short horizons (certainly less than one year), the logistic distribution is the best fit, and for relatively long horizons, the log-normal distribution is

Table 2.8: The skewness and best fit distributions of various assets for a horizon of $N = 5$ years.

Stock	Skewness	Distribution	Density Function
Treasury Bills	0.60	Beta	
10-Year Treasury Bonds	0.73	Log-normal	
S&P 500 Stock Index	0.80	Beta	
Decile 10	1.20	Log-normal	
Market Portfolio	1.28	Log-normal	
Decile 1	2.91	Log-normal	

the best fit. From all of these results, we can draw the following conclusions:

(a) For relatively short horizons, the M–V rule may be the appropriate investment rule;

(b) For relatively long horizons, with log-normal distributions, the mean coefficient of variation (M–C) rule may be the appropriate investment rule, where $C = E/\sigma$ is the coefficient of variation;[12]

(c) For other horizons (generally intermediate horizons), we have that beta, gamma, and other distributions constitute the best fit distribution, and for these distributions, we do not have optimal investment rules that are consistent with the expected utility

---

[12]For a proof of this claim, see, Levy, H. (1973). Stochastic dominance among log-normal prospects. *International Economic Review* 14(3), 601–614.

paradigm; hence, stochastic dominance rules should be employed (see Chapter 3).

Finally, note that we use "may be" in conclusions a and b which needs clarification. The reason is that it may be that, say, the logistic distribution is the best fit, yet it does not provide a perfect fit; hence, employing the M–V does not necessarily maximize the expected utility. Yet, it is reasonable to assume that by employing the investment rule that best fits the empirical distribution, the potential errors and therefore the economic losses are relatively small.

2.3. Skewness and the Best Fit Distribution: Autocorrelation is Incorporated

In the previous analysis, we employed the bootstrapping technique which assumes *i.i.d.* We next relax the *i.i.d.* assumption and measure the skewness of three assets as follows: for a horizon of $N = 2$ months, we take the first two months as the first observation; hence, the accumulated returns corresponding to these two months is the first observation. Then the returns corresponding to the third and fourth months form the second observation, and so forth. Thus, if returns are autocorrelated, it will be reflected in the data. We employ the same procedure up to a horizon of five years. Of course, with this procedure, the number of observations is limited. For example, having, say, 100 years of data and a horizon of $N = 5$ years, we have only 20 observations. The advantage of this approach in comparison to the previous results is that the *i.i.d.* assumption is relaxed. The disadvantage of this approach is that we cannot use this approach to investigate very long horizons as we end up with a very small number of observations. Table 2.9 presents the results when possible autocorrelation is considered.

We cover three assets: large stocks (Decile 10), small stocks (Decile 1), and the market portfolio, all taken from French's website (see footnote 10), covering monthly rates of returns for the period July 1927–October 2020. We investigate the distributions for 1–6 month alternate horizons, and then for 1–5 year alternate horizons. For example, for a five-year horizon, the first observation is the

Table 2.9: The skewness and best fit for various assets and various horizons with autocorrelation.

Stock	Skewness	Best Fit Distribution	Density Function
For a horizon of $N = 1$ month			
Decile 10	0	Logistic with mean = 1.0102 and scale 0.03	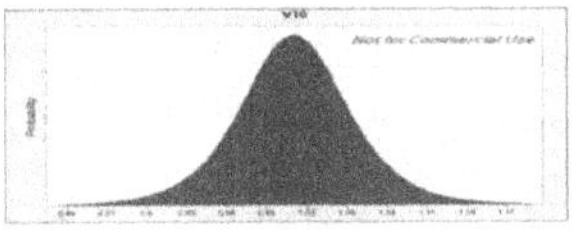
Market Portfolio	0	Logistic with mean = 1.0111 and scale 0.03	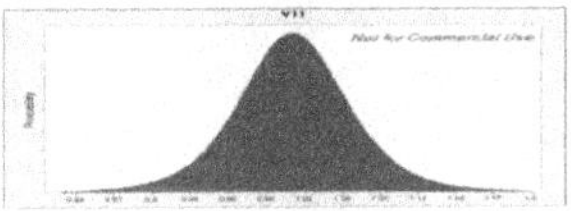
Decile 1	0	Student's t	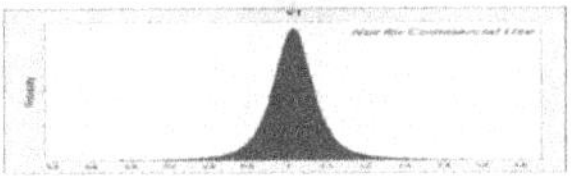
For a horizon of $N = 2$ months			
Decile 10	0	Logistic with mean = 1.0202 and scale 0.04	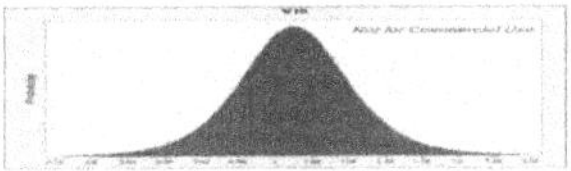
Market Portfolio	0	Logistic with mean = 1.0213 and scale 0.04	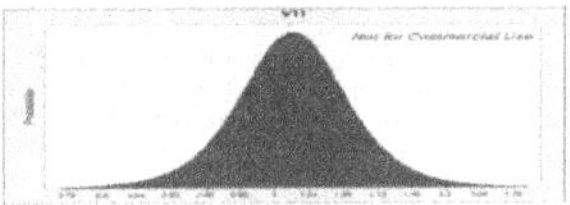
Decile 1	0	Logistic with mean = 1.0212 and scale 0.07	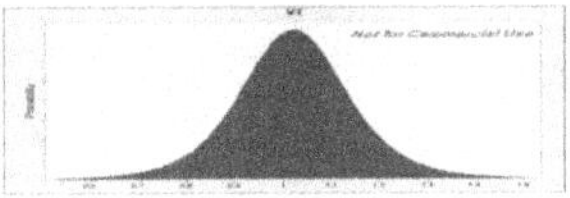
For a horizon of $N = 3$ months			
Decile 10	0	Student's t	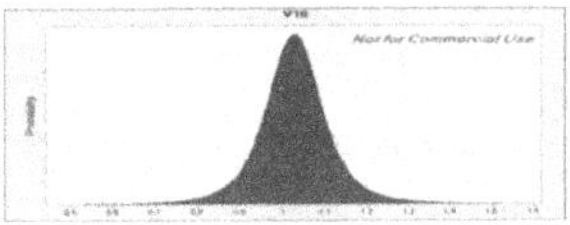
Market Portfolio	0	Student's t	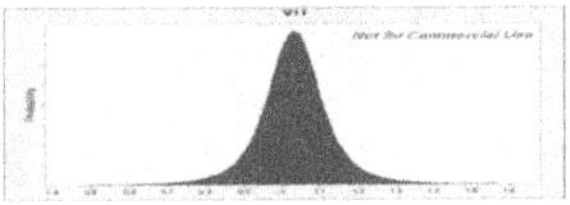

(*Continued*)

Table 2.9: (*Continued*)

Stock	Skewness	Best Fit Distribution	Density Function
Decile 1	0	Logistic with mean = 1.0336 and scale 0.1	
For a horizon of $N = 4$ months			
Decile 10	0	Student's t	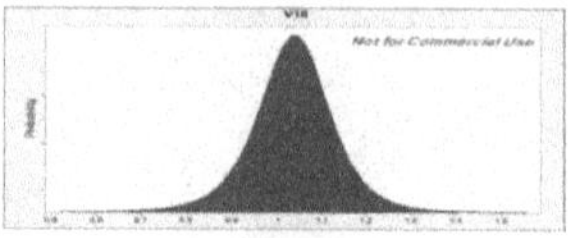
Market Portfolio	0	Logistic with mean = 1.0401 and scale 0.06	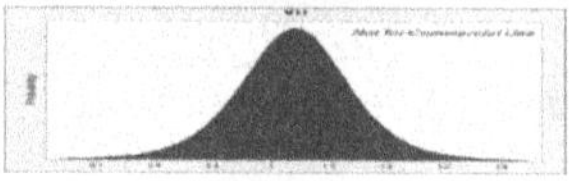
Decile 1	0	Logistic with mean = 1.0409 and scale 0.1	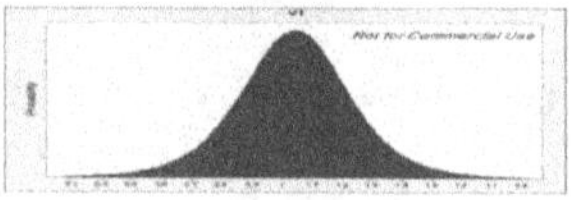
For a horizon of $N = 5$ months			
Decile 10	0.0117	Logistic with mean = 1.0470 and scale 0.06	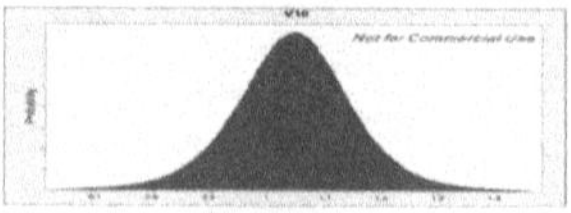
Market Portfolio	0	Student's t	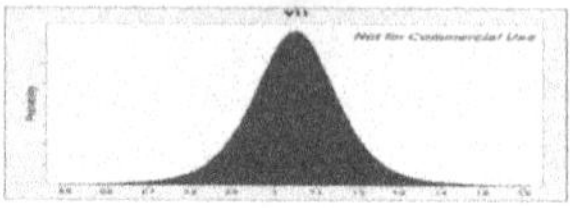
Decile 1	0	Logistic with mean = 1.0526 and scale 0.13	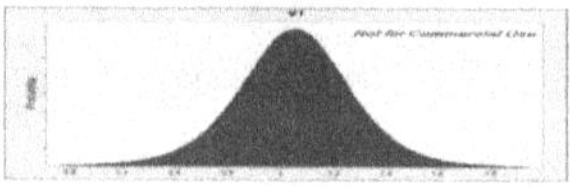
For a horizon of $N = 6$ months			
Decile 10	0	Logistic with mean = 1.0587 and scale 0.14	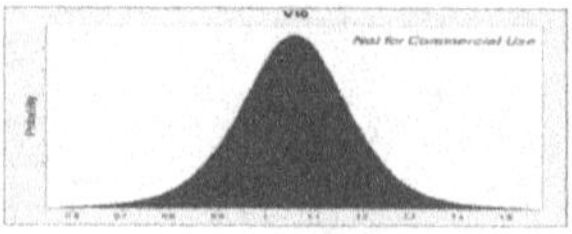

Table 2.9: (*Continued*)

Stock	Skewness	Best Fit Distribution	Density Function
Market Portfolio	0	Logistic with mean = 1.0609 and scale 0.08	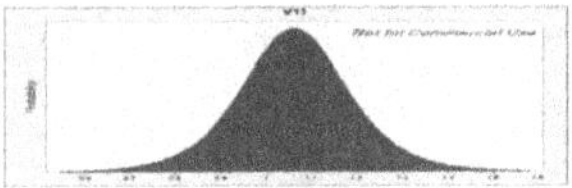
Decile 1	0	Logistic with mean = 1.0717 and scale 0.14	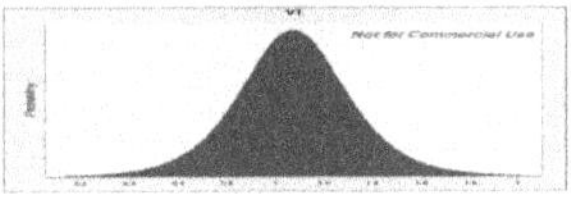
For a horizon of $N = 1$ year			
Decile 10	0	Student's t	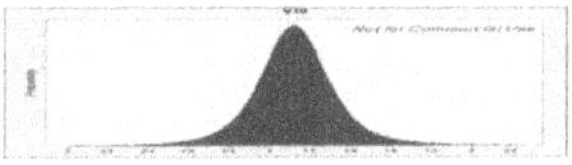
Market Portfolio	0	Student's t	
Decile 1	0.1940	Maximum extreme with likeliest = 1 and scale = 0.34	
For a horizon of $N = 2$ years			
Decile 10	0	Student's t	
Market Portfolio	0	Student's t	
Decile 1	1.1395	Maximum extreme with likeliest = 1.1 and scale = 0.53	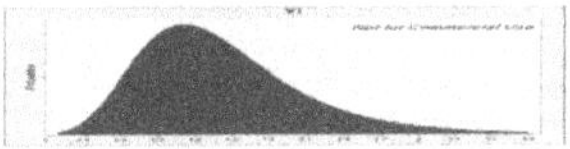
For a horizon of $N = 3$ years			
Decile 10	0.00	Logistic with mean = 1.3914 and scale 0.25	

(*Continued*)

Table 2.9: (*Continued*)

Stock	Skewness	Best Fit Distribution	Density Function
Market Portfolio	0.00	Logistic with mean = 1.4216 and scale 0.25	
Decile 1	1.1395	Maximum extreme with likeliest = 1.27 and scale = 0.69	

For a horizon of $N = 5$ years

Stock	Skewness	Best Fit Distribution	Density Function
Decile 10	1.5085	Log-normal with location = 0.52, mean = 1.64, Std. Dev. = 0.52	
Market Portfolio	1.4153	Log-normal with location = 0.47, mean = 1.67, Std. Dev. = 0.53	
Decile 1	6.5859	Log-normal with location = 0.42, mean = 2.45, Std. Dev. = 2.75	

cumulative return for the first five years, the second observation is for years 6–10, and so forth.

For a 1–6 month horizon, the distributions are symmetrical (with one exception — the five-month horizon for Decile 10). The logistic distribution is the dominating theoretical distribution that best fits the empirical distributions for this relatively short horizon. Increasing the horizons for one year or more, skewness appears and for a horizon of $N = 5$ years, the best fit distribution is log-normal. The main result, however, is that introducing autocorrelation does not change much the previous results: for relatively short horizons, the distributions have zero skewness, and the logistic distribution in most cases is the best fit. Thus, for short horizons, it is reasonable to employ the M–V rule. However, for longer horizons, a positive skewness emerges and the best fit distribution is the log-normal distribution. For a horizon of one-year or more, employing the M–V rule is not consistent with expected utility maximization; hence, an economic loss may occur by investing according to this rule.

2.4. Summary

Optimal investment decision criteria that are consistent with the expected utility paradigm depend on the shape of the distributions of the returns that investors face. For example, if the distributions of returns are elliptic (when the normal and logistic distributions belong to this family), then the M–V is an optimal investment rule in the face of risk aversion. Most theoretical and empirical studies in economics and finance employ this rule, hence implicitly or explicitly assuming normal (or elliptic) distributions of returns.

This chapter reveals that assuming an elliptical distribution is generally incorrect, as the return distributions are positively skewed; hence, the skewness (the third moment) that determines the expected utility cannot be ignored. Specifically, for relatively short horizons (up to 6–9 months, depending on the asset under consideration), the distributions of returns on various assets are symmetric (the logistic distribution is the best fit in many cases), and for longer horizons, a positive skewness is built up, and for a horizon longer than one year, in many related cases, the log-normal distribution is the best theoretical fit to the empirical distributions.

These results are intact for a variety of assets: Treasury bills, 10-year Treasury bonds, the S&P 500 stock index, the market portfolio, and the decile of the 10% smallest stocks as well as for the 10% largest stocks. We find that the longer the horizon, the larger the positive skewness, and the more volatile the asset (e.g., small firms), the faster the increase in the skewness and in the approximation to the log-normal distribution.

Finally, as most investors plan their investment for one year or more, for retirement, employing the M–V rule and the CAPM that relies on this rule should be done very carefully, being aware of the fact that the M–V rule may lead to an economic loss, as by this rule, the skewness is ignored.

Chapter 3

Mean–Variance, Stochastic Dominance, and the Investment Horizon

Most economic and financial models of choices under risk assume, implicitly or explicitly, a one-period investment decision-making process and, in addition, that all investors have the same one-period investment horizon, e.g., one month or one year. Having a set of risky assets to choose from, researchers who develop equilibrium pricing generally first analyze theoretically the investors' optimal choices of risky assets. Then under some additional assumptions, e.g., homogenous expectation, a theoretical asset pricing equilibrium model, such as the capital asset pricing model (CAPM), is derived. In virtually all of these models, it is assumed that there are two dates common to all investors: the asset purchasing date and the liquidation date. For example, the most influential study of Markowitz,[1] a Nobel laureate in Economics who is considered the father of modern portfolio selection theory, assumes a one-period investment from which the efficient set of all portfolios is derived. Sharpe,[2] another Nobel laureate in Economics, likewise based his theory on the one-period investment assumption framework. He suggests *beta* as a measure of the risk of an individual asset that is included in the held optimal diversified portfolio and the well-known equilibrium CAPM.

---

[1]Markowitz, H. M. (1952). Portfolio selection. *The Journal of Finance* 7(1), 77–91.

[2] Sharpe, W. F. (1964). Capital asset prices: A theory of market equilibrium under conditions of risk. *The Journal of Finance* 19(3), 425–442.

99

Thus, these models explicitly assume a one-period investment. In other words, the investors invest at t_0 and sell the asset at t_1, and the time difference $t_1 - t_0$ is called the one-period investment horizon.[3] Note, however, that while the one-period investment assumption is crucial to the derivation of the CAPM, Markowitz's portfolio efficiency analysis can be tailored such that each investor faces an efficient set of portfolios, which may vary from one investor to another depending on their planned investment horizon. However, if an investment company, e.g., a mutual fund, wishes to derive Markowitz's efficient set of portfolios for all of its customers, it must rely, like in the CAPM derivation, on the one-period investment horizon assumption that is common to all its customers. Similarly, virtually all the empirical studies that either apply the various theoretical models to some specific economic issues, e.g., testing the validity of theoretical models like the CAPM or testing for the existence of the small firm effect (SFE), employ monthly or annual data. Thus, once again, a one-period investment horizon is assumed. For a few influential empirical studies that implicitly assume the one-period common investment horizon (generally one month), see, for example, Fama and MacBeth[4] and Fama and French.[5]

In contradiction to the common one-period investment horizon assumption, in practice, investors have various planned investment horizons. For instance, an investor who needs the money to buy a house within three months needs to make optimal investment decisions in the financial market for these three months. Hence, he needs information on the distribution of the quarterly rates of returns corresponding to the various assets under consideration.[6] Those who

---

[3]There are also continuous time models where the investment period is very small, approaching zero, see, for example, Merton, R. (1973). An intertemporal capital asset pricing model. *Econometrica* 41(5), 867–887.

[4]Fama, E. F. and J. D. MacBeth (1974). Tests of the multiperiod two-parameter model. *Journal of Financial Economics* 1(1), 43–66.

[5]Fama, E. F. and K. R. French (1992). The cross-section of expected stock returns. *The Journal of Finance* 47(2), 427–465.

[6]To make an investment decision, one needs information on the future rates of return. This future distribution generally is estimated by the *ex-post* distribution. Note, however, that based on the same set of historical data, generally the distribution of the returns depends on the assumed investment horizon. For example,

need the money back in one year are interested in the distributions of the annual rates of returns on the various assets. In the extreme case, those who invest for retirement need to make decisions based on distributions of about 30–40 years' rates of returns.

As various investors have different investment horizons, adhering to the one-period mean–variance (M–V) analysis as well as to other investment decision rules could lead to misspecification. In practice, one needs to derive the M–V efficient frontier for various horizons. The multi-period parameters employed in deriving various efficient frontiers are generally derived by employing the one-period parameters, assuming that the one-period return of each asset is identical and independent over time, well known as the identical independent distribution denoted as *i.i.d.*

Thus, we have a sharp gap between the theoretical common one-period investment assumption and the various horizons which characterize investors' practice. Does this difference between the one-period assumed horizon in economic research and the horizon employed in practice matter? Does the assumed length of the horizon affect choices? Do the optimal choices of the same investor change when the investment horizon changes (changes which may emerge for various reasons, e.g., with aging)? Does the observed empirical heterogeneous horizon affect equilibrium prices? Does it affect the risk index (e.g., the variance or beta) of individual assets? Another measure that may be affected by the assumed investment horizon is the well-known risk premium, also known as the "risk premium puzzle" analyzed by Mehra and Prescott.[7] Is it possible that this puzzle exists with annual data and vanishes with a longer horizon? And what is the effect of having investors with various horizons on the risk premium puzzle?

---

a quarterly rate of return distribution is different than, say, the annual rate of return distribution. Thus, the assumed investment horizon is crucial information for investment decision-making.

[7] Mehra, R. and E. C. Prescott (1985). The equity premium: A puzzle. *Journal of Monetary Economics* 15(2), 145–161. They assume constant relative risk aversion (CRRA) utility function. With this function, under some assumptions, the optimal investment choice is unaffected by the horizon. However, as we shall see in what follows, the risk premium is affected by the horizon.

In the case where the rates of returns on a given asset are *dependent* over time, it is obvious that the assumed horizon may affect optimal choices and, hence, may affect asset pricing. For example, an asset which goes either up or down in one year and with a high probability goes in the opposite direction the next year may be considered less risky by the two-year horizon investors relative to the risk perceived by the one-year investors (we demonstrate this case with a specific numerical example). Thus, it is obvious that dependence over time (negative or positive) may create a connection between the magnitude of the risk index of an asset and the assumed investment horizon that, in turn, may determine the risk premium and the equilibrium asset pricing. Thus, this possible dependence of returns over time is a sufficient condition for investors with various investment horizons to invest in different bundles of risky assets even if they have homogenous expectations, let alone heterogeneous expectations regarding the future distributions of returns.

Generally, the type of dependency over time, if it exists, is hard to economically exploit. Moreover, empirical studies, albeit not all of them, support the hypothesis that rates of returns (or changes in prices) of assets are independent over time, hence the well-known Random Walk Theory.[8] Indeed, the independency over time assumption is commonly employed in empirical and theoretical studies. However, there are empirical studies revealing a short-term serial correlation of returns, and some studies also reveal stock price trends known as momentum and even long-term stock reversals.[9] Since most standard models cannot explain these phenomena, they

---

[8]See, Malkiel, B. (2007). *Random Walk Down Wall Street,* 9th ed., W.W. Norton and Company.

[9]Short-term stock return in some empirical studies reveals positive autocorrelation and long-term mean reversion. For example, see Fama, E. and K. French (1988). Permanent and temporary components of stock prices. *Journal of Political Economy* 96(2), 246–273; Poterba, J. M. and L. H. Summers (1988). Mean reversion in stock returns: Evidence and implications. *Journal of Financial Economics* 22(1), 27–59; Levy, H. and K. C. Lim (1988). The economic significance of the cross-sectional autoregressive model: Further analysis. *Review of Quantitative Finance and Accounting* 11(1), 37–51.

are classified as "anomalies" or "puzzles."[10] Moreover, if one can predict these anomalies, an investment model can be employed to exploit this information, and it will be employed again and again until these anomalies (like the well-known Monday effect) vanish.

We assume in most of the analytical derivations that the Random Walk Theory is intact, keeping in mind that autocorrelation may affect the results. For example, we assume independence over time to derive the multi-period variance of the return on an asset, knowing that adding a serial correlation may decrease or increase the multi-period variance. We also examine empirically the effect of possible serial correlation on the multi-period variance of the asset under consideration and on our multi-period analyses. Yet, independence over time is the basis for the various multi-period calculations given in this book.

If one accepts the Random Walk Theory, and adopts the common practice that rates of returns are independent (and identical) over time, intuitively, it seems that the investment choices should be invariant to the assumed investment horizon; in other words, the assumed horizon does not matter. Surprisingly, this is a misleading intuition. The main reason for the effect of the assumed investment horizon on the optimal choices, even in the *i.i.d.* case, is that the two-period actual return is given by $x_1 x_2$, which is not equal to $(x_1 + x_2) - 1$ [11] where x is 1 + rate of return. Thus, the compounding effect is crucial and, of course, the longer the horizon, the larger

---

[10]Most of these puzzles and anomalies which deviate from the *i.i.d.* assumption are explained by behavioral models, like overreaction to news, loss aversion, investor over confidence, etc. For studies focusing on behavioral economics to explain these anomalies, see, for example, De Bondt,De Bondt, Werner W. and R. Thaler (1985). Does the stock market overreact? *The Journal of Finance* 40(3), 793–805; Shefrin, H. and M. Statmen (1985). The disposition to sell winners too early and ride losses too long: Theory and evidence. *The Journal of Finance* 40(3), 777–790; Barberis, N., A. Shleifer, and R. Vishny (1998). A model of investors sentiment. *Journal of Financial Economics* 49(3), 307–343.

[11]Note that x stands for the return, namely 1 + rate of return or $(1 + R)$, where R is the rate of return. Therefore,

$$x_1 x_2 = (1 + R_1)(1 + R_2) = 1 + R_1 + R_2 + R_1 R_2.$$

the magnitude of the compounding effect on the investment choices. Some researchers overcome this technical difficulty by considering the log of the terminal value of the investment; that is, they consider the value given by $log(x_1x_2) = log(x_1) + log(x_2)$, which under the *i.i.d.* assumption is simply equal to $2log(x_1)$. Note that with the log-return, for one-period investors, it is simply $log(x)$, where x is the one-period return, a random variable that is the same for each one-period horizon; therefore, multiplying by the constant, 2, should not affect the optimal investment choices as the horizon changes. Indeed, with an *i.i.d.* assumption and with log-return, the optimal choices are invariant to the assumed investment horizon. However, this is a technical result with no economic meaning because by the von-Neumann and Morgenstern[12] expected utility paradigm, the investor's goal is to maximize the expected utility of wealth, $EU(w_T)$, and not $EU(log(w_T))$, where w_T, the wealth, is a random variable the investor faces at time T. Specifically, in the given example, the goal in the expected utility framework is to maximize $EU(w_0x_1x_2)$ and not $EU(\log(w_0x_1x_2))$, where w_0 is the initial invested wealth. As most economic and financial models are analyzed in the expected utility framework, shifting from x_1x_2 to $log(x_1x_2)$ is economically wrong and may induce an economic loss to the investors who make decisions by the log-return, $log(x_1x_2)$. Moreover, the longer the horizon, the greater the loss induced by such a shift to the log-return. In other words, maximizing $EU(log(w_T))$ generally implies investing non-optimally in the expected utility framework. However, note that for very small returns and a very short one-period horizon, say, one day, x_1x_2 generally provides a good approximation of $(x_1+x_2) - 1$, an approximation which is not intact for relatively long horizons.

By the other calculation method, we have

$$(x_1 + x_2) - 1 = (1 + R_1) + (1 + R_2) - 1 = 1 + R_1 + R_2.$$

Therefore, the difference between the two calculation methods is the term R_1R_2. When the rates of return are relatively small, e.g., the daily rate of return, then the two calculation methods generally yield almost the same numbers.

[12]von Neumann, J. and O. Morgenstern (1953). *Theory of Games and Economic Behavior*, 3rd ed., Princeton University Press, New Jersey.

One can employ various investment rules for choice under uncertainty, where the horizon varies from one investor to another. In this chapter, we discuss the M–V and stochastic dominance (SD) rules. Both rules are consistent with an expected utility paradigm with one difference: the M–V rule is optimal only in the case where the distributions of the returns corresponding to the risky assets under consideration are normal (or elliptic when the normal distribution belongs to the elliptic family), while the SD rules are distribution-free, that is, no assumption on the shape of the distribution is required.

Yet, each rule has its pros and cons. The M–V rule is easy to apply, and there is a technique for finding the optimal diversification for each assumed investment horizon. In contrast, the SD rules do not suggest a path for finding the optimal SD portfolios. Even so, the M–V rule cannot be optimal for all investment horizons because if the one-period distribution is normal, the multi-period distribution is no longer normal, whereas the SD rules are optimal for all horizons, as they are distribution-free. Thus, one has to weigh the technical advantage of employing the M–V rule against the economic loss induced by using a non-optimal rule. However, if one does not seek an optimal diversification and decides to invest in one of the well-known traded funds that mimic some stock indices, e.g., the S&P 500 stock index or any other available traded funds, it is optimal to employ the SD rules to choose between these funds. Also, if one wishes to invest, let's say 25%, in each of four available stock indices versus investing 50% in each of two stock indices, once again, the SD rules can be employed to choose between these two portfolios. However, the SD rules do not provide the optimal diversification as the M–V rule does; hence, they do not tell us what optimal weight to invest in each of the above stock indices.[13] We further discuss all of these issues in this chapter.

---

[13] However, like the M–V rule, also with the SD rules, we may have no dominance between two compared portfolios; thus, we have partial rather than a complete prospect ordering.

3.1. The M–V Rule and the Horizon

The most popular investment rule under uncertainty is the M–V rule, suggested and developed by Markowitz (see footnote 1) and Tobin,[14] two Nobel laureates in Economics. Facing two uncertain prospects (stocks, bonds, mutual funds, or any other pair of investments) denoted by F and G, prospect F dominates prospect G by the M–V rule if the following two conditions hold:

$$\text{(a) } E_F(x) \geq E_G(x)$$
$$\text{(b) } \sigma_F(x) \leq \sigma_G(x). \tag{3.1}$$

To avoid trivial cases, it is required to have at least one strict inequality, either in condition (a) or in condition (b) given above. Condition (a) requires that to have dominance by the M–V rule, prospect F must have a larger (or equal) expected return than prospect G, i.e., on average, it is more profitable than prospect G. Condition (b) requires that prospect F is also less risky than prospect G, as having a smaller (or equal) variance implies that its future return is more stable or that it has less volatility. Nevertheless, in the rest of this chapter, we ignore the trivial case where equality holds, and when no misunderstanding may arise, we simplify the notation and assume that dominance exists if strict inequality holds in both conditions (a) and (b). This will facilitate the discussion and exposition of the mathematical formulas without losing from the generality of the results. Generally, in the M–V analysis, it is assumed that the investor considers investing either in prospect F or in prospect G for one period, say one year, and the above means and variances correspond to the rate of return corresponding to this one-period investment horizon.

The interesting question to which we devote this chapter, among others, is whether the assumed investment horizon affects the M–V dominance relationship and the SD relationship. The SD rules will be

---

[14]Tobin, J. (1958). Liquidity preferences as behavior toward risk. *Review of Economic Studies* 25(2), 65–86.

defined and explained later in the chapter.[15] Moreover, we analyze whether the assumed investment horizon's effects, as determined by the M–V rule and by the SD rules, are in the same direction. If the effects are in different directions, one needs to explain the reason for this result and, even more importantly, to analyze which one of the two rules is the correct one to be employed when the horizon varies. This is theoretically, as well as practically, important, as in the market, there are investors with various investment horizons; some may wish to invest for only one year, whereas others may wish to invest for retirement, corresponding to a relatively long horizon of 30–40 years.

In most analyses in economics and finance, it is assumed that the return of each asset is identical and independent (*i.i.d.*) over time. Keeping in mind the possible serial correlations, we also analyze empirically for the possible effect of autocorrelation on the multi-period variance.

Note that if the *i.i.d.* assumption is only mildly violated, our main theoretical results (e.g., the increase in the multi-period variance with the horizon) may be still intact, albeit not precisely, as predicted by the mathematical formula given in this chapter. Indeed, we empirically show later in the chapter that this is the case. Thus, for practical investment decisions with various horizons, we do not require the strict *i.i.d.* assumption to hold. However, in cases where the independence over time assumption is extremely violated, the M–V rule (as well as other investment rules) may be strongly dependent on the assumed horizon, and the correlation over time strongly affects the ranking of the prospects under consideration. Let us first demonstrate the effect of possible extreme dependency over the time of the return on the prospect-ranking relationship by the M–V rule. Later on, we develop similar analyses with regard to the SD rules. We argue that, with an extreme dependency over time, very little can be said regarding the relationship between the one-period and multi-period M–V dominance.

---

[15]In this book, we deal mainly with the first-degree stochastic dominance and second-degree stochastic dominance, but most of the results hold also for higher degree stochastic dominance rules.

Suppose that one investor considers investing either in prospect F or in prospect G for one year, and another investor considers investing in one of these two prospects for two years. Is it possible that for a one-year investment horizon F dominates G by the M–V rule, but for a two-year investment horizon, this dominance vanishes? Furthermore, is it possible to obtain the opposite result, that is, for a one-year horizon, there is no M–V dominance of one prospect over the other, but for a two-year horizon such dominance emerges? The answer to such questions, which are of crucial importance to investors with various investment horizons, generally depends on one key variable: the assumed correlation over time, or more simply, the kind of dependency of the return corresponding to the two prospects under consideration over time. However, as we shall see later in this chapter, even if returns are independent over time, the length of the assumed horizon generally affects the M–V dominance results.

To illustrate the role of the dependency between the returns in consecutive periods on the M–V prospect ranking, let us first employ a very simple example with an extreme dependency. Suppose that the one-year return on prospect F is with an equal probability of 0.5, either -10% or $+20\%$. The return on prospect G is $+2\%$ with certainty. Obviously, the mean and variance of F are both larger than the corresponding parameters of prospect G; therefore, for the one-year investor, neither F nor G dominates the other by the M–V rule. Thus, the one-year investor may choose either F or G depending on the degree of their tolerance to risk. In financial jargon, we say that both F and G are included in the M–V *efficient set*.

Let us now turn to the two-year investment horizon case. Is there M–V dominance? Is it possible that for an investor who invests for two years, one prospect is definitely better than the other as long as this choice is done by the M–V rule? To answer this question, we need information on the dependency of the returns over time. As mentioned above, we demonstrate this issue with an extreme example that is simple to follow. The advantage of the extreme case given in what follows is its simplicity and transparency. However, the same results may hold for less extreme cases, depending on the assumed dependency and assumed parameters.

In this example, the dependency over time of the returns is assumed to be as follows: if the rate of return on F in the first year is $+20\%$, then in the second year, the rate of return is -10%. If the rate of return on prospect F in the first year is -10%, then in the second year, the rate of return is $+20\%$. Thus, with F, we have a perfect negative dependency over time of the returns. With prospect G, the return is also $+2\%$ in the second year. With this assumption, we have the following two-year end of period wealth for a \$1 initial investment.

Prospect F: $\$1(1 - 0.1)\ (1 + 0.2)$ with a probability of 0.5 and $\$1(1 + 0.2)(1 - 0.1)$ with a probability of 0.5.

In other words, due to perfect negative dependency, we obtain at the end of the second year \$1.08 with certainty.

Prospect G: We obtain $\$1(1.02)\ (1.02) = \$1.0404$ with certainty.

As the variance of the return on both F and G is zero with the longer horizon, we obtain that for the two-year investors, prospect F with the higher (mean) return dominates prospect G according to the M–V rule.

In conclusion, due to the negative dependency over time of the return on F, we obtain M–V dominance for the two-year investor, while for the one-year investor, such dominance does not exist. Of course, we demonstrated that the role that dependency over time plays on the M–V dominance results with an extreme case, but as mentioned above, this dependency effect on prospect ranking also prevails in many other less extreme cases of dependency and even in the "neutral" case where returns are independent over time.

As we shall see in the following, the opposite can also occur: we may have that for a one-year investment horizon, prospect F dominates prospect G by the M–V rule, but for a longer investment horizon, say two years, neither F nor G dominate the other by the M–V rule. We will show this case after presenting the multi-period formulas corresponding to the M–V rule. Thus, the main result we can draw from this example and from the mathematical analyses given in what follows is that the assumed horizon affects the M–V investment efficiency analysis.

Knowing that with dependency over time, almost any result is possible depending on the type of assumed dependency, we adhere below to the commonly employed *i.i.d.* assumption in economics and finance, keeping in mind that the results may change with the introduction of possible dependency over time.

Denote by x_i the *return* (namely, $1 +$ the rate of return) corresponding to period $i = 1, 2$. According to the independence assumption, if x_1 and x_2 are the returns corresponding to periods 1 and 2, respectively, then

$$f(x_1, x_2) = f_1(x_1)f_2(x_2) \tag{3.2}$$

where f stands for the density functions. This implies that regarding the expected return, we have due to the independence assumption

$$E(x_1 x_2) = E(x_1)E(x_2)$$

and due to the "identical" component of the *i.i.d.* assumption, we have

$$E(x_1 x_2) = E(x_1)E(x_2) = [E(x)]^2$$

where x_1 and x_2 are the same random variable denoted by x. These relationships, which are demonstrated above for $N = 2$ periods, are also intact for all $N > 2$. This property will be employed in the derivation of the multi-period M–V rule.

3.2. The Multi-Period Variance as a Function of the One-Period Parameters

Tobin,[16] to the best of our knowledge, was the first to analyze the relationship between the one-period and multi-period mean and variance. Let us elaborate on the derivation of these multi-period

---

[16]Tobin, J. (1965). The theory of portfolio selection, in Hahn, F. Y. and F. P. Brechling (eds.), *The Theory of Interest Rates*, London.

parameters. Suppose that the multi-period investment horizon consists of N "one-periods." Then, due to the independence assumption, the multi-period mean is given by

$$E(X_N) = E(x_1 x_2 \ldots \ldots x_N) = E(x_1)E(x_2)\ldots\ldots E(x_N)$$

where X_N stands for the end of period wealth, x_i is the return in period i, and there are altogether N periods.

Due to the "identical" assumption, we have

$$E(X_N) = [E(x_1)]^N = (1+\mu)^N \tag{3.3}$$

where μ is the one-period mean *rate of return* that is identical across all periods, and N denotes the number of one-periods that in this chapter is also called the investment horizon. Thus, $E(X_N)$ is the multi-period mean return, and $E(x_1)$ is the one-period mean return (to distinguish from the mean *rate* of return). The derivation of the multi-period variance is a little more involved. Define by σ_N^2 the multi-period variance and by σ_1^2 the one-period variance. We have the following statistical relationship:

$$\sigma_N^2 = E(x_N^2) - [E(x_N)]^2.$$

This can be rewritten as

$$\sigma_N^2 = E[(x_1 x_2 \ldots x_N)^2] - [E(x_1)E(x_2)\ldots E(x_N)]^2, \tag{3.4}$$

and due to the *i.i.d.* assumption, it can be rewritten as

$$\sigma_N^2 = E(x_1^2)E(x_2^2)\ldots E(x_N^2) - [E(x_1)]^{2N}.$$

Recalling that for each period i, we have

$$\sigma^2(x_i) = E(x_i^2) - [E(x_i)]^2 \quad \text{where } i = 1, 2, \ldots, N, \tag{3.5}$$

the multi-period variance can be rewritten as

$$\sigma_N^2 = (\sigma^2(x_1) + [E(x_1)]^2)(\sigma^2(x_2) + [E(x_2)]^2)$$
$$\cdots (\sigma^2(x_N) + [E(x_N)]^2) - [E(x_1)]^{2N},$$

and finally, due to the "identical" component in the *i.i.d.* assumption, we have

$$\sigma_N^2 = [\sigma^2 + (1+\mu)^2]^N - (1+\mu)^{2N} \tag{3.6}$$

where σ^2 and $1 + \mu = E(x_1)$ are the one-period variance and mean *return* (which are identical for all periods $i = 1, 2, \ldots, n$), respectively, and σ_N^2 is the multi-period variance.

From this equation, it is clear that the M–V dominance relationship may be a function of the horizon, as the multi-period variance increases in the one-period mean. Let us illustrate numerically the case where, under the *i.i.d.* assumption, F dominates G by the M–V rule for one-period, and this M–V dominance vanishes once the two-period investment is considered. Suppose that we have the following one-period parameters:

Prospect F:

    Mean $\mu_1 = 0.50$, namely 50%

    Variance $\sigma_1^2 = 0.04$ (which implies a standard deviation

    of 0.2 or 20%)

Prospect G:

    Mean $\mu_1 = 0.10$, namely 10%

    Variance $\sigma_1^2 = 0.05$ (which implies a standard deviation

    of .223 or about 22.3%)

Note that we add the subscript 1 to emphasize that these are the one-period parameters. Obviously, for one-period investors F dominates G by the M–V rule, as it has a higher mean and a smaller variance.

We show now that for the two-period investors, the dominance of F over G by the M–V rule vanishes. We employ the multi-period formulas for the means and variances. Obviously, the two-period mean of F is larger than the two-period mean of G, as the following calculation confirms:

$$E(F) = (1.5)\,(1.5) = 2.25 > E(G) = (1.1)\,(1.1) = 1.21,$$

where $E(F)$ and $E(G)$ are the terminal expected returns rather than rates of return.

To calculate the two-period variance, we employ Eq. (3.6) for the case $N = 2$:

$$\sigma_2^2 = [\sigma_1^2 + (1 + \mu_1)^2]^2 - (1 + \mu_1)^4,$$

where $E(F)$ and $E(G)$ are the terminal expected returns rather than rates of return.

This formula can be reduced to

$$\sigma_2^2 = \sigma_1^4 + 2[\sigma_1^2(1+\mu_1)^2] + (1+\mu_1)^4 - (1+\mu_1)^4 = \sigma_1^4 + 2[\sigma_1^2(1+\mu_1)^2].$$

Plugging in the formula above the various parameters corresponding to the one-period parameters of prospects F and G, respectively, we obtain

$$\sigma_2^2(F) = 0.04^2 + 2[0.04 \times 1.5^2] = 0.0016 + 0.18 = 0.1816$$

and

$$\sigma_2^2(G) = 0.05^2 + 2[0.05 \times 1.1^2] = 0.0025 + 0.121 = 0.1235.$$

Thus, with this example, neither F nor G dominates the other by the M–V rule because

$$E(F) = 2.25 > E(G) = 1.21$$

and

$$\sigma_2^2(F) = 0.1816 > \sigma_2^2(G) = 0.1235.$$

To sum up, earlier in the chapter, we saw a case with a negative dependence, revealing that there is no one-period M–V dominance, but there is two-period M–V dominance. With the above example (which assumes *i.i.d.*), we showed that the opposite is also possible: F dominates G by the M–V rule for one-period investors, but not for two-period investors. From these results, we may conclude that the one-period investors choose F, but the two-period investors can choose either F or G, depending on their risk tolerance. Note that at this point, we present these results merely technically, but do not take a stand regarding which results are economically valid. This will be discussed later on in the chapter.

We have seen in the given example that prospect F, which dominates prospect G by the M–V rule for one-period investors, does not dominate G for two-period investors. How can this be explained? As can be seen from Eq. (3.6), and as we demonstrate in the following, the multi-period variance is an increasing function of the one-period mean; that is, other things being equal, the higher the one-period mean, the larger the multi-period variance. To see that this assertion is generally true, let us employ the binomial formula by writing Eq. (3.6) as follows (we add the subscript 1 to emphasize that these are the one-period parameters):

$$\sigma_N^2 = [\sigma_1^2 + (1 + \mu_1)^2]^N - (1 + \mu_1)^{2N}$$

$$= \sum_{i=0}^{i=N} \binom{N}{i} (\sigma_1^2)^{N-i}[(1 + \mu_1)^{2i}] - (1 + \mu_1)^{2N}.$$

And as for $i = N$, the first term on the right-hand side of the equation is reduced to $(1 + \mu_1)^{2N}$, the multi-period formula for the variance, and after canceling terms it becomes

$$\sigma_N^2 = [\sigma_1^2 + (1 + \mu_1)^2]^N - (1 + \mu_1)^{2N}$$

$$= \sum_{i=0}^{i=N-1} \binom{N}{i} (\sigma_1^2)^{N-i}(1 + \mu_1)^{2i}. \tag{3.6'}$$

The advantage of the last formula for presenting the multi-period variance is that, from this equation, it is straightforward to see that the larger the one-period mean μ_1, the larger the multi-period variance, σ_N^2, and similarly, the larger the σ_1^2, the larger the σ_N^2. In other words,

$$\partial \sigma_N^2 / \partial \mu_1 > 0 \quad \text{and} \quad \partial \sigma_N^2 / \partial \sigma_1^2 > 0. \tag{3.7}$$

Furthermore, it is simple to show that for a given set of parameters (μ_1, σ_1^2), $\partial \sigma_N^2 / \partial N > 0$. Thus, in a comparison of two prospects F and G by the M–V rule under the *i.i.d.* assumption, we have the following possibilities (in this discussion, we allow equality of some parameters in the M–V analysis, as it is important to the issue under discussion):

(a) $\mu_1(F) = \mu_1(G)$ and $\sigma_1^2(F) < \sigma_1^2(G)$, namely F dominates G by the one-period M–V rule. As the one-period means are identical by Eq. (3.6), this dominance is also intact for all $N > 1$.

(b) $\mu_1(F) > \mu_1(G)$ and $\sigma_1^2(F) = \sigma_1^2(G)$. In this case, as in case (a) above, F dominates G for the one-period horizon by the M–V rule. However, the M–V dominance prevailing for one-period vanishes as N increases because $\partial \sigma_N^2 / \partial \mu_1 > 0$ (see Eq. (3.6$'$)).

(c) $\mu_1(F) > \mu_1(G)$ and $\sigma_1^2(F) < \sigma_1^2(G)$. In this case, we have M–V dominance for $N = 1$, and this dominance may vanish for a larger N.

(d) $\mu_1(F) > \mu_1(G)$ and $\sigma_1^2(F) > \sigma_1^2(G)$. In this case, there is no one-period M–V dominance, and there is no M–V dominance for any $N > 1$ because $\partial \sigma_N^2 / \partial \sigma_1^2 > 0$ and $\partial \sigma_N^2 / \partial \mu_1 > 0$ (see Eq. (3.6$'$)).

Thus, under the *i.i.d.* assumption, if there is no M–V dominance for $N = 1$, there is also no M–V dominance for $N > 1$. However, if there is dominance for $N = 1$, this dominance may vanish for $N > 1$, and the precise value of N for which this dominance vanishes is a function of the various parameters of the two prospects under consideration.

Figure 3.1 illustrates the changes in the multi-period variance calculated by Eq. (3.6) for three hypothetical stocks. We consider asset a with one-period parameters ($\mu_1 = 0.30, \sigma_1^2 = 0.02$), asset b with one-period parameters ($\mu_1 = .10, \sigma_1^2 = 0.04$), and asset c with one-period parameters ($\mu_1 = .10, \sigma_1^2 = 0.06$). First, note that all the multi-period variances increase monotonically as a function of the one-period mean and one-period variance, as well as a function of the horizon, N.

At $N = 1$, the variance of asset c is larger than the variance of asset b which, in turn, is larger than the variance of asset a. However, as the mean of asset a is the largest, its multi-period variance increases very rapidly, and at $N > N_1$, its multi-period variance becomes larger than the multi-period variance of asset b,

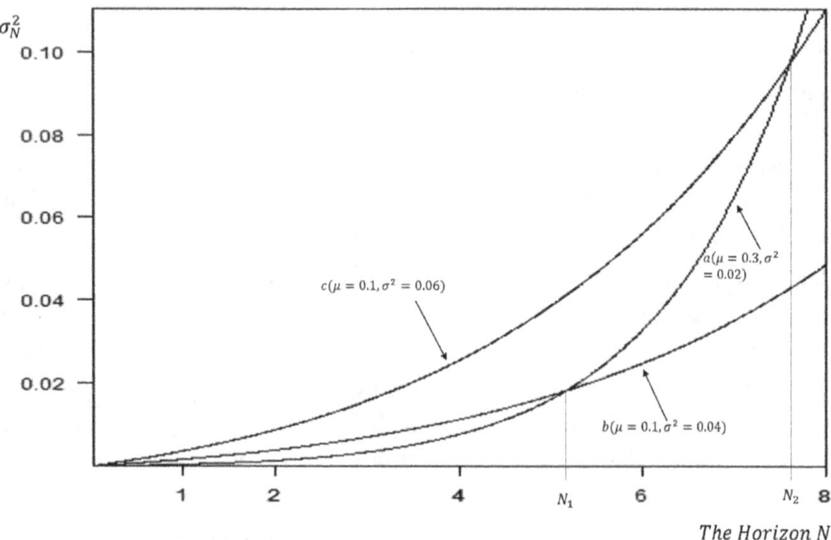

Figure 3.1: The multi-period variance σ_N^2 of three assets.

while at $N > N_2$, its variance also becomes larger than the variance of asset c. Finally, note that although assets b and c have equal one-period means, the multi-period variance of asset c grows faster than the multi-period variance of asset b, as the one-period variance of asset c is also larger (see Figure 3.1).

Let us explain the consequences of these results regarding the changes in the size and content of the M–V efficient set as a function of the length of the investment horizon. To illustrate this issue, suppose that you have 100 mutual funds (portfolios), and you wish to find the M–V efficient set for various horizons. The common procedure is to compare the means and variances of all possible pairs of the funds under consideration. Suppose that for $N = 1$ we find that, say, 40 funds are included in the M–V efficient set and 60 funds are included in the inefficient set. By definition of the efficient set and the inefficient set, this implies that for each fund included in the inefficient set, there must be at least one fund in the efficient set which dominates it by the M–V rule. Assuming *i.i.d.*, one can use one-period parameters to calculate the multi-period mean and variance of each fund. This can be done by employing the multi-period equations for the mean and variance (see Eqs. (3.3) and (3.6)). Using the results regarding the one-period and multi-period M–V dominance, we conclude that the size of the M–V efficient set may increase, in the weak sense, with the increase in the assumed horizon, N. This is immediate, as one-period M–V dominance cannot be reversed by increasing the horizon since if the mean return on the dominating prospect is larger than the mean return of another prospect for one-period, it will be larger for any multi-period horizon. Thus, a one-period M–V efficient portfolio cannot be relegated to the inefficient set by increasing the horizon.

Figure 3.2 illustrates the possibility of changes in the size of the M–V efficient set as a function of the assumed investment horizon, measured in years (or in periods). Note that the M–V efficient set increases in the weak sense as N increases. Although Figure 3.2 illustrates a smooth increase in the size of the efficient set, in practice, we may have a case where the size of the efficient set remains identical for some values of N and increases for some larger values of N.

We next show that with the SD rules and the *i.i.d.* assumption, we obtain just the opposite result: the SD efficient set cannot increase with the horizon, and it may even decrease with the increase in the investment horizon. We first show this claim technically and then analyze the economic differences between the M–V approach and the SD approach, advocating that although the M–V results are technically correct, they may be economically misleading, and only

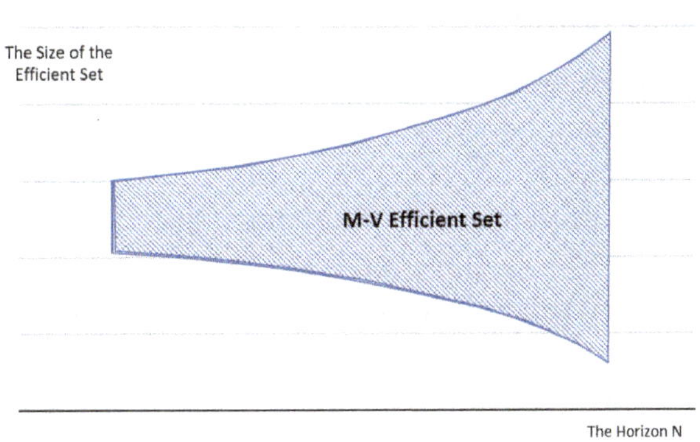

Figure 3.2: The size of the M–V efficient set increases with the horizon.

the SD result can be justified economically. As we wish to analyze the multi-period stochastic dominance efficient set, as done with the M–V rule, let us first define the one-period SD rules.

3.3. Stochastic Dominance Rules

3.3.1. *First-degree SD*

Let F and G be the cumulative distribution functions (CDFs) of the returns on two prospects under consideration. Then F dominates G for all non-decreasing utility functions $U(x)$ if and only if $F(x) \leq G(x)$ for all values x, and there is at least one value x for which there is a strict inequality. This means that

$$F(x) \leq G(x) \quad \text{for all } x \Longleftrightarrow EU_F(x) \geq EU_F(x), \qquad (3.8)$$

and there is at least one strict inequality on both sides of the above formula, and the right-hand side of the equation holds for all monotonic non-decreasing utility functions, namely, for all utility functions U with $U' \geq 0$. Graphically, the first-degree stochastic dominance (FSD) of prospect F over prospect G implies that the cumulative distribution F is located, in the weak sense, below the cumulative distribution G. We do not rule out the possibility that there is a range (or ranges) of returns where $F(x) = G(x)$. It can be easily proved that if F dominates G by FSD, then the mean return of F must be larger than the mean return of G. However, the variance of F may be either larger or smaller than the variance of G.

3.3.2. *Second-degree SD*

This rule is more relevant for a comparison to the M–V rule because these two rules assume risk aversion, that is, these rules apply to all monotonic non-decreasing concave utility functions. For simplicity and without loss of generality, we assume that the range of return is finite ($a \leq x \leq b$). However, the results are also intact with infinite returns. By this rule, prospect F dominates prospect G if and only if

$$\int_a^x [G(t) - F(t)]dt \geq 0 \qquad (3.9)$$

for all values x, and there is at least one value x for which there is a strict inequality. By the second-degree stochastic dominance (SSD) rule, we have the following relationships:

$$\int_a^x [G(t) - F(t)]dt \geq 0 \quad \text{for all } x \iff EU_F(x) \geq EU_F(x)$$

for all risk-averse U, namely, for all U with $U' \geq 0$ and $U'' \leq 0$, and there is at least one strict inequality on both sides of the above equation.

It can be shown that if F dominates G by SSD, then the mean of prospect F must be larger than or equal to the mean return of prospect G. However, as with the FSD rule, there is no constraint on the variances because the dominating prospect may have a smaller, equal, or larger variance than the variance of prospect G. With SSD, the two cumulative distributions may cross many times, yet SSD dominance is possible. Also, we have the following relationship:

$$\text{FSD} \Rightarrow SSD \text{ but SSD} \nRightarrow \text{FSD}.$$

This implies that the SSD efficient set is a subset, in the weak sense, of the FSD efficient set. However, generally, there is no systematic relationship between the M–V efficient set and the FSD, the M–V, and the SSD efficient sets. For the FSD and SSD rules, see Hadar and Russell,[17] Hanoch and Levy,[18] and Rothschild and Stiglitz.[19]

3.4. The One-Period and Multi-Period FSD

We have shown above that with the M–V rule and the *i.i.d.* assumption that if for $N = 1$, there is no M–V dominance then for any $N > 1$, there is also no M–V dominance. This result corresponds

---

[17]Hadar, J. and W. Russell (1969). Rules for ordering uncertain prospects. *American Economic Review* 59(1), 25–34.

[18] Hanoch, G. and H. Levy (1969). The efficiency analysis of choices involving risk. *Review of Economic Studies* 36(3), 335–346.

[19]Rothschild, M. and J. Stiglitz (1970). Increasing risk: I. A definition. *Journal of Economic Theory* 2(3), 225–243.

to the M–V rule. However, for the more general rules, the FSD and the SSD rules, which are distribution-free, this result does not necessarily hold. Let us illustrate this claim with an example referring to the FSD rule.

Example 1. Suppose that the one-period outcomes of prospects G and F are as follows:

$G_1 = G_2$: in each one-period, the outcome is 1 with a probability of 1/4 and 4 with a probability of 3/4.

$F_1 = F_2$: In each one-period, the outcome is 2 with a probability of 1/2 and 10 with a probability of 1/2. Note that G_1 and G_2 refer to periods 1 and 2, respectively, and as we assume *i.i.d.*, these two one-period distributions are identical. The same is intact for the distributions of the other prospect, F. Assuming independence over time, we calculate the two-period distributions of F^2 and G^2 where the superscript 2 indicates that we are dealing with the two-period distributions. A simple calculation reveals that we have:

The two-period distribution G^2: outcome 1 is obtained with a probability of 1/16, outcome 4 is obtained with a probability of 6/16, and outcome 16 is obtained with a probability of 9/16.

The two-period distribution F^2: Outcome 4 is obtained with a probability of 1/4, outcome 20 is obtained with a probability of 1/2, and outcome 100 is obtained with a probability of 1/4.

Figure 3.3(a) provides the one-period distributions of F and G. As the one-period cumulative distributions of F and G cross, neither dominates the other by FSD in the one-period case. Figure 3.3(b) provides two-period distributions of these two prospects calculated, as with the M–V rule under the *i.i.d.* assumption. Here, the two-period distribution F^2 dominates the two-period distribution G^2 by FSD, as we have $F^2(x) \leq G^2(x)$ for all values x, and there are some values x for which a strict inequality holds.

In a nutshell, we have seen that if we have no one-period dominance with the M–V rule, there is also no M–V dominance in

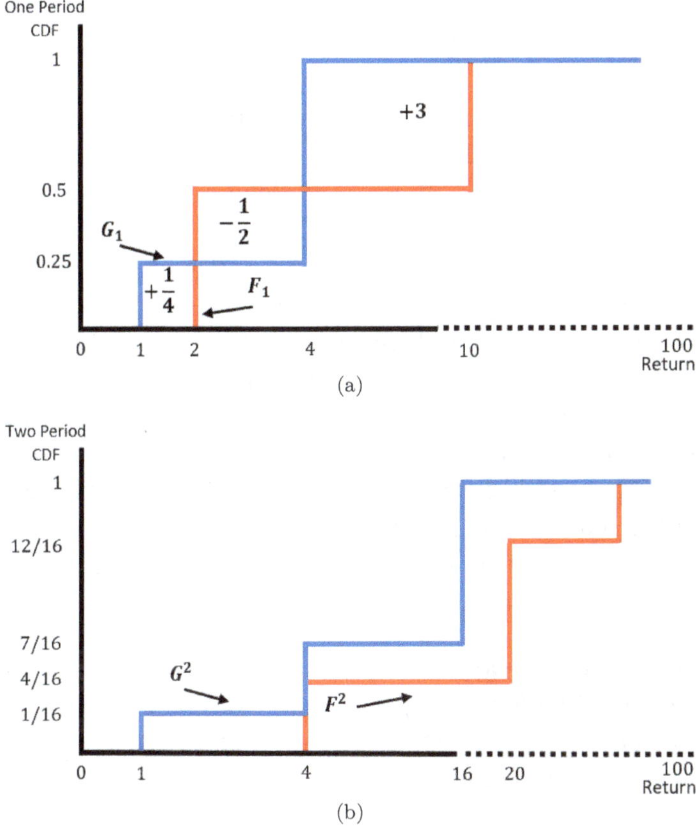

Figure 3.3: (a) The one-period cumulative distributions; neither F_1 nor G_1 dominates the other by FSD; (b) The two-period prospect F^2 dominates the two-period prospect G^2 by FSD.

the multi-period case. However, in contrast, with FSD, we may have no one-period FSD dominance, but for a multi-period case, we may have FSD. These are technical results, and we discuss the economic consequences of these M–V and FSD contrasting results later in this chapter.

Let us generalize the relationship between the one-period and multi-period FSD. We first compare the cumulative distributions of the one-period and the two-period — two prospects investors face. The generalization to the N-period case is straightforward.

Denote the two-period distributions of the two prospects under consideration by $F^2(x)$ and $G^2(x)$, and for simplicity and when no confusion can arise, we denote $F^2(x)$ by $F(x)$ and $G^2(x)$ by $G(x)$. The one-period cumulative distributions are denoted by $F_1(x_1)$ and $F_2(x_2)$, and $G_1(x_1)$ and $G_2(x_2)$ with density functions f_i and g_i, respectively, where $i = 1, 2$. We also denote by F and G the two prospects under consideration.

In the following proposition, we prove that if prospect F dominates prospect G in one-period horizon, it is sufficient to insure (in contrast to the M–V results) that prospect F dominates prospect G by FSD for the two-period horizon as well. We prove this claim by assuming independence of the returns over time, but the "identical" component of the *i.i.d.* assumption is not needed for this proof. This claim, combined with the example showing that we may have no one-period FSD but a two-period FSD, is sufficient to conclude that the size of the FSD efficient set decreases, in the weak sense, with the horizon.

Proposition 1. *Assuming independence over time of the returns, a sufficient condition for a two-period dominance of prospect $F(x)$ over prospect $G(x)$ by FSD is that there is FSD in each period, that is, F_i dominates G_i by FSD for $i = 1, 2$.*

Proof. First note that $x = x_1 x_2$ (where x is the *return*, namely $1 +$ rate of the return, which is always greater or equal to zero). Using this definition, we employ the independence over time assumption to obtain the two-period cumulative distribution of $F(x)$. The cumulative distribution is given by

$$F(x) = \Pr(X \le x) = \int_a^b \int_a^{x/t_1} f_1(t_1) f_2(t_2) dt_1 dt_2$$

$$= \int_a^b F_2(x/t_1) f_1(t_1) d\,t_1. \tag{3.10}$$

Note that due to the independence assumption, we have $f(t_1, t_2) = f(t_1) f_2(t_2)$. In the integral formula, the first integral is with respect to the first period return, t_1. The second integral is with respect to t_2, where the range of this variable is bounded from above by x/t_1. Thus, for each possible value x, the two-period return goes up to $t_1 t_2 = t_1(x/t_1) = x$, as required by the cumulative distribution formula $F(x) = \Pr(X \le x)$. Note that the range of t_1 is $a \le t_1 \le b$ and, therefore, if $t_1 > x$, then the variable t_2 must be smaller than x, such that the constraint required by the cumulative distribution $F(x) = \Pr(X \le x)$, namely, $t_1 t_2 = x$ is intact.

Similarly, we obtain for the two-period distribution $G(x)$ that

$$G(x) = \Pr(X \le x) = \int_a^b \int_a^{x/t_1} g_1(t_1)g_2(t_2)dt_1 dt_2$$

$$= \int_a^b G_2(x/t_1)g_1(t_1)dt_1 \tag{3.11}$$

where $t_1 t_2 = x$; hence, $t_2 = x/t_1$. We need to prove that if for each one-period prospect F dominates prospect G by FSD, then we also have two-period FSD dominance, that is, for all values x, the following holds:

$$F(x) = \Pr(X \le x) = \int_a^b F_2(x/t_1)f_1(t_1)dt_1 \le$$

$$\tag{3.12}$$

$$G(x) = \Pr(X \le x) = \int_a^b G_2(x/t_1)g_1(t_1)dt_1.$$

As there is FSD of prospect F over prospect G in each period, we also have for the second period that $F_2(x/t_1) \le G_2(x/t_1)$ for all values x/t_1, and there is at least one strict inequality. Therefore, we can write the following equation:

$$G_2(x/t_1) = F_2(x/t_1) + \delta(x/t_1) \tag{3.13}$$

where $\delta(x/t_1) \ge 0$, and there is at least one value x/t_1 with a strict inequality.

Thus, we need to prove that for all values x

$$F(x) - G(x) = \int_a^b F_2(x/t_1)f_1(t_1)d(t_1)$$

$$- \int_a^b [F_2(x/t_1) + \delta(x/t_1)]g_1(t_1)dt_1 \le 0.$$

Therefore, the following inequality (which guarantees two-period FSD of F over G) holds:

$$F(x) - G(x) = \int_a^b F_2(x/t_1)f(t_1)d(t_1) - \int_a^b G_2(x/t_1)g_1(t_1)d(t_1) \leq 0$$

$$(3.14)$$

if and only if the following inequality holds:

$$\int_a^b [F_2(x/t_1)[f_1(t_1) - g_1(t_1)] - \int_a^b \delta(x/t_1)g_1(t_1)dt_1 \leq 0. \quad (3.15)$$

And there is at least one strict inequality. As $\delta(x/t_1)$ and $g(t_1)$ are non-negative, to show that $F(x) - G(x) \leq 0$ for all values x, it is sufficient to show that for all values x,

$$\int_a^b [F_2(x/t_1)[f_1(t_1) - g_1(t_1)]dt_1 \leq 0. \quad (3.16)$$

Integrating by parts, Eq. (3.16) with respect to t_1, we obtain

$$[F_2(x/t_1)(F_1(t_1) - G_1(t_1)]_a^b$$

$$- \int_a^b \{[F_1(t_1) - G_1(t_1)]\partial F_2(x/t_1)/\partial t_1\}dt_1.$$

Finally, as $F_1(b) = G_1(b) = 1$ and $F_1(a) = G_1(a) = 0$, the first term is equal to zero; therefore, we can safely assert that the two-period prospect F dominates the two-period prospect G by FSD if the following holds:

$$- \int_a^b [F_1(t_1) - G_1(t_1)]\partial[F_2(x/t_1)]/\partial t_1]dt_1 \leq 0.$$

However,

$$- \int_a^b [F_1(t_1) - G_1(t_1)][\partial[F_2(x/t_1)]/\partial t_1]\,dt_1$$

$$= - \int_a^b [F_1(t_1) - G_1(t_1)]f_2(x/t_1)(-x/t^2)dt_1$$

$$= \int_a^b [F_1(t_1) - G_1(t_1)]f_2(x/t_1)(x/t^2)dt_1.$$

This term is non-positive because $f_2(x/t_1)(x/t^2) \geq 0$ (note that x, being the return and not the rate of return, is non-negative), and by assumption of the one-period FSD, we have $F_1(t_1) - G_1(t_1) \leq 0$ for all values t_1. As $\delta(x/t_1)$ is also non-negative, and for at least one value x/t_1, it is strictly positive, we finally conclude that the term given by Eq. (3.15) is non-positive, and for at least one value, it is strictly negative. Therefore, we can safely conclude that with the two-period distribution $F(x) \leq G(x)$ for all x, there is at least one strict inequality. Thus, if in each one-period, prospect F dominates prospect G by FSD, such dominance also prevails for the two-period horizon as claimed by Proposition 1. So far, we have analyzed and compared the one-period FSD to the two-period FSD. The generalization of these results to the N-period FSD is straightforward and given in Proposition 2.

Proposition 2. *Denote by $F^N(x)$ and $G^N(x)$ the N-period investment cumulative distribution of terminal wealth of prospects F and G, respectively. Then, assuming independence over time, a sufficient condition for FSD of the N-period prospect $F^N(x)$ over the N-period prospect $G^N(x)$ is that there is FSD in each one-period, namely $F_i(x) \leq G_i(x)$ for all periods, $i = 1, 2, \ldots, N$ (and as usual, to avoid trivial cases, we need to have at least one strict inequality).*

Proof. The proof is by induction. For $N = 2$, we have the proof given by Proposition 1. Let us assume that Proposition 2 is intact for $N - 1$ periods. We need to prove that it also holds for N periods. Thus, by assumption, $F^{N-1}(x)$ dominates $G^{N-1}(x)$, and for the last period, F_N dominates G_N (namely there is a dominance for the last one-period specific case $i = N$). Employing the independence assumption of the return $\prod_{i=1}^{N-1} x_i$ and x_N (as all x_i are independent, $Y \equiv \prod_{i=1}^{N-1} x_i$ and x_N are also independent), we can apply Proposition 1 corresponding to Y and x_N to prove that prospect F dominates prospect G for the N-period case also as claimed by Proposition 2.

So far, we have not assumed that returns are identical over time. Therefore, we can say very little about the changes in the size and content of the FSD efficient set as a function of the investment horizon. To see this claim, assume that the same prospects may have different one-period distribution. To illustrate, suppose that we have 100 portfolios in the feasible set, and we conduct pair-wise FSD comparisons for all 100 portfolios. Furthermore, assume that we analyze the relationship between the one-period and two-period FSD efficient sets. Suppose that for the first period we find, say, 50 portfolios are included in the FSD efficient set, and in the second period, there is no FSD; hence, all 100 portfolios are included in the FSD efficient set. In this case, the condition required that in each period there is FSD, say, prospect F dominates prospect G by FSD, is not intact, and the sufficient condition required by Proposition 1 does not hold; hence, the two-period efficient set may include all 100 portfolios. Thus, in order to have N-period dominance of, say, F over G, we need prospect F to dominate G in all the one-periods $i = 1, 2, \ldots, N$. If even in one period there is no FSD dominance, we cannot safely assert that F dominates G for the two-period case and, of course, also not for the more general N-period case. In the next proposition, we assume, as is generally assumed by financial economists, that $i.i.d.$ not only becomes independent over time, but also that the "identical" component of this assumption is intact.

Proposition 3. *If returns of each prospect under consideration are i.i.d., the multi-period efficient set decreases, in the weak sense, with the horizon and, therefore, any FSD-dominated prospect for one-period is also FSD-dominated for the N-period where $N > 1$.*

Proof. The proof is trivial. Due to the $i.i.d.$ assumption, we have for prospect F and prospect G under consideration that $F_i = F$ for $i = 1, 2, \ldots, N$ and $G_i = G$ for $i = 1, 2 \ldots, N$, where N denotes the last one-period under consideration. Therefore, a dominance in the first period implies a dominance in all other one-periods, and as the conditions of Proposition 2 are intact, a dominance in one-period of F over G by FSD implies that prospect F dominates prospect G by FSD for any arbitrary N-period. In addition, since we may have multi-period dominance even if there is no one-period dominance, we have the following relationship: $S_1 \supseteq S_N$, where S_1 and S_N are the one-period and the N-period FSD efficient sets, respectively.

3.5. Risk-Aversion: The Multi-Period SSD

While the most general prospect ranking rule is the FSD rule (as it only assumes $U' \geq 0$), the more interesting and more economically relevant rule is the SSD rule, as generally, risk aversion is commonly assumed in most models in finance and economic research. Furthermore, the FSD and the M–V dominance and efficiency analyses are not economically comparable, as the M–V rule assumes risk aversion and the FSD rule does not. Therefore, it is economically more relevant to compare the M–V and SSD multi-period analysis, as both rules assume risk aversion.

We find that the result corresponding to the one-period and multi-period SSD are very similar to those corresponding to the FSD presented above, albeit the proofs are a little more involved. We first demonstrate with a numerical example that with the independence over time assumption, we may have no one-period SSD, but we may have a multi-period SSD. With the *i.i.d.* assumption, namely adding the "identical" component of this assumption, the multi-period SSD efficient set is a subset of the one-period SSD efficient set — a result which is in sharp contradiction to the M–V results presented earlier in this chapter.

Before we turn to the general multi-period SSD analysis, let us illustrate the one-period SSD and the two-period SSD with the two prospects given in Example 1, showing that we may have no one-period SSD, but have a two-period SSD. We employ in the following the SSD condition given in Eq. (3.9).

As we can see from Figure 3.3(a), for $N = 1$, neither F nor G dominates the other by the SSD.

Specifically,

$$\int_1^4 [G_1(x) - F_1(x)]dx = -1/4 \quad \text{and}$$

$$\int_1^{10} [F_1(x) - G_1(x)]dx = -2.75.$$

Therefore, both prospect F and prospect G are included in the one-period SSD efficient set. However, as we can see from Figure 3.3(b), prospect F dominates prospect G for all two-period investors because the SSD dominance condition $\int_1^x [G^2(t) - F^2(t)]dt \geq 0$ is intact for all values x, and there is at least one strict inequality (actually, we have here FSD which implies SSD). This example indicates that the SSD efficient set may decrease with the horizon, as in this example, there are two prospects in the one-period SSD efficient set and only one prospect, prospect F, in the two-period SSD efficient set. The opposite cannot occur: Proposition 4 that follows states that if prospect F dominates prospect G by SSD in each one-period, such dominance is maintained for the two-period horizon.

We turn now to the formal relationship between the one-period SSD and the multi-period SSD with an emphasis on the changes in the SSD efficient set with the investment horizon. We start with a comparison of the one-period and two-period SSD relationship, and then we extend the results, as done in the analysis of the FSD, to the N-period case.

Proposition 4. *Assuming independence over time, if prospect F dominates prospect G by SSD in each one-period, then prospect F also dominates prospect G by SSD for the two-period horizon.*

Proof. The two-period prospect F dominates the two-period prospect G by SSD if and only if $\int_a^x [G(t) - F(t)]dt \geq 0$ for all values of x, and there is a strict inequality for at least one value x_0, where F and G are the two-period cumulative distributions of the two prospects under consideration. As with the FSD analysis, by the independence assumption we have

$$G(x) = \Pr(X \leq x) = \int_a^b \int_a^{x/t_1} g_1(t_1)g_2(t_2)dt_1 dt_2$$

$$= \int_a^b G_2(x/t_1)g_1(t_1)dt_1 \tag{3.17}$$

and

$$F(x) = \Pr(X \le x) = \int_a^b \int_a^{x/t_1} f_1(t_1) f_2(t_2) dt_1 dt_2$$

$$= \int_a^b F_2(x/t_1) f_1(t_1) dt_1. \tag{3.18}$$

(For these formulas, see the FSD analysis, Eqs. (3.10) and (3.11).)

Thus, with this formulation, we need to prove that

$$\int_a^{x_i} [G_i(t_i) - F_i(t_i)] dt_i \ge 0 \quad for \ all \ x_i \ (i = 1, 2)$$

$$\Rightarrow \int_a^x [G(t) - F(t)] dt \ge 0 \tag{3.19}$$

for all values x, and there is at least one strict inequality, namely there is a two-period dominance. Employing Eqs. (3.17) and (3.18) to have a two-period SSD of prospect F over prospect G, we need to prove that

$$\int_a^x G(t) dt = \int_a^x \int_a^b G_2(x/t_1) g_1(t_1) dt_1 dt$$

$$\ge \int_a^x F(t) dt = \int_a^x \int_a^b F_2(x/t_1) f_1(t_1) dt_1 dt$$

for all $x = t_1 t_2$, and there is at least one strict inequality. Note that the first integration is with respect to t_1, and the second integration is with respect to t.

However, by the second-year SSD of prospect F over prospect G (as assumed by Proposition 4), we have

$$\int_a^{x/t_1} G_2(x/t_1) dt_1 \ge \int_0^{x/t_1} F_2(x/t_1) dt_1 \text{ for all } x/t_1,$$

which can be rewritten as

$$\int_a^{x/t_1} G_2(x/t_1) dt_1 = \int_a^{x/t_1} F_2(x/t_1) dt_1 + \delta(x/t_1) \tag{3.20}$$

where $\delta(x/t_1) \geq 0$, and there is at least one value for which $\delta(x/t_1) > 0$.

Thus, we need to prove that

$$\int_a^x \int_a^b [F_2(x/t_1)g_1(t_1)dt_1 dt + \delta(x/t_1) \geq \int_a^x \int_a^b F_2(x/t_1)f_1(t_1)dt_1 dt$$

$$(3.21)$$

where $\delta(x/t_1)$ changes with x/t_1, but it is non-negative for all values of x/t_1, and it is strictly positive for at least one value. Once again, the first integration is with respect to t_1 for the range $(a,\ b)$, and the second integration is with respect to t for the range (a,x), and the inequality should hold for all values x.

Therefore, if the following inequality holds, then *a fortiori* (3.21) holds, and F dominates G by SSD in the two-period case

$$\int_a^x \int_a^b [F_2(t/t_1)g_1(t_1)dt_1 dt \geq \int_a^x \int_a^b F_2(t/t_1)f_1(t_1)dt_1 dt \quad (3.22)$$

and this inequality should hold for all $x = t_1 t_2$. Inequality (3.22) can be rewritten as

$$\int_a^x \int_a^b F_2(t/t_1)[g_1(t_1) - f(t_1)]dt_1 dt \geq 0,$$

which can be rewritten as

$$\int_a^b [g_1(t_1) - f(t_1)] \left(\int_a^{x/t_1} [F_2(t/t_1)]dt \right) dt_1 \geq 0. \quad (3.23)$$

Integrating by parts with respect to t_1, the last equation yields

$$\int_a^b [g_1(t_1) - f(t_1)] \int_a^{x/t_1} [F_2(t/t_1)]dt_1 dt$$

$$= \left\{ [G_1(t_1) - F_1(t_1)] \int_a^{x/t_1} [F_2(t/t_1)]dt_1 \right\}_b^a$$

$$- \int_a^b [G_1(t_1) - F_1(t_1)] \left[\partial \int_a^{x/t_1} [F_2(t/t_1)dt_1]/\partial t_1 \right].$$

As the first term on the right-hand side is equal to zero, what is left to prove is that

$$-\int_a^b [G_1(t_1) - F_1(t_1)] \left[\partial \int_a^{x/t_1} [F_2(t/t_1)dt_1]/\partial t_1 \right] \geq 0,$$

or

$$\int_a^b [G_1(t_1) - F_1(t_1)] \left[-\partial \int_a^{x/t_1} [F_2(t/t_1)dt_1]/\partial t_1 \right] \geq 0$$

$$= \int_a^b [G_1(t_1) - F_1(t_1)] \int_a^{x/t_1} [-\partial[F_2(t/t_1)dt_1]/\partial t_1] \geq 0.$$

Suppose that $[-\partial[\int_a^{x/t_1} [F_2(t/t_1)dt_1/\partial t_1] \equiv A(x,t_1)$ is positive, and $A'(x,t_1)$ is negative. We argue that, in this case, the above inequality is intact; therefore, the two-period prospect F dominates the two-period prospect G by SSD. The explanation for this claim is as follows: by the one-period SSD assumption $\int_a^x [G_1(t_1) - F_1(t_1)] \geq 0$, up to any value of x (and also for the specific value $x = b$). This implies that when we draw the cumulative one-period distributions of F_1 and G_1, for any negative area enclosed between F_1 and G_1, there must be a preceding positive area (namely in a preceding range of the returns) that is at least as big as the negative area (in absolute terms). As $A(x,t_1)$ is non-negative, and $A'(x,t_1)$ is negative, we multiply in this case all areas enclosed between F and G, positive and negative alike, by positive numbers that are declining as we shift to the right. Therefore, as by assumption $\int_a^b [G_1(t_1) - F_1(t_1)]dt \geq 0$, then *a fortiori* the above integral is non-negative, as for each negative area multiplied by some positive number, there is a larger positive area located before the negative area that it is multiplied by a larger positive number.

To illustrate the above claim, suppose that G yields either 2 or 3 with an equal probability of 0.5, and F yields 2 with certainty; see Figure 3.4 for the two cumulative distributions. Obviously, F dominates G by SSD. Now, suppose that we multiply the positive area enclosed between G and F, say, by 5, and the negative area enclosed between G and F, say, by 4 (note that $A(x,t_1)$ is positive

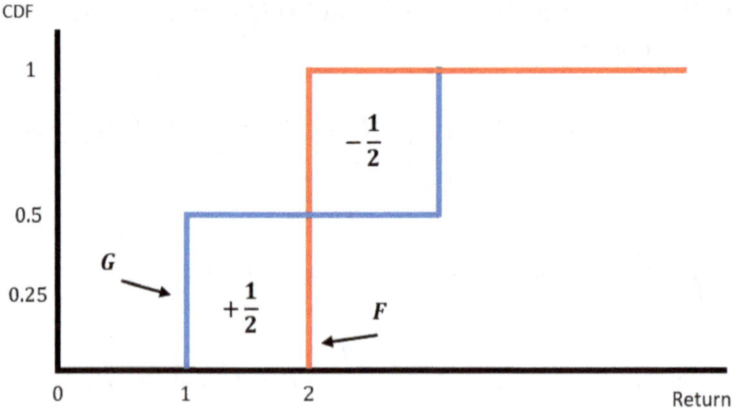

Figure 3.4: Prospect F dominates prospect G by SSD.

and decreasing as x increases). Thus, by multiplying by $A(x, t_1)$, we only enhanced the SSD relationship as the positive area becomes $0.5 \times 5 = 2.5$, and the negative area becomes $-0.5 \times 4 = -2.0$ (see Figure 3.4).

The proof of Proposition 4 hinges on the assumption that $A(x, t_1)$ is positive, and $A'(x, t_1)$ is negative. Indeed, this assumption is valid. As the proof of this claim is technical and relatively long, we do not provide it here, and the reader can find the detailed proof in Levy.[20]

Proposition 5 extends the two-period SSD results to the general N-period case.

Proposition 5. *Denote by $F^N(x)$ and $G^N(x)$ the N-period cumulative distribution of terminal wealth of prospects F and G, respectively. Then, assuming independence over time, a sufficient condition for SSD of $F^N(x)$ over $G^N(x)$ is that there is SSD in each one-period for all periods, $i = 1, 2, \ldots, N$ (and as usual, to avoid trivial cases, we need to have at least one strict inequality).*

---

[20]Levy, H. (1973). Stochastic dominance, efficiency criteria, and efficient portfolios: The multi-period case. *The American Economic Review* 63(5), 986–994.

Proof. The proof is by induction and very similar to the proof of the multi-period FSD case. For $N = 2$, we have the proof given by Proposition 4. Let us assume that Proposition 5 is intact for $N - 1$ periods. We need to prove that it also holds for N periods. As by the induction assumption $F^{N-1}(x)$ dominates $G^{N-1}(x)$ by SSD, and for the last period F_N dominates G_N by SSD (that is, there is an SSD dominance for the last one-period case $i = N$), using the independence assumption of the return $\prod_{i=1}^{N-1} x_i$ and x_N (as all x_i are independent and $\prod_{i=1}^{N-1} x_i$ and x_N are also independent) we can apply, once again, Proposition 4 to prove the claim given in Proposition 5.

Note that we assume in the above proof independence over time, but the distributions are not necessarily identical over time. Therefore, like in the multi-period FSD case, we cannot determine whether the size of the SSD efficient set decreases or increases over time. Yet, by adding the "identical" part of the *i.i.d.* assumption, we can conclude that the multi-period SSD efficient set decreases, in the weak sense, with the horizon, in contradiction to the M–V results. This is summarized in the following proposition.

Proposition 6. *If returns of each prospect under consideration are i.i.d., the multi-period SSD efficient set decreases, in the weak sense, with the horizon. Specifically, any dominated prospect for one-period is also dominated for the N-period where $N > 1$.*

Proof. The proof is trivial and very similar to the multi-period FSD case. Due to the *i.i.d.* assumption, we have for prospect F and prospect G under consideration that $F_i = F$ for $i = 1, 2, \dots, N$ and $G_i = G$ for $i = 1, 2, \dots, N$. Therefore, SSD dominance in the first period implies SSD dominance in all other one-periods and the conditions of Proposition 5 are intact; hence, the multi-period prospect $F(x)$ dominates by SSD the multi-period prospect $G(x)$ for any arbitrary N-period horizon. In this case, $S_1 \supseteq S_N$ where S_1 and S_N are the SSD one-period and the N-period efficient sets, respectively.

3.6. The FSD, SSD, and the M–V Multi-Period Efficient Sets

In this section, we illustrate various cases of the changes in the SD and M–V efficient sets as a function of the investment horizon. In the following Figures 3.5 and 3.6, we compare the changes in the FSD, SSD, and M–V efficient sets as a function of the investment horizon. We analyze various cases corresponding to the one-period relationships of these three sets. Figure 3.5 illustrates the FSD (and SSD) and M–V one-period possible dominance relationship. In Figure 3.5(a), prospect F dominates prospect G by both the M–V rule and the FSD rule, and obviously also by the SSD rule. In Figure 3.5(b), prospect F does not dominate prospect G by the M–V rule, but F dominates G by the FSD as well as SSD rules. Finally, Figure 3.5(c) demonstrates the case where prospect F dominates prospect G by the M–V rule and by the SSD rule, but not by the FSD rule (see the intersection of the two cumulative distributions which avoids the FSD). Thus, by Figure 3.5(a), only F is both the M–V and FSD (and SSD) one-period efficient set. By Figure 3.5(b), the one-period M–V set includes both F and G, but the FSD and SSD efficient sets contain only one prospect, F. Finally, by Figure 3.5(c), both F and G are in the FSD efficient set, but by the M–V and SSD rules, only F is included in the efficient set (note that the area where F is below G is drawn such that it is larger than the area where G is below F; hence, we obtain the SSD of F over G). From these three examples, we can conclude that if normality is not assumed with the one-period return, the one-period M–V efficient set may be smaller, equal, or larger than the one-period FSD and SSD efficient sets.

Despite these varieties of the one-period efficiency possibilities, as described in Figure 3.5, under the *i.i.d.* assumption, we can have stronger results concerning the size and content of the efficient set as a function of the investment horizon, namely in the multi-period analysis. In Figure 3.6, we assume that many prospects are compared, rather than only two as in Figure 3.5, and we focus only on the FSD and M–V efficient sets, although the discussion can easily be extended to the SSD efficient set. Assuming *i.i.d.*, as the

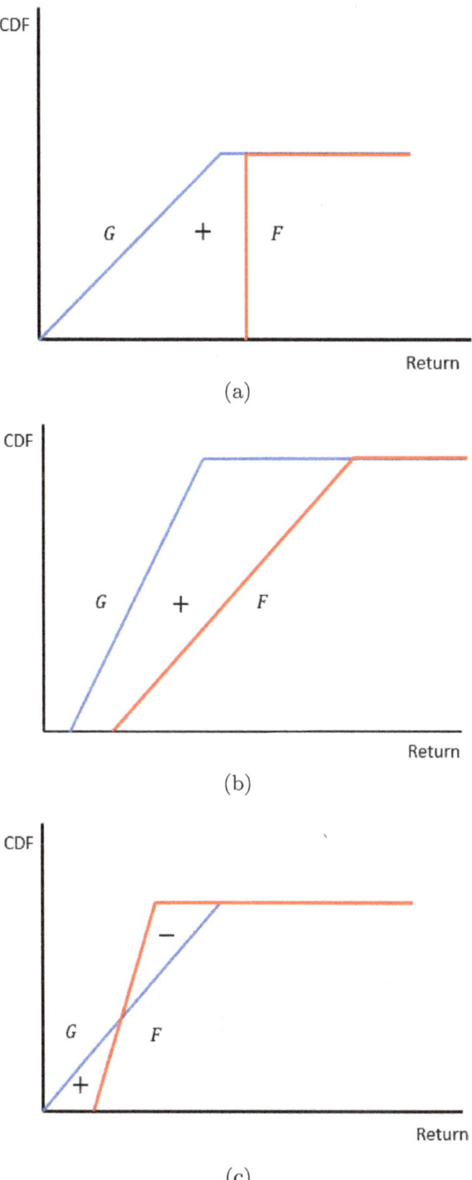

Figure 3.5: (a) F dominates G by both M–V and FSD; (b) F dominates G by SSD but not by M–V; (c) F dominates G by M–V and SSD but not by FSD.

investment horizon increases, the M–V efficient set increases, and the FSD (and SSD) efficient set decreases (see Propositions 3 and 6). The three one-period possibilities described by Figure 3.5 are presented in Figure 3.6 as a function of the assumed investment horizon. In Figure 3.6(a), the one-period M–V and FSD efficient sets are identical. Thus, we generalize the result given by Figure 3.5(a) and assume that many prospects are available where in the one-period there are, say, n prospects in the FSD, as well as the M–V efficient sets, and these are the same prospects in both sets. As the horizon increases, the FSD efficient set shrinks, and the M–V efficient set expands. In Figure 3.6(b), the one-period FSD and SSD efficient sets are smaller than the one-period M–V efficient set (corresponding to Figure 3.5(b), but with many assets), and as before, the M–V efficient set expands with the horizon, and the FSD efficient set shrinks with it. In Figure 3.6(c), the one-period FSD efficient set is larger than the one-period M–V and SSD efficient sets (corresponding to Figure 3.5(c), but with many assets). As can be seen, in this specific case, the curves representing the size of the M–V and FSD efficient sets may cross.

As mentioned before, the horizon's effect on the multi-period efficient set is economically more interesting when we compare the SSD and M–V rules, as both assume risk aversion. We elaborate on the M–V and SSD comparison first with a numerical example, then analyze the multi-period case where the one-period distribution is assumed to be normal and alternatively log-normal, as these two distributions are commonly employed in economic research.

In the following example, we show that the existence of the one-period SSD implies a two-period SSD (as proven in Proposition 6), but one-period M–V dominance vanishes as we shift to two-period M–V analysis.

Example 2. *One-period dominance*: Suppose that prospect G yields either 1 or 3 with equal probability, and prospect F yields either 2 or 4 with equal probability. These are the returns, namely the $1 +$ rate of return. A simple calculation reveals that

$$E_F \equiv (1 + \mu_F) = 3 > E_G \equiv (1 + \mu_G) = 2$$

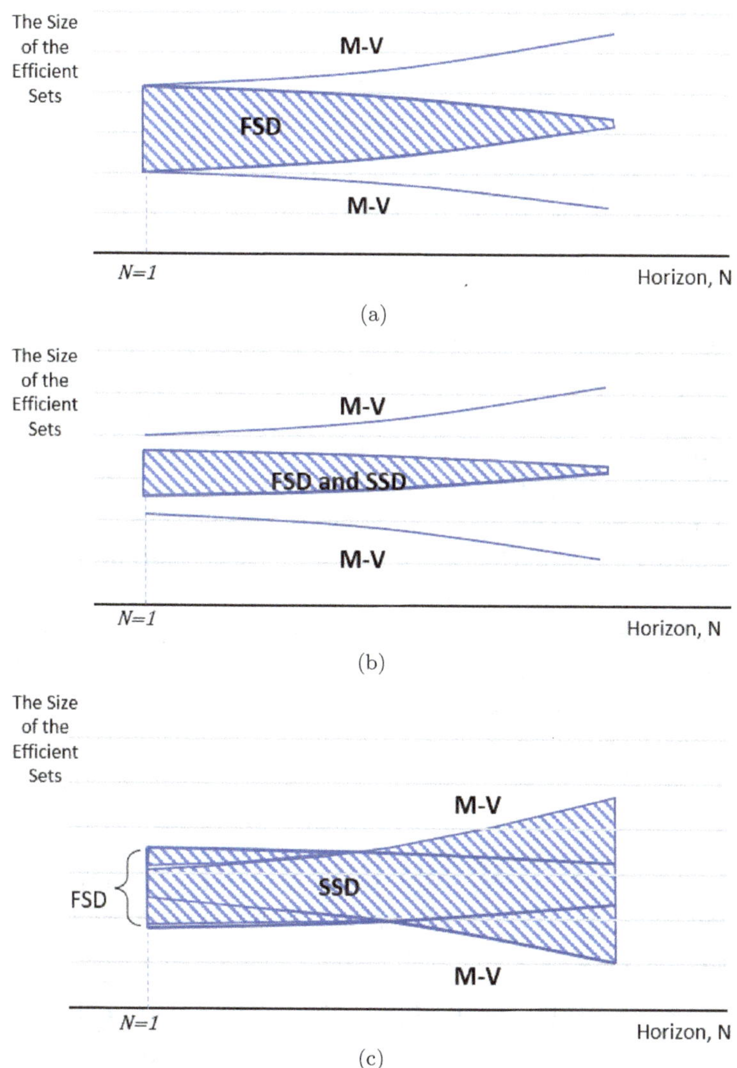

Figure 3.6: (a) The one-period M–V, FSD, and SSD efficient sets are identical; (b) The one-period FSD and SSD efficient sets are smaller than the M–V efficient set; (c) The one-period M–V and SSD efficient sets are smaller than the FSD efficient set.

and

$$\sigma_F^2 = 1/2(2-3)^2 + 1/2(4-3)^2$$

$$= 1 \text{ and } \sigma_G^2 = 1/2(1-2)^2 + 1/2(3-2)^2 = 1.$$

Therefore, F dominates G by the M–V rule for one-period investors. It is obvious that F dominates G also by the SSD rule (actually, F dominates G by the FSD rule, let alone by the SSD rule).

Two-period dominance: Assuming *i.i.d.* prospect G yields 1 with a probability of 0.25, 3 with a probability of 0.50, and 9 with a probability of 0.25. A similar calculation reveals that F yields 4 with a probability of 0.25, 8 with a probability of 0.50, and 16 with a probability of 0.25. Drawing the two cumulative distributions, it is clear that the two-period prospect F dominates as before the two-period prospect G by FSD, let alone by SSD. This result is not surprising as a one-period FSD and SSD under *i.i.d.* implies a two-period FSD and SSD, respectively (see Propositions 3 and 6). We turn now to calculate the two-period mean and variance of prospects F and G. We have, as expected, a two-period mean of F that is larger than the two-period mean of G:

$$E_F = 0.25 \times 4 + 0.5 \times 8 + 0.25 \times 16$$

$$= 9 > E_G = 0.25 \times 1 + 0.50 \times 3 + 0.25 \times 9 = 4.$$

However, while the one-period variances of the two prospects are identical, with the two-period variances, the variance of F is larger than the variance of G because

$$\sigma_F^2 = .25(4-9)^2 + .50(8-9)^2 + .25(16-9)^2 = 19$$

and

$$\sigma_G^2 = .25(1-4)^2 + .50(3-4)^2 + .25(9-4)^2 = 9.$$

Thus, in the one-period case, F dominates G by both SSD and M–V, in the two-period case, the SSD relationship, as expected, remains intact. However, the M–V dominance vanishes as F has a higher mean and higher variance than G. The reason for the relatively fast increase in the variance of prospect F is that it has a relatively large mean, and the larger the mean, other things being held constant, the larger the multi-period variance. These figures can also be obtained directly from Eq. (3.6) for the case $N = 2$, where the direct effect of the mean on the multi-period variance is more transparent. By Eq. (3.6), we have

$$\sigma_N^2 = [\sigma_1^2 + (1 + \mu_1)^2]^N - (1 + \mu_1)^{2N}$$

and for $N = 2$ we obtain

$$\sigma_2^2 = [\sigma_1^2 + (1 + \mu_1)^2]^2 - (1 + \mu_1)^{2x2} = \sigma_1^4 + 2\sigma_1^2(1 + \mu_1)^2.$$

Note that in our example, $\sigma_2^2(F) = \sigma_2^2(G) = 1$; hence, also $\sigma_2^4(F) = \sigma_2^4(G) = 1$. Therefore, Eq. (3.6) reveals that

$$\sigma_2^2(F) = 1 + 2(3)^2 = 19, \quad \text{and}$$
$$\sigma_2^2(G) = 1 + 2(2)^2 = 9$$

exactly as obtained with the direct calculation of the two-period variances. As can be seen from Eq. (3.6), the fact that F has a higher one-period mean than G induces a faster increase in the two-period variance of F relative to the increase in the variance of G. Therefore, in this example, the M–V dominance of F over G in the one-period case vanishes in the two-period case.

Thus, this example confirms the theoretical results: the one-period SSD dominance in this example is not affected by the horizon, while the M–V is affected: as the horizon increases, the M–V efficient set increases, as it contains two prospects in comparison to the one-period M–V efficient set containing only one prospect, prospect F. In general, with many prospects and with the *i.i.d.* assumption, the M–V efficient set increases, in the weak sense, and the SSD efficient set decreases, in the weak sense, with the horizon.

3.7. The SSD Rule with One-Period Normal Distribution and the Horizon Effect

To analyze the changes in the efficient set with the horizon where the one-period distribution is assumed to be normal, let us first shed more light on the one-period M–V dominance rule and its relationship to the SSD rule. As we have seen in Figures 3.5 and 3.6, the relationship between the SSD and M–V multi-period efficient sets corresponding to various horizons generally depends on the assumption regarding the one-period efficient sets. In the following analysis, we assume that the one-period distributions are normal (actually, the same conclusions are intact for a one-period elliptic distribution family where the normal distribution belongs to this family). We first show that, for normal distributions, the M–V rule and the SSD rule coincide, that is,

$$F \text{ dominates } G \text{ by the SSD rule}$$

$$\Longleftrightarrow F \text{ dominates } G \text{ by the M–V rule.}$$

As the detailed mathematical proof of this claim is given in Tobin (see footnote 14), Hanoch and Levy (see footnote 18), and Levy,[21] we briefly discuss this proof here. In a nutshell, this result is induced by the fact that two cumulative normal distributions with different variances intersect only once, and the one with the lower variance intersects the other one from below, and if the mean of the distribution with the lower variance is also larger than the mean of the other distribution, then by definition, we have dominance by the M–V rule. We claim that in such a case, we also have dominance of F over G by the SSD rule. To see this, recall that by the definition of expected utility we have

$$E_F U(x) - E_G U(x) = \int_a^b [f(x) - g(x)]U(x)dx$$

where $f(x)$ and $f(x)$ are the density functions of the two prospects under consideration.

Integrating part by part, we have

$$E_F U(x) - E_G U(x) = [(G(x) - F(x))U'(x)]_a^b$$
$$- \int_a^x [G(x) - F(x)]U'(x)dx$$

---

[21]Levy, H. (2016). *Stochastic Dominance: Investment Decision-Making Under Uncertainty,* Springer, New York.

and as the first term on the right-hand side of the equation is equal
to zero, we obtain

$$E_F U(x) - E_G U(x) = \int_a^x [G(x) - F(x)]U'(x)dx$$

for all utility functions U. This also holds in the specific case where
$(x) = x$, and as for this function, $U' = 1$, we obtain in this specific
case where $U(x) = x$ that

$$\mu_F - \mu_G = \int_a^b [G(x) - F(x)]dx. \tag{3.24}$$

By assumption of M–V dominance of F over G, we have $\mu_F - \mu_G \geq 0$. Due to the fact that two cumulative normal distributions
with different variances intersect exactly once, where F with the
lower variance intersects G from below, Eq. (3.24), and the fact that
$\mu_F - \mu_G \geq 0$ implies that the following holds: $\int_a^x [G(x) - F(x)]dx \geq 0$
for all values of x (with at least one strict inequality). Thus a
dominance of F over G by the M–V rule, implies that F also
dominates G by the SSD rule, so long as the distributions are normal
(see Eq. (3.9)). To further see this claim, note that $\mu_F - \mu_G \geq 0$
implies that the total area enclosed between the two distributions
$[G(x) - F(x)]$ is positive where the positive area up to the intersection
point is larger (in absolute terms) than the negative succeeding
area; hence $\int_a^x [G(x) - F(x)]dx \geq 0$, implying SSD of F over G. By
similar argument, it can be shown that with normal distribution, SSD
dominance implies M–V dominance. Thus, with normal distributions,
the M–V and the SSD one-period efficient sets are identical. As we
shall see in what follows, this relationship changes as we extend the
analysis to the multi-period case as the multi-period distribution is
no longer normal.

We turn now to analyze the size and content of the efficient
sets as a function of the horizon in the case of one-period normal
distributions. The one-period normal distribution case is very simple:
as the one-period M–V and SSD rules are identical for a horizon
$N = 1$, the one-period M–V and SSD efficient sets coincide (see
Figure 3.7). As we proved that the SSD efficient set decreases with

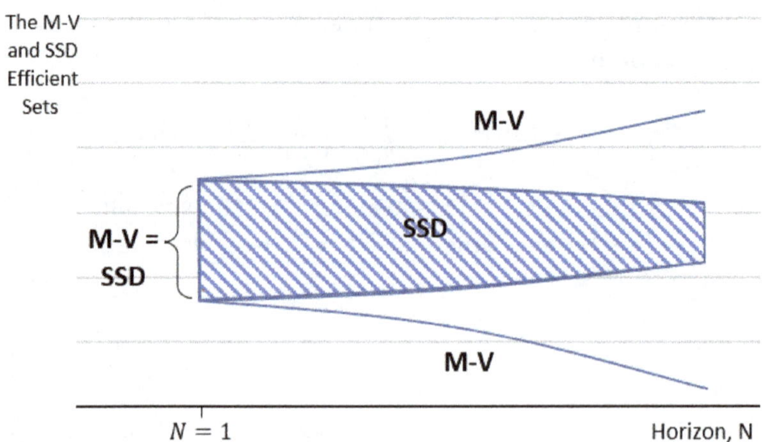

Figure 3.7: The efficient sets with one-period normal distributions.

the horizon, and the M–V efficient set increases with it, we obtain the changes in these two efficient sets with the increase in the horizon, as illustrated in Figure 3.7.

3.8. The SSD Rule with One-Period Log-Normal Distributions and the Horizon Effect

We turn now to analyze dominance relationship where the one-period distributions are assumed to be log-normal. Suppose that the one-period distributions of F and G are log-normal. Thus, $\log(x)$ is normally distributed. In this case, F dominates G for all risk averters if and only if the following two conditions hold:

(a) $E_F(x) \geq E_G(x)$,

(b) $Var_F(\log x) \leq Var_G(\log x)$, and there is at least one strict inequality.

In other words, if the one-period distributions are log-normal, the above two conditions imply that the SSD condition $\int_a^x [G(t) - F(t)]dt \geq 0$ holds for all values of x, and there is at least one strict inequality. Therefore,

(a) $E_F(x) \geq E_G(x)$ and

(b) $Var_F(\log x) \leq Var_G(\log x) \iff$ SSD of F over G.

Note that condition (b) above is equivalent to the condition $\sigma_F(x)/E_F(x) \leq \sigma_G(x)/E_G(x)$, where x stands for the return, and not log-return. For the proof of the SSD in the log-normal case and the above equivalent formulation of condition (b), see Levy.[22]

To analyze the one-period SSD efficient set with one-period log-normal distributions and its relationship to the M–V one-period efficient set, we need a little more delicate analysis. First, note that the mean and variance of the log-normal distribution are given by

$$E(x) = e^{\mu + 1/2\sigma^2} \quad \text{and} \quad Var(x) = e^{2\mu + \sigma^2}(e^{\sigma^2} - 1) = [E(x)]^2(e^{\sigma^2} - 1)$$

$$(3.25)$$

where $E(x)$ and $Var(x)$ are the parameters of the returns x, and μ and σ^2 are the parameters of $log(x)$. Namely, $Var(logx) \equiv \sigma^2$. Suppose that F dominates G by the M–V rule. Then,

$$E_F(x) \geq E_G(x), \quad \text{and} \quad Var_F(x) \leq Var_G(x). \tag{3.26}$$

Equation (3.25) implies that if Eq. (3.26) holds then $E_F(x) \geq E_G(x)$, and that $\sigma^2(F) \leq \sigma^2(G)$ (these are the variances of $log(x)$); therefore, we conclude that in the one-period distributions,

$$F \text{ dominates } G \text{ by M–V} \Rightarrow F \text{ dominates } G \text{ by SSD.} \tag{3.27}$$

Let us now assume that F dominates G by SSD. As the one-period distributions are assumed to be log-normal, SSD dominance implies that

$$E_F(x) \geq E_G(x) \quad \text{and} \quad \sigma^2(F) \leq \sigma^2(G)$$

(recall that these are the variances of $log(x)$).

---

[22] Levy, H. (1973). Stochastic dominance among log-normal prospects. *International Economic Review* 14(3), 601–614.

From Eq. (3.25), we find that

$$Var_F(x) \gtrless Var_G(x); \text{ therefore,}$$

$$F \text{ dominates } G \text{ by SSD} \nRightarrow F \text{ dominates } G \text{ by M–V.} \quad (3.28)$$

From (3.27) and (3.28), we conclude that with log-normal one-period distributions, the one-period SSD efficient set is a subset of the one-period M–V efficient set. We employ this property in drawing Figure 3.8.

Figure 3.8 corresponds to the assumption that the one-period distributions are log-normal. In this case, as proven above, the one-period SSD efficient set is smaller than the one-period M–V efficient set. The M–V efficient set, as in all other cases given before, expands with the horizon. However, with one-period log-normal distribution, the SSD efficient set remains the same regardless of the horizon. The explanation of this unique result is that if x is log-normally distributed, then the multi-period return $\prod_{i=1}^{N} x_i$ is also log-normally distributed, and as the multi-period variance of $\log\left(\prod_{i=1}^{N} x_i\right)$ is equal to $N[Var(\log(x_i))]$, the one-period and multi-period SSD efficient sets are identical. That is, any prospect that is eliminated from the one-period SSD efficient set is also eliminated from the N-period SSD

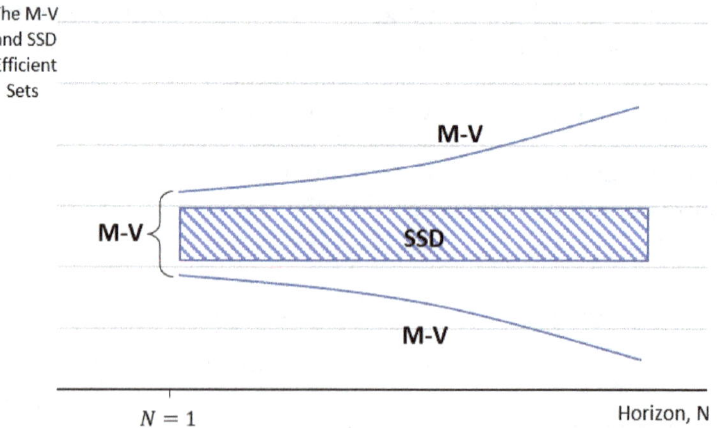

Figure 3.8: The efficient sets with one-period log-normal distributions.

efficient set. Moreover, if F does not dominate G by SSD in one-period, such dominance also does not exist for the N-period horizon. The explanation for these results is that all multi-period distributions are log-normal and that

$$E_F(x) \geq E_G(x), \ \sigma^2(F) \leq \sigma^2(G) \Longleftrightarrow$$

$$E_F\left(\prod_{i=1}^{N} x_i\right) \leq E_G\left(\prod_{i=1}^{N} x_i\right), \ \text{and } N\sigma^2(F) \leq N\sigma^2(G)$$

where $\sigma^2(F)$ and $\sigma^2(G)$ are the variances of $log(x)$.

3.9. The Economic Loss Induced by Employing the M–V Rule for Long Horizons

Investors who adhere to the M–V rule in their investment selection process may incur an economic loss in cases where the distributions are not normal. The possible loss is induced by the fact that the selected investment by the M–V rule may be SSD inefficient, that is, every risk averter may benefit from switching from the investment selected by the M–V rule to another investment that is SSD efficient. In this section, we demonstrate this potential economic loss.

Tables 3.1 and 3.2 demonstrate the relationships of the FSD, SSD, and M–V size and content of the efficient sets and the length

Table 3.1: The mean and standard deviation of 10 assets distributed normally.

Asset	$1 + \mu$	σ
1	1.02	0.03
2	1.04	0.04
3	1.06	0.03
4	1.08	0.05
5	1.09	0.10
6	1.10	0.12
7	1.10	0.08
8	1.11	0.10
9	1.12	0.08
10	1.30	0.30

Table 3.2: Assets included in the FSD, SSD, and M–V efficient sets for various horizons.

Horizon N	FSD	SSD	M–V
1	2,3,4,6,8,9,10	3,4,9,10	3,4,9,10
2	3,4,6,8,9,10	3,4,9,10	3,4,7,9,10
3	3,4,6,8,9,10	3,4,9,10	3,4,7,9,10
4	3,4,6,8,9,10	3,4,9,10	3,4,7,9,10
5	3,4,6,8,9,10	3,4,9,10	3,4,7,9,10
6	4,6,8,9,10	3,4,9,10	3,4,7,9,10
7	4,6,8,9,10	4,9,10	3,4,7,9,10
$\vdots$	$\vdots$	$\vdots$	$\vdots$
10	4,6,8,9,10	9,10	3,4,7,9,10
11	6,8,9,10	9,10	3,4,7,9,10
$\vdots$	$\vdots$	$\vdots$	$\vdots$
17	6,8,9,10	9,10	2,3,4,7,9,10
$\vdots$	$\vdots$	$\vdots$	$\vdots$
25	6,8,9,10	9,10	2,3,4,7,9,10
$\vdots$	$\vdots$	$\vdots$	$\vdots$
27	6,8,9,10	9,10	2,3,4,6,7,9,10
28	6,8,9,10	9,10	2,3,4,6,7,9,10
29	6,8,9,10	9,10	2,3,4,5,6,7,9,10
30	6,8,9,10	9,10	2,3,4,5,6,7,9,10

of the assumed investment horizon, where the one-period ($N = 1$) distributions of all assets under consideration are assumed to be normal. The procedure for finding the various efficient sets is as follows: for $N = 1$ year, we draw from each of the 10 normal distributions given in Table 3.1 a total of 100,000 observations (with replacement) and apply the pairwise FSD, SSD, and M–V rules to examine whether there is dominance of one asset over the other[23]

---

[23] We order the returns from the smallest to the largest return of each prospect. To have FSD of, say, x over y, we need $x_i \geq y_i$ for all $i = 1, 2, \ldots\ldots 100,000$ observations with at least one strict inequality. For SSD of x over y, we need $\sum_{i=1}^{K} x_i \geq \sum_{i=1}^{K} x_i$ for all $K = 1, 2, \ldots 100,000$ and that there is at least one strict inequality where, once again, x_i and y_i are ranked from the lowest value to the highest value.

(for more details, see Levy, footnote 21). For $N = 2$, we draw from 100,000 sets two independent observations (one after the other with replacement) from each normal distribution and calculate the two-period return given by $x = x_1 x_2$. Having this two-period distribution based on the simulated 100,000 observations of two-periods, once again, we examine the two-period dominance relationship between each pair of the 10 assets included in the feasible set (see Table 3.1). The same procedure is repeated for various horizons, N, up to $N = 30$ years.

Employing the simulation described above, we find that for $N = 1$, asset 3 dominates asset 1 by FSD (see Table 3.2). Thus, the simulation confirms the theoretical result asserting that with normal distributions, there is FSD if and only if the variances of the two prospects under consideration are equal (otherwise, the two cumulative normal distributions under consideration intersect; hence, we do not have FSD), and the mean of the superior prospect is larger.[24] Indeed, this is the case with these two assets as $\sigma_3 = \sigma_1 = 0.03$ and $(1 + \mu_3) = 1.06 > (1 + \mu_1) = 1.02$ (see Table 3.1). By a similar argument, asset 9 dominates asset 7 by FSD, and asset 8 dominates asset 5 also by FSD. Thus, for $N = 1$, the FSD efficient set contains 7 assets (see Table 3.2). As the assumed investment horizon N increases, the FSD efficient set decreases, in the weak sense, as predicted by the theoretical analysis given above. Table 3.2 reports the results for selected N (for the specific horizons omitted from the table, there are no changes in the FSD, SSD, or the M–V efficient sets; hence, no information is lost by this omission). Note that for $N \geq 11$, the FSD efficient set contains only 4 assets, and this efficient set does not change up to $N = 30$. Thus, the FSD efficient set decreases from 7 assets for $N = 1$ to 4 assets for $N = 11$, and is unchanged up to $N = 30$. Also, note that asset 10 with the highest one-period mean also has the highest multi-period mean;

---

[24]For normal distributions with equal variances, the CDF of the distribution with the larger mean is located below the other distribution's CDF in the whole range of returns; hence, we have FSD of the distribution with the larger mean over the other distribution.

therefore, it is always included in the FSD and SSD efficient sets. This result is also predicted by the theoretical analysis as a necessary condition for FSD dominance in that the dominating asset must have a higher mean than the mean of the dominated one; and by the SSD dominance, the dominating prospect must have a mean that is equal to or larger than the mean of the dominated prospect. Thus, no asset can dominate asset 10 by the FSD or SSD rules. Moreover, by the definition of the M–V rule, asset 10 must be included in the M–V efficient sets for all horizons.

Obviously, for $N = 1$ and with the normal distribution assumption, one does not need the simulation and can determine FSD, SSD, and M–V dominance theoretically, based on the fact that the distributions are normal. Thus, not surprisingly for $N = 1$, the SSD and M–V efficient sets are identical, as predicted theoretically. However, for consistency, we employ the same simulation for $N = 1$ as for $N > 1$.

Table 3.2 presents the various efficient sets as a function of the assumed investment horizon. As mentioned above, for $N = 1$, there are no surprises, and the efficient sets obtained with 100,000 observations are exactly as predicted theoretically, based on the normality assumption. However, for $N > 1$, the normality assumption no longer holds. In addition, the multi-period distributions are unknown and, therefore, the simulations are necessary to figure out the size and content of the three multi-period efficient sets. The main results from Table 3.2 are as follows:

(a) The FSD and SSD efficient sets decrease, in the weak sense, as the horizon increases, whereas the M–V multi-period efficient set, as predicted by Eq. (3.6), increases with the horizon.

(b) Shifting from $N = 1$ to $N = 30$, the FSD efficient set decreases from 7 assets to 4, the SSD efficient set decreases from 4 assets to 2 and, in contrast, the M–V efficient set increases from 4 assets to 9.

(c) As mentioned above, conforming with theory, asset 10 with the largest mean return is always included in all three efficient sets regardless of the assumed investment horizon.

We now turn to measure the economic loss induced by choosing a prospect from the M–V efficient set, a prospect which is SSD inefficient. First, suppose that for $N = 1$, indeed, the distributions are normal, and investors are risk averters. Then for $N = 1$, one can safely employ the M–V rule for investment selection as it coincides with the SSD rule, which is an optimal investment rule for all risk averters. Therefore, for $N = 1$, no economic loss is possible when choosing from the M–V efficient set, which is identical to the SSD efficient set. In this case, each risk averter chooses one prospect from the SSD = M–V efficient set depending on their risk-averse preference. However, as the horizon increases, the normality no longer holds, and employing the M–V rule rather than the SSD rule may incur an economic loss. Let's demonstrate the loss induced by employing the M–V rule for investors with an $N = 10$ years horizon.

As can be seen from Table 3.2, for $N = 10$ years, all risk averters should select the optimal choice from two assets only (assets 9 and 10), while those investors who choose by the M–V rule may mistakenly select other assets, namely assets 3, 4, or 7, which are M–V efficient but SSD inefficient (see Table 3.2). We demonstrate the economic loss involved in making the wrong choice by employing the following procedure: Suppose that the risk averse investor is myopic, with a preference given by the formula $U(x) = x^{1-\alpha}/(1-\alpha)$. Furthermore, suppose that for $N = 10$, the risk averse investor chooses prospect 3 from the M–V efficient set (the same procedure applies to assets 4 and 7). We calculate the expected utility, as well as the certainty equivalent (CE) corresponding to asset 3, as follows:

$$EU(x) = (1/100,000) \sum_{i=1}^{100,000} x_i^{1-\alpha}/(1-\alpha)$$

where x_i is the return corresponding to the 100,000 times N observations (depending on the assumed horizon N) drawn at random from the normal distribution corresponding to asset 3, and each observation measures the 10-year compounded return. In the second stage, find the CE as follows:

$$EU(x) = \left(\frac{1}{100,000}\right) \sum_{i=1}^{100,000} \frac{x_i^{1-\alpha}}{1-\alpha} = \frac{(CE)^{1-\alpha}}{1-\alpha}.$$

Then we conduct the same calculation for an asset taken from the SSD efficient asset, say asset 10, and the difference in the two CE values — the one of asset 10 and the one of asset 3 — measures the monetary loss from employing the wrong M–V rule when normality does not exist. Tables 3.3(a) and (b) report the CE loss when choosing by the wrong M–V rule rather than the correct SSD rule for alternate assumed horizons $N = 1$ year and $N = 10$ years. To measure the loss, we first assume that $\alpha = 1$, a case where the above myopic utility function is reduced to the log-function.[25]

Table 3.3: (a) The economic loss induced by investing in SSD-inefficient assets with $U(x) = \log x$ for $N = 1$; (b) The economic loss induced by investing in SSD-inefficient assets with $U(x) = \log x$ for $N = 10$.

(a)

Asset	$E[U(x)]$	CE	$\frac{CE}{CE_{10}} - 1$	$\frac{CE}{CE_9} - 1$
3	0.0578	1.0595	−0.162	−0.0517
4	0.076	1.078	−0.146	−0.0343
7	0.056	1.0576	−0.163	−0.0534
9	0.1109	1.117	−0.116	0
10	0.2341	1.263	0	0.1311

(b)

Asset	$E[U(x)]$	CE	$\frac{CE}{CE_{10}} - 1$	$\frac{CE}{CE_9} - 1$
3	0.579	1.78	−0.826	−0.410
4	0.759	2.14	−0.792	−0.294
7	0.554	1.74	−0.831	−0.425
9	1.107	3.02	−0.706	0
10	2.329	10.27	0	2.397

---

[25]Note that the log-function is not defined for negative values. However, as the standard deviation is small relative to the return (1 + rate of return), in all simulations, we obtained positive values. Hence, this technical obstacle in our specific calculations is avoided.

As we can see, the loss in CE terms increases rapidly with the horizon, reaching astonishing values. For example, if one mistakenly invests in asset 3 rather in asset 9, the CE loss is about 5% for $N = 1$ year, and if one invests mistakenly in asset 3 rather than in asset 10 (which is also SSD efficient and may be optimal for some risk averters, and for the log utility function, it is indeed the optimal choice), the loss is about 16%. The CE loss for $N = 10$ jumps to about 41% in the case where asset 9 is selected for $N = 10$ and about 83% where asset 10 is the optimal selection. Thus, if the CE of investing in asset 10 for $N = 10$ years is, say, \$100, by investing in asset 3, the CE is only \$17 — quite a dramatic loss induced by adhering to the M–V rule in selecting the investment. We would like to emphasize, at this point, that asset 3 is an M–V efficient asset; therefore, those investors who adhere to this rule when normality is violated incur this dramatic economic loss.

One may wonder whether these results are specific to the log-utility preference, which reveals extreme negative values when the return becomes close to zero. Table 3.4 repeats the same analysis for $N = 10$, but this time we assume that the preference is the myopic function with $\alpha = 0.5$, rather than $\alpha = 1$. The results are very similar: when investing in asset 3, rather than asset 10, the loss in terms of the CE is about 85% for a 10-year investor. In the comparison of assets 3 and 9, the loss is about 42%. Finally, note that all figures reported in these tables are negative with the exception of the bottom figure reported on the right-hand side of each table. This figure reports the loss of investing in asset 10 rather than in asset 9,

Table 3.4: The economic loss induced by investing in SSD inefficient assets for $U(x) = \sqrt{x}$ for $N = 10$.

Asset	$E[U(x)] = E[\sqrt{x}]$	CE	$\frac{CE}{CE_{10}} - 1$	$\frac{CE}{CE_9} - 1$
3	1.337	1.788	−0.851	−0.416
4	1.465	2.146	−0.821	−0.299
7	1.329	1.765	−0.853	−0.424
9	1.750	3.063	−0.744	0
10	3.461	11.981	0	2.912

and as both are included in the SSD efficient set, and as asset 10 has a larger expected utility with the two preferences we employ, a gain rather than a loss is obtained by investing in asset 10 rather than in asset 9. Obviously, it is possible to obtain an economic loss with other risk-averse utility functions, as both assets are included in the SSD efficient set.

This large economic loss induced by investing in asset 3, which is M–V (but not SSD) efficient, rather than in asset 10 which is SSD efficient, at first glance, is quite surprising. However, drawing the cumulative distributions of assets 3 and 10 corresponding to an $N = 10$ years horizon sheds light on this large economic loss result. As we can see from Figure 3.9(a), for $N = 1$, the two cumulative distributions (of assets 3 and 10) intersect, which implies that there is no FSD. There is also no SSD as the CDF of asset 3 with the lower mean intersects the distribution of asset 10 with the higher mean from below (see Eq. (3.9) which provides the SSD dominance condition). The intersection of the two CDFs occurs in the vicinity of the point where the return value is equal to 1, namely at about a zero rate of return. However, for $N = 10$, the distribution of asset 10 is located to the right of the distribution of asset 3, almost in the whole range of return, which explains the large economic loss induced by investing in asset 3 for a relatively long horizon. Yet, even in this case, we do not have SSD of asset 10 over asset 3, as in the left tail, the two distributions intersect (see the close-up part of the left tails of the distributions given in Figure 3.9(c) and Eq. (3.9) that states the SSD dominance condition). The intersection point takes place at a return of about 1.5, namely at about a 50% rate of return. At first glance, having an intersection point at about 1 in the case of $N = 1$ and at about 1.5 for $N = 10$ may be surprising in light of the comparison of Figures 3.9(a) and (b). However, to put things in perspective, recall that for $N = 1$, the mean return of asset 10 is 1.3, while for $N = 10$, the mean return of this asset is $1.3^{10} = 13.78$. Thus, the intersection in the case of $N = 10$ is located much further in the left tail of the distributions relative to the location in the case of $N = 1$.

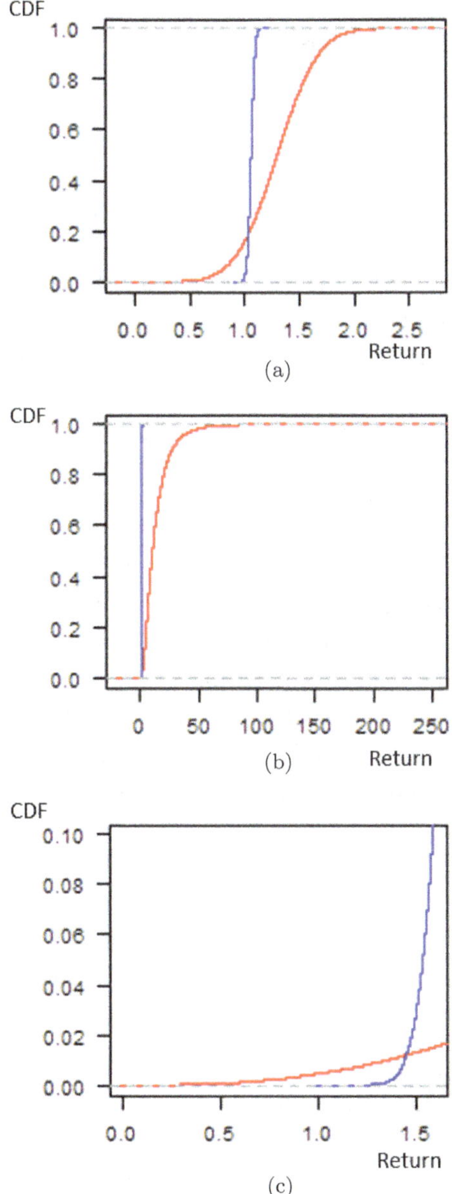

Figure 3.9: (a) The CDF of the return on assets 3 and 10 for $N = 1$; (b) The CDF of the return on assets 3 and 10 for $N = 10$; (c) The left tail of the CDF of the return on assets 3 and 10 for $N = 10$.

3.10. The Arrow–Pratt Risk Premium and the Investment Horizon

Although this chapter is focused mostly on the changes in the various efficient sets with the horizon, we devote this section to changes in the risk premium as a function of the assumed investment horizon. Recall, however, that if the risk premium changes with the horizon, it implies changes in the desirability of the risky asset under consideration with the horizon, which is related to changes in the optimal choices with the horizon (here, between the risky and the risk-free asset, rather than between two risky assets) as a function of the horizon.

Arrow[26] and Pratt[27] define the risk premium π as follows:

$$EU(W + x) = U(W + E(x) - \pi) = U(CE)$$

where CE denotes the certainty equivalent, W is the initial wealth, and x is the return $(1 + \text{rate of return})$ on a risky asset, which is a random variable. Obviously, the required risk premium varies from one investor to another as a function of their preference, U, and as a function of the initial wealth, W. In the following, we calculate the risk premium with myopic utility functions, assuming that $W = 0$, but the same analysis is similar for any other U and any other assumed wealth W.

We calculate the required risk premium on the S&P 500 stock index as a function of the assumed investment horizon. For example, for the log-utility function (which is also a myopic function) for $N = 1$, we calculate the empirical parallel of the above Arrow–Pratt risk premium by

$$\sum_{i=1}^{100,000} log\,(x_i)/100,000 = log\,(\bar{x} - \pi)$$

---

[26] Arrow, K. J. (1971). *Essays in the Theory of Risk Bearing*, Markham Publishing Company, Chicago.

[27] Pratt, J. W. (1964). Risk aversion in the small and in the large. *Econometrica* 32(1), 122–136

where 100,000 is the number of observations drawn from the distribution of the annual rates of return on the S&P 500 stock index for the years 1928–2019,[28] x_i is the ith observation, and $\bar{x}$ is the mean return of all these 100,000 observations. The value π which solves this equation is the Arrow–Pratt risk premium required by this investor who invests in stocks for $N = 1$ year. By the same methodology, we calculate the required risk premium, π_N, for an investor with an N-years horizon. The only difference is that if an investor invests for N years, in the risk-premium equation, we have, instead of x_i, the N-years return $\prod_{i=1}^{N} x_i$, and instead of $\bar{x}$, we have the N-period mean return given by the average of $\prod_{i=1}^{N} x_i$. Thus, the value π in this case is replaced by π_N, the risk premium required by the investors who invest for N years. For example, if $N = 10$, we draw 10 observations (with replacement) from the distribution of return on stocks, multiply them to obtain the 10-year return, $\prod_{i=1}^{10} x_i$, and repeat this procedure 100,000 times. In this case, the mean return is the average of $\prod_{i=1}^{10} x_i$ across all 100,000 times that we repeat this procedure. Thus, in general, for any N, we have the following equation:

$$\sum_{j=1}^{100,000} \log \left(\prod_{i=1}^{N} x_{ji} \right) / 100,000 = \log(\bar{x}_N - \pi_N)$$

where x_{ji} is the return in period i of observation j (which consists of N periods), $\bar{x}_N$ is the mean of $\prod_{i=1}^{N} x_i$ across all 100,000 observations, and π_N is the N-years required risk premium by the N-period investor with the log utility function.

We analyze the change in the risk premium as a function of the investment horizon. Table 3.5 reports the results for various risk-aversion parameters as a function of the investment horizon.

Note that, as expected, for each horizon N, the risk premium π increases as the risk aversion parameter α increases. Thus, the more risk averse the investor, the readier they are to pay to get rid of the risk. The second observed phenomenon from this table is that for each α, the risk premium increases with the horizon. For example,

---

[28] *Source*: http://people.stern.nyu.edu/adamodar/pc/datasets/histretSP.xls.

Table 3.5: Risk premiums for CRRA utility functions and different horizons. (Returns are sampled from the S&P500 stock index historical data.)

N	$\overline{\mu}$	$\alpha = 0.5$: $E[\frac{X^{0.5}}{0.5}]$	$\alpha = 1$: $E[log(x)]$	$\alpha = 1.5$: $E[\frac{x^{-0.5}}{-0.5}]$	$\alpha = 2$: $E[\frac{x^{-1}}{-1}]$	π_1	π_2	π_3	π_4	$\frac{\pi_1}{\mu}$	$\frac{\pi_2}{\mu}$	$\frac{\pi_3}{\mu}$	$\frac{\pi_4}{\mu}$
1	1.1152	2.1035	0.0921	-1.9188	-0.9296	0.0091	0.0187	0.0288	0.0396	0.0082	0.0168	0.0259	0.0355
2	1.2458	2.2142	0.1862	-1.8391	-0.8623	0.0201	0.0412	0.0632	0.0862	0.0162	0.0330	0.0507	0.0692
3	1.3901	2.3295	0.2791	-1.7636	-0.8007	0.0335	0.0681	0.1040	0.1412	0.0241	0.0490	0.0748	0.1016
4	1.5499	2.4497	0.3711	-1.6922	-0.7445	0.0496	0.1006	0.1529	0.2067	0.0320	0.0649	0.0987	0.1334
5	1.7268	2.5751	0.4621	-1.6246	-0.6932	0.0690	0.1394	0.2112	0.2841	0.0400	0.0807	0.1223	0.1645
10	2.9874	3.3182	0.9256	-1.3187	-0.4799	0.2348	0.4641	0.6873	0.9036	0.0786	0.1553	0.2301	0.3025
20	8.9413	5.5073	1.8515	-0.8691	-0.2296	1.3587	2.5717	3.6454	4.5856	0.1520	0.2876	0.4077	0.5129
30	26.7721	9.1618	2.7843	-0.5706	-0.1089	5.7876	10.5829	14.4859	17.5931	0.2162	0.3953	0.5411	0.6571

for $\alpha = 0.5$, it is 0.0091 for $N = 1$, 0.0690 for $N = 5$, and it jumps to 5.7876 for $N = 30$.

Economically, the increase in the risk premium with the horizon is not a necessary result; therefore, its intensity is, at first glance, quite surprising. To see this claim, recall that the basic equation for solving the risk premium is

$$EU(x) = U(CE) = U(E(x) - \pi).$$

As the horizon increases, generally, $EU(x)$ increases, the variability of x increases, and $E(x)$ increases; hence, the horizon effect on the risk premium is ambiguous. It can decrease or increase with the horizon without violating the above risk premium equation. The evidence reported in Table 3.5 reveals a large increase in the risk premium with the horizon, at least for the myopic preference.

Note that for $N = 1$, the average return on the S&P 500 stock index is 1.1152, implying an annual rate of return for the covered period of 11.52%. For $\alpha = 1$ and $N = 1$, the risk premium is 0.9% (see Table 3.5). For $N = 30$, this risk premium jumps to about 579%. However, as the mean return also increases dramatically with the horizon, we also calculate the relative risk premium — the risk premium divided by the corresponding mean return. The four columns on the right of Table 3.5 show that the relative risk premium also increases with the horizon. For example, for $\alpha = 1$, the relative risk premium increases from 0.8% for $N = 1$ to 21.6% for $N = 30$.

We demonstrate here the changes in the risk premium for a specific utility function. While the results may change with other utility functions, with this specific preference, the increase in the relative risk premium with the horizon indicates that stocks become less desirable as the horizon increases. Obviously more research should be done in this area, as along with other preferences, the results may reverse.

3.11. Diversification: Markowitz's Efficient Frontier in the Multi-Period Case

So far, we assumed that the investor faces two prospects and wishes to invest in one of them. In this section, we assume many available assets and that diversification is allowed. We analyze the one-period M–V efficient frontier that is identical to the one-period SSD efficient frontier when the one-period distribution is assumed to be normal. Then we analyze the optimal choices when one shifts from the one-period case to the multi-period case, knowing that the multi-period distributions are no longer normal. In this case, the M–V and SSD models depart. Figure 3.10 illustrates the well-known M–V frontier and the M–V efficient and inefficient sets. Curve *abc* is the M–V frontier where segment *ab* is M–V inefficient and only segment *bc* is the efficient curve. Thus, with normal distributions, all risk-averse investors (by M–V and SSD alike) would choose the optimal portfolios from segment *bc*, where the optimal portfolio of each individual investor is selected from this segment depending on their risk tolerance, that is, depending on their personal preference. As for normal distribution, the M–V rule and the SSD rule coincide; thus, we can safely conclude that all the SSD one-period efficient portfolios are also located on segment *bc*.

Shifting to the multi-period case, the M–V rule and the SSD rule yield different results induced by the fact that normality no longer holds. Let us first start with the multi-period M–V case. Note that

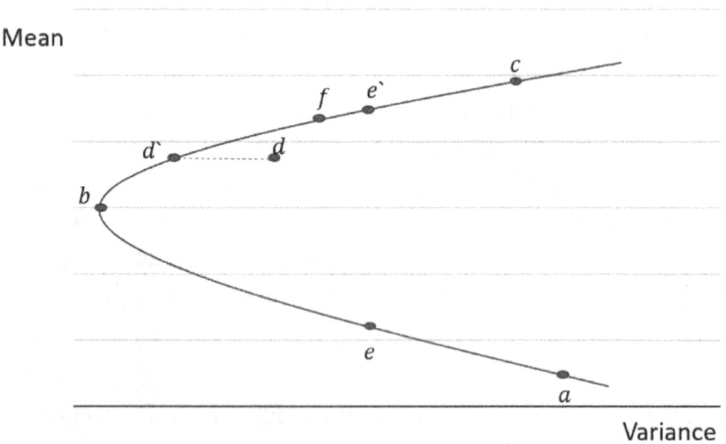

Figure 3.10: The M–V and SSD one-period and multi-period efficient portfolios with one-period normal distributions.

any interior portfolio in the one-period M–V inefficient set also is included in the multi-period M–V inefficient set. For example, for any one-period interior portfolio like portfolio d, there is a portfolio d' which dominates it by the multi-period M–V rule. To see this claim, note that the multi-period means of d and d' are identical (just as the one-period means are identical). As the means (the one-period, as well as the multi-period) are identical, and for the one-period variances, we have $\sigma^2(d) > \sigma^2(d')$, employing Eq. (3.6) we conclude that the multi-period variance of d' is smaller than the multi-period variance of portfolio d; therefore, portfolio d' dominates portfolio d by the multi-period M–V rule. Using the same logic, we can safely conclude that all interior portfolios are M–V inefficient both in the one-period and multi-period cases.

We turn now to segment ab, which is M–V inefficient with a one-period horizon. Actually, in the one-period case, portfolio b dominates all portfolios located on segment ab as it has a larger mean and a smaller variance of all these portfolios. This M–V dominance is not intact in the multi-period case. To see this, let us compare portfolios e and b given in Figure 3.9. It is obvious that the mean of portfolio b is also larger than the mean of portfolio e in the multi-period case. However, as the multi-period variance is an increasing function of the mean, we may find that the multi-period variance of portfolio b is larger than the multi-period variance of portfolio e; hence, both may be M–V multi-period efficient.

One is tempted to believe that although portfolio b does not dominate portfolio e by the M–V multi-period rule, portfolio e' may dominate portfolio e. However, this assertion also does not hold, as these two portfolios have the same one-period variance, and portfolio e' has a larger mean, and by Eq. (3.6), portfolio e' has a larger multi-period variance than portfolio e. Hence, portfolio e' does not dominate portfolio e according to the multi-period M–V rule.

Thus, in principle, all portfolios located on the one-period bc segment are multi-period M–V efficient, and some or all portfolios (depending on the specific parameters) located on segment ab may also be M–V efficient in the multi-period case. In the extreme case, all of the frontier *abc*, unlike in the one-period case, may be M–V efficient in the multi-period case.

We turn now to the multi-period SSD. As for normal distribution, the SSD and M–V rules coincide, the one-period SSD efficient set is, like the one-period M–V efficient set, the segment *bc*. However, as by Proposition 5, SSD in one-period implies SSD in the multi-period case, we can safely conclude that all portfolios not located on segment *bc* are relegated to the SSD inefficient set both in the one-period as well as in the multi-period case. However, as in the example illustrated before, we may have no SSD in the one-period case, but may have SSD in the multi-period case. Therefore, we may have "holes" in segment *bc* where the holes represent multi-period SSD inefficient portfolios. For example, portfolio *f* may be one-period SSD efficient, but multi-period SSD inefficient. The determination of these potential holes depends on the data under consideration, and for some sets of data, we may not observe them.

In conclusion, there is very little in common between the multi-period M–V and SSD efficient sets, despite the fact that both rules are identical in the one-period case, so long as normality is assumed. The M–V multi-period efficient set may include all portfolios located on segment *abc*, while the SSD multi-period efficient set is a subset of segment *bc*.

The economic consequence of the above analysis is clear: If one employs the M–V rule regardless of the assumed horizon, an economic loss may emerge. For example, it is well-known that for relatively short horizons, say up to one year, the distributions are close to normal; hence, one can employ the M–V rule, at least as an approximation to make the optimal choice. However, for longer horizons, the distributions deviate from normality and a positive skewness is created, and for very long horizons, the distributions become close to log-normal distributions (see the discussion on the distributions of rates of returns in Chapter 2). Thus, in the multi-period case, an investor who employs the M–V rule may choose portfolio *e* which may be M–V efficient. However, by the SSD rule portfolio *e* is multi-period inefficient, as we can safely conclude that for all risk averters, there is at least one portfolio, say portfolio *e'*, located on segment bc, with a higher expected utility than $EU(e)$. Thus, every risk averter loses by investing in a portfolio like portfolio e rather than choosing a portfolio from segment bc. Note, however, that this loss is not necessary, as it is possible for the risk averter to choose a portfolio, say d', which is included in both the M–V and SSD multi-period efficient sets.

Finally, note that in Tables 3.3(a), 3.3(b) and 3.4, we measure the economic loss by deviation from normality for some specific prospects when diversification is not specifically emphasized. In contrast, in Figure 3.10, we refer to all diversified and non-diversified portfolios, efficient and inefficient alike.

3.12. The Multi-Period Variance Where Returns May be Dependent Over Time: The Empirical Evidence

Assuming independence over time, the multi-period variance increases with the horizon quite rapidly. If returns are not independent over time, the multi-period variance may increase faster or slower than what is obtained under the independence assumption, or may not even change at all with the horizon. Recall that the main reason for the increase in the M–V efficient set with the horizon is the increase in the variance with the horizon, as given in Eq. (3.6). If there is dependency and the variance calculated by Eq. (3.6) deviates substantially from the empirical multi-period variance, the M–V of the multi-period efficient set may even decrease with the horizon (which casts doubt on the analyses and results given in this chapter regarding the M–V analysis). To examine the effect of the possible empirical dependency over time on the multi-period variance, we employ data corresponding to the annual rates of returns on the S&P 500 stock index and on 10-year Treasury bonds for the period 1928–2019.[29] We conduct the following various calculations of the multi-period variance. We first calculate the mean and variance based

---

[29]See footnote 28.

on annual data and then employ Eq. (3.6) to calculate the multi-period variance for various horizons, N. Thus, by this calculation, we obtain the multi-period variance derived under the independence assumption. We next conduct similar calculations by simulations. For $N = 1$, we draw 100,000 annual observations of rates of returns with replacement and calculate the variance corresponding to $N = 1$. For $N = 2$, we draw two observations at random (with replacement) and calculate first the two-period return with 100,000 pairs and then the variance across these 100,000 pairs. By the same procedure, we calculate the multi-period variance corresponding to various assumed investment horizons.

So far, we have not incorporated possible dependence over time. To examine the effect of the possibility of such dependence, for $N = 2$, we took two consecutive years and calculated the bi-annual rates of returns. In other words, the return across 1928 and 1929 is the first observation, the return corresponding to years 1930 and 1931 is the second observation, etc. Then we calculate the variance across all of these bi-annual returns. This is different from the simulation procedure as we also consider possible autocorrelations between consecutive two-year periods. For $N = 3$, the first observation is the return corresponding to the period 1928–1930, the second observation is the return for the period 1931–1934, and so forth. Obviously, by this procedure, the longer the investment horizon, the smaller the number of observations. In the last calculation procedure, we allow overlapping. For example, for $N = 2$, the first observation corresponds to years 1928–1929, the second observation corresponds to years 1929–1930, and so forth. The overlapping procedure is inferior to the non-overlapping calculation, but it allows us to have more observations. Moreover, we create artificial autocorrelation even if it does not exist in practice because the same year, say 1929, appears in the first two observations in the case of $N = 2$.

Tables 3.6 and 3.7 provide the multi-period variance calculated by the four methods described above. Table 3.6 corresponds to the S&P 500 stock index, and Table 3.7 corresponds to the 10-year Treasury bonds. In both tables, we confine the calculation only to $N = 1, 2, 3$, and 4, as for longer horizons, we get too few observations, which

Table 3.6: The multi-period variance calculated by various methods for the S&P 500 stock index.

Horizon, years	As Calculated by Eq.(3.6)	As Calculated by Simulation	Variance (No Overlap)	Degrees of Freedom (No Overlap)	Statistic-χ^2 (No Overlap)	Variance (with Overlap)	Degrees of Freedom (with Overlap)	Statistic-χ^2 (with Overlap)
1	0.038	0.038	0.038	91	91.000	0.038	91	91.000
2	0.097	0.095	0.079	45	36.717	0.088	90	81.932
3	0.184	0.179	0.156	29	24.645	0.144	90	70.273
4	0.310	0.296	0.232	22	16.497	0.241	90	70.004

Table 3.7: The multi-period variance calculated by various methods for the 10-year US Treasury bond.

Horizon, years	As Calculated by Eq.(3.6)	As Calculated by Simulation	Variance (No Overlap)	Degrees of Freedom (No Overlap)	Statistic-χ^2 (No Overlap)	Variance (with Overlap)	Degrees of Freedom (with Overlap)	Statistic-χ^2 (with Overlap)
1	0.006	0.006	0.006	91	90.996	0.006	91	90.966
2	0.013	0.013	0.011	45	37.235	0.013	90	87.581
3	0.022	0.021	0.024	29	31.665	0.021	90	88.316
4	0.032	0.031	0.032	22	21.938	0.036	90	100.629

makes the analysis meaningless. Thus, we estimate the effect of the autocorrelation on the multi-period variance up to $N = 4$ years. As we can see from both tables, the variances calculated by Eq. (3.6) and by the simulations are very similar. This is not surprising as the simulations implicitly assume independency over time, and the small differences are due to the random deviation of the finite size of the sample simulation from the precise formula, given by Eq (3.6). When we calculate the variance with the actual data, we get the following results: in both cases, with and without overlapping, the variance strictly increases with the horizon. For example, for the S&P returns, the multi-period variance increases in the non-overlapping case from 0.038 for $N = 1$ to 0.232 for $N = 4$, while the increase by the multi-period variance calculated by Eq. (3.6) increases from 0.038 to 0.296. With overlapping, we get a little larger deviation between the calculated variance by Eq. (3.6) and the empirical variance, which is not surprising in light of the autocorrelation induced by the overlapping procedure. The result reported in Table 3.7, corresponding to the 10-year Treasury bonds, reveals even more impressive results showing very minor effects of the possible dependency over time, as the multi-period variance calculated by the various methods are very similar.

The two tables also report the Chi-square statistic, where the null hypothesis is that the variances calculated with possible dependency are not significantly different from the variance calculated by Eq. (3.6), which assumes perfect independence over time. We find that we cannot reject the null hypothesis in any of the cases. Even in the worst case, from a statistical point of view where we have only 22 degrees of freedom (see the non-overlapping observation for the case $N = 4$), we obtain the Chi-square statistics of 16.497 for stocks, and the corresponding number of 21.938 for bonds, where the two-sided test critical values for 5% significance levels are 10.98 and 36.78, respectively. Thus, the results are highly insignificant. For the other cases, the null hypothesis cannot be rejected even at a very high and generally unaccepted significant level in research, e.g., for stocks for $N = 2$, the sample statistics with the non-overlapping observation is 36.717, where the lower and upper critical level for a 5% significance level with $N = 2$ are about 29 and 66, respectively.

The main conclusion from the results appearing in Tables 3.6 and 3.7 is that, indeed, there is no perfect independence over time, and the multi-period variance calculated with a perfect independence assumption may somewhat differ from the empirical multi-period variance calculated with and without overlapping observations. However, a few important results emerge from the empirical analysis, even in the case that the independence assumption is relaxed:

(a) The multi-period variance increases with the horizon in all cases.
(b) The variance of the S&P index increases percentage-wise faster with the horizon than the variance of the bonds. This result conforms with the mathematical result asserting that the higher the mean, the higher the increase in the multi-period variance.
(c) The empirical variance with dependence is not significantly different from the variance calculated under the independence assumption.

Finally, recall that to support the multi-period results regarding the (weak) expansion of the M–V efficient set as a function of the horizon presented in this chapter, it is sufficient to show that the multi-period variance increases as a function of the mean. Hence, investment choices selected by the M–V rule may be misleading and, therefore, may incur economic loss, particularly for long-horizon investors.

Having said that, we are not ruling out that autocorrelation exists, particularly for short horizons, say, when daily or weekly returns are considered. Moreover, we may have some weak annual serial correlation, but this does not affect the conclusions and results obtained under the independence assumption — particularly regarding the changes and size of the M–V efficient sets as a function of the investment horizon.

3.13. Discussion

So far, we assumed in most of the analyses in this chapter that the one-period return distribution is normal, and we analyzed the effect of the horizon on the M–V and SSD efficient sets and the induced economic loss by employing the M–V rule corresponding to horizons longer than one year. The assumption that the short horizon is normal, or at least approximately normal (or elliptic), has some empirical support (see Chapter 2). This implies that using the M–V rule, rather than the SSD rule, does not incur a substantial economic loss for relatively short-horizon investors. However, for some assets, even the one-period return is not normal (e.g., the return on options) — a case where SSD remains the optimal investment rule for all risk averters, but the M–V rule does not. The reason for failure of the M–V rule in such cases is that, generally, higher distribution moments also affect expected utility, which the SSD rule considers and the M–V rule ignores.

We have the following relationships:

$$F \text{ dominates } G \text{ by SSD} \Rightarrow E_F U(x) \geq E_G U(x)$$

for all risk-averse utility functions.

However, unless the distributions of returns are normal (or elliptic), we have

$$F \text{ dominates } G \text{ by M–V} \nRightarrow E_F U(x) \geq E_G U(x)$$

for all risk-averse utility functions.

The example where the skewness of the distribution plays an important role in determining expected utility is given by Hanoch and Levy (see footnote 18), and is reproduced here:

G: 1 with a probability of 0.80 and 100 with a probability of 0.20

F: 10 with a probability of 0.99 and 1,000 with a probability of 0.01

Using these figures, we find that G dominates F by the M–V rule because

$$E_G(x) = 20.8 > E_F(x) = 19.9$$

and

$$\sigma_G^2 = 1{,}468 < \sigma_F^2 = 9{,}703.$$

Yet, for the commonly employed *log* function $(log_{10}(x))$, we have

$$E_F U(x) = 1.02 > E_G U(x) = 0.4.$$

Thus, by the M–V rule, G has a higher mean and a lower variance than F, yet, it has a lower expected utility than F for the log-utility function. Note that F has a very large positive skewness which the expected utility and the SSD rules consider, but the M–V rule ignores. To see this claim, one can expand the expected utility to Taylor's series as follows:

$$EU(W + x) = U(W + Ex) + U''(W + Ex)\left[\frac{\sigma^2}{2!}\right]$$

$$+ U'''(W + Ex)\left[\frac{\mu_3}{3!}\right] + \cdots$$

where μ_3 stands for the third central moment measuring the skewness of the distribution, which is equal to zero for normal distributions. As decreasing absolute risk aversion implies that $U''' > 0$, we obtain that the larger the skewness, all else being held constant, the larger the risk-averse investor's expected utility. In the above example, F has a lower mean and a larger variance than G; hence, ignoring the skewness, as the M–V does, G would be preferred to F by the M–V rule. However, expected utility considers all distribution moments, and we obtain that F, which has a very large skewness, is preferred to G.

If the M–V rule may be misleading and may incur economic loss as SSD inefficient investments may be selected, why is it so popular and widely employed by researchers, as well as by practitioners? The answer to these questions is that the M–V rule is mathematically more developed than the SSD rules, allowing the investor to find the M–V optimal bundle of risky assets, which cannot be done using the SSD rules. Specifically, the advantage of the M–V rule over the SSD rules is that one can find the optimal M–V diversification, define the risk of each individual asset in a portfolio context, and the equilibrium CAPM can be derived. With SSD, we cannot achieve all these results and cannot even define the SSD risk of an individual asset in the context of the portfolio held. However, this technical advantage of the M–V rule may lead to a choice of a non-optimal investment that may incur a monetary loss.

To sum up, the M–V rule is an optimal rule for risk averters if the distributions of returns are normal or elliptic.[30] It also provides an excellent approximation of expected utility where the range of return is not too wide, say, in the range of –0.30 to +0.60, as shown by Levy and Markowitz.[31] These two justifications for the employment of the M–V rule are very important for short-horizon investors and should be carefully employed in certain cases when the above conditions are intact.

For long-horizon investors, we have a completely different story. Moreover, even if the short-horizon distribution is approximately or precisely normal, for longer horizons, a positive skewness is built up and cannot be ignored. Although this topic is covered in detail in Chapter 2, it is worthwhile to repeat it briefly here as it is strongly related to the subjects dealt with in this chapter.

To see this, assume that x_1, which stands for the one-period return (say, one year) is indeed normal (or elliptic), or at least close enough to the normal distribution to justify precisely or approximately employing the M–V rule. Similarly, the second period return x_2 is also normal. Thus, each one-period investor can safely employ the M–V rule for portfolio selection, and even enjoys the M–V recommendation for selecting the optimal diversification. However, for the two-period investor, employing the M–V rule may incur a loss because even if x_1 and x_2 are normally distributed, the two-period return $x = x_1 x_2$ is not normally distributed. Therefore, for the two-period investor, choosing the optimal portfolio by the M–V rule may induce an economic loss, and generally the longer the horizon, the larger the deviation from normality, and the larger the loss. Actually,

---

[30]See Chamberlain, G. (1983). A characterization of the distributions which imply Mean–Variance utility functions. *Journal of Economic Theory* 29(1), 185–201.

[31]Levy, H. and H. M. Markowitz (1979). Approximating expected utility by a function of the mean and variance. *American Economic Review* 69(3), 308–317.

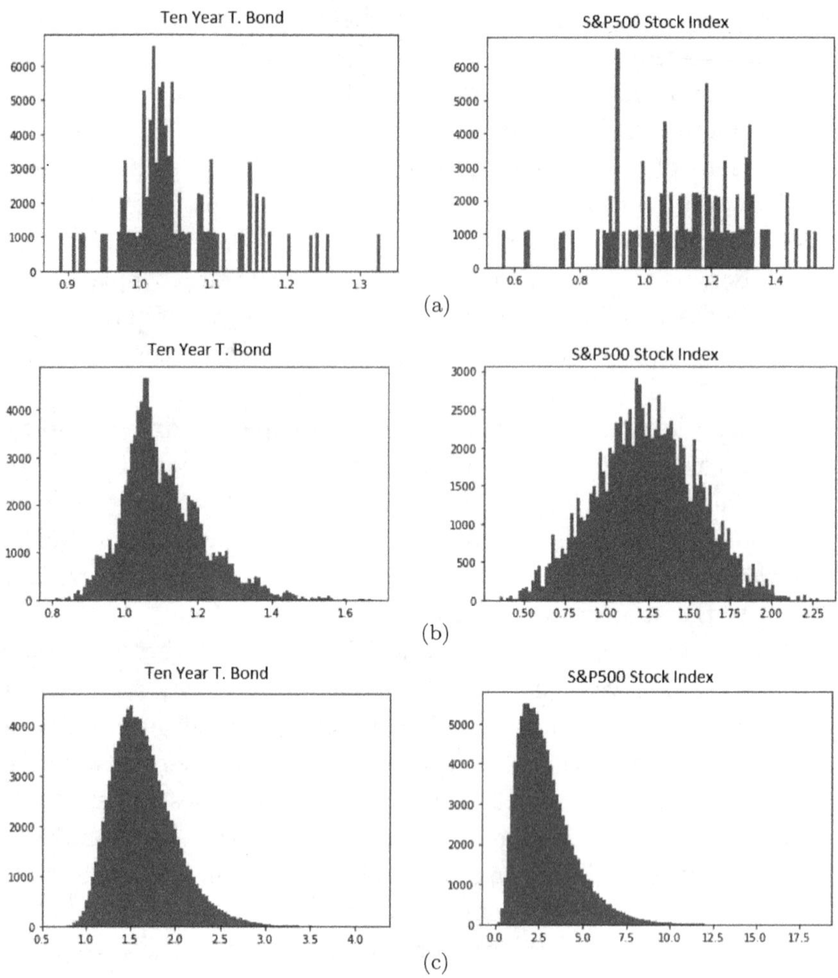

Figure 3.11: (a) Density function of rate of return for horizon $N = 1$; (b) Density function of rate of return for horizon $N = 2$; (c) Density function of rate of return for horizon $N = 10$.

a positive skewness is mathematically built up for relatively long investment horizons. Figure 3.11 provides the density function of the return on the S&P 500 stock index and for 10-year Treasury bonds for one year (x_1), two-year $(x = x_1 x_2)$, and 10-year horizons $(x = x_1 x_2 \ldots \ldots x_{10})$. As we can see from both figures, even for $N = 1$, there is some positive skewness, but for $N = 10$, a strong positive skewness emerges, particularly for the stock index. Thus, even if one can use the M–V rule for short horizons (probably even less than a year), for relatively long horizons, employing the M–V rule is inappropriate and may lead to economic loss. Hence, the SSD rule should be employed in such cases. Note that the preference for skewness is supported theoretically and empirically, as Arrow[32] shows decreasing absolute risk aversion implies a preference for skewness, a fact that is ignored by the M–V rule.

Thus, the M–V and SSD have pros and cons. For relatively short horizons, the M–V rule can be employed, and the investor may benefit from a clear-cut path for finding the optimal diversification. For a relatively long horizon, by employing the M–V rule, an investor may end up investing in an inefficient asset; therefore, a very large economic loss may occur. Thus, for relatively long horizons, only the SSD rule should be employed by all risk averters. This rule does not suggest an optimal diversification, but if one considers investing in a stock index, bond index, or alternative portfolios, say 0.5 in a stock index and .5 in a bond index, the SSD rule can tell us which of these portfolios are SSD efficient and which are inefficient. It also indicates the portfolios that are efficient for relatively short horizons and likely to become inefficient as the horizon increases.

3.14. Summary

Numerous theoretical and empirical studies in economics and finance assume that all investors have the same investment horizon, typically one month or one year. In practice, various investors have different investment horizons; hence, there is a gap between the theoretical models and the investment behavior in practice. Does the investment horizon matter? In this chapter, we discussed the effect of the investment horizon on prospect ranking under the condition of

---

[32] Arrow claims that decreasing absolute risk aversion (DARA) commonly prevails. This implies a preference for skewness, as $U''' > 0$ is a necessary condition for DARA; see Arrow, K. J. (1971). *Essays in the Theory of Risk-Bearing*, Markham Publishing Company, Chicago.

risk. Specifically, we analyzed the merits of the M–V and SSD rules for decision-making as a function of the assumed investment horizon.

The most popular investment decision rule for choosing among risky prospects is by far the M–V rule developed by Markowitz. This is also the optimal decision rule in an expected utility framework, so long as the distributions are elliptic, where the normal distribution belongs to the elliptic family. If normality is not intact, one should employ the SD rules, as these rules are consistent with the expected utility maximization even if normality does not prevail. Obviously, if normality prevails, the SSD and the M–V rules coincide.

For relatively short investment horizons, generally less than a year, the distribution is approximately normal, and one can employ the M–V rule for investment decisions. In such a case, the M–V rule has an advantage over the SSD rule, as there is an algorithm for finding the optimal M–V diversification.

We show in this chapter that even if the one-period return is normally distributed, the multi-period return distribution cannot be normal, and the distribution tends to be positively skewed; hence, employing the M–V rule may induce an economic loss. On the other hand, the SD rules are distribution-free; hence, they can be safely employed for all possible horizons. Specifically, the SSD rule considers the skewness, and the M–V rule ignores it.

We find that the SSD and the FSD efficient sets decrease with the horizon, while the M–V efficient set increases with it. As the M–V rule is not the optimal rule for various horizons, when employing it with a relatively long horizon, investors may incur an economic loss, as an M–V efficient prospect, which is SSD inefficient, may be selected. We find that for investors with a 10-year horizon, the economic loss (in terms of the certainty equivalent) induced by employing the M–V rule may be as high as 80%!

To sum up, each of these two rules, M–V and SSD, has some advantages and some disadvantages. It seems that for relatively short horizons, the technical advantages of the M–V rule outweigh its disadvantages, and the opposite holds for relatively long horizons. The critical horizon for which one method is better than the other depends on the distributions of the returns of the specific prospects under consideration.

Chapter 4

Performance Indices and the Investment Horizon

There are several employed performance indices, of which the most well-known are Jensen's alpha (JA), the Treynor ratio (TR), and the Sharpe ratio (SR). Probably the most popular performance index is the SR, published in 1966,[1] following Sharpe's seminal work deriving the capital asset pricing model (CAPM)[2] and defining beta (β) as the risk index of each individual asset held within the optimal diversified portfolio, known as the *market portfolio*. The popularity of the SR is probably due to its simplicity and generality, as it does not need to assume that the CAPM holds, as the TR and the JA performance indices do. The SR is published by financial services companies ranking mutual funds, exchange-traded funds (ETFs), hedge funds, iShares, etc. by their performance (considering the mean return and the risk of the fund under consideration) in the last year, in the last three years, and sometimes the SR is published even corresponding to longer periods, e.g., the last five years. As many investors invest in these traded funds, the SR presumably is employed as a tool for choosing among all the available managed funds, hence its popularity among investors.

---

[1] Sharpe, W. F. (1966). Mutual funds performance. *Journal of Business* 39(1), 119–138.

[2] Sharpe, W. F. (1964). Capital asset pricing: A theory of market equilibrium under conditions of risk. *The Journal of Finance* 19(3), 425–442.

175

In this chapter, we first analyze the possible changes in the *SR* with changes in the investment horizon, and then we analyze the horizon's effect on the *TR* and *JA*, where these two performance indices rely on the CAPM. The horizon's effect on *JA* has a direct implication on the reported small firm effect (SFE). We show that when annual rates of return, rather than monthly rates of return, are employed to calculate the *JA*, about half of the SFE vanishes. This issue is discussed in Section 4.6.

A word of caution: We saw in Chapter 2 that for short horizons, say less than one year, one can use the mean–variance (M–V) rule as the distributions are symmetric, and for some horizons they are elliptic (logistic) — a case where employing the M–V rule is optimal. However, as the horizon increases, the distributions tend to be log-normal, which are positively skewed; hence, there is no economic justification for employing the M–V rule for these relatively long horizons. Note that all three indices discussed in this chapter rely on the optimality of the M–V rule, which may be inconsistent with expected utility maximization. The only reason for doing so is because these indices are widely published, and investors presumably use them despite their shortcomings for long horizons. As there are no other reasonable simple performance indices to replace these three indices, we would like investors to at least recognize the possible changes in the fund ranking with the horizon. Adhering (with no economic justification for relatively long horizons, see Chapter 3) to the performance indices that rely on the M–V rule, we would like investors to be aware of changes in the performance ranking of assets with the investment horizon.

Let us first define these three performance indices and demonstrate their use by practitioners.

4.1. The Three Main Performance Indices: Definitions

Having Markowitz's M–V efficient frontier, Sharpe suggests to add the riskless asset (borrowing and lending at the riskless interest rate) to the available risky assets as a possible investment. By mixing the

M–V tangency portfolio with the riskless interest rate located on the vertical axis, every risk-averter can also maximize their expected utility, so long as the distributions of returns are normal (or more generally elliptical). Thus, one seeks to maximize the slope of the line given by

$$Sharpe\ Ratio \equiv SR = \frac{E(R) - r}{\sigma_R} \qquad (4.1)$$

where R is the random return of the selected portfolio of risky assets with mean $E(R)$ and standard deviation σ_R, and r stands for the riskless interest rate. In calculating the SR, the return, R, may be the return on a portfolio which includes all available risky assets, or alternatively the return on a subset of all available risky assets, and in the extreme, it may correspond to one individual asset.

As the TR and JA rely on the validity of the CAPM or at least on the concept that the beta (β) measures the risk involved, we first need to define these two concepts. Assuming that each investor maximizes the SR, and a full diversification is allowed (namely R, given in Eq. (4.1), refers to the return on a portfolio which includes all available risky assets), Sharpe derives the CAPM, where the equilibrium expected return of asset i is given by

$$E(R_i) = r + [E(R_m) - r]\beta_i. \qquad (4.2)$$

Thus, in equilibrium, we have for each asset i

$$\frac{E\left[(R_i) - r\right]}{\beta_i} = [E(R_m) - r] = \text{constant} \qquad (4.3)$$

where $E(R_m)$ is the expected return on the market portfolio, and β_i is the risk[3] of asset i, where it is assumed that all investors hold the optimal portfolio composed of all available risky assets, which is given

---

[3]The risk index, beta, is estimated by the following time series regression: $R_{it} = \alpha_i + \beta_i R_{mt} + e_t$, where R_{it} and R_{mt} are the rates of returns on the ith asset and the market portfolio, respectively, in month t. When the riskless interest rate varies across time, R_{it} and R_{mt} are defined as the excess returns, namely the return of the risky asset less the riskless interest rate in period t.

by the tangency point of the straight line raising from point r on the vertical axis with the M–V efficient frontier. Under the CAPM, all risky assets are held by investors, and they hold the same portfolio of risky assets called the *market portfolio*. The only difference among various investors is with regard to the proportion of the riskless asset (borrowing or lending) in the optimal portfolio of each investor.

In practice, however, as the expected return $E(R_m)$ and the true beta are unknown, one generally employs the empirical estimates of these two values and the sample parallel of Eq. (4.2) becomes

$$\bar{R}_i = r + (\bar{R}_m - r)\hat{\beta}_i + \alpha_i \tag{4.4}$$

where the sample estimate parameters ($\bar{R}_i, \bar{R}_m$, and $\hat{\beta}_i$) substitute for the unknown parameters given by Eq. (4.2). As, in practice, the riskless interest rate varies with time, it is common to run the regression for estimating the beta with an excess return; therefore, Eq. (4.4) is rewritten as follows[4]:

$$\bar{R}_{ie} = (\bar{R}_m)\hat{\beta}_{ie} + \alpha_i \tag{4.4'}$$

where $\bar{R}_{ie}$ is the average return on stock i less the average riskless interest rate and, similarly, $\bar{R}_{me}$ is the average return on the market portfolio less the average riskless interest rate, and the subscript e stands for "excess return."

Note first that even if one would know the parameters needed for the derivation of the CAPM, this equilibrium model empirically does not perfectly hold, and some deviations from the CAPM are possible, e.g., deviations due to the fact that some investors do not hold the market portfolio, or due to possible heterogeneous expectations. Secondly, the CAPM does not necessarily perfectly hold with empirical estimates of the various true unknown parameters. Therefore, we also generally have the term α_i for each asset i that can be negative, positive, or equal to zero. The larger the alpha, the

---

[4]In practice, the interest rate is not constant over time; therefore, it is common to run this regression with excess returns, namely $\bar{R}_{ie} = (\bar{R}_{me})\hat{\beta}_i + \alpha_i$ where $\bar{R}_{ie}$ and $\bar{R}_{me}$ are the average returns in *excess* to the average risk-free interest rate.

better the performance of the asset under consideration, as its mean rate of return is higher than what is predicted by the CAPM, namely by the asset's risk measured by the beta. This is called Jensen's alpha (JA).

Thus, Eq. (4.4) can be rewritten as

$$\frac{\bar{R}_i - r}{\hat{\beta}_i} = \left(\bar{R}_m - r\right) + \frac{\alpha_i}{\hat{\beta}_i} \tag{4.5}$$

Stocks and other risky assets are, therefore, commonly ranked either by α_i, which is also called JA, or by the TR given by $TR \equiv \frac{\bar{R}_i - r}{\hat{\beta}_i}$. Note that if a given stock outperforms its expected risk-adjusted return by TR, such outperformance is also recorded by JA and vice versa as

$$\frac{\bar{R}_i - r}{\hat{\beta}_i} > \left(\bar{R}_m - r\right) \Longleftrightarrow \frac{\alpha_i}{\hat{\beta}_i} > 0,$$

and as stocks rarely have a negative beta, a relatively good performance measured by the TR generally implies a relatively good performance measured by JA, namely $\alpha_i > 0$.

Thus, there are three main performance indices: the SR, TR, and JA. In this chapter, we analyze the effect of the investment horizon on each of these, as well as the relationship between them. However, at the outset, we would like to stress that we technically analyze the changes of these performance indices with the horizon and not with the consistency of the rules with the expected utility paradigm, which is widely discussed in Chapter 3.

We start with the SR, which is the most popular performance index. Then we discuss the effect of the investment horizon on the TR and JA. As the TR and JA depend on the beta, we first need to analyze the horizon's effect on the beta.

We devote a substantial portion of this chapter to the SR analysis. Before analyzing each of the three performance indices in detail, one question emerges: Why is the SR so popular, particularly among practitioners, relative to the other two performance measures? The reason for this, in our view, is that the TR and JA are the appropriate performance indices for individual assets (or portfolios) held within a well-diversified portfolio — the market portfolio — which contains all available risky assets in the market. Thus, by employing these two performance indices, one assumes explicitly or implicitly that the CAPM holds, albeit not perfectly. In other words, the assumption is that a very well-diversified portfolio is held, even if the CAPM does not perfectly hold. At the minimum, it is assumed that the CAPM's beta is the correct measure of risk. In contrast, the SR does not rely on the assumption that a perfect diversification, or even on the assumption that a very intensive diversification, takes place.

In practice, there are many mutual funds, ETFs, hedge funds, etc. traded in the market, suggesting that investors hold these diversified portfolios, although these assets are not perfectly diversified. Thus, generally, investors who invest in these funds do not hold all available risky assets in the market in contradiction to the CAPM assumption, which served as a springboard for the development of the TR and JA. Furthermore, some of these traded funds specialize in some industries (e.g., the oil industry, the aviation industry, etc.); hence, the funds' managements implicitly declare that they do not even attempt to achieve perfect diversification as suggested by the CAPM. In addition, some of these traded funds specialize in asset picking, and the SR measures the performance of the management of these funds exactly according to their declared mission.

Since the typical investor is not an expert in the stock market, they commonly diversify indirectly by investing in one of these traded funds. For those investors who wish to have some diversification by investing in mutual funds, ETFs, etc., the SR is the appropriate performance ranking index. As there are many mutual funds and ETFs traded in the market, it indicates that, presumably, a large group of investors simply decides to invest in one of these funds rather than to diversify directly in all assets available in the market. Moreover, some funds simply mimic one of the stock indices, e.g., the S&P 500 stock index, the Dow–Jones index, etc.; hence, investors can indirectly diversify in all stocks composing these indices by investing in these funds. In such cases, in the M–V framework, the risk of the mutual fund held in isolation is simply σ_R (and not by β), and one maximizes their expected utility, given the constraint that only one fund is selected, simply by choosing the fund which maximizes the slope given in Eq. (4.1), provided that the investor is also allowed to borrow and lend money at the riskless interest rate.

Figure 4.1 demonstrates a case where there are several available funds, and the line with the highest SR slope provides the highest expected utility.

Assuming that the conditions under which employing the M–V rule and expected utility maximization coincide, the SR maximization also maximizes the expected utility. As we can see from Figure 4.1, Fund A is the best as it provides the largest SR; therefore, each investor investing in this fund also maximizes their expected utility (see indifference curve U_3). Investing in Funds B or C implies a lower slope, and as we can see from this figure, a lower expected utility is obtained by investing in these funds in comparison to the expected utility achieved by investing in Fund A.

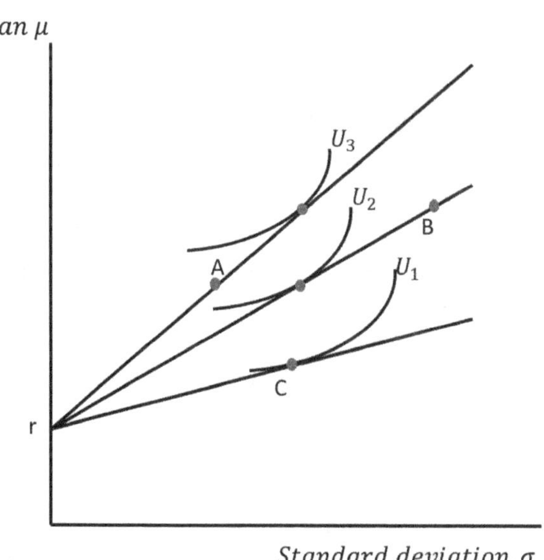

Figure 4.1: The SR of funds A, B, and C.

For investment decisions in practice, if the investor has their subjective estimates of the expected value and standard deviation of each potential investment (e.g., mutual fund), they simply need to calculate the subjective SR for each fund under consideration and invest in the one with the largest SR. Generally, however, such subjective estimates are not employed, and one commonly employs the published SR, calculated based on the *ex-post* rates of return of the fund in the last year or the last few years. If a good performance in the past indeed predicts a good performance in the future, namely the quality of the fund's management, choosing a fund by its *ex-post* performance constitutes a reasonable investment strategy. However, if past performance does not predict good performance in the future, the SR is economically worthless for investors in practice. As for an individual investor, it is hard to examine the consistency of performance, and it is common to rely on the past SR as published by the services companies, hoping that it reflects the ability of the management to pick up promising stocks and bonds in the market.

Given the widespread employment of the SR to rank mutual funds, ETFs, and other funds, in this chapter we analyze whether employing monthly, annual, or even longer period rates of returns to calculate the SR affects the ranking order of the mutual funds. In other words, we ask the following question: Is it possible that for an investor with, say, a one-year investment horizon, Fund A has a higher SR than Fund B, and for an investor with, say, a two-year investment horizon, just the opposite ranking is obtained, where both use the same set of data, say the last 10 years' rates of returns? We emphasize at the outset that in the following analysis, we assume that both investors face the same information. The only difference between the SR calculated for various horizons is that the historical data are cut into different slices, say monthly rates of returns, semi-annual rates of returns, annual rates of returns, and so on. If the ranking depends on the horizon, it is meaningless to publish one ranking list for all investors, as in practice different investors have different investment horizons.

4.2. The Employment of the *SR* in Practice

The *SR* is commonly employed for ranking mutual funds, ETFs, *i*Shares, and many other investment portfolios. Most published rankings are based on monthly rates of returns (see, for example, the famous published ranking by Morningstar). Thus, the ranking companies employ *monthly* rates of returns to calculate the mean rate of return and the standard deviation, which are the inputs to the *SR* calculation. To illustrate the use of the *SR* for funds' rating, we cite a few examples in what follows.

Table 4.1 provides some data, including the various performance indices corresponding to the Canara Robeco Bluechip Equity Fund. As we can see, based on the three-year performance, the *SR* is 0.12 and the *JA* is equal to 5.29. Some publications also provide the Treynor ratio and the Sortino ratio.[5] These various performance indices are not comparable. The only common feature of the *TR* and *JA* is that both must have the same sign. The *SR*, however, does not give us any information unless we compare it to other funds, e.g., to the S&P 500 stock index or even to changes in the *SR* over time in the same fund.

Table 4.1: Various ratios of the Canara Robeco Bluechip Equity Fund.

Portfolio Beta	0.91
R^2	96.12
Standard Deviation	8.80
Sharpe Ratio	0.12
Treynor Ratio	0.03
Jensen's Alpha	1.13
Sortino Ratio	-0.26

Source: Morningstar, November 30, 2021.

---

[5]Some publications also provide the Treynor ratio and the Sortino ratio. The less common Sortino ratio is different from the *SR* as we have in the denominator the standard deviation downside risk.

Let us turn to one more example, the Lee Conrad[6] report, ranking the best 20 mutual funds (the detailed table with all 20 funds is not given here) based on the *SR*. The main message of this article is that return by itself is only one dimension for investment decision-making, and to establish a performance ranking, one must also incorporate the risk involved, ending up with the *SR*. As the article clarifies, the fund with the highest *ex-post* mean return and with the highest standard deviation is not necessarily the best fund for future investment. The reason is that the large standard deviation implies that the next year's future realized return, which is relevant for one-year investors, may be very low as the realized future return may deviate from the *ex-post* mean return. This deviation can even get to the negative territory of returns that spells out losing money, despite the high historical mean return. In contrast, a fund with a relatively low mean and relatively small standard deviation may have a relatively large *SR*; hence, it is preferred to the investment with the large mean but smaller *SR*. The following quote from Conrad's report describes how practitioners perceive the *SR* and the ranking of a sample of funds using it.

> Greg McBride, chief financial analyst at Bankrate, illustrates this idea with a story that any client can relate to. "It's one thing to get to the airport in time for your flight, but what did it take to get there? Was it a white-knuckle ride weaving in and out of traffic, or a leisurely, low-stress ride with plenty of time to spare? The ride that gets you to the airport without the stress is the one with the higher Sharpe ratio."
>
> So in the name of metaphorical low-stress rides to the airport — i.e., returns without the volatility — we collected the mutual funds and ETFs with the best risk-adjusted returns.
>
> The Sharpe ratio is a popular way to measure the return of an investment compared to the amount of risk taken. Risk is measured as volatility or standard deviation. So, the equity managers with the highest Sharpe ratios in the WhaleWisdom database have demonstrated skill in picking stocks with market-beating returns. However, their picks have shown relatively tame price fluctuations.

---

[6]Conrad, L. (June 2019). Facebook.

Name	13FMKT Value	Total Holdings	3 Yr Sharpe	1 Yr Perf	Q3 (2019) Perf
Reilly Herbert Faulkner III	238,174,000	50	2.064	19.58	4.38
Junto Capital Management LP	1,682,556,000	40	1.9357	17.82	5.88
Blair William & Company	17,355,103,000	1692	1.9161	24.66	2.83
Douglass Winthrop Advisors, LLC	2,614,301,000	260	1.6971	23.45	7.4
Lannebo Fonder AB	329,357,000	24	1.6926	20.88	8.02
Security Asset Management	152,001,000	80	1.6922	19.81	3.41

These hedge funds, as reported in the table, provided for three years report a very high SR in comparison to the S&P 500 stock index with an SR of only 1.07. Yet, recall that only funds with a consistent SR may indicate the ability of stock picking. For example, if the top ranking fund in a given time interval becomes a low SR fund, we attribute the good performance to luck rather than to stock picking ability. Yet, in this chapter, we do not discuss this issue, but rather assume that the SR indeed reflects the quality of the management, and analyze how the horizon affects his SR ranking.

As the SR is considered to be a very important investment ranking tool, in the next section, we analyze how the assumed investment horizon affects the ranking of funds by the SR.

4.3. The One-Period and Multi-Period SRs: Mathematical Analysis of Horizon Mismatch

In this section, we first assume that there are several mutual funds (or any other assets, but for simplicity, we refer to all of these assets as mutual funds) with identical SRs for a given horizon, say one year, and investigate whether the SRs remain identical as the horizon increases, and if not, what the direction of the changes is. Are the changes in the *SR* systematic or random? What are the implications and interpretation of published mutual fund rankings? These issues are important because if practitioners rank mutual funds and other traded portfolios by employing, say, monthly rates of returns to calculate the means and standard deviations that are the inputs for the *SR* calculation, and if this ranking changes by shifting to, say, quarterly or annual rates of returns, it casts doubts on the economic validity of the published *SR* ranking. This is particularly important as investors who invest in traded funds available in the market typically invest for a long run, on average, certainly for more than one month.

We show in the following that indeed the ranking of the various funds by *SR* is affected by the assumed investment horizon. For simplicity, we start with the case where all funds have identical *SR*s for a given horizon. Having these results, we then analyze the more common case where we assume that with monthly data, one fund outperforms the other by the *SR*, and analyze whether the performance ranking may reverse with changes in the horizon. Specifically, we show that, say, Fund *A* may have a higher *SR* than Fund *B*, where monthly rates of returns are employed to calculate the *SR*, and the opposite ranking is obtained with, say, quarterly rates of returns. The implication of this reversed ranking is that investors who intend to invest for one month should prefer Fund *A* over Fund *B*, and those who invest for three months should prefer Fund *B* rather than Fund *A*, so long as both investors employ the *SR* to select their funds. In other words, there is no meaning in the publication of the *SR* index with one horizon for all investors who typically have different investment horizons. Let us show this claim formally:

Suppose that there are two mutual funds, *A* and *B*, and for a one-year horizon, both have identical performances, namely

$$SR(A) = \frac{\mu_A - r}{\sigma_A} = \frac{\mu_B - r}{\sigma_B} = SR(B). \qquad (4.6)$$

With these one-period parameters and one-period equal SR, the investor is indeed indifferent about investing either in Fund A or Fund B. Suppose now that another investor who invests for N-periods, say N-years, employs the same set of historical data to calculate the SR. However, they do not use the one-period rates of returns to calculate the SR, but rather the N-period rates of returns. For example, an investor with a two-year investment horizon would employ the bi-annual rates of returns to calculate the SR. Is the N-period investor also indifferent about Funds A and B? And if not, what is the horizon's effect on the ranking of these two funds as the horizon changes? To answer these important questions, which are crucial from the investor's point of view, we first need to define the multi-period SR. Under the identical independent distribution ($i.i.d.$) assumption, the N-period SR is given by

$$SR = \frac{[(1+\mu)^N - 1] - [(1+r)^N - 1]}{\{[\sigma^2 + (1+\mu^2)]^N - (1+\mu)^{2N}\}^{\frac{1}{2}}}. \tag{4.7}$$

For the formula of the standard deviation given in the denominator, see Eq. (3.6) in Chapter 3. As for the one-period, the SR is assumed to be identical for both funds, we omit the notation for the funds, as it is not necessary for the proofs given below, therefore we have

$$\frac{(1+\mu) - (1+r)}{\sigma} = c,$$

where c is some constant that is equal for both funds. Therefore,

$$\sigma = [(1+\mu) - (1+r)]/c. \tag{4.8}$$

Define

$$\frac{\sigma}{1+\mu} = \frac{1 - (1+r)/(1+\mu)}{c} \equiv \frac{1-V}{c}, \quad \text{where } \frac{1+r}{1+\mu} \equiv V < 1. \tag{4.9}$$

Having these definitions, we can rewrite the multi-period SR given by Eq. (4.7) as follows:

$$SR(N) \equiv \frac{[(1+\mu)^N - 1] - [(1+r)^N - 1]}{\{[\sigma^2 + (1+\mu)^2)]^N - (1+\mu)^{2N}\}^{\frac{1}{2}}}$$

$$= \frac{1 - (1+r)^N/(1+\mu)^N}{\{[(\sigma/(1+\mu))^2 + 1]^N - 1\}^{1/2}} = \frac{1 - V^N}{\{[((1-V)/c)^2 + 1]^N - 1\}^{1/2}}.$$

$$(4.10)$$

Note that we divide each term in the denominator by $(1+\mu)^2$, which implies dividing the whole dominator by $(1+\mu)^N$, considering the N and $\frac{1}{2}$ power terms appearing in the denominator of Eq. (4.7).

Denoting by B the following term:

$$B \equiv (1-V)/c)^2 + 1,$$

we find that the multi-period SR can be rewritten as

$$SR(N) = (1 - V^N)/[(B^N - 1)]^{\frac{1}{2}} \qquad (4.11)$$

where $SR(N)$ stands for the N-period SR.

However, we can express the terms appearing in Eq. (4.11) as follows:

$$1 - V^N = (1 - V)[1 + V + V^2 + \cdots V^{N-1}]$$

$$1 - B^N = (1 - B)[1 + B + B^2 + \cdots B^{N-1}]$$

and

$$B^N - 1 = (B - 1)[1 + B + B^2 + \cdots B^{N-1}].$$

As $B - 1 = ((1 - V)/c)^2$, the SR can be rewritten as

$$SR(N) = \frac{(1 - V)[1 + V + V^2 + \cdots V^{N-1}]}{((1 - V)/c)[1 + B + B^2 + \cdots B^{N-1}]^{\frac{1}{2}}}.$$

Note that we have only the term $((1 - V)/c)^2$ without the power of 2 because of the power of $\frac{1}{2}$, which cancels it. Hence, after canceling by (1–V), which appears in both the numerator and the denominator, we obtain

$$SR(N) = \frac{c[1 + V + V^2 + \cdots V^{N-1}]}{[1 + B + B^2 + \cdots B^{N-1}]^{\frac{1}{2}}}. \qquad (4.11')$$

To analyze how the SR changes with the increase in the horizon, recall that $V = \frac{1+r}{1+\mu}$ and $B = \frac{1-V}{c^2} + 1$. Moreover, as it is safe to assume that the expected return on the fund is larger than the riskless interest rate (otherwise no investor will buy the fund), we also have that

$$0 < V = (1+r)/(1+\mu) < 1 \quad \text{and} \quad B = \left[\frac{1-V}{c^2} + 1\right] > 1.$$

Thus, for a given multi-period N and for a given positive constant c, an increase in μ induces a decrease in V; hence, the numerator of Eq. (4.11$'$) decreases. By a similar argument, as the mean μ increases, B increases. As the numerator decreases and the denominator increases, we can safely conclude from Eq. (4.12) that we have $\partial(SR(N))/\partial\mu < 0$. As we hold constant the one-period SR, we have that $c = \frac{(1+\mu)-(1+r)}{\sigma}$; therefore, when $(1 + \mu)$ increases, σ also must increase; therefore, we also have that $\partial(SR(N))/\partial\sigma < 0$. Thus, in the case where the one-period SR is constant for all funds, for a given multi-period horizon, N, the $SR(N)$ is a decreasing function of the one-period mean and the one-period standard deviation of the fund under consideration. Thus, we expect that the riskier one-period funds will have a relatively small multi-period $SR(N)$.

We next calculate the $SR(N)$ values corresponding to various scenarios. Specifically, we assume that for a given horizon (one-month, one-year, and 10-years), all funds have identical SRs, and analyze the effect of deviating from this horizon on the SR, where the deviation can be by increasing or decreasing the horizon relative to the benchmark horizon for which the SRs are assumed to be identical. Particularly, we analyze whether there are some systematic changes in the SR as N changes. Later on, we will also analyze the more realistic case where for a given horizon, not all funds have the

Table 4.2: The changes in the SR for various scenarios.

Scenario	The Horizon for Which the SR is Assumed to be Constant	The Calculated SR for Various Horizons
Case a	1 year	More than 1 year
Case b	1 month	More than 1 month
Case c	10 years	More than 10 years
Case d	1 year	Less than 1 year

identical SR, and we analyze possible changes in the funds' ranking by the SR as the horizon changes.

Table 4.2 reports the four cases we first analyzed in this chapter. Each case may be relevant to some segment of investors, and to the best of our knowledge, Segment d is the most relevant one for the largest segment of investors.

In Case a, for a one-year horizon, all funds have identical SRs, and we analyze the effect on the SR corresponding to various horizons longer than one year. In Case b, it is assumed that the SR is constant for the one-month horizon, and we analyze the effect on the SR induced by increasing the horizon to more than one month. In Case c, the SR corresponding to the 10-year horizon is assumed to be constant, and we analyze the changes in the SR corresponding to longer than a 10-year horizon. Finally, Case d is the most relevant, as the SR is assumed to be constant for the one-year horizon, and the SR is calculated and reported for horizons less than one year. In our view, this is the most important case because investors' typical horizon is about one year (or longer), and the financial services generally report the SR corresponding to a one-month horizon. Therefore, from this case, we can see the possible economic distortion caused by relying on the published monthly SR by investors with longer investment horizons.

Figure 4.2 illustrates the horizon effect on the SR in Case a, namely in the hypothetical case where it is assumed that for a one-year horizon all funds have identical SRs. In drawing Figure 4.2(a), we assume that the annual interest rate is 0.05 (namely 5%), and the market portfolio mean return and the standard deviation are

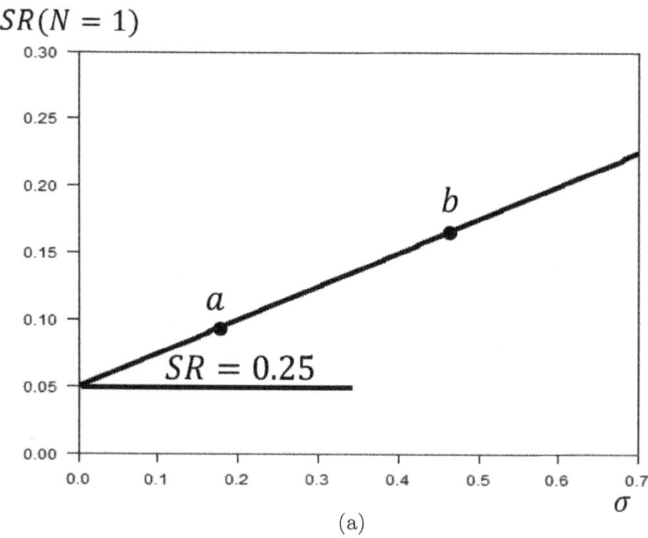

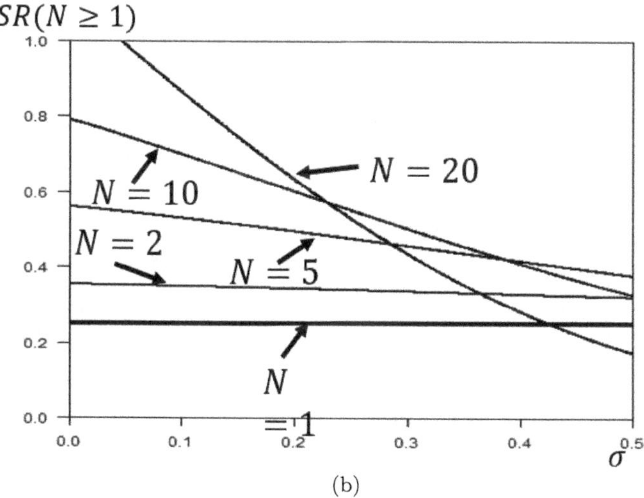

Figure 4.2: (a) The SR of funds with annual rates of returns for a horizon of $N = 1$ year; (b) The SR as a function of σ for horizons $N \geq 1$ year.

10% and 20%, respectively. Thus, the slope of the straight line a–b given in this figure is $(0.1 - 0.05)/0.20 = 0.25$. It is assumed that all portfolios (mutual funds) are located on this straight line. Therefore, they have an identical SR of 0.25. In Figure 4.2(b), we draw the

SR curves for various horizons. These SR values are calculated by employing Eq. (4.7), where the one-period parameters corresponding to the various funds are taken from the line given in Figure 4.2(a). Obviously, for $N = 1$, by construction, all funds have a constant SR of 0.25. Therefore, investors with a horizon of an $N = 1$-year investment period are indifferent about all the funds located on the straight line, so long as they make their investment decision by the SR criterion. For all longer horizons, namely $N > 1$ year, the SR curves are downward sloping as a function of the fund's standard deviation, and the larger the number of years N, the steeper the decrease in the SR. Thus, for a given horizon $N > 1$, funds located close to point b in Figure 4.2(a) have a lower SR than funds located close to point a. The findings illustrated in Figure 4.2(b) are consistent with the mathematical analysis given before, as funds with a relatively large standard deviation and large mean (namely taken from the right-hand side on the line given in Figure 4.2(a)) reveal a lower multi-period SR than funds with a relatively small mean and small standard deviation. Of course, each curve intersects the horizontal SR line at a different point depending on the selected N. Also, note that for the relevant annual standard deviation on stocks, say, a standard deviation smaller than 0.4 (namely, smaller than 40%), the multi-period SR is always larger than the SR corresponding to $N = 1$.

So far, we assumed ranking of funds by SR, which is based on annual rates of return, and we calculated the SR for horizons longer than one year. In practice, most ranking services companies employ monthly rates of returns to calculate the SR; hence, they report the monthly SR, but investors typically invest for a horizon longer than one month. Figure 4.3(a), which is similar to Figure 4.2(a), corresponds to this case. It is assumed that with monthly rather than annual rates of returns, the SRs are identical in all funds, namely all funds are located on the straight line given in Figure 4.3(a) with a slope (SR) that is equal to 0.1. This monthly SR is calculated at a monthly riskless interest rate corresponding to an annual riskless interest rate of about 3.5%, and with monthly parameters corresponding to the annual mean rate of return and standard deviations of the market portfolio of 10% and 22%, respectively.

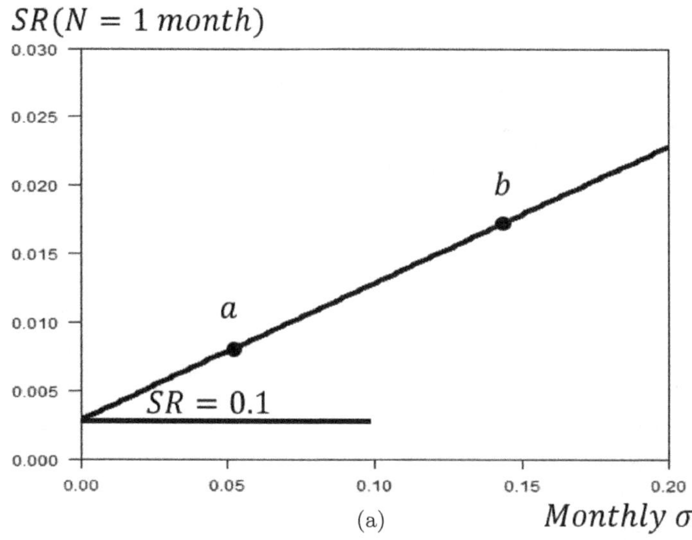

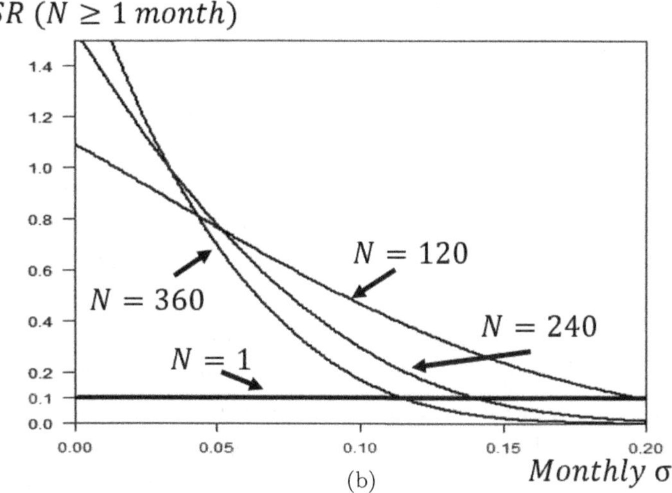

Figure 4.3: (a) The *SR* of funds with monthly rates of returns for a horizon of $N = 1$ month; (b) The *SR* as a function of σ for horizons $N \geq 1$ month.

Any reasonable changes in these parameters do not change the basic changes in the *SR* pattern reported in what follows.

Figure 4.3(b) presents the *SR* curves of all the funds located on the straight line a–b given in Figure 4.3(a) calculated, once again, by the formula given in Eq. (4.7) for various horizons $N \geq 1$ month. Note that if we plug monthly parameters and also $N = 1$ into Eq. (4.7), we obtain, as expected, that $SR = 0.1$.

We obtain in Case b (see Table 4.2) very similar results as those obtained in Case a. The SR curves decrease for all horizons $N > 1$ month. As before, funds with a relatively low one-month standard deviation and lower one-month mean reveal a larger multi-period SR than funds with a relatively large standard deviation and large mean. In sum, the results corresponding to Cases a and b are very similar: assuming that all funds have the same SR calculated with monthly or annual rates of returns, increasing the horizon yields downward sloping SR curves as a function of the standard deviation, and the larger the standard deviation, the lower the SR.

We turn now to Case c, given in Table 4.2. We assume in this case that the SR is constant for a horizon of $N = 10$ years and analyze the changes in the SR, where these performance indices are calculated for shorter horizons, say one or two years. We employ Eq. (4.7) to calculate the annual parameters of various portfolios with a constant SR and examine how the SR changes, where we plug $N < N = 10$ years into Eq. (4.7) for various portfolios, namely those with various annual means and annual standard deviations. This analysis corresponds to long-term investors (in our example, 10-year horizon investors), namely those who invest in life cycle mutual funds, typically investors who save money for retirement. We show that these long-term investors are indifferent about the various funds so long as the investment horizon is 10 years, but they may make an investment error based on relatively short horizon SR ranking. Hence, they are exposed to an economic loss by following the reported ranking of the funds by the SR index calculated for shorter horizons.

The precise procedure for calculating the SR for $N < 10$ in Case c is as follows: We first plug $N = 10$ into Eq. (4.7) to obtain

$$SR(N = 10) = \frac{[(1+\mu)^{10} - 1] - [(1+r)^{10} - 1]}{\{[\sigma^2 + (1+\mu^2)]^{10} - (1+\mu)^{20}\}^{\frac{1}{2}}} \equiv c = 0.25.$$

$$(4.12)$$

It is assumed that all funds with $N = 10$ years have the same SR, which is equal to $c = 0.25$ (the pattern of the results are the same for other reasonable values of c). Then we plug into Eq. (4.12) various values for the annual σ and solve for the corresponding annual value μ which guarantees that the SR remains equal to $c = 0.25$. We cover these calculations with a wide range of annual parameters where the minimum value of the annual mean is 0.05, the maximum annual mean return is .75, and the average annual mean return of all portfolios covered in this calculation is .23, or 23%. These values are not crucial, and the whole purpose of this exercise is to take various funds with equal SRs for $N = 10$ years and calculate the annual mean and annual standard deviation of various portfolios with this constant SR, and with these annual parameters we calculate the SR for shorter horizons, $N < 10$ years. Thus, for a sample of funds located on the $N = 10$ years horizon line, we calculate the SR for the shorter horizon by employing the following formula:

$$SR_i(N_j) = \frac{[(1+\mu_i)^{N_j} - 1] - [(1+r)^{N_j} - 1]}{\{[\sigma_i^2 + (1+\mu_i^2)]^{N_j} - (1+\mu_i)^{2N_j}\}^{\frac{1}{2}}} \qquad (4.13)$$

where (μ_i, σ_i) are the annual parameters of the ith fund, and N_j is the assumed horizon for which the SR is calculated, where $N_j < N = 10$. Note that we have two indices in Eq. (4.13): i which stands for asset i and N_j where j stands for the number of years, $1, 2, \ldots, 10$.

Figure 4.4 provides the SR curves. Obviously, for $N = 10$, we obtain a horizontal line, as by construction all funds have the same SR of 0.25. For all $N_j < 10$ years, we have upward sloping SR curves as a function of the standard deviation. The larger the standard deviation, the larger the SR. This is just the opposite of what is obtained in Figure 4.3, where it is assumed that for a short horizon the SR is constant, and we calculate the SR corresponding to larger horizons.

The economic interpretation of these results is as follows: suppose that for $N = 10$, which is relevant for long-term investors, all portfolios perform equally by the SR criterion. However, the financial services companies calculate the SR based on shorter horizons, say

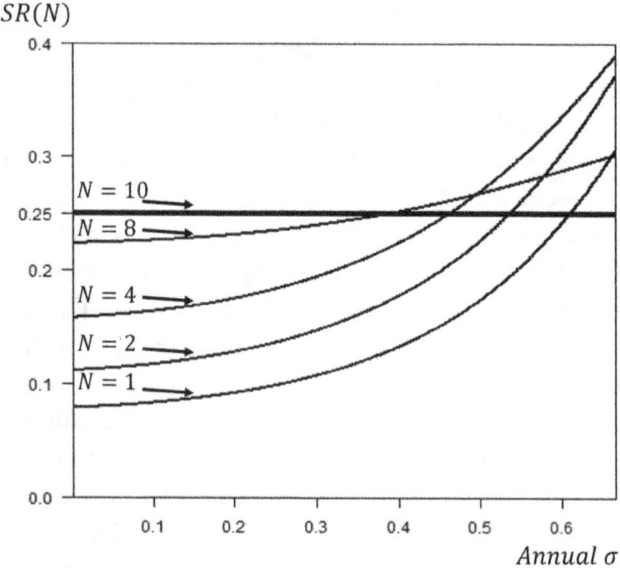

Figure 4.4: The $SR(N)$ of funds with $N_i < N = 10$ years.

$N = 1$ year. Then they report that portfolios with a relatively large σ perform relatively well, and those funds with a relatively small σ perform relatively poorly. Thus, investors with an $N = 10$ years horizon, relying on the published SR for $N < 10$, would invest in the riskier funds and avoid, with no economic justification, the low-risk funds.

One may correctly argue that, in this specific case, no economic harm is done as investors are assumed to invest for $N = 10$, and for this horizon, all funds have identical SRs regardless of the published SR for $N < 10$. Therefore, any selected fund is as good as any another, so long as the investors' horizon in practice is indeed 10 years. However, as we shall show in what follows, the same bias occurs even in the more widespread case, where not all funds are located on the same straight line, and in this case, a mismatch between the investors' horizon and the SR calculated horizon generally induces an economic loss.

We turn now to Case d, given in Table 4.2, a case which, in our view, is the most relevant one for investors in practice. Recall that the actual investment horizon is about one year, and may be even more than one year, but the SR is reported by the services companies for a shorter horizon, typically for one month. For this relevant case, we conduct the same analysis as in Figure 4.4, but this time, the horizon for which the SR is assumed to be constant for all funds is 12 months, and for this 12-month horizon, we assume that $SR = 0.25$ (the patterns of the results presented in what follows are insensitive to reasonable changes in this SR value). We then calculate the SR for shorter horizons of 1, 2, 4, and 8 months.

Recalling that for a 12-month horizon, we have for the *ith* asset (see Eq. (4.13))

$$SR_i(12) = \frac{[(1+\mu_i)^{12} - 1] - [(1+r)^{12} - 1]}{\{[\sigma_i^2 + (1+\mu_i^2)]^{12} - (1+\mu_i)^{2x12}\}^{\frac{1}{2}}},$$

and as by assumption for the 12-month horizon the SR is constant across all funds, we have that $SR_i(12)$ is constant for all assets i. Thus, given this constant SR for all assets, for any monthly mean return μ_i, we can calculate the corresponding monthly σ_i^2, guaranteeing that $SR_i(12)$ remains unchanged. Then we can plug into the above formula each pair $(\mu_i,\ \sigma_i^2)$ and calculate

$$SR_i(N_j) = \frac{[(1+\mu_i)^{N_j} - 1] - [(1+r)^{N_j} - 1]}{\{[\sigma_i^2 + (1+\mu_i^2)]^{N_j} - (1+\mu_i)^{2N_j}\}^{\frac{1}{2}}}$$

where the index i stands for asset i and N_j is the number of months for which the SR is calculated, where $N_j = 1, 2, \ldots, 12$ months, namely for a shorter horizon than that for which the SR performance index is assumed to be constant.

Figure 4.5 presents the results, and they are very similar to those reported in Figure 4.4. By construction, for a 12-month horizon, the SR is identical for all funds (see the horizontal line in Figure 4.5), and then the SR increases with the increase in the standard deviation. This phenomenon is intact for all horizons shorter than 12 months. The same result holds for other horizons shorter than one year that are not reported in this figure. In sum, in all cases where the investors' horizon is longer than the SR calculated horizon, the SR curves are upward sloping as a function of the standard deviation.

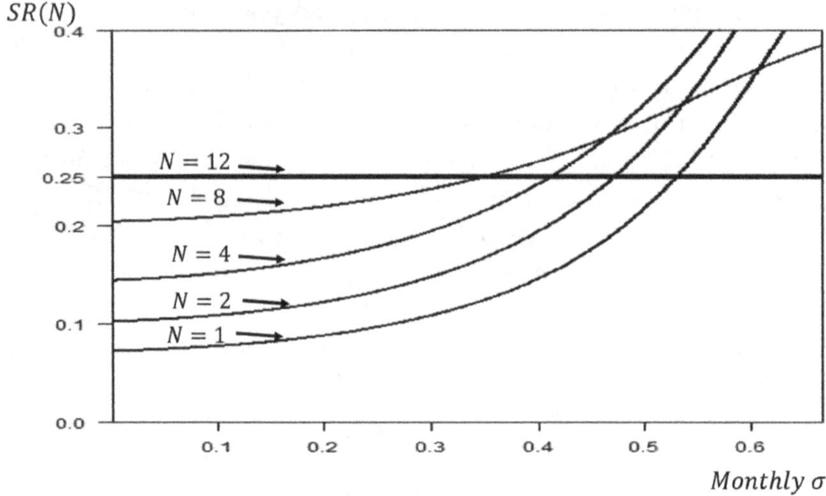

Figure 4.5: The $SR(N)$ for various horizons for $N_i \leq 12$ where for a 12-month horizon the SR is identical for all funds. For a 12-month horizon the SR is 0.25.

So far, for simplicity, and to obtain a transparent presentation of the effect of a possible mismatch in the horizons, we assume that for a given horizon the SR is identical for all funds. In this case, for investors with the horizon for which the SR is identical for all funds, there is no economic loss induced by choosing to invest in funds with shorter horizon high SR rankings, as for their relevant horizon all funds have the same SR. The more interesting and realistic case, to which we turn next, is where there is no horizon for which the SR is identical for all funds.

Having the effect of a possible mismatch in the horizons on the SR ranking in the constant SR case under our belt, we turn now to the more realistic case where for a given horizon not all funds are located on the same straight line, implying that they have different SRs. Indeed, in practice, looking at the SR ranking, we generally have different rankings for different funds, and only rarely do two funds have the identical SR ranking (see the two articles written by practitioners given at the beginning of this chapter that report the SR for various funds). We show in what follows that, for this most

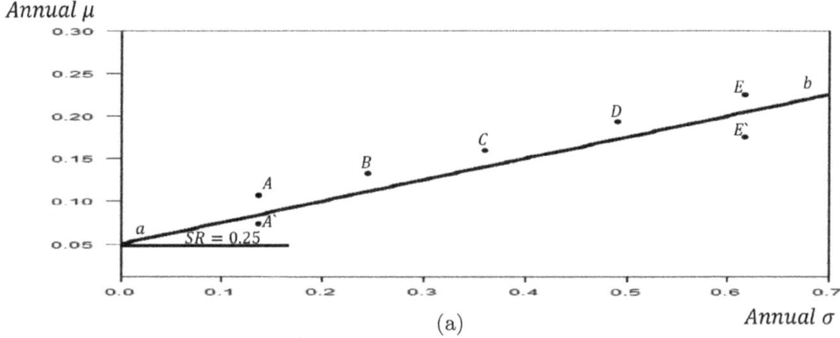

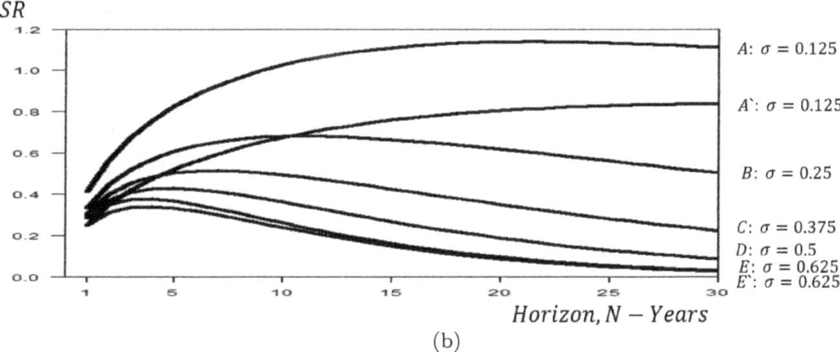

Figure 4.6: (a) SR with annual rates of returns. All funds on the line $a - b$ have $SR = 0.25$. Funds A, B, C, D, and E are above the line $a - b$; hence they have a higher SR. The mean μ of the funds which are located above the line is 0.02 (2%) above the line $a - b$; (b) The SR of funds A, B, C, D, and E given in Figure 4.6(a) for various horizons greater than one year. Funds A' and E' have the same σ as funds A and E, respectively, but lie beneath the SR line.

relevant case for investors, it is possible that for one horizon one fund may have a higher SR than another, and that this SR ranking is reversed for another horizon.

Figure 4.6 illustrates the possible economic distortion created by relying on an SR calculated for one period when the actual horizon is longer, say two periods. Now, we relax the assumption that for the one-period case all funds have the identical SR, which certainly conforms better with real empirical data. Indeed, a glance at the published SR reveals that, as expected, different funds have different SR rankings even in the case where all the SR calculations rely on one horizon, say monthly rates of returns, and cover the same period (see the examples given earlier in the chapter).

Figure 4.6(a) presents the straight line corresponding to funds with the SR calculated with annual parameters. As shown in this figure, there are a few points (funds) located above the line, indicating that in practice not all funds have identical SRs even for the same horizon. If investors indeed have a one-year investment horizon, the funds that are located above the line are those with the best SR performance. Indeed, for a relatively short horizon of one year, these are the best funds. Actually, Fund A is the best by the SR ranking, as it creates the largest slope (SR), with a line connecting it with the riskless interest rate on the vertical axis (this line is not drawn in the figure). As we shall see in what follows, for long-horizon investors, the choice of some of the one-year good performance funds may be a mistake, resulting in economic loss. For example, for $N > 10$, Fund E with $\sigma = 0.625$, which has an excellent SR for the one-year horizon (as it is located above the straight line, it performs better than all the funds located on the line), performs very poorly with relatively long horizons, see Figure 4.6(b). Thus, for investors with very long horizons, some funds that perform very well with $N = 1$ underperform in the very long run. An even more striking result is that Fund A', which has a lower SR than Fund B with annual rates of returns, also has a larger SR for investors with about $N > 10$ years, and a larger SR than other funds that perform very well for a one-year horizon for relatively long horizons. Thus, having a relatively low standard deviation implies that for a relatively long horizon, this is an advantage as these funds typically have relatively large SRs. This phenomenon provides the first indication that bonds with a relatively small standard deviation may outperform stocks by the SR, provided that the horizon is relatively long.

Notwithstanding, if two funds have identical standard deviation, the fund with the larger mean will always have a larger SR, regardless of the horizon, as long as it is larger than the horizon employed in drawing the straight line (compare Funds E and E', or Funds A and A' in Figures 4.6(a) and (b)). Finally, note that in the specific numerical example given in Figure 4.6, if all investors choose Fund

A, which is the best for a horizon of $N = 1$ year, no economic loss occurs as this is also the best fund for all horizons $N > 1$ (see Figure 4.6(b)). However, in the case that Fund A does not exist, an economic loss may occur for long-horizon investors who rely for their investment choices on the published annual SR conducted with short horizons. For example, in the absence of Fund A, the fund with the largest annual SR is Fund B, yet for a horizon larger than about 10 years, Fund A' outperforms Fund B. Thus, relying on the annual SR, investors will choose Fund B, which incurs a loss with a horizon of more than 10 years (see Figure 4.6(b)).

Finally, note that in Figure 4.6, we compare the one-year SR with the SR corresponding to longer horizons. However, similar results are intact where we compare the monthly SR (with some funds having a larger SR than the others) with the SR corresponding to horizons longer than one month. Thus, an economic loss may incur for investors who choose their investment by the monthly SR ranking when their horizon is longer than one month, as long as they believe that the SR is the best rule for investment choices.

From all the above reported results, we conclude that a horizon mismatch affects the SR ranking; hence, it may induce an economic loss. Moreover, we find that the standard deviation strongly affects the relationship between the SR and the horizon. If for a given horizon N_0 two funds have the same SR, then for $N < N_0$ the fund with the larger standard deviation by SR outperforms the fund with the smaller standard deviation, and just the opposite holds for horizon $N > N_0$. This result is presented in Figure 4.7.

We turn now to the relationship of the SR and the horizon for stocks and bonds corresponding to the period 1928–2019. Obviously, bonds have a lower standard deviation than stocks. Figure 4.8 provides the results. In this figure, we employ the annual rates of returns for the period 1928–2019.[7] We first calculate the average return and standard deviation of the S&P 500 stock index, the US 10-year Treasury bonds, and the mean of the Treasury bills which serves as the mean riskless interest rate. The historical mean and standard

---

[7] *Source*: http://people.stern.nyu.edu/adamodar/pc/datasets/histretSP.xls.

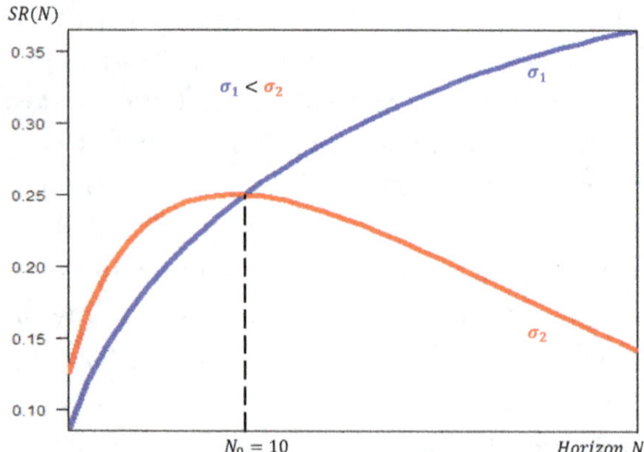

Figure 4.7: The *SR* of the two funds is constant for horizon $N_0 = 10$. For $N < N_0$, the fund with the larger σ has a larger *SR*, and for $N > N_0$ the fund with the smaller σ has the larger *SR*.

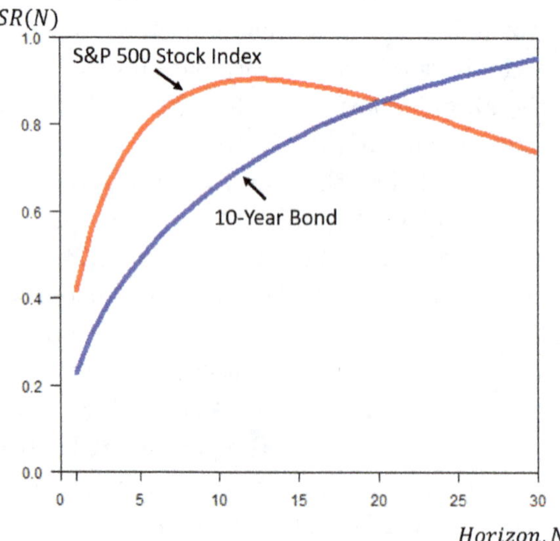

Figure 4.8: The *SR* of 10-year Treasury bonds and the S&P 500 stocks index as a function of the horizon, N.

deviation of the annual rates of returns on the S&P 500 stocks are 11.6% and 19.6%, respectively. For bonds, the corresponding figures are 5.4% and 7.7%, respectively.

We calculate the SR for stocks and bonds for various horizons using Eq. (4.7). As we can see, the SR varies with the assumed investment horizon, and the SR of stocks is larger than the SR of bonds up to about a 20-year investment horizon. However, for about $N > 10$, the SR of stocks starts declining, but the SR of bonds continues to increase with N, and for about $N > 20$, bonds outperform stocks by the SR. Thus, for very long-horizon investors, e.g., those investing for retirement, bonds provide a higher SR than stocks.[8]

Of course, this result implies that bonds are a better investment than stocks for the very long run, as long as, indeed, the SR is the optimal investment criterion. However, as mentioned before and as we have seen in Chapter 3, the M–V rule may be misleading for investors with relatively long horizons as the distributions of returns are not elliptic (see also Chapter 2), also implying that the SR which relies on the M–V rule is not the optimal investment rule for the long run. To examine whether bonds outperform stocks in the long run, one should measure the expected utility corresponding to these two assets as a function of the horizon and not rely solely on the SR performance index. Yet, we realize that the SR ranking is very popular and that many investors use it in practice for investment choices. Accepting this practice of employing the SR rule for investment choices, the purpose of the $SR(N)$ analysis is to pinpoint the effect of the horizon mismatch on the SR ranking. Specifically, the SR ranking for a given horizon is meaningless for all investors who have in practice different investment horizons. In sum, there is no one suit that fits all investors.

---

[8]For similar results, see Hodges, C. W. Taylor, R. L. Walton and J. A. Yoder (1997). Stocks, Bonds, the Sharpe ratio and the investment horizon. *Financial Analysts Journal* 53(6), 74–80.

4.4. The Changes in the Beta, Treynor Ration (*TR*), and Jensen's Alpha (*JA*) with the Increase in the Horizon

We turn now to analyze the horizon's effect on two performance indices, the *TR* and the *JA*. However, as the beta is an important ingredient of these two performance indices, we need first to analyze the effect of the horizon on it. Moreover, the horizon's effect on beta is interesting by itself, as it is employed in other areas in finance, e.g., estimating a firm's cost of capital, classifying stocks as aggressive and defensive, etc.

4.4.1. *The horizon effect on the beta*

The beta is well-known as the measure for risk of an asset held within a diversified portfolio. It also plays an important role in determining the *TR* and *JA*, which we discuss in detail in the rest of this chapter. For simplicity, we deal here with a given risky asset, asset i, whose one-period beta is denoted by β_{i1} and the corresponding multi-period beta of this asset is denoted by β_{iN}. Having the formula connecting these two risk indices, we analyze the effect of the horizon on the multi-period beta for defensive, neutral, and aggressive stocks.

Suppose that we would like to study the effect of the horizon on the beta of stock i. The one-period beta is given by

$$\beta_{i1} = \frac{cov(R_i, R_m)}{\sigma_m^2} \tag{4.14}$$

where R_i and R_m stand for the return on the ith stock and on the market portfolio, respectively, and σ_m^2 stands for the market portfolio's variance.

We turn now to calculate the multi-period beta. First note that for N-period, the return (namely, $1 +$ rate of return) on the ith stock and on the market portfolio is given by

$$R_{iN}^* = R_{i1}, R_{i2} \ldots \ldots R_{iN} \text{ and}$$

$$R_{mN}^* = R_{m1}, R_{m2} \ldots \ldots R_{mN}, \text{ respectively,}$$

where N stands for the number of periods under consideration, and R_{iN}^* and R_{mN}^* denote the terminal wealth accumulated after N periods of investment. By definition, the N-period beta is given by β_{iN},

$$\beta_{iN} = \frac{cov(R_{iN}^*, R_{mN}^*)}{\sigma_{mN}^2} \tag{4.15}$$

where σ_{mN}^2 stands for the market portfolio N-periods' variance. Therefore,

$$\beta_{iN} = \frac{cov(R_{i1}, R_{i2} \ldots \ldots R_{in}, R_{m1}, R_{m2} \ldots \ldots R_{mn})}{\sigma_{mN}^2},$$

which can be rewritten as

$$\beta_{iN} = \frac{\begin{matrix} E[(R_{i1}, R_{i2} \ldots R_{in})(R_{m1}, R_{m2} \ldots R_{mn})] \\ - E[(R_{i1}, R_{i2} \ldots R_{in})]E[(R_{m1}, R_{m2} \ldots R_{mn})] \end{matrix}}{\sigma_{mN}^2}.$$

Using the independence assumption, we obtain that β_{iN} can be rewritten as

$$\frac{\begin{matrix} E[(R_{i1}R_{m1})]E[(R_{i2}R_{m2})] \ldots E[(R_{in}R_{mn})] \\ - E[(R_{i1})]E[(R_{i2})] \ldots E[(R_{in})]E[(R_{m1})]E[(R_{m2})] \ldots E[(R_{mn})] \end{matrix}}{\sigma_{mN}^2},$$

and with the *i.i.d.* assumption, β_{iN} finally reduces to

$$\beta_{iN} = \frac{[E(R_{i1}R_{m1})]^N - E(R_{i1})^N E(R_{m1})^N}{\sigma_{mN}^2}. \tag{4.16}$$

As we assume *i.i.d..*, we can drop the index 1 (as all periods are identical) and simply rewrite this formula as

$$\beta_{iN} = \frac{[E(R_i R_m)]^N - E(R_i)^N E(R_m)^N}{\sigma_{mN}^2} \tag{4.17}$$

where all the parameters appearing in the numerator correspond to any one-period selected arbitrary. Employing the relationships

$$cov(R_i, R_m) = E(R_i R_m) - E(R_i)E(R_m),$$

Eq. (4.16) can be rewritten as

$$\beta_{iN} = \frac{[E(R_i R_m)]^N - E(R_i)^N E(R_m)^N}{\sigma^2_{mN}}$$

$$= \frac{[cov\ (R_i, R_m) + E(R_i)E(R_m)]^N - [E(R_i)E(R_m)]^N}{\sigma^2_{mN}}.$$

Using the multi-period formula for the variance of the market portfolio (see Eq. (3.6) in Chapter 3), and denoting $E(R_i) = \mu_i$ and $E(R_m) = \mu_m$, the multi-period beta can finally be rewritten as

$$\beta_{iN} = \frac{[cov(R_i, R_m) + \mu_i \mu_m]^N - [\mu_i \mu_m]^N}{[\sigma^2_m + \mu^2_m]^N - \mu^{2N}_m}. \tag{4.18}$$

Recalling that $\beta_{i1} = cov(R_i, R_m)/\sigma^2_m$, we can rewrite the multi-period beta as a function of the one-period beta as follows:

$$\beta_{iN} = \frac{[\beta_{i1}\sigma^2_m + \mu_i \mu_m]^N - [\mu_i \mu_m]^N}{[\sigma^2_m + \mu^2_m]^N - \mu^{2N}_m}. \tag{4.19}$$

It is obvious from Eq. (4.19) that if the CAPM holds for one period and $\beta_{i1} = 1$ (a neutral stock), also $\beta_{iN} = 1$, as in this case, also $\mu_i = \mu_m$. Thus, for a neutral stock, the beta does not change with the horizon. As we shall see in what follows, unlike the case of neutral stocks, the beta of aggressive stocks increases with the horizon and the beta of defensive stocks decreases with the horizon. These patterns in the multi-period beta affect the multi-period CAPM, as well as the *TR* and *JA* performance indices. Specifically, we show that the CAPM may hold for the one-period case, but not for the multi-period case, implying that *JA* may be equal to zero for one period and not for other periods.

We analyze the changes in the beta with the horizon in two alternative ways. First, we assume that the CAPM holds for $N = 1$ and analyze theoretically the changes in the beta with the horizon by employing Eq. (4.19). As these results depend on the assumption that for one period the CAPM is intact, we also measure empirically the changes in the beta with the horizon, which yields results that do not depend on the validity of the CAPM. Obviously, we do not expect the two methods to yield identical results, but we are more interested in finding out whether the two methods yield the same pattern, particularly corresponding to changes of the beta with the horizon of assets classified as defensive, neutral, and aggressive.

We employ Eq. (4.19) to analyze theoretically the relationship between the one-period beta and the multi-period beta. We first assume that for the one-period, the CAPM is intact. Therefore, to analyze the relation between these two betas, we can assume any hypothetical one-period mean rate of return corresponding to the market portfolio and any hypothetical riskless interest rate — parameters that one needs to employ in Eq. (4.19). Using the assumed parameters, we calculate for each one-period beta (which also determines the one-period mean return on the asset under consideration, as the CAPM is assumed to hold for one period) the multi-period beta. However, to have realistic figures, we estimate the needed parameters based on historical data. We use the 1928–2019 period to estimate the mean annual rate of return on the market portfolio rate of return (we employ the S&P 500 stock index as a proxy to the market portfolio) and by annual average interest rate on Treasury bills as a proxy to the annual riskless interest rate. For this period, we obtain that the average rates of returns on stocks and Treasury bills are 11.57% and about 3.340%, respectively (see footnote 8). With these estimated parameters, and assuming that the CAPM holds for one period, we can determine for each hypothetical one-period β_i the corresponding one-period μ_i. Thus, we have all the required parameters to calculate β_{iN} for each given β_i, and for each horizon, N (see Eq. (4.19)).

Figure 4.9 presents β_N as a function of β_1 for various horizons, N, and Table 4.3 provides some selected values taken from Figure 4.9. As we can see from this figure, as predicted by the mathematical analysis, for one period, $\beta_1 = 1$, also for the multi-period, $\beta_N = 1$ for all horizons, N (see the intersection point of all curves given in Figure 1.0).

For $\beta_1 < 1$ (defensive stocks), β_N decreases with the horizon as all curves are below the 45-degree line, and for $\beta_1 > 1$, β_N increases with the horizon as all curves are above the 45-degree line. Moreover,

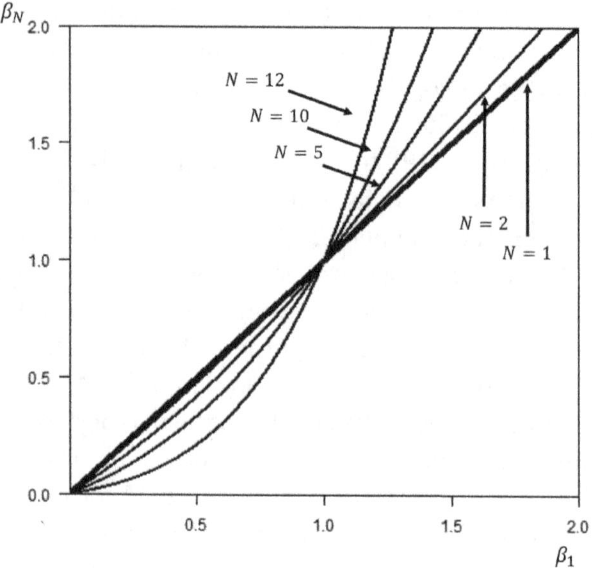

Figure 4.9: β_N as a function of β_1 and the horizon N years.

Table 4.3: β_N as a function of β_1 and the horizon N years.

	$N = 1$	$N = 2$	$N = 5$	$N = 10$	$N = 20$
$\beta_1 = 0.5$	0.5	0.478208	0.41823	0.334148	0.212433
$\beta_1 = 1$	1	1	1	1	1
$\beta_1 = 1.5$	1.5	1.565376	1.779958	2.208448	3.419799
$\beta_1 = 2$	2	2.174336	2.796941	4.270618	10.08742

the larger the N, the more intensive these changes. These findings
have a strong implication for investors. To illustrate, suppose that
for one period the risk of a given stock is $\beta_1 = 1.5$. Thus, one-period
investors require a risk premium based on the fact that $\beta_1 = 1.5$.
However, if another investor considers investing in the same stock
for, say, $N = 5$ years, they face a risk index of about $\beta_{N=5} \cong 1.78$
(see Table 4.3); hence, the required risk premium from the same stock
is larger. Just the opposite holds for defensive stocks (see Table 4.3).
We would like to stress at the outset that these changes in the beta as
a function of the horizon are based on the fact that for the one-period
horizon the CAPM is intact.

However, as we shall see in what follows, these patterns of changes in the beta are quite general, irrespective of the CAPM being intact. Thus, we obtain empirically that the beta of aggressive stocks typically increases with the horizon and the beta of defensive stocks typically decreases with the horizon, albeit not exactly as documented in Figure 4.9, which is derived under the assumption that the CAPM is intact for the one-period horizon.

4.4.2. *The effect of an increase in the horizon on the multi-period TR*

The Treynor ratio (TR), which is commonly employed by researchers and practitioners alike, is also affected by the assumed investment horizon. Changes in the TR, which are due to changes in the horizon (as compared to a baseline horizon), follow a systemic pattern. Recall that the one-period TR is defined as $TR = \frac{\mu-r}{\beta}$, and as each of the parameters appearing in this TR formula changes with the assumed investment horizon, the TR also changes with the assumed horizon. However, while the effect of the increase in the horizon on the numerator is obvious as it increases with the horizon (recall that for risky assets generally $\mu > r$), the horizon's effect on the denominator is ambiguous; hence, the horizon effect on TR is also ambiguous. To see this claim, let us first write the multi-period TR as a function of the horizon, N:

$$TR_N = \frac{(1+\mu)^N - (1+r)^N}{\beta_N}. \tag{4.20}$$

Given that $\mu > r$, the numerator increases with N. However, the changes in β_N are as follows: for defensive stocks with $\beta_1 < 1$, β_N decreases with the horizon, and for neutral stocks with $\beta_1 = 1$, β_N does not change with the horizon; hence, it remains equal to 1, and for aggressive stocks with $\beta_1 > 1$, β_N increases with the horizon. Thus, for neutral stocks with $\beta_1 = 1$, we expect the TR to increase with the horizon as the numerator increases and the denominator remains constant. For defensive stocks, we expect the change in the TR with the horizon to be in the same direction as with neutral stocks, as the numerator increases with the horizon and the denominator decreases with it. However, the effect of the horizon on the TR for aggressive stocks is ambiguous, as both the numerator and denominator increase with the horizon, and the change in TR with the horizon in this case depends on the relative speed of the changes in these two components of the TR.

Figure 4.10 and Table 4.4 reveal the $TR(N)$ as a function of the one-period beta and the horizon, N. As we assume that for $N = 1$ the CAPM is intact, we get for $N = 1$ a horizontal line, that is, the TR is identical for all assets regardless of the one-period beta. With the annual parameters employed before, we have that the TR is equal to 0.08173 regardless of the value of the beta (see Table 4.4 for the case $N = 1$). For all horizons $N > 1$, the TR is larger than this figure.

For all values N, the TR curves are downward sloping (see Figure 4.10). As the curves do not intersect, we obtain that the ranking of all assets by their TR is invariant to the assumed

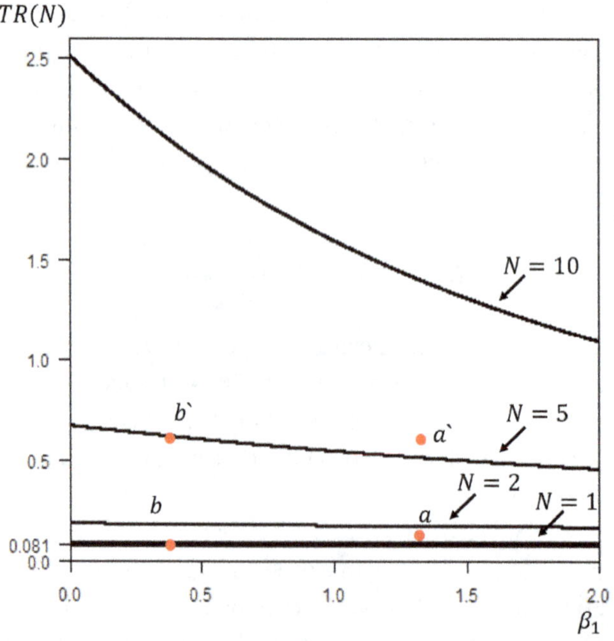

Figure 4.10: The $TR(N)$ as function of β_1 and the horizon N.

Table 4.4: The $TR(N)$ as a function of β_1 and the horizon N (years).

	$N = 1$	$N = 2$	$N = 5$	$N = 10$	$N = 20$
$\beta_1 = 0.5$	0.08173	0.18021	0.60431	1.97891	10.75292
$\beta_1 = 1$	0.08173	0.17569	0.54698	1.59202	6.98144
$\beta_1 = 1.5$	0.08173	0.17156	0.49869	1.30676	4.79254
$\beta_1 = 2$	0.08173	0.16775	0.45764	1.09206	3.44765

investment horizon, which is a positive feature of the TR performance index. For example, an investor with $N = 2$-year horizon would rank all the assets under consideration by their performance ratio in the same order as an investor with another investment horizon, say $N = 5$ years.

Notwithstanding, an incorrect investment decision incurring an economic loss may also occur in this case. To see this, suppose that the services companies rank assets by the TR. As expected by the CAPM assumption, all assets yield identical TRs given by the horizontal line corresponding to $N = 1$. Suppose now that the CAPM does not precisely hold, and that there is one fund which outperforms the others with a horizon $N = 1$ (see point a in Figure 4.10). Following the annual TR ranking, the investor would choose to invest in Fund a, as it has a higher TR than the other funds. Specifically, with a TR ranking corresponding to $N = 1$, asset a is preferred to asset b (see Figure 4.10). However, if the actual investor's horizon is $N = 5$ years, investing in asset a rather than in asset b induces an economic loss, as with a 5-year horizon, it would be better to invest in an asset with a lower beta — compare points b' and a' in Figure 4.10 corresponding to an $N = 5$-year horizon. Once again, this economic loss exists only under the assumption that the TR, which is widely employed, is the correct investment rule.

4.4.3. *The effect of an increase in the horizon on the multi-period JA*

Suppose that the CAPM is intact for one period; hence, JA is equal to zero for all risky assets. Does it remain equal to zero as the horizon increases? To answer this question, recall that with one period we have

$$\mu_i = r + (\mu_m - r)\beta_i + \alpha_i,$$

and if the CAPM is intact, all α_i are equal to zero. However, in the multi-period case we have

$$(1 + \mu_i)^N = (1 + r)^N + [(1 + \mu_i)^N - (1 + r)^N]\beta_{iN} + \alpha_{iN},$$

and even if the CAPM is intact, it does not imply that $\alpha_{iN} = 0$. Once again, when we analyze the effect of the horizon on α_{iN}, we also take into account the effect of the horizon on β_{iN} discussed before, which is an important factor in determining α_{iN}.

Figure 4.11 and Table 4.5 present JA as a function of the one-period beta and the horizon. Obviously, for $N = 1$, JA is equal to zero, as we assume that for this horizon the CAPM is intact. For one-period betas smaller than 1, all alphas are positive, and they become negative for betas larger than 1. For example, suppose that the ranking services rank the various assets by their alpha, and all assets have an identical ranking, as given in Figure 4.11 in the case

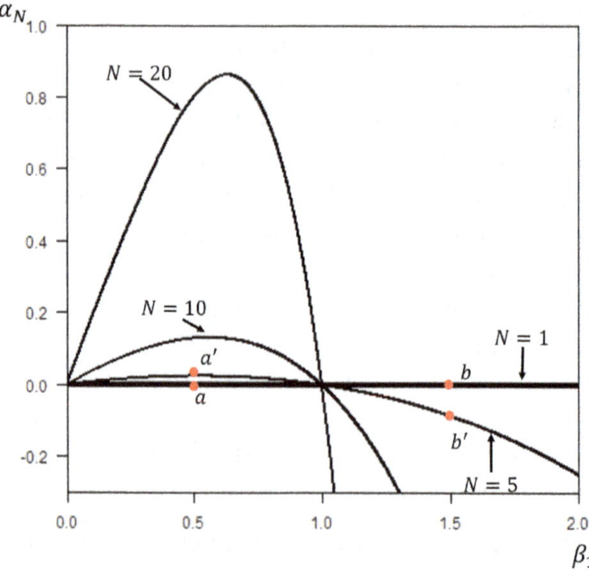

Figure 4.11: JA as a function of β_1 and the horizon N.

Table 4.5: α_N as a function of β_1 and the horizon N (years).

	$N = 1$	$N = 2$	$N = 5$	$N = 10$	$N = 20$
$\beta_1 = 0.5$	0.000	0.002	0.024	0.129	0.801
$\beta_1 = 1$	0.000	0.000	0.000	0.000	0.000
$\beta_1 = 1.5$	0.000	−0.006	−0.086	−0.630	−7.486
$\beta_1 = 2$	0.000	−0.017	−0.250	−2.135	−35.647

where $N = 1$. Thus, an investor with an $N = 1$-year horizon is indifferent regarding the selected assets, and therefore may randomly choose asset a rather than asset b (see Figure 4.11 and Table 4.4), corresponding to the horizon $N = 1$. What are the *JAs* for an investor with an $N = 5$-year horizon? Making choices based on the ranking services, they may invest in an asset with a beta equal to 1.50, ending up with a negative excess return of −0.086 (namely, a loss of almost −10% in comparison to the expected CAPM's predicted return (see point b' in Figure 4.11)). They would be better off investing in an asset with a beta equal to 0.5, making an excess return (alpha) of 0.024, that is, about 2% (see point a' in Figure 4.11).

4.5. The Changes in the Beta and the Performance Indices with a Horizon Shorter than the CAPM Horizon

4.5.1. *The effect of a decrease in the horizon on the beta*

So far, we have assumed that the CAPM is intact for one period, and analyzed the effect of an increase in the horizon on the beta and on several performance indices. We turn now to analyze the opposite case: for a relatively long horizon (say, one year) it is assumed that the CAPM is intact, and we calculate the beta as well as the performance indices for shorter horizons. This case is probably the most interesting as the services companies commonly calculate and report the performance indices based on monthly rates of returns, whereas the typical investment horizon in practice is much longer, a year or even more than one year. We assume in what follows that for a 12-month horizon, the CAPM is intact; however, the same analysis is intact for a longer period as long as the performance indices are calculated and reported for shorter horizons.

We employ Eq. (4.19) connecting the one-period beta and the multi-period beta, but this time we assume that the CAPM corresponding to $N = 12$ months is intact and solve for the one-period beta. Figure 4.12 and Table 4.6 provide the results. As we can see, starting with $N = 12$ months and decreasing the horizon, the beta of the defensive stock increases from 0.5 for $N = 12$ months to 0.521 for $N = 1$ month, and the increase in the beta of the defensive stock is consistent; the smaller the N, the larger the beta. Just the opposite occurs with aggressive stocks. For example, for beta $= 3$ with a 12-month CAPM, we find that the beta decreases from 3 to 2.590 for a one-month horizon. Note that as the changes in betas are relatively small, in this specific case Table 4.6 presents the results more transparently than Figure 4.12. These results, which are obtained under the *i.i.d.* assumptions, are consistent with the

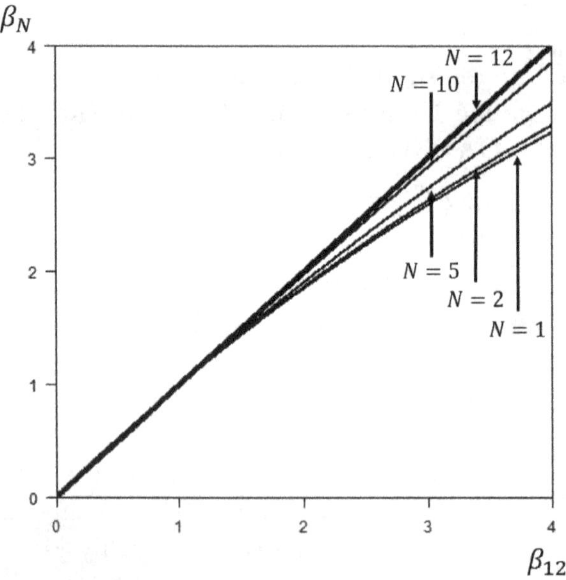

Figure 4.12: β_N (N in months) as a function of β_{12} and the horizon N.

Table 4.6: β_N as a function of the annual β and the horizon N when $N = 1, 2, 5, 10,$ and 12 months.

	Monthly μ	$N = 1$	$N = 2$	$N = 5$	$N = 10$	$N = 12$
$\beta_{12} = 0.5$	1.006	0.521	0.519	0.513	0.504	0.5
$\beta_{12} = 1$	1.009	1.000	1.000	1.000	1.000	1
$\beta_{12} = 1.5$	1.012	1.443	1.448	1.463	1.489	1.5
$\beta_{12} = 2$	1.015	1.853	1.866	1.905	1.972	2
$\beta_{12} = 2.5$	1.018	2.234	2.257	2.327	2.449	2.5
$\beta_{12} = 3$	1.021	2.590	2.625	2.732	2.921	3
$\beta_{12} = 3.5$	1.023	2.923	2.971	3.121	3.387	3.5
$\beta_{12} = 4$	1.026	3.235	3.298	3.494	3.848	4

mathematical analyses of this chapter, as well as the mathematical results of Levhari and Levy.[9]

4.5.2. *The effect of a decrease in the horizon on the TR*

Figure 4.13 and Table 4.7 provide the *TR* figures for a horizon smaller than 12 months, where for $N = 12$ months it is assumed that the CAPM is intact. The betas corresponding to relatively short horizons are employed to calculate the *TR* for relatively short horizons. These betas are taken from Table 4.6 and Figure 4.12, discussed before. Obviously, for $N = 12$ months we have identical TRs for all assets, as we assume that the CAPM is intact for this horizon. As we decrease the horizon to less than 12 months, we find that the *TR* decreases systematically for all assets, defensive and aggressive alike. Yet, even in this case, an economic loss may occur due to the mismatch in the horizons. To see this, consider the relevant case where the services companies rank assets by employing monthly rates of returns, and there is an outlier: with monthly data, asset b underperforms relative to the other assets; hence, it is not recommended to investors. Note, in our example, that asset a outperforms asset b (see Figure 4.13 with the monthly (see $N = 1$ month) reported *TR*). However, as

---

[9]See Levhari, D. and H. Levy (1977). The capital asset pricing model and the investment horizon. *The Review of Economics and Statistics* 59(1), 92–104.

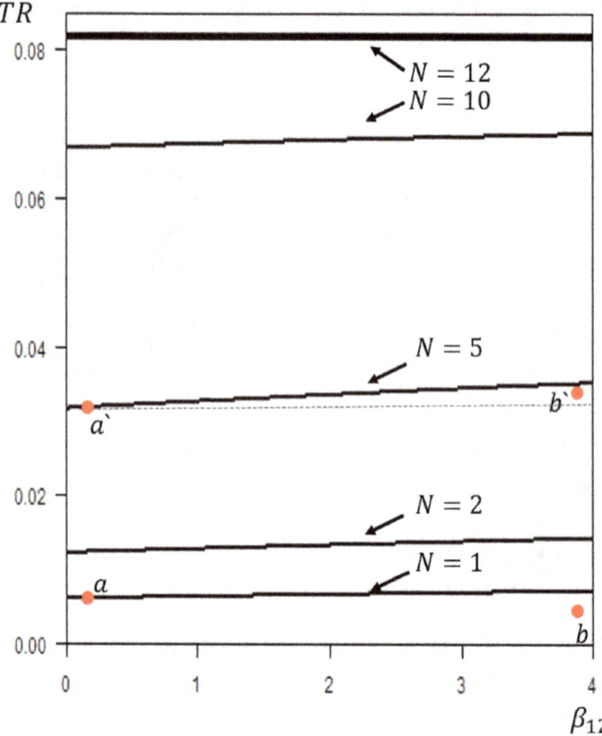

Figure 4.13: The TR as a function of β_{12} and the horizon N (in months).

Table 4.7: The TR as a function of the horizon N (measured in months) when for $N = 12$ the CAPM holds.

	Monthly μ	$N = 1$	$N = 2$	$N = 5$	$N = 10$	$N = 12$
$\beta_{12} = 0.5$	1.006032	0.006229	0.01256	0.032173	0.067011	0.08173
$\beta_{12} = 1$	1.009165	0.006378	0.012831	0.032658	0.067297	0.08173
$\beta_{12} = 1.5$	1.012195	0.006521	0.013094	0.033122	0.067568	0.08173
$\beta_{12} = 2$	1.015128	0.00666	0.013347	0.033568	0.067826	0.08173
$\beta_{12} = 2.5$	1.017971	0.006796	0.013593	0.033998	0.06807	0.08173
$\beta_{12} = 3$	1.020729	0.006927	0.013831	0.034412	0.068304	0.08173
$\beta_{12} = 3.5$	1.023407	0.007055	0.014062	0.034811	0.068527	0.08173
$\beta_{12} = 4$	1.026011	0.007179	0.014287	0.035196	0.06874	0.08173

an investor's horizon is assumed to be longer, say 5 months, asset b outperforms asset a (see points a' and b' in Figure 4.13, where point b' is located above point a'). Thus, following the assets' ranking, which is based on monthly data, may induce an economic loss for investors who have a longer investment horizon.

4.5.3. *The effect of a decrease in the horizon on JA*

Figure 4.14 and Table 4.8 report JA for horizons $N < 12$ months. As for $N = 12$ months, it is assumed that the CAPM is intact, therefore all assets, regardless of their beta, have a zero alpha at the horizon $N = 12$ months. Moreover, all the SR performance curves cross the horizontal line at a beta equal to 1. To see the reason for this phenomenon, recall that if the beta is equal to 1 for a 12-month horizon, it remains equal to 1 for all other horizons under consideration (see Figure 4.9). As with $N = 12$ months, the CAPM

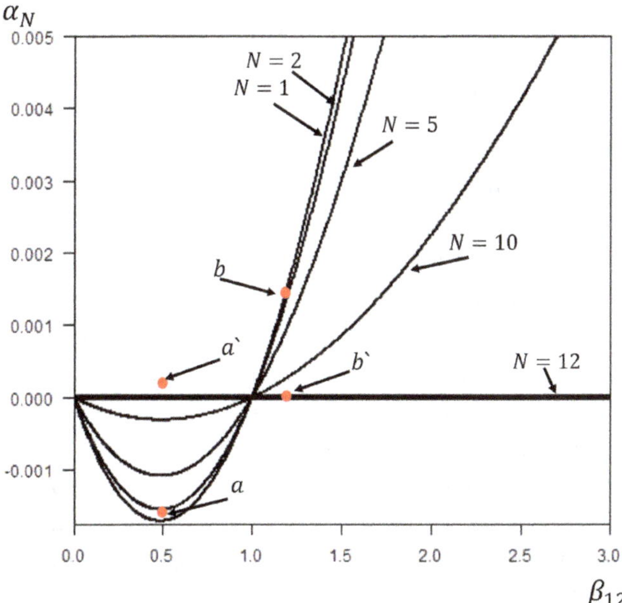

Figure 4.14: Jensen's α_N as a function of β_{12} and the horizon N (in months) used to calculate β.

Table 4.8: *JA* as a function of the horizon N (measured in months) when for $N = 12$, $\alpha_N = 0$.

	Monthly μ	$N=1$	$N=2$	$N=5$	$N=10$	$N=12$
$\beta_{12} = 0.5$	1.0060	-0.0017	-0.0015	-0.0011	-0.0003	0.0000
$\beta_{12} = 1$	1.0092	0.0000	0.0000	0.0000	0.0000	0.0000
$\beta_{12} = 1.5$	1.0122	0.0047	0.0043	0.0030	0.0009	0.0000
$\beta_{12} = 2$	1.0151	0.0120	0.0110	0.0078	0.0023	0.0000
$\beta_{12} = 2.5$	1.0180	0.0217	0.0198	0.0141	0.0041	0.0000
$\beta_{12} = 3$	1.0207	0.0335	0.0307	0.0219	0.0065	0.0000
$\beta_{12} = 3.5$	1.0234	0.0472	0.0432	0.0310	0.0092	0.0000
$\beta_{12} = 4$	1.0260	0.0625	0.0574	0.0413	0.0124	0.0000

is assumed to be intact, and for beta $= 1$, the mean return on the stock under consideration is equal to the mean return on the market portfolio we have for all assets with a beta equal to 1 so that the following holds for all horizons:

$$\beta_{i,1} = \beta_{i,N} = 1, \text{ and also that } \mu_i = \mu_m.$$

Hence, for any horizon N, we have

$$(1 + \mu_i)^N = (1 + r)^N + [(1 + \mu_m)^N - (1 + r)^N]\beta_{iN} + \alpha_{iN},$$

and as in this specific case $\mu_i = \mu_m$ and $\beta_{i,1} = \beta_{i,N} = 1$, it implies that $\alpha_{iN} = 0$ for all horizons N (measured in months), as revealed in Figure 4.14.

Note, however, that for a beta different from 1, we obtain negative alphas for defensive stocks and positive alphas for aggressive stocks, which is consistent with the well-known SFE phenomenon.

Here again, with a possible horizon mismatch, an economic loss may occur. To illustrate, suppose that indeed the investor makes their choice by the one-month published alphas. According to this criterion, asset b is preferred to asset a (see the location of these two points in Figure 4.14 corresponding to the $N = 1$-month horizon). However, for investors with an $N = 12$-month horizon, it possible that a', which is an outlier, is better than asset b' (compare points a' and b' in Figure 4.14 with the $N = 12$-month horizon).

4.6. The Empirical Evidence: Relaxing the *i.i.d.* and the CAPM Assumptions: The Implication for the Reported SFE

The analyses so far rely on the mathematical formulas developed under the *i.i.d.* assumption, and some of the results also rely on the existence of the CAPM. In practice, the distribution of returns may vary over time; hence, the "identical" component of the *i.i.d.* assumption may not hold, and the returns may also be dependent, so the "independence" assumption may not hold. Moreover, it is empirically well documented that the CAPM does not hold, and it certainly does not hold perfectly. Yet, the ranking services companies still adhere to the CAPM'S beta as the risk measure of risky assets, particularly when the performance of individual assets is involved. Therefore, the interesting question, which has an important implication to investors in practice, is the robustness of the theoretical results presented in this chapter where empirical historical rates of returns are employed that certainly do not obey perfectly the *i.i.d.* assumption, let alone the validity of the CAPM assumption. Do betas of defensive stocks typically decrease with the horizon and betas of aggressive stocks increase with it empirically, as theoretically predicted under the *i.i.d.* and CAPM assumptions? We next empirically explore this issue.

To examine these important questions, we employ historical rates of returns which may or may not obey the *i.i.d.* and the CAPM assumptions. We use the rates of returns of stocks covering the period from June 1926 to October 2020[10] corresponding to each decile, where the deciles are determined by the market value of the stocks. Decile 1 corresponds to the smallest 10% of stocks ranked by market value, Decile 2 includes the next 10% of stocks ordered by market size, and so on, and finally, Decile 10 corresponds to the 10% of largest firms. To estimate the beta corresponding to various horizons, we run

---

[10] *Source*: https://mba.tuck.dartmouth.edu/pages/faculty/ken.french/data_libra ry.html.

a regression of the excess return of each decile on the excess return on the market portfolio by employing rates of returns corresponding to various horizons from 1-month to 24-month horizons. For $N = 1$ month, we simply include all monthly observations in the regression and estimate empirically the monthly beta of each decile. For the two-month horizon, the first observation is the compounded return corresponding to the first two months (months 1 and 2), the second observation corresponds to the compounded return corresponding to months 3 and 4, and so forth. Running the regression with bi-monthly rates of returns, which does not assume independence over time, we obtain the empirical bi-monthly beta. We repeat this procedure up to a horizon of 24 months. Obviously, the larger the assumed horizon, the smaller the number of available observations included in the regression analysis which, in turn, imposes a limit on the length of the horizon we can examine by this method. Thus, we run the following regression:

$$R_{iN} - r_N = \alpha_{N_i} + \beta_{N_i}(R_{mn} - r_N)$$

where R_{iN} is the N-period return of decile i: if $N = 2$, we take the product of each two consecutive observations (with no overlap): $R_{i2} = (1 + R_{i1})(1 + R_{i2})$ and, similarly, we calculate the market return and the risk-free return, r_N, for this horizon.

By this procedure, in beta estimation, we consider the possible autocorrelations, and we do not rely on the validity of the CAPM. For example, if two consecutive rates of returns are correlated, the suggested procedure takes this autocorrelation into account, which may affect the changes in the beta with the horizon. Thus, this empirical analysis does not rely on the validity of the *i.i.d.* assumption.

Table 4.9 reports the results. As we can see from this table, two phenomena emerge: first, not surprisingly, the table reveals that the beta of the small firms' decile is generally larger than that of the large firms' decile. This conforms with the well-known result asserting that the return on small firms is generally more volatile than that on large firms. However, the more interesting result emerging from this table is that the beta of the small firms' decile increases with

Table 4.9: The changes in beta as a function of the horizon for various deciles.

	1 month	2 months	3 months	4 months	5 months	6 months	7 months	8 months	9 months	10 months	11 months	12 months	24 months
D_1	1.409	1.738	1.865	2.000	2.054	1.720	1.698	1.637	1.694	1.581	1.396	2.155	1.929
D_2	1.381	1.586	1.718	1.899	1.859	1.669	1.627	1.515	1.569	1.522	1.389	1.973	1.894
D_3	1.325	1.528	1.588	1.715	1.676	1.469	1.435	1.388	1.410	1.385	1.268	1.662	1.552
D_4	1.257	1.397	1.464	1.562	1.521	1.399	1.382	1.302	1.312	1.279	1.239	1.524	1.389
D_5	1.228	1.304	1.394	1.461	1.369	1.340	1.324	1.250	1.262	1.236	1.202	1.432	1.262
D_6	1.203	1.290	1.320	1.376	1.317	1.273	1.261	1.211	1.224	1.210	1.193	1.375	1.298
D_7	1.153	1.187	1.222	1.290	1.277	1.207	1.198	1.188	1.187	1.207	1.170	1.235	1.183
D_8	1.113	1.164	1.156	1.191	1.170	1.148	1.146	1.120	1.099	1.112	1.071	1.249	1.188
D_9	1.062	1.083	1.089	1.103	1.079	1.053	1.051	1.065	1.070	1.061	1.018	1.103	1.080
D_10	0.932	0.913	0.908	0.891	0.900	0.914	0.918	0.922	0.916	0.928	0.934	0.903	0.938

Note: Based on a monthly rate of return for the period of July 1927–October 2020. See footnote 11.

the horizon, which is consistent with the theoretical results that rely on the *i.i.d.* assumption, as well as on the CAPM. Specifically, the beta is equal to 1.409 for a 1-month horizon reaching about 2 for the 12–24-month horizon. The change in the beta with the horizon for Decile 10, the decile of the largest firms, seems at first glance not to be consistent with the theoretical result, as we expect the beta of large firms to decrease with the horizon. In contrast, we find that the beta corresponding to this decile almost does not change with the horizon. However, a deeper look into these results leads to an opposite conclusion that is rather consistent with the theory: the one-month beta of large firms is about 1, and we have proved theoretically that assets with beta $= 1$ are not affected by the horizon. Hence, as expected theoretically, the empirical beta of large firms remains equal to 1 for all horizons, even in the case where the *i.i.d.* assumption is relaxed.

To examine the changes in beta with the horizon of large firms, we need a more delicate division of all stocks into groups, say the group of the 1% or 5% largest firms with a beta which is substantially smaller than 1, to be able to analyze empirically the effect of the horizon on the beta of large firms that are classified as defensive stocks. Since this delicate division of all stocks into groups by size is not available on French's data website, we rely next on another source that provides this division of all firms into groups by market value.

A study by Handa, Kothari, and Wasley[11] fills this void. Covering the period 1926–1982, they divided all stocks by size into 20 groups where group 20 includes the largest 5% of the firms, rather than the largest 10% as in Table 4.9. These results are given in Table 4.10.

Unlike the decile case reported in Table 4.9, here, the monthly beta of the top 5% largest firms is substantially smaller than 1, allowing us to examine empirically the horizon's effect on the beta. Although Table 4.10 covers horizons ranging from one day to 12

---

[11]Handa, P., S. P. Kothari and C. Wasley (1989). The relation between the return interval and betas: Implication for the size effect. *Journal of Financial Economics.* 23(1), 79–100.

Table 4.10: Beta and the horizon with 20 classes of stocks divided by size[*].

Portfolio	1 year	6 months	4 months	3 months	2 months	1 month	1 week	1 day
MV 1	1.66	1.60	1.57	1.51	1.53	1.41	1.18	0.99
MV 2	1.38	1.41	1.42	1.37	1.33	1.27	1.13	1.02
MV 3	1.31	1.31	1.35	1.32	1.29	1.23	1.12	1.04
MV 4	1.18	1.20	1.21	1.21	1.17	1.18	1.13	1.08
MV 5	1.16	1.19	1.17	1.16	1.17	1.14	1.11	1.08
MV 6	1.22	1.14	1.15	1.12	1.11	1.11	1.10	1.10
MV 7	1.10	0.11	1.11	1.08	1.08	1.08	1.10	1.09
MV 8	1.10	1.09	1.07	1.06	1.05	1.04	1.10	1.10
MV 9	1.04	1.01	1.02	1.03	1.01	1.03	1.08	1.09
MV 10	0.94	0.98	0.97	0.99	0.99	1.00	1.05	1.05
MV 11	1.00	0.97	0.96	0.99	0.99	0.99	1.02	1.03
MV 12	0.97	0.94	0.93	0.94	0.94	0.96	0.96	0.98
MV 13	0.88	0.88	0.88	0.88	0.89	0.92	0.95	0.96
MV 14	0.87	0.87	0.88	0.88	0.88	0.91	0.93	0.97
MV 15	0.83	0.86	0.85	0.86	0.87	0.88	0.91	0.95
MV 16	0.79	0.79	0.79	0.81	0.82	0.85	0.90	0.93
MV 17	0.72	0.73	0.74	0.77	0.80	0.81	0.87	0.90
MV 18	0.70	0.73	0.71	0.77	0.77	0.79	0.85	0.90
MV 19	0.59	0.62	0.63	0.66	0.68	0.71	0.79	0.86
MV 20	0.56	0.58	0.58	0.61	0.63	0.67	0.78	0.90

Note: [*]These data are reproduced from Handa, Kothari, and Wasley (1989).

months, for a fair comparison with Table 4.9, we also focus here mainly on the range of one month to 12 months, which is common to both tables. While the monthly beta of the largest 10% of the firms is 0.932, the beta of the top 5% of the firms is 0.67 (compare Tables 4.9 and 4.10). Once we have a group of defensive stocks, we are able to examine the horizon's effect on the betas of large firms.

As Table 4.10 reveals, the beta of the largest firms decreases with the horizon: from 0.90 with a horizon of one day to .56 with a horizon of one year. When we compare the monthly and annual betas, they decease from .67 for a 1-month horizon to .56 for a 1-year horizon. Consistent with the theory and with the results reported in Table 4.10, the beta of the most aggressive stocks (small stocks) increases from .99 with a one-day horizon to 1.66 with the 1-year horizon.

Thus, relaxing the *i.i.d.* and the CAPM assumptions does not change theoretically the pattern in the beta results obtained with *i.i.d.* and the CAPM assumptions: the beta of aggressive stocks generally increases with the horizon, whereas the beta of defensive stocks generally decreases with it, and finally the beta of neutral stocks is unaffected by changes in the assumed horizon (see Tables 4.9 and 4.10). The astonishing results are that by assuming *i.i.d.*, and even the more unrealistic assumption that the CAPM holds perfectly, and by relaxing these assumptions, we get the same pattern, albeit not at the same magnitude: the theoretical and empirical results reveal that for aggressive stocks, the beta increases with the horizon, it is unaffected by the horizon in neutral stocks, and it increases with the horizon with defensive stocks. To illustrate the importance of these findings to investors, suppose that they wish to take some risk (for the expected return and not for the risk itself), but impose a limit asserting that the beta cannot exceed, say, 1.5. Looking at the Decile 1 and the commonly employed monthly data, they may invest in these stocks with beta = 1.41. However, if their investment horizon is, say, one year, they end up with an investment with beta = 1.66, which is in contrast to the declared investment strategy (see Table 4.10). Finally, recall that for those investors who invest in individual stocks (and not in a decile of stocks), these changes in the beta with the horizon may be much more extreme; hence, the distortion in the investment decision is much more severe.

In deriving Table 4.9, we assume that neither the *i.i.d.* nor the CAPM hold. The disadvantage of this procedure is that for a relatively long horizon, we have a limited number of observations. For example, with 100 years' annual data, for a horizon of 2 years, we have only 50 observations. Table 4.11 reports the effect of the horizon on the beta where the CAPM assumption is relaxed as before, but we assume *i.i.d.* in such a case, we can create, as explained before, 100,000 observations for each horizon (see footnote 12). As we can see from Table 4.11, the beta of Decile 1 still increases with the horizon, but with less intensity in comparison to the result given in Table 4.9. The beta of Decile 1 increases from 1.400 for a 1-month horizon to

Table 4.11: Changes in the beta as a function of the horizon, where *i.i.d.* is assumed.

	1 month	2 months	3 months	4 months	5 months	6 months	7 months	8 months	9 months	10 months	11 months	12 months	24 months
D_1	1.400	1.414	1.423	1.429	1.439	1.453	1.439	1.467	1.462	1.466	1.479	1.475	1.550
D_2	1.384	1.387	1.389	1.395	1.390	1.407	1.406	1.413	1.427	1.419	1.431	1.439	1.504
D_3	1.325	1.327	1.333	1.336	1.342	1.344	1.352	1.356	1.355	1.363	1.372	1.370	1.429
D_4	1.249	1.253	1.271	1.270	1.272	1.282	1.278	1.287	1.285	1.287	1.293	1.301	1.346
D_5	1.226	1.230	1.236	1.236	1.243	1.243	1.245	1.247	1.251	1.253	1.260	1.257	1.295
D_6	1.204	1.206	1.210	1.215	1.215	1.220	1.219	1.228	1.228	1.229	1.233	1.236	1.273
D_7	1.153	1.156	1.158	1.161	1.161	1.166	1.167	1.166	1.169	1.171	1.176	1.175	1.199
D_8	1.113	1.116	1.116	1.118	1.121	1.120	1.122	1.123	1.127	1.129	1.128	1.131	1.148
D_9	1.063	1.061	1.065	1.064	1.066	1.067	1.066	1.068	1.068	1.069	1.068	1.071	1.082
D_10	0.931	0.931	0.931	0.930	0.931	0.930	0.929	0.928	0.928	0.928	0.927	0.926	0.921

Note: Based on monthly rates of returns for the period of July 1927–October 2020. See footnote 11.

1.475 for a 24-month horizon. Similar changes occur in Deciles 2 and 3. For Decile 10, as before, the beta does not change much with the horizon, which is explained by the fact that the beta of this decile is about 1.

Finally, Table 4.12 reports the empirical JA corresponding to various horizons. To have a large number of observations in deriving JA, we assume *i.i.d.*, but not the CAPM; hence, for each horizon, we have 100,000 observations. We obtained that for Decile 1 all JA are positive, which is consistent with the well-known SFE. For Decile 10, some of the JA are negative and some are positive. As most empirical studies regarding the SFE employ monthly rates of returns, focusing on the one-month horizon is important; the JA is about 0.14% (very small) for Decile 1 and about negative 0.002% for Decile 10.

One more interesting result emerging from Table 4.12 is that for the first decile, JA seemingly increases with the horizon. For example, it is 0.1411% (very small) for the one-month horizon and 2.4404% for the 24-month horizon. We say "seemingly" because in such a comparison, one needs first to equalize the investment horizon. For example, an excess return for one-month of 0.1411% (very small) repeated for a 24-month investment accumulates to $(1+0.001411)^{24} - 1 = 1.0344 - 1 = 0.0344$ or about 3.4%. This is much larger than JA for 24 months, which is about 2.4%, see Table 4.12.

What is the implication of this difference? To answer this question, suppose that the typical investment horizon is 2 years, but the SFE is measured as commonly done by employing monthly rates of returns. Then the recorded SFE overstates the true SFE, as about half of it is induced by employing monthly rates of returns which are irrelevant for 2-year investors. This overstating the SFE by employing monthly rates of returns rather than longer horizon rates of returns was documented by Levy and Levy.[12]

---

[12]Levy, M. and H. Levy (2011). The small firm effect: A financial mirage? *The Journal of Portfolio Management* 37(2), 128–129.

Table 4.12: Jensen's α_N, in percent, for various horizons with *i.i.d.* assumption.

	1 month	2 months	3 months	4 months	5 months	6 months	7 months	8 months	9 months	10 months	11 months	12 months	24 months
D_1	0.1411	0.2883	0.4396	0.5315	0.6396	0.8295	0.9966	1.0689	1.1363	1.3190	1.4105	1.6041	2.4404
D_2	0.0282	0.1048	0.1239	0.1892	0.1954	0.1791	0.2343	0.2667	0.2224	0.2356	0.3329	0.2892	−0.0439
D_3	0.0570	0.1492	0.2114	0.2670	0.2920	0.3513	0.3719	0.4949	0.5645	0.5673	0.5379	0.7037	0.8569
D_4	0.0699	0.1614	0.2332	0.3259	0.4059	0.4922	0.5831	0.5654	0.7077	0.7259	0.7758	0.8960	1.3620
D_5	0.0642	0.1200	0.1803	0.2427	0.2443	0.3351	0.4013	0.4274	0.4458	0.4579	0.6067	0.6295	0.8335
D_6	0.0807	0.1662	0.2565	0.3467	0.4364	0.5148	0.5710	0.6880	0.7880	0.8363	0.9252	0.9785	1.8275
D_7	0.0488	0.1155	0.1646	0.2295	0.2701	0.3132	0.3454	0.3856	0.4579	0.5183	0.5725	0.6177	1.0672
D_8	0.0556	0.1178	0.1714	0.2113	0.2776	0.3442	0.3998	0.4255	0.5035	0.5086	0.5949	0.6529	1.2605
D_9	0.0224	0.0524	0.0715	0.0897	0.1263	0.1372	0.1497	0.1835	0.1984	0.2158	0.2555	0.2421	0.4366
D_10	−0.0019	0.0022	−0.0020	0.0054	0.0112	0.0089	0.0205	0.0204	0.0063	0.0245	0.0252	0.0193	0.1019

4.7. Summary

For future investment decision-making, one needs to estimate the future distribution rates of returns on various assets. Each investor may create their subjective beliefs regarding the future return. Notwithstanding, investors commonly look at the past published performance that is objective and common to all investors as an indicator of future performance. Indeed, there are numerous service companies evaluating the performance of risky assets (generally of various funds) in the last year, the last two to three years, and some ranking publication corresponds even to the last five years. This indicates that investors choose their investment based on the reported past performance of the various funds.

The three most popular performance indices are the SR, TR, and JA. Because the SR does not rely on the CAPM assumptions, it can be applied to individual stocks or to portfolios that are diversified, albeit not fully diversified. Indeed, the service companies publish the SR of mutual funds, iShares, hedge funds, etc. Thus, investors who are not experts in the stock market trust the investment abilities of these fund managers and diversify in the market indirectly by investing in one of them.

In contrast to the SR ranking index, an important parameter appearing in the TR and JA performance measures is the CAPM's beta; hence, these two performance indices can be applied to individual assets as well as to portfolios. However, if the CAPM is not intact, and if the beta does not measure the risk of the individual asset under consideration, these two performance indices may be misleading, particularly when they are applied to individual assets. The SR performance measure is very popular because it does not rely on the CAPM, but its usefulness is limited and has no economic meaning when applied to individual stocks.

In this chapter, we analyzed, theoretically and empirically, the effect of the assumed investment horizon on the performance indices. The main result is that these indices are not invariant to the assumed investment horizon. Therefore, the published performance indices which rely mainly on monthly rates of returns cannot fit all investors, as investors generally have various planned investment horizons.

Specifically, the *SR* of Fund *A* may be larger than that of Fund *B* with monthly rates of returns, and the opposite holds with, say, annual rates of returns. We would like to emphasize that in both calculations of the *SR*, we employ the same set of data, say rates of returns corresponding to the last 10 years. The only difference, in this 10-year example, is that in one we slice the data into 120 monthly rates of returns and in the other we slice the data into 10 annual rates of returns. While it is obvious that, with autocorrelation, cutting the data into slices of different sizes may affect the volatility, it also may affect the volatility of the *SR* even in the absence of autocorrelation. Hence, we show that the horizon's effect on the performance indices is valid and substantial even if returns are assumed to be identical and independent over time.

As the *TR* and *JA* depend on the CAPM's beta, we first show that the beta is also not invariant to the assumed investment horizon. We find that the beta of defensive stocks decreases with the horizon, and the beta of aggressive stocks increases with it. For example, a beta of 1.5 calculated with monthly rates of returns may reveal a beta of 2.5 with annual rates of returns. As the beta measures the risk of the asset under consideration, the investor with a one-year planned investment horizon may consider this asset much riskier than the investor whose planned investment horizon is one month. Moreover, as the beta is a crucial component in the *TR* and *JA*, we find that these two performance measures are also not invariant to the assumed investment horizon.

When we relax the *i.i.d.* assumption and employ historical rates of returns that may not obey this assumption, we obtain very similar results: the beta of aggressive stocks increases with the assumed horizon, and the opposite holds for the beta of defensive stocks. Therefore, the performance indices are also not invariant to the assumed investment horizon, and this result is intact both theoretically and empirically.

The results of this chapter are not very encouraging: they imply that one size cannot fit all. The published performance indices, which are based on one horizon (generally one month), cannot fit investors with a planning investment horizon that is different than one month.

Actually, given that the *ex-post* performance also predicts future investment, each investor should calculate the performance indices with rates of returns that fit their investment horizon — not an easy task considering the large number of available assets in the market. Relying on the monthly published performance indices may lead to the incorrect investment choice, hence to an economic loss. The larger the investor's investment horizon, the larger the economic loss.

Finally, all the popular investment indices rely on the M–V rule which, in turn, assumes normal (or more generally elliptical) distribution of returns. As the horizon increases, there is evidence that the normal distribution assumption is invalid, which casts doubt on the validity of these performance indices. However, as these indices are widely published by the media, and as they are very popular, investors who use these performance measures should be aware of the distortion implied by mismatch of the horizons.

Chapter 5

Stocks Versus Bonds: Mean–Variance and Expected Utility Paradigms

The mean–variance (M–V) investment rule is by far the portfolio investment criterion most commonly employed by academic researchers and professional investors. However, there is little research on the horizon's effect on optimal M–V diversification. Therefore, regardless of existing criticism of the application of the M–V rule for all horizons, as the M–V rule is widely used in practice, it is important to analyze the recommended optimal M–V choices for various horizons. Therefore, we devote this chapter to the changes in the optimal M–V choices with the horizon.

To derive the M–V optimal portfolio choices, one needs, as an input, the future distributions of rates of returns on all assets under consideration. However, as the future distributions of returns are unknown, to derive the M–V optimal portfolios, one commonly uses historical distributions of rates of returns as the best estimates of future distributions. Given that one needs to rely on distributions of rates of returns, the question one faces in practice is in regard to the appropriate holding period returns to be employed in the M–V analysis. There is no one recipe regarding the appropriate holding period rates of returns that should be employed in the derivation of the M–V efficient frontier and in the derivation of the optimal M–V portfolio of risky assets. Recall that even if one employs some subjective beliefs regarding the distributions of future rates of return, the historical returns serve as the basis of the creation of these subjective beliefs. Markowitz[1] provides examples revealing that there are unexpected future risks that even a history since 1926 cannot predict (e.g., the October 1987 Black Monday). Yet, even Markowitz admits that the historical data are important for future investment decision-making (for more details, see footnote 1). Notwithstanding, regardless of whether one employs subjective or objective distributions of rates of returns, the horizon's effect remains and needs a discussion.

What rates of returns (subjective, objective, or historical) are relevant for constructing the optimal M–V portfolio: daily rates of returns, weekly, annual, or maybe bi-annual rates of returns? If the optimal M–V portfolio is invariant to the employed holding period rates of return, this issue is practically irrelevant. However, if the optimal M–V choices vary with these various rates of returns, the following issues that need a detailed discussion emerge:

(a) What is the effect of the employed holding period rates of returns on the optimal M–V choices? On the optimal M–V diversification?

(b) What is the appropriate holding period rates of returns that should be employed in the derivation of the optimal M–V investment choices?

(c) What is the economic distortion induced by employing the M–V rule, rather than the expected utility maximization for relatively long horizons?

Unfortunately, the financial literature devotes very little attention to these important issues. We hope that this and the next chapters will fill this void. Indeed, as we shall see in what follows, the assumed investment horizon is of crucial importance, as it greatly affects the selected M–V portfolio.

Specifically, we show that the way one "slices" all available data into small pieces may affect the theoretical and empirical results. To illustrate the horizon issue, suppose that one relies on the past

---

[1]Markowitz, H. M. (2020). *Risk–Return Analysis: The Theory and Practice of Rational Investing,* Vol. 3, McGraw Hill, New York.

50 years' rates of return series corresponding to various risky assets. For future investments, should one employ the weekly, monthly, annual, or even longer horizon rates of returns to estimate the various needed parameters? In other words, does the way one slices the available data corresponding to the last 50 years into pieces affect the obtained M–V optimal investment? Suppose that two investors relying on the past 50 years' rates of return distribution select their portfolio based on this set of historical rates of returns. Furthermore, suppose that one investor employs monthly rates of returns to derive the optimal portfolio and the other employs annual rates of returns. Would they select the same optimal M–V portfolio? And if the answer is negative, can we say what the relationship is between the way one slices the given 50 years' data into small pieces and the selected M–V portfolio?

Thus, the horizon's effect dilemma discussed in previous chapters also emerges when one employs the M–V methodology to find the best investment in this framework. The horizon issue is important because, as we shall see in this chapter, the optimal M–V portfolio of risky assets is not invariant to the assumed investment horizon. Specifically, even when one assumes that returns are identical and independent over time (the *i.i.d.* assumption), the optimal M–V portfolio composition generally changes with the horizon, let alone when the *i.i.d.* assumption does not hold, and autocorrelations in the series of returns prevail, namely, in the case where returns are dependent over time.

The reason for the strong horizon's effect on the optimal M–V portfolio is that the asset's mean and variance increase with the assumed horizon in some complex manner, where the multi-period variance of each asset increases not only as a function of the one-period variance, but also as a function of the mean return; the larger the mean return, the faster the increase in the multi-period variance with the horizon. Thus, assets with a relatively large mean may be attractive in the short run, but not in the long run, as their variance also increases as a function of the mean. Moreover, all pair-wise correlations vary with the horizon in a peculiar way: positive correlations decrease with the horizon, and negative correlations increase with it. Thus, focusing solely on the correlations' effect on the M–V portfolio selection, we find that stocks with a positive correlation, other things being held constant, become more attractive with the horizon, whereas stocks with a negative correlation become less attractive with the horizon — quite a surprising result!

As we find that the optimal M–V investment weight in the less risky asset (bonds rather than stocks) increases with the horizon, we also calculate the expected utility of stocks and bonds for various horizons for commonly employed utility functions. We obtain with the expected utility just the opposite results — the expected utility of stocks is larger than the expected utility of bonds for the commonly employed utility functions and for the relevant risk-aversion parameters, and in a diversified stocks–bonds portfolio the weight of stocks is relatively large. Moreover, the superiority of stocks over bonds in the expected utility maximization is enhanced with the horizon. Thus, it seems that the M–V and expected utility reveal contrasting results that will be discussed in this chapter.

A word of caution: In this chapter, we analyze the horizon's effect on optimal M–V diversification, not because we advocate that the M–V rule should be employed for all horizons, but simply because the M–V rule is the most popular investment rule used by theoretical researchers as well as practitioners, and there is no elaborate discussion in the literature on the horizon's effect on optimal M–V portfolio choices. Moreover, as the M–V rule is widely employed, even in cases where there is no theoretical justification to employ it, it is of crucial importance to know how the optimal M–V portfolio of risky assets changes with the horizon and the possible economic distortion induced by employing this rule for all horizons. Moreover, in Chapter 2 we showed that the distributions of returns vary with the horizon and a positive skewness is built up with it. Hence, it is clear if the relatively long horizon's distributions of returns are not symmetrical, let alone not normal. Therefore, the M–V rule, which may be optimal for a short investment horizon, may lead to non-optimal choices for a relatively long horizon — certainly for horizons longer than one year. Thus, the reader should examine the results presented in the present chapter with a grain of salt, as employment of the M–V rule in some cases is economically not justified. However, presenting the results to investors is of crucial importance, as the M–V rule is widely used also in cases where it leads to non-optimal results. We believe that investors should be aware of the potential error and, hence, economic loss in their investment decision-making in which relying on the M–V rule may be avoided.

5.1. Changes in the Correlation with the Horizon

The correlation between economic variables is widely employed both in academic research and in investment in practice. For finding the optimal M–V diversification, the correlation (or the covariance plus the standard deviations) plays a central role. We analyze the horizon's effect on optimal diversification first by analyzing the changes in the correlations with the horizon. In the second stage, we also incorporate other parameters that also change with the horizon; hence, these also affect the changes in the optimal M–V diversification with the horizon.

5.1.1. *The definition of the one-period and multi-period correlations*

Correlation is an important parameter employed in economics and finance. When the variables under consideration are multiplicative (e.g., rates of returns on stocks, interest rates, population growth, inflation, gross domestic product (GDP) growth, etc.), the correlation may change with the assumed interval horizon over which the various variables are measured. Using the same dataset (say the last 20 years of data), we may obtain different correlations for, say, monthly and annual variables, e.g., rates of returns. In other words, the way we cut the given dataset (namely, given information) into intervals affects the calculated correlation. Therefore, selecting the appropriate horizon for measuring the correlation is very important.

Although this book focuses on portfolio investment decision-making, the implications of the results presented in this section may be relevant to studies in various research areas such as chemistry, biology, medicine, physics, and, mainly, economics. Whenever one of the two variables under consideration is multiplicative, the horizon, or the selected interval unit for measurement, affects the obtained correlation. When the two variables under investigation are additive, such problems generally do not arise. Just to mention a few economic phenomena where the variables are, by their nature, multiplicative, consider, as mentioned before, the studies that analyze the relationship between the growth rate in the economy, say, in the growth of the GDP and the growth rate in the population. Exactly like with financial assets, a growth rate of 5% in the GDP in each of two consecutive years implies a growth rate for the two years of 10.25%, rather than 10%, as would be obtained with an additive measurement. This seemingly small difference has an accumulated effect and may drastically affect the obtained correlation. Despite the horizon's effect on many multiplicative phenomena, in this book we focus on the effect related to the capital market, particularly to financial assets.

Suppose that, based on the last 50 years of data, for two random variables, say the return on two risky assets with given one-period returns (say, one-year returns), the obtained correlation is $\rho_1 = 0.6$. What would be the correlation for a longer interval horizon measurement, say a bi-annual rate of return? Thus, based on 50 years of available data, we can calculate the correlation, once based on 50 annual rates of returns, and once based on 25 bi-annual rates of returns. Adhering to the above example, it is obvious that if the returns are dependent over time, the bi-annual correlation may increase or decrease depending on the type of dependency over time of the return of each of the two assets under consideration. However, the intuition is that if returns are *i.i.d.*, the correlation would be invariant to the assumed investment horizon. As we shall see in what follows, this intuition is misleading, and the correlation changes with the horizon in some peculiar way even in the *i.i.d.* case. Let us elaborate the effect of the horizon on the correlation with financial assets that are relevant for the issues with which we deal in this book.

Given two random variables X and Y, the correlation between these two random variables is given by

$$\rho_1 = \frac{Cov(x,y)}{\sigma_x \sigma_y} = \frac{E(xy) - E(x)E(y)}{[Ex^2 - (Ex)^2]^{\frac{1}{2}} [Ey^2 - (Ey)^2]^{\frac{1}{2}}}. \tag{5.1}$$

As in our case, X and Y stand for the returns $(1 +$ rate of return$)$ on the two prospects under consideration, both variables are non-negative.

The N-period random returns $(1 +$ rate of return$)$ are given by

$$X_N \equiv x_1, x_2, \ldots, x_N \text{ and } Y_N \equiv y_1, y_2, \ldots, y_N, \text{ respectively.} \tag{5.2}$$

Assuming *i.i.d.* of x as well as y, we also have that the following pairs are *i.i.d.*:

$$(x_1\, y_1), (x_2\, y_2), \ldots, (x_N\, y_N). \tag{5.3}$$

The multi-period correlation ρ_N is given by

$$\rho_N = \frac{cov(X_N, Y_N)}{\sigma_{X_N} \sigma_{Y_N}}. \tag{5.4}$$

We show in what follows that ρ_N and ρ_1 are generally different even when returns are *i.i.d.*

5.1.2. *With i.i.d., the multi-period correlation converges to zero*

We turn now to analyze the relationship between the one-period correlation, ρ_1, and the multi-period correlation, ρ_N, showing that apart from one specific case, the multi-period correlation, ρ_N, approaches zero with N, regardless of the assumed one-period correlation ρ_1.

Assuming *i.i.d.*, for convenience only, we can safely delete the subscripts of the random variables as all one-period variables are identical. Using the above mathematical relations, the multi-period correlation can be rewritten as

$$\rho_N = \frac{cov(X_N, Y_N)}{\sigma_{X_N}\sigma_{Y_N}} = \frac{[E(xy)]^N - [E(x)E(y)]^N}{\{[E(x^2)]^N - [(Ex)^2]^N[E(y^2)]^N - [(Ey)^2]^N\}^{\frac{1}{2}}}.$$

$$(5.5)$$

To facilitate the mathematical analysis, we define the following variables:

$$A = \frac{E(x^2)}{[E(x)]^2}, \quad B = \frac{E(y^2)}{[E(y)]^2} \quad \text{and} \quad C = \frac{E(xy)}{E(x)E(y)}. \qquad (5.6)$$

Plugging Eq. (5.6) in Eq. (5.5), we obtain

$$\rho_N = \frac{cov(X_N, Y_N)}{\sigma_{X_N}\sigma_{Y_N}} = \frac{C^N - 1}{[(A^N - 1)(B^N - 1)]^{\frac{1}{2}}}.$$

Therefore,

$$\rho_N^2 = \frac{(C^N - 1)^2}{(A^N - 1)(B^N - 1)}.$$

In the next theorem, we claim that the correlation, ρ_N^2, approaches zero (with the exception of one case) as N increases, regardless of the assumed one-period correlation. Theorem 1 was proven by Levy and Schwartz.[2]

Theorem 5.1. *Let ρ_N be the N-period correlation as defined above of two multiplicative random variables that are non-negative and non-constant, and that each variable has a finite variance. Then, as N approaches infinity, we have $\lim \rho_N = 0$, apart from one case where $y = kx$ (for some positive k), a case where the correlation is $+\,1$ for all horizons and the regression line of y on x passes through the origin.*

Proof. First note that by the Schwarz inequality, we have $E(xy) \leq (E(x^2)E(y^2))^{\frac{1}{2}}$, and equality holds only in the case $y = kx$, which

---

[2]Levy, H. and G. Schwarz (1997). Correlation and time interval over which the variables are measured. *Journal of Econometrics* 76(1–2), 341–350.

we rule out.[3] The Schwarz inequality can be also rewritten as

$$\frac{E(xy)}{(E(x))^2(E(y))^2} \leq \frac{(E(x^2)E(y^2))^{1/2}}{(E(x))^2(E(y))^2},$$

which can be rewritten in terms of $A, B,$ and C defined above as

$$C \leq (AB)^{\frac{1}{2}}.$$

We prove the claim given in Theorem 5.1 corresponding to three separate cases, which together cover all possibilities.

(a) *Case a:* $1 < C < (AB)^{\frac{1}{2}}$

In this case, we rewrite the multi-period correlation as

$$\rho_N^2 = \frac{(C^N - 1)^2}{(A^N - 1)(B^N - 1)} = \left(\frac{C^2}{AB}\right)^N \left[\frac{(1 - C^{-N})^2}{(1 - A^{-N})(1 - B^{-N})}\right].$$

First, note that $lim \left(\frac{C^2}{AB}\right)^N = 0$ (see the condition given in a above), and to complete the proof we show that

$$\lim \left[\frac{(1 - C^{-N})^2}{(1 - A^{-N})(1 - B^{-N})}\right] = 1.$$

To see this, recall that by definition $1 < C$; hence, $limC^{-N} = 0$, and the numerator of the above term is equal to 1. The denominator of the above term is also equal to 1 as

$$A^{-N} = \left[\frac{E(x^2)}{[E(x)]^2}\right]^N = \left[\frac{E(x^2)}{E(x^2) + \sigma_X^2}\right]^N, \text{ hence } lim \, A^{-N} = 0.$$

By the same argument, we also have that $limB^{-N} = 0$; therefore,

$$\lim \left[\frac{(1 - C^{-N})^2}{(1 - A^{-N})(1 - B^{-N})}\right] = 1.$$

---

[3]By plugging $y = kx$ in all the above formulas, it is easy to see that the correlation remains equal to 1 for all horizons.

In sum, as $lim = \left(\frac{C^2}{AB}\right)^N = 0$, and the second term approaches 1 as N increases indefinitely, in this specific case (Case a), we have $lim\rho_N = 0$.

Case b: $C = 1$. In this trivial case, $C^{-N} = 1$ for all N; hence $\rho_N = 0$ for all N.

Case c: $C < 1$. In this case, we rewrite the ρ_N^2 coefficient as follows:

$$\rho_N^2 = \left(\frac{1}{AB}\right)^N \left[\frac{(1 - C^{-N})^2}{(1 - A^{-N})(1 - B^{-N})}\right].$$

As before, $lim = \left(\frac{1}{AB}\right)^N = 0$, $lim(1 - C^{-N})^2 = 1$, and $\lim(1 - A^{-N})(1 - B^{-N}) = 0$, we also obtain in this case $lim\rho_N = 0$.

Levy and Schwarz also prove that the decrease in ρ_N^2 is *monotonic* with N, as shown in Figure 5.1. This figure illustrates a hypothetical horizon's effect on the correlation for four hypothetical cases. When the correlation is positive, $\rho_N > 0$, ($+1$ or $+\frac{1}{2}$ in our hypothetical example), ρ_N decreases with the horizon, and when the correlations are negative $\rho_N < 0$ (-1 or $-\frac{1}{2}$ in our example), the multi-period

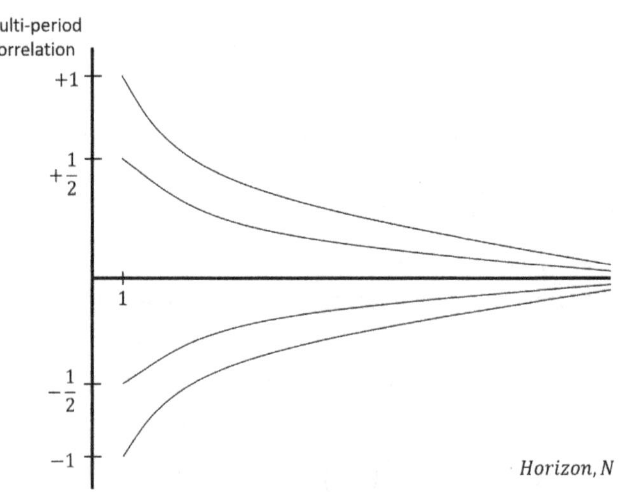

For $\rho_1^2 = 1$, we rule out the case $y = kx$, namely, where the regression line rises from the origin. In this case, $\rho_N = \rho_1 = 1$ for all N.

Figure 5.1: Multi-period correlation for various one-period correlations.

correlations increase with the horizon. We selected $+\frac{1}{2}$ and $-\frac{1}{2}$ correlations for illustration only, but the same pattern is valid for all possible correlations.

Note, however, that if the regression line passes through the origin (the case $y = kx$, as mentioned in Theorem 1), the correlation is unaffected by the horizon and remains $+1$, regardless of the assumed horizon.

Example. Table 5.1 provides a hypothetical case where for the one period, we have only two possible returns on stocks and on bonds. As we have only two points located on a given straight line, the correlation between the two hypothetical variables is obviously $+1$. However, as shown in Figure 5.2, the points are selected in this example such that the straight line does not pass through the origin; hence, the case $y = kx$ does not hold with this example. We have in this example the relationship $y = a + bx$, where in the specific case under consideration, $a < 0$ and $b > 0$.

We turn now to the two-period return distributions on stocks and bonds. Assuming *i.i.d.*, the lower part of Table 5.1 provides the two-period probability distributions. For example, assuming independence over time, we obtain twice a return (namely a $1 + \text{rate}$ of return) of 0.90 on stocks with a probability of $0.5 \times 0.5 = 0.25$; hence the obtained two-period return is 0.81 with probability of 0.25. Similarly, on bonds, we obtain twice the return of 0.98 with

Table 5.1: One- and two-period hypothetical returns on stocks and bonds.

Stocks	Bonds	Probability
(a) One period		
0.9	0.98	0.5
1.2	1.1	0.5
(b) Two period		
0.81	0.9604	0.25
1.08	1.078	0.5
1.44	1.21	0.25

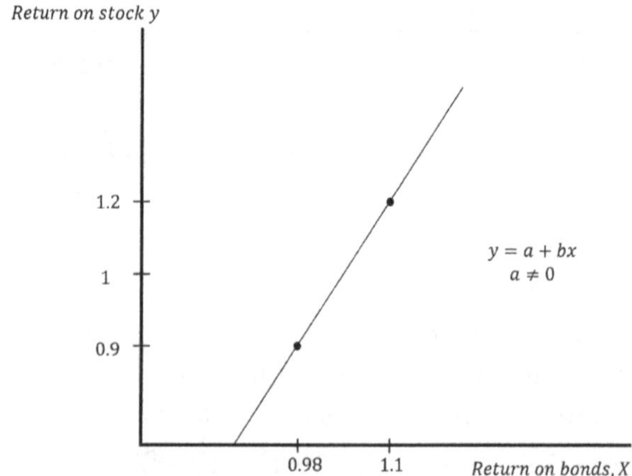

Figure 5.2: The one-period hypothetical returns on stocks and bonds.

probability of 0.25; hence, at the end of the second period return, we get $.98 \times .98 = .9604$ with a probability of .25. In a similar way, we calculate the detailed two-period distributions of returns on stocks and bonds. We find that for the two-period returns, the correlation slightly decreases from $+1$ for $N = 1$ to .996455 for $N = 2$. However, recall that the purpose of this example is to show that the correlation does not remain $+1$ as the horizon increases even with *i.i.d.*, rather than to investigate the magnitude of the decrease in the correlation. Moreover, when we further increase the horizon, the correlation corresponding to this example continues to decrease monotonically: the longer the horizon, the smaller the multi-period correlation, despite the fact that for $N = 1$, the correlation is $+1$.

In the above example, we have seen that the correlation is only slightly reduced as the horizon increases from $N = 1$ to $N = 2$. Thus, despite the theorem's claim, it is possible that, in practice, the reduction in the correlation with the horizon does not substantially affect the optimal M–V investment choices, particularly when the horizon only slightly increases. Obviously, the magnitude of the horizon's effect on the optimal M–V diversification is an empirical question, and depends not only on the correlation, but also on changes in the expected return and variance of each asset under consideration with the horizon, as well as with the changes in the pair-wise correlations with the horizon. Moreover, recall that one of the inputs employed in the derivation of the optimal M–V portfolio is $\sigma_{ij} = \rho_{ij}\sigma_i\sigma_j$ (see what follows). Therefore, we need to consider apart from the changes in the correlations, ρ_{ij}, with the horizon, also the changes in the standard deviations, which increase with the horizon. Yet, recall that for, say, a positive one-period correlation, the term $\rho_{ij}\sigma_i\sigma_j$ would increase for $\rho_{ij} > 0$ faster (or decrease slower with $\rho_{ij} < 0$) with the horizon if the correlation did not change with the horizon.

The most interesting issue is how the pairwise correlation changes with the horizon with relevant investment in the capital market rather than with hypothetical examples. To investigate empirically this issue, we employ the first and the 10th deciles of stocks taken from French's website.[4] The first decile (Decile 1) contains the smallest 10% of all stocks as measured by their market value, and the 10th (Decile 10) contains the 10% of largest firms, once again, measured by their market value.

The procedure for finding the correlations corresponding to various horizons is as follows: for $N = 1$ year, we simply draw at random 100,000 observations (with replacement) from the two deciles under consideration and calculate the correlation. Note that we draw both return observations of Decile 1 and of Decile 10 simultaneously; hence, each pair corresponds to the same year. For $N = 2$ years, we draw two years at random, calculate the compounded return corresponding to the two deciles, and repeat this procedure 100,000 times. Having these 100,000 pairs of observations, we calculate the correlation for these two series of observations. This procedure implicitly assumes *i.i.d.*, but the results may deviate somewhat from the theoretical results expected by the *i.i.d.* assumption as long as the number of repetitions is finite. Of course, the larger the number of observations drawn from the historical distribution, the closer the result is to what is expected under the *i.i.d.* assumption.

---

[4]https://mba.tuck.dartmouth.edu/pages/faculty/ken.french/data_library.html

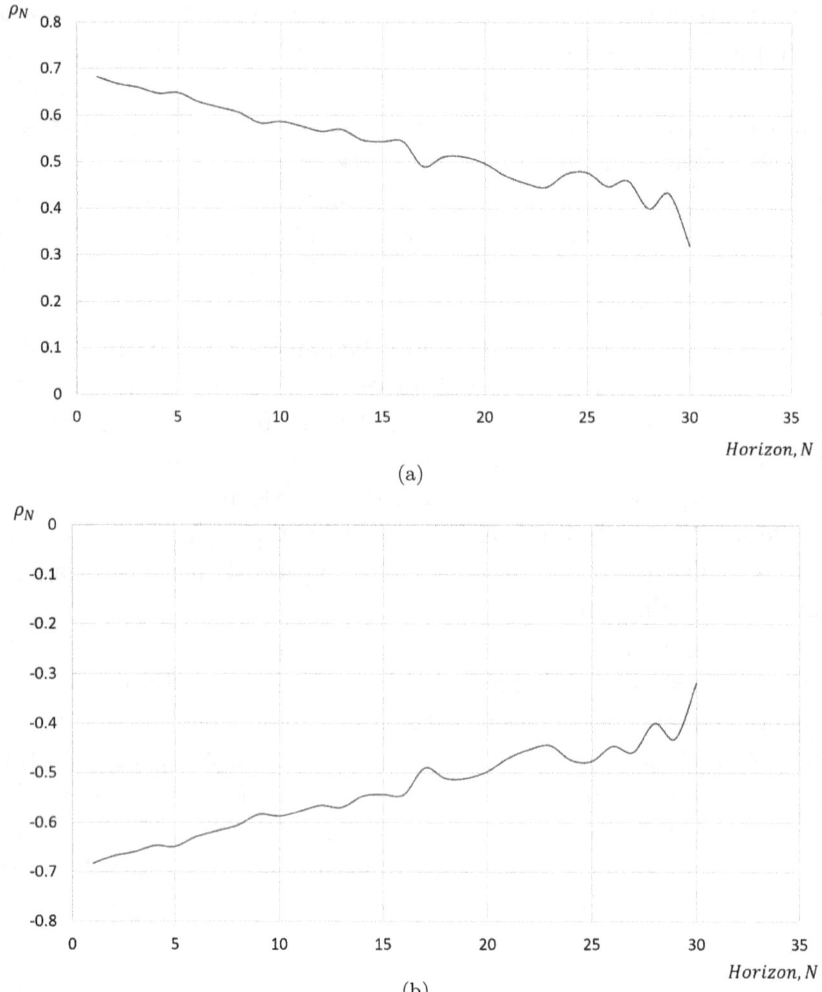

Figure 5.3: The multi-period correlations between Decile 1 (small stocks) and Decile 10 (large stocks): (a) Long position in both deciles; (b) Short position in Decile 10 and long position in Decile 1.

Figure 5.3 presents the results. In Figure 5.3(a), it is assumed that one holds a long position in both stock deciles. In Figure 5.3(b), it is assumed that one stock decile (say, Decile 10) is held in a short position, and the other decile (Decile 1) is held in a long position.

As we can see from Figure 5.3(a), the multi-period positive correlations decrease with the horizon with these two specific assets from 0.68211 for $N = 1$ year to 0.319034 for a horizon of $N = 30$ years. Thus, considering solely the correlation, those who invest for one year may have a different optimal diversification than those who save for retirement, that is, $N = 30$ years. Obviously, the correlation horizon's effect on optimal diversification is more complex where we consider the effect of the other parameters on the optimal M–V diversification, and certainly when more than two assets are considered. We will elaborate later in this chapter on the joint effect of all relevant parameters on changes in the optimal M–V diversification with the horizon.

Figure 5.3(b) is a mirror image of Figure 5.3(a). Here, one stock decile is held in a short position; therefore, the correlations are negative, increasing with the horizon from $-.68211$ for $N = 1$ year to $-.319034$ for $N = 30$ years. Thus, the negative correlation's effect on diversification diminishes with the horizon.

Figure 5.4 is similar to Figure 5.3(b), with the exception that it reports the changes in the correlations with two assets that are both

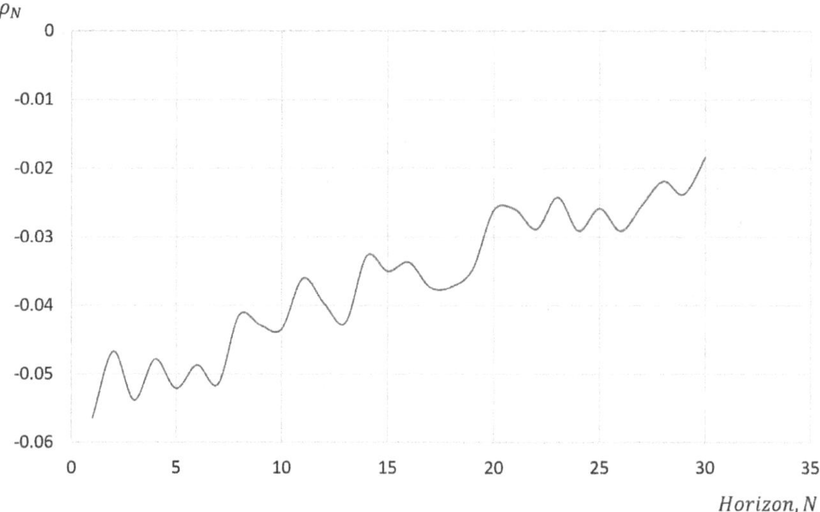

Figure 5.4: The multi-period correlation between the return on Decile 1 (small stocks) and Treasury bills.

held in a long position, where for the one-period, the correlation is negative. Based on the same source of data and the same procedure, we calculate the correlation between the interest on Treasury bills and the return on stocks. With this data, the correlation increases from -0.05646 for $N = 1$ year to $-.01846$ for a horizon of $N = 30$ years. Note that the changes here are very small, as the one-period correlation is relatively small, but the direction of the changes conforms with what is claimed in Theorem 1.

Thus, the example given above, as well as Figures 5.3 and 5.4, conform empirically with the theoretical claim given in Theorem 1: the negative correlations, as well as the positive correlations, tend to zero from both sides as the horizon increases. Note, however, that in both Figures 5.3 and 5.4, we do not have monotonicity, but this would certainly be obtained were we to precisely mimic the *i.i.d.* assumption, namely to increase the number of observations indefinitely. Any deviations from monotonicity are due to the fact that the number of observations in the simulation are finite.

5.2. The Optimal M–V Diversification and the Horizon

In Section 5.1, we discussed how the correlations change with the horizon. However, to analyze how the optimal M–V portfolio changes with the horizon, we also need as inputs the multi-period means and variances of all assets under consideration. In order to find the M–V frontier, for various horizons with the constraint of no short selling, we solve the following system:

$$\text{Minimize } \boldsymbol{X}' \sum \boldsymbol{X}$$

Subject to:

(a) $x_i \geq 0 \quad i = 1, 2, \ldots, n$

(b) $\boldsymbol{X}'\boldsymbol{u} = \mu_p$

(c) $\boldsymbol{X}'\boldsymbol{1} = 1$

where with the bold figures, we have the following notation: $\boldsymbol{X}'$ stands for the vector of the investment proportions, $\boldsymbol{u}$ stands for the vector of the means of the n assets under consideration, and 1 stands for the unit vector. The other variables are: Σ is the variance–covariance matrix, and μ_p is the predetermined mean return on the portfolio for which one wishes to minimize the variance. Thus, the frontier contains all portfolios with a minimum variance for a given mean. Of course, for each horizon, we plug in the formula the relevant multi-period parameters. If one wishes to derive the M–V efficient frontier with short sells, simply eliminate Constraint (a) given in the maximization procedure. In the formula, we do not consider the riskless asset; hence, the obtained result is the known M–V curve or the M–V frontier. However, when we also consider borrowing and lending at the riskless interest rate, the obtained efficient frontier is a straight line (see the elaboration that follows).

Incorporating some of the constraint into one formula, and also considering the horizon effect on the M–V efficient frontier, the vector-matrix formula can be rewritten in a more transparent way as follows:

$$
C_N = \left[\sum_{i=1}^{n} x_i^2 \sigma_i^2 + 2 \sum_{i=1}^{n} \sum_{j=1,j>i}^{n} x_i x_j \sigma_{ij} \right.
$$
$$
\left. + \lambda_1 \left(1 - \sum_{i=1}^{n} x_i \right) + \lambda_2 \left(\mu_p - \sum_{i=1}^{n} x_i \mu_i \right) \right]_N
$$
$$
\text{Subject to } x_i \geq 0 \quad \text{for all } i. \tag{5.7}
$$

With this formulation, we emphasize the assumed investment horizon, where the subscript N indicates that all parameters, and the function C_N, correspond to the N-period horizon. For example, if $N = 10$ years, it implies that σ_i^2 appearing in Eq. (5.7) is the variance of the ith asset corresponding to a 10-year investment horizon.

In Eq. (5.7), we have the following variables:

x_i is the investment weight in asset i, which can be zero or positive.

n is the number of risky assets under consideration.

σ_i^2 is the variance of the return on the ith asset.

σ_{ij} is the covariance of the returns on asset i and asset j.

μ_i is the mean return on asset i.

μ_p is the selected portfolio mean return.

λ_1 and λ_2 are Lagrange multipliers.

N is the assumed investment horizon.

To investigate empirically the horizon's effect on the M–V frontier, we employ Eq. (5.7), where the inputs are the parameters corresponding to the N-period horizon. Specifically, for each asset i ($i = 1, 2, \ldots, n$), we have the following N-period parameters:

N-period variance:

$$\sigma_N^2 = [\sigma^2 + (1 + \mu)^2]^N - (1 + \mu)^{2N}$$

where μ stands for the one-period mean, and σ^2 stands for the one-period variance (see Chapter 3).

The N-period mean return:

$(1 + \mu)^N$ where μ, as before, is the one-period mean.

The N-period covariance:

$$\sigma_{ij\,(N)} = \rho_N \sigma_{iN} \sigma_{jN}$$

where ρ_N is given by Eq. (5.5), and the individual asset standard deviation is simply the square root of the N-period variance given above.

As N stands for the assumed horizon, for each N we plug into Eq. (5.7) the appropriate N-period variances, means, and correlations, as given above. Thus, for each horizon, we can minimize the portfolio's variance and solve for the M–V frontier. However, as in the empirical investigation, we also consider the riskless asset, we turn to Eq. (5.8), which considers possible lending and borrowing at the riskless interest rate. When the riskless asset is also an available function given by Eq. (5.7), it becomes

$$C_N = \sum_{i=1}^{n} x_i^2 \sigma_i^2 + 2 \sum_{i=1}^{n} \sum_{j=1, j>i}^{n} x_i x_j \sigma_{ij}$$

$$+ \lambda \left[\mu_p - \sum_{i=1}^{n} x_i \mu_i - \left(1 - \sum_{i=1}^{n} x_i \right) r \right]_N$$

Subject to $x_i \geq 0$ for all i. (5.8)

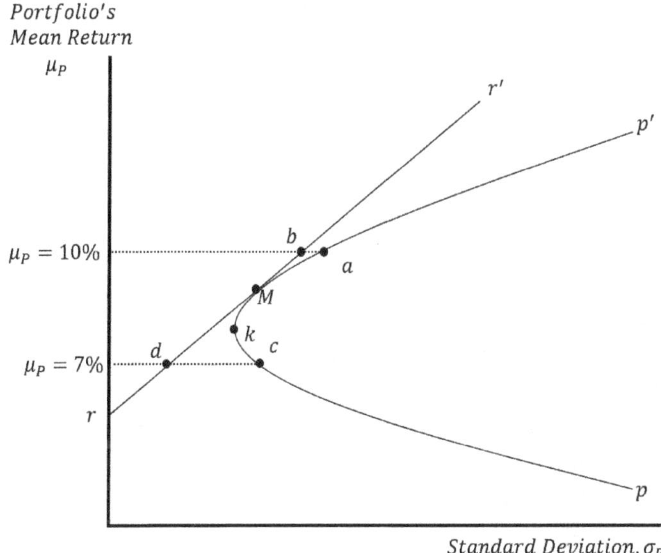

Figure 5.5: The efficient frontier.

With this formulation, λ is a Lagrange multiplier, and r is $1 +$ the interest rate. If one wishes to avoid short selling, the constraint $x_i \geq 0$ for all assets i is added to Eq. (5.8). We employ Eq. (5.8) both with and without the no short selling constraint to derive all portfolios given on line rr' shown in Figure 5.5.

Thus, Eq. (5.7) is employed to solve for the M–V frontier (see curve pMp' in Figure 5.5) and Eq. (5.8) is employed to solve for all the efficient M–V portfolios where the riskless lending and borrowing is available, namely finding all efficient portfolios that are located on line rr'. By Eq. (5.8), we also solve for the optimal portfolio of risky assets, known as the *market portfolio* (see point M in Figure 5.5). Let us elaborate on the optimal M–V portfolio selection by focusing on Eq. (5.8).

Deriving C_N with respect to x_i for $i = 1, 2, \ldots, N$ and with respect to λ, and equating each equation to zero, we have $n + 1$ equations with $n + 1$ unknowns; hence, the system is generally solvable. Thus, we find the investment weights that minimize the portfolio's variance for a given mean return on the selected portfolio. Note that taking the derivative with respect to λ and equating the derived equation to zero implies that

$$\frac{\partial C_N}{\partial \lambda} = \mu_p - \sum_{i=1}^{n} x_i \mu_i - \left(1 - \sum_{i=1}^{n} x_i\right) r = 0 \Rightarrow$$

$$\mu_p = \sum_{i=1}^{n} x_i \mu_i + \left(1 - \sum_{i=1}^{n} x_i\right) r.$$

Thus, this optimization procedure provides the investment weights which minimize the portfolio variance (risk) for a given mean rate of return μ_p, which is predetermined. Figure 5.5 graphically illustrates this optimization procedure. Suppose that an investor wishes to minimize the portfolio's variance for a given mean return of, say, 10%. Then, if the riskless asset is not available, the optimal portfolio for this specific investor is given by portfolio a (see Figure 5.5). If the riskless asset is available, the investor's welfare increases as they can shift to Portfolio b, yielding the same mean rate of return of 10%, but with lower risk. Consider another investor who prefers to take less risk; hence, as there is no free lunch, they must have a predetermined mean rate of return on the selected portfolio of less than 10%, say of 7%. In this case, the risk is also reduced, and they obtain in this case Portfolio c with no riskless asset and Portfolio d with the riskless asset. Finally, Portfolio M is the optimal portfolio composed of *only risky assets*, called the market portfolio. All M–V investors mix this market portfolio with the riskless assets by shifting on the straight line rr'.

If one minimizes the portfolio variance by deriving Eq. (5.7), the frontier pMp' is obtained. Only the segment kp' of this frontier is M–V efficient, where k stands for the minimum variance portfolio. If one takes the derivatives of Eq. (5.8), the obtained results are all efficient M–V portfolios that are located on the line rMr'. Each point on pMp' yields a vector of optimal investment in the n available risky assets, and each point on line rr' yields optimum M–V investment weights in $n + 1$ assets, the n risky assets, and the riskless asset. If, in addition, one also adds in the minimization of the variance the constraint $x_i \geq 0$, we obtain optimal portfolios with no short selling.

5.3. Asset Allocation and the Horizon in the M–V Framework: The Empirical Evidence

In this section, we investigate the changes in asset allocation with the horizon as implied by the M–V rule, which may be a non-optimal investment rule for relatively long investment horizons, and may mislead investors who mistakenly rely on this rule. In other words, generally, there are portfolios with larger expected utility than the optimal M–V portfolio; hence, one can increase the expected utility by shifting from the optimal M–V portfolio to another portfolio, which may be even inferior to the M–V frontier. Thus, we technically analyze the M–V optimal diversification for various horizons, and no economic recommendation is attached to these technical results, particularly for relatively long investment horizons.

We investigate empirically the horizon's effect on the M–V recommended diversification with two alternative datasets. One dataset includes the S&P 500 stock index and 10-year Treasury bonds covering the period 1928–2019, and the other dataset includes 10 stock portfolios constructed by their market values, covering the period of July 1926–October 2020. Thus, we have 10 deciles of stocks ranked by their size (which also are generally ranked by their risk) taken from French's website.

5.3.1. *The stock–bond M–V optimal allocation and the horizon with i.i.d. assumption*

We first employ the annual rates of returns on the S&P 500 stock index and the 10-year Treasury bills for the period 1928–2019.[5] We draw 100,000 observations corresponding to various assumed investment horizons; thus, *i.i.d.* is implicitly assumed. Figure 5.6 provides the efficient frontiers (with no short selling) corresponding to six selected horizons from $N = 1$ year to $N = 30$ years. The annual selected risk-free interest rate is about 3.379%, which is the actual average interest rate on short-term Treasury bills prevailing during the covered period. Indeed, for $N = 1$ year, the line rr' intersects

---

[5]http://www.stern.nyu.edu/~adamodar/pc/datasets/histretSP.xls

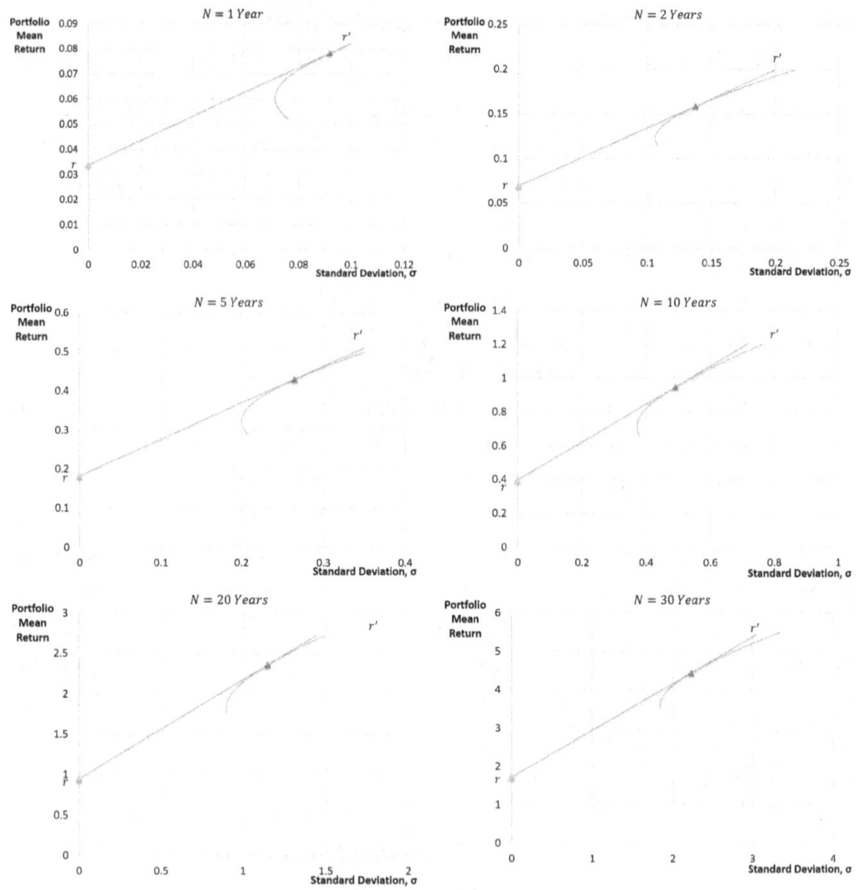

Figure 5.6: The efficient frontier for various horizons.

the vertical axis at this point. For the $N = 30$ years horizon, line rr' intersects the vertical axis at

$$(1 + .033779)^{30} - 1 \cong 1.71 \text{ (see Figure 5.6).}$$

Looking at Figure 5.6, the effect of the assumed investment horizon on the M–V efficient frontier is not transparent, as each figure has a different scale. In Figure 5.7, we focus only on two horizons: $N = 1$ and $N = 5$. Both efficient frontiers are depicted in this figure with the same scale, allowing us to see the horizon's effect on the

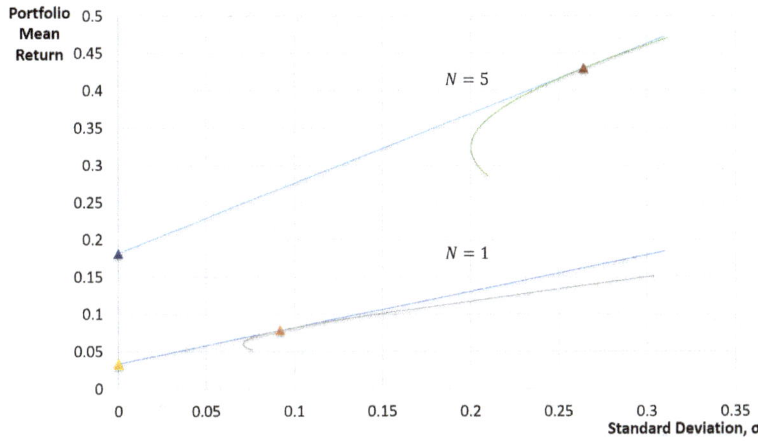

Figure 5.7: The efficient frontier for $N = 1$ and $N = 5$ years.

location of the M–V frontier. As we can see, increasing the horizon from one year to five years induces a dramatic change in the location of the M–V frontier. The M–V frontier shifts upward and to the right with the horizon. While increasing the horizon, the means and the variances of the rates of returns increase, the variances increase at a faster rate than the mean, hence the dramatic shift in the frontier to the right with the horizon. This phenomenon is typical to all cases where the investment horizon increases.

Table 5.2 provides the optimal stock–bond M–V parameters, as well as the optimal investment weights corresponding to the tangency portfolio (TP) for various horizons. The table also provides the weights corresponding to the minimum variance portfolio. As can be seen from Table 5.2(a), as expected, the mean return and standard deviation on stocks are substantially larger than these parameters for bonds. The correlations between stocks and bonds are very close to zero for all horizons appearing in Table 5.2(a).[6]

---

[6]Note that we do not have a monotonic increase in the negative correlation as predicted by Theorem 1, a phenomenon which can be explained by the finite sample size employed in the simulation. In other words, we do not have a perfect *i.i.d.*

Table 5.2: The stock–bond M–V portfolios: parameters and investment weights.

(a) The annual parameters of rates of returns on stocks (S&P 500 stock index) and 10-year Treasury bonds (1928–2019)

Horizon	Risk-Free Rate	Mean SP500	SD SP500	Mean Bonds	SD Bonds	Correlation
1 Year	0.034	0.117	0.196	0.052	0.077	−0.013
2 Years	0.069	0.242	0.310	0.106	0.113	−0.015
5 Years	0.182	0.731	0.695	0.285	0.210	−0.013
10 Years	0.397	1.987	1.779	0.649	0.383	−0.017
20 Years	0.950	7.933	8.057	1.726	0.906	−0.016
30 Years	1.725	26.618	32.103	3.495	1.847	−0.011

(b) The M–V investment weights in stocks and bonds corresponding to the minimum variance portfolio (MVP) and the optimal tangency portfolio (TP)

Horizon	Weight of SP500 in TP	Weight of SP500 in MVP Portfolio	Mean of the MVP Portfolio	SD of the MVP Portfolio
1 Year	0.413	0.136	0.060	0.071
2 Years	0.385	0.122	0.122	0.106
5 Years	0.324	0.087	0.324	0.200
10 Years	0.224	0.047	0.713	0.373
20 Years	0.102	0.014	1.814	0.899
30 Years	0.043	0.004	3.581	1.843

Table 5.2(b) provides the optimal M–V investment weights in the minimum variance portfolio (MVP) and in the investment weights of the optimal portfolio of risky assets given by the TP. For $N = 1$ year, the optimal TP contains about 41% stocks and 59% bonds. The weight allocated to stocks monotonically decreases with the horizon, reaching only about 4% for the $N = 30$ years' horizon. The MVP reveals similar results: stock weight decreases from about 14% in stocks for the $N = 1$-year horizon, becoming closer to zero for the $N = 30$-year horizon.

Based solely on the M–V rule, we find that stocks become less attractive than bonds with the horizon as their proportion in the optimal portfolio decreases with the horizon. Thus, the M–V results seemingly contradict the assertion of "stocks for the long run."

Do stocks really become less attractive than bonds with the horizon, or are the M–V results merely technical with no economic meaning? What is the explanation of the contradiction between the obtained M–V results and the "stocks for the long run" common investment strategy? Clarifying this issue is important as the M–V results are also in contradiction to the popular life cycle mutual funds investment strategy, as these funds invest a relatively large proportion of their assets in stocks for long horizons and less for short horizons (for a detailed discussion of the life cycle funds, see Chapter 1).

We next show that the M–V results have very few economic consequences, and do not necessarily contradict the "stocks for the long run" investment strategy. The reason is that for the long run, the investment in stocks becomes very positively skewed, a desired property by risk-averse expected utility maximizers — a property which the M–V rule ignores. Thus, it is possible that stocks become more attractive in the long run despite the unfavorable reported M–V results. Finally, recall that in Chapter 2 we have seen that for relatively short horizons (generally less than one year), it is reasonable to employ the M–V rule, but this rule loses ground for longer horizons as the elliptical distribution (let alone the normal distribution) does not fit the empirical distributions of returns for relatively long horizons. Thus, the M–V results for relatively long horizons have no economic merit. Therefore, employing the M–V rule for such horizons may induce economic distortions.

Nevertheless, one may suspect that the *i.i.d.* assumption in deriving the M–V optimal portfolio for the long run is the source for the above-mentioned contradiction. As we shall see next, similar results are obtained even when one relaxes the *i.i.d.* assumption. Thus, we rule out the *i.i.d.* assumption as the source for the difference between the M–V results and the "stocks for the long run" assertion.

5.3.2. *The stock–bond optimal M–V asset allocation where autocorrelations are considered*

According to the simulation technique explained previously, we have 100,000 observations where the returns of each asset are approximately *i.i.d.* In practice, we may have autocorrelations of returns over time; hence, in practice, the investor may face different results regarding the optimal stock–bond asset allocation when autocorrelations are considered. From Figure 5.8, we see that the M–V optimal portfolio allocations do not hinge on the *i.i.d.* assumption. Figure 5.8 provides the stock–bond efficient frontier for the $N = 5$ years' horizon, once where, as before, *i.i.d.* is assumed (with 100,000 observations), and once where possible empirical autocorrelations are considered. Specifically, with possible autocorrelations, the first observation is the compounded return for the first five years, namely the years 1928–1932, the second observation is the compounded return for the years 1933–1937, and so forth. Thus, if there is an autocorrelation effect (over a 5-year interval) on the M–V optimal diversification, this autocorrelation may affect the optimal M–V diversification. However, recall that with this method, we have only a limited number of observations — even where a full century is

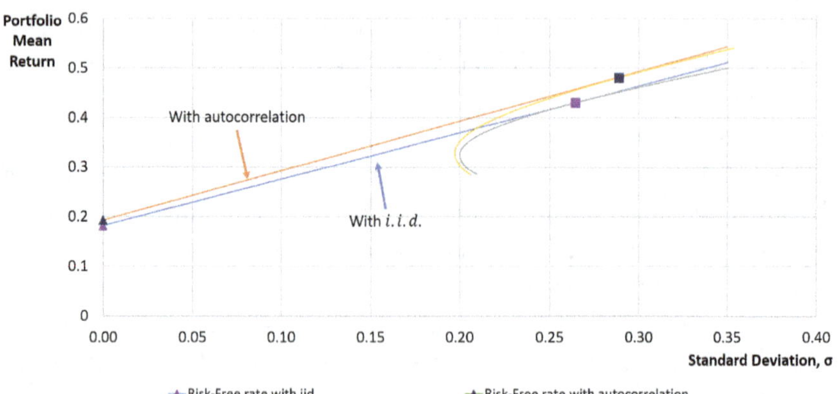

Figure 5.8: The efficient frontier for $N = 5$ years with *i.i.d.* and alternatively with autocorrelation.

covered, we have only 20 observations. Thus, statistical errors with such a number of observations may occur.

Figure 5.8 presents side by side the two efficient frontiers: with *i.i.d.* and with autocorrelations corresponding to the $N = 5$ years' horizon. As we can see from this figure, relaxing the *i.i.d.* assumption only slightly affects the efficient frontier.

The results appearing in Table 5.3 are even more relevant for measuring the *i.i.d.* assumption's effect on the optimal M–V portfolios. First, note that the MVP is almost identical with and without the *i.i.d.* assumption: the investment weight in stocks with *i.i.d.* is about 8.6% (that is, about 91.4% is allocated to bonds), while with *i.i.d.*, the optimal weight in stocks is about 10.6% (hence, 89.4% is allocated to bonds). When we shift to the TP, a larger gap is revealed: with the *i.i.d.* assumption, about 32% is allocated to stocks, and with possible autocorrelation, this optimal weight increases to about 48%. Thus, incorporating autocorrelations somewhat closes the gap between the optimal M–V rule and the "stocks for the long run" investment strategy. Yet, recall that with the relaxation of the *i.i.d.* assumption, we have very few observations. Hence, the increase

Table 5.3: The investment weights in stocks and bonds in the MVP and the TP with *i.i.d.* and with autocorrelation for $N = 5$ year horizon.

(a) The MVP

	MVP–SP500 Weight	SD of the MVP	Mean Return MVP
With *i.i.d.*	0.087	0.200	0.324
With Autocorrelation	0.106	0.197	0.327

(b) The TP

	TP–SP500 Weight	SD of the TP	Mean Return TP
With *i.i.d.*	0.324	0.264	0.429
With Autocorrelation	0.480	0.289	0.480

in the weight invested in stocks from 32% to 48% might vanish with more observations.

Are the M–V results intact only with stocks and bonds or are the results typical to all assets with different risk characteristics? We address this issue in the following section.

5.4. Optimal M–V Diversification with 10 Portfolios of Risky Assets

So far, we compared portfolios composed of stocks and bonds revealing that as the horizon increases, the optimal portfolio contains a larger proportion of bonds, which is counterintuitive and contradicts the "stocks for the long run" common view. To see whether this is a typical characteristic of the M–V horizon's effect, we now examine the portfolio composition of 10 deciles of risky stocks, as provided by French's website (see footnote 4). Decile 1 includes 10% of the smallest market value, and Decile 10 includes the largest 10% of stocks. Generally, as we shift from Decile 1 toward Decile 10, both the variance and the mean rate of return decrease. Thus, if indeed there is a trend by the M–V rule to take less risk with the horizon, we expect to find an increase in the weight allocated to Decile 10, the safer stocks, with the horizon.

Figure 5.9 provides the M–V efficient frontier of portfolios composed of 10 deciles of stocks for various horizons. As we can see from this figure, there is not much curvature in any of these frontiers. This relatively little curvature of the frontiers stems from the characteristics of the data under consideration; the correlations of the returns on the 10 deciles of stocks are all positive and relatively large, inducing the relatively low curvature in the efficient frontiers. Moreover, the frontiers are derived with no short selling constraint, which also induces a decrease in the curvature of the frontiers.

Indeed, Table 5.4 reveals relatively large correlations between the returns on the various stock deciles, which at least partially explains why the M–V frontiers have relatively little curvature, inducing in several cases 100% optimal M–V investment in the large stocks.

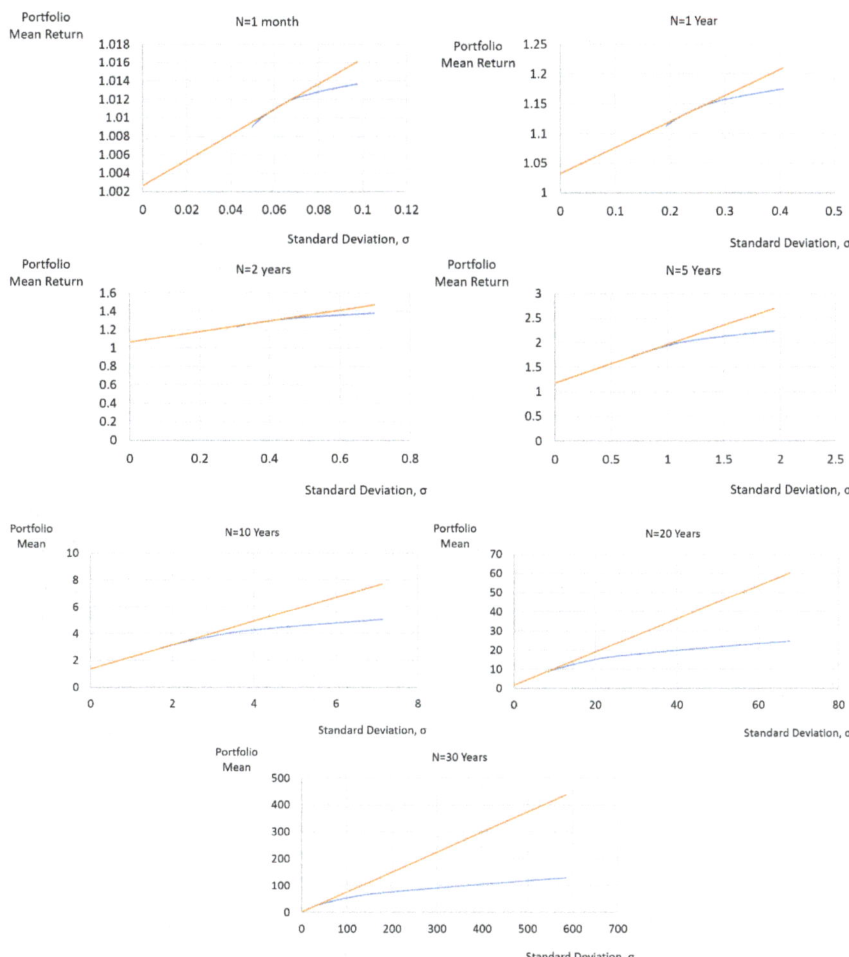

Figure 5.9: Efficient frontiers of the 10 deciles of stocks.

Table 5.5 reports the optimal M–V investment weights in the 10 deciles to the MVP, as well as the optimal investment weights in the optimal portfolio, the TP, where short selling is not allowed. Quite surprisingly, the MVP is a specialized portfolio where 100% is invested in Decile 10, the decile of the 10% largest stocks. This decile is a relatively low-risk, low-return decile relative to the others. Note that the derivation of the figures appearing in Table 5.5 is conducted

Table 5.4: The correlation matrix for the 10 deciles for the horizon of $N = 1$ year.

D1	D2	D3	D4	D5	D6	D7	D8	D9	D10	RF
1.000	0.953	0.924	0.903	0.874	0.851	0.835	0.796	0.773	0.685	−0.052
0.953	1.000	0.973	0.962	0.946	0.925	0.911	0.880	0.855	0.775	−0.042
0.923	0.973	1.000	0.981	0.971	0.959	0.944	0.925	0.900	0.822	−0.035
0.903	0.962	0.981	1.000	0.979	0.971	0.958	0.938	0.915	0.836	−0.032
0.874	0.946	0.971	0.979	1.000	0.980	0.971	0.959	0.940	0.871	−0.026
0.851	0.925	0.959	0.971	0.980	1.000	0.977	0.971	0.958	0.893	−0.035
0.835	0.911	0.944	0.958	0.971	0.977	1.000	0.977	0.965	0.908	−0.024
0.796	0.880	0.925	0.938	0.959	0.971	0.977	1.000	0.977	0.927	−0.0251
0.773	0.855	0.900	0.915	0.940	0.958	0.965	0.977	1.000	0.949	−0.017
0.685	0.775	0.822	0.836	0.871	0.893	0.908	0.927	0.949	1.000	−0.011
−0.052	−0.042	−0.035	−0.032	−0.026	−0.035	−0.024	−0.025	−0.017	−0.011	1.000

Note: D_i: the ith decile, $i = 1, 2, \ldots, 10$.

with no short selling constraint. Nevertheless, as we shall see in what follows, with short selling, the preference for Decile 10 even increases.

Shifting to the optimal TP, there is some diversification, but, once again, there is a tendency to increase the allocation to large stocks with the horizon. While this investment weight in large stocks is only about 6.5% for a one-month horizon, it grows monotonically with the horizon, and for a horizon of 20 years or more, it is 100%.

Figure 5.10 reveals the M–V efficient frontier with short selling with the 10 deciles of stocks for a horizon of $N = 10$ years. As can be seen from this figure and the table attached to it, the MVP contains a 155% investment in Decile 10, that is, the funds obtained from short selling other deciles are used mainly for investing in Decile 10. With the optimal TP, the investment weight in Decile 10 is about 94%.

In sum, the M–V rule reveals that the longer the horizon, more should be invested in the less risky asset, namely in bonds in the stock–bond portfolio, and in Decile 10 in the 10 decile portfolios. Thus, by the M–V rule, it is recommended to decrease the stock weight in the stock–bond portfolio or to decrease the riskier decile (Decile 1) of stocks (in the 10 decile portfolios) with the horizon. This investment strategy is clearly in contradiction to the "stocks for the long run" investment strategy. We will explain these contradictory results in the next section.

Table 5.5: The M–V portfolio composition for various horizons.

Horizon	d1 weight	d2 weight	d3 weight	d4 weight	d5 weight	d6 weight	d7 weight	d8 weight	d9 weight	d10 weight	Portfolio Mean	Portfolio SD
(a) The *MVP*												
1-Month MV	0.000	0.000	0.000	0.000	0.000	0.000	0.000	0.000	0.000	1.000	1.009	0.050
1-Year MV	0.000	0.000	0.000	0.000	0.000	0.000	0.000	0.000	0.000	1.000	1.112	0.193
2-Year MV	0.000	0.000	0.000	0.000	0.000	0.000	0.000	0.000	0.000	1.000	1.237	0.307
5-Year MV	0.000	0.000	0.000	0.000	0.000	0.000	0.000	0.000	0.000	1.000	1.705	0.681
10-Year MV	0.000	0.000	0.000	0.000	0.000	0.000	0.000	0.000	0.000	1.000	2.911	1.719
20-Year MV	0.000	0.000	0.000	0.000	0.000	0.000	0.000	0.000	0.000	1.000	8.390	7.517
30-Year MV	0.000	0.000	0.000	0.000	0.000	0.000	0.000	0.000	0.000	1.000	24.501	29.331
(b) The optimal *TP*												
1-Month Tangency	0.000	0.000	0.000	0.000	0.000	0.671	0.000	0.264	0.000	0.065	1.011	0.063
1-Year Tangency	0.000	0.000	0.000	0.000	0.000	0.493	0.000	0.254	0.000	0.253	1.137	0.237
2-Year Tangency	0.000	0.000	0.000	0.000	0.000	0.338	0.000	0.272	0.000	0.390	1.279	0.367
5-Year Tangency	0.000	0.000	0.000	0.000	0.000	0.088	0.000	0.249	0.000	0.663	1.778	0.764
10-Year Tangency	0.000	0.000	0.000	0.000	0.000	0.000	0.000	0.068	0.000	0.932	2.958	1.770
20-Year Tangency	0.000	0.000	0.000	0.000	0.000	0.000	0.000	0.000	0.000	1.000	8.390	7.517
30-Year Tangency	0.000	0.000	0.000	0.000	0.000	0.000	0.000	0.000	0.000	1.000	24.501	29.331

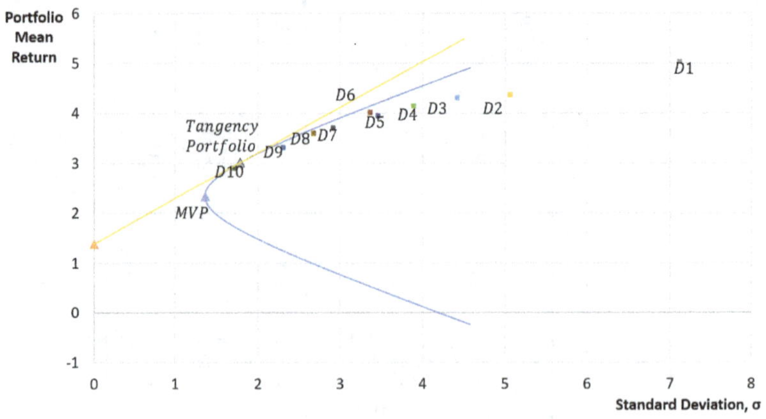

The investment weights in the minimum variance portfolio.

D1	D2	D3	D4	D5	D6	D7	D8	D9	D10	Return	SD
0.0134	−0.016	−0.111	0.257	0.0258	−0.543	−0.095	−0.218	0.137	1.550	2.336	1.365

The investment weights in the tangency portfolio.

D1	D2	D3	D4	D5	D6	D7	D8	D9	D10	Return	SD
0.101	−0.232	−0.203	0.213	−0.049	0.168	0.044	0.245	-0.227	0.940	3.014	1.785

Figure 5.10: The efficient frontier of the 10 deciles for $N = 10$ with short sales.

5.5. Contrasting the M–V and Expected Utility Results for Various Horizons

Which approach provides the correct results from an economic point of view? Should one increase or decrease the weight of the risky assets with the horizon? To examine this issue empirically, we employ two datasets. The first set includes the 10 deciles of stocks, where Decile 1 contains the "small stocks" which are the riskiest (and on average more profitable than the other deciles), and Decile 10 contains the "large stocks" which are characterized by a relatively low risk–low expected return profile. The other set of data includes the S&P 500 stock index and the 10-year Treasury bonds.

We first employ the decile data to calculate the expected utility of "small stocks" and "large stocks," and then we employ the stock–bond data to calculate the expected utility of stocks (the S&P 500 index) and bonds (10-year Treasury bonds) for various utility functions and for various risk-aversion parameters. With the expected utility analysis, we show that, in contrast to the M–V analysis, stocks are superior to bonds, and "small stocks" are superior to "large stocks," particularly for relatively long investment horizons. Next, we also consider diversified portfolios, analyzing the optimal investment weights in stocks and bonds as a function of the employed utility function, degree of risk aversion, and the investment horizon. This procedure allows us to compare M–V diversified portfolios with expected utility diversified portfolios.

To better understand the relative attractiveness of assets with different risk profiles for relatively long horizons, we first draw the density and cumulative distribution functions of "small stocks" and "large stocks." Figure 5.11 reveals that the density functions of the returns on the two deciles of stocks under consideration are not normal, and they actually are positively skewed, which casts doubt on the economic validity of the M–V results which assume a symmetrical distribution (more precisely elliptical distributions), a property which does not hold for relatively long horizons. Figure 5.12 provides the cumulative distributions of the returns corresponding to Decile 1

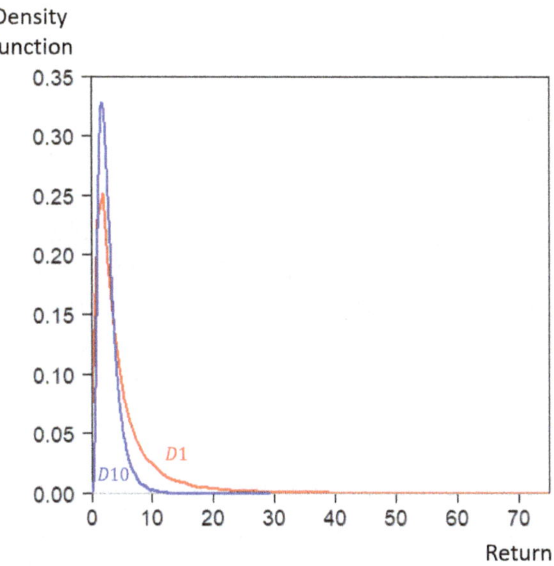

Figure 5.11: The density function of the return on Decile 1 and Decile 10 of stocks for the horizon of $N = 10$ years.

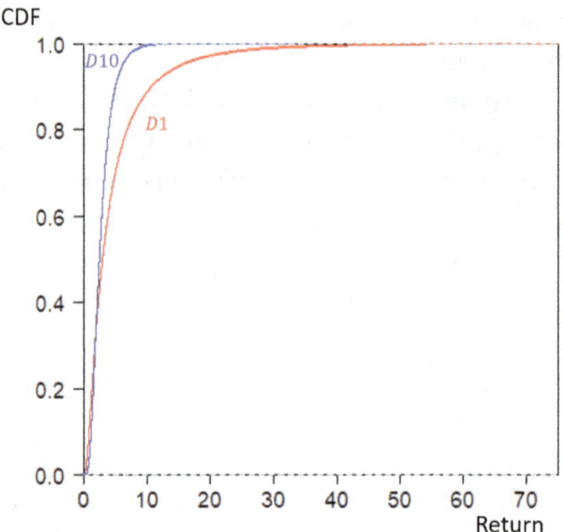

Figure 5.12: The cumulative distribution of the returns on Decile 1 and Decile 10 of stocks for the horizon $N = 10$ years.

and Decile 10, respectively, for the $N = 10$ years' horizon. As we can see from this figure, the cumulative distribution corresponding to Decile 1 is located in most of the range to the right of the distribution of Decile 10, indicating that for a 10-year horizon, Decile 1 is more attractive than Decile 10 — a result that conforms with the strategy asserting that the weight of the riskier asset should be relatively large for a long horizon.

Figure 5.13 focuses on the left tails of the distributions given in Figure 5.12, allowing us to better see the range of returns over which Decile 10 outperforms Decile 1. Looking solely at this range of returns, one may advocate that if investors typically assign a relatively large weight to the left tails of the distributions, the M–V results reported above in favor of the less risky assets in the long run (in our case, $N = 10$ years) may have economic justification. As we shall see in what follows, for most relevant preferences, this assertion is invalid.

Generally, investors do not consider only the left tails of the distributions, as the right tails are also important because these represent the large potential profit. Considering these two ranges of returns simultaneously, which asset dominates the other? The way

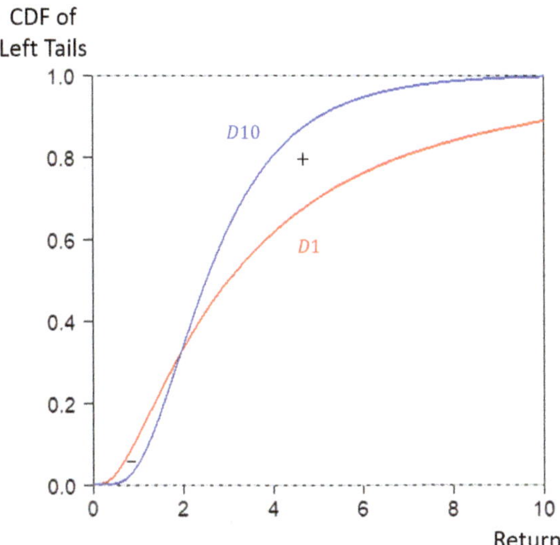

Figure 5.13: The left tails of the cumulative distributions of Decile 1 and Decile 10, respectively.

to examine whether the left tail given in Figure 5.13 is the reason for the superiority of Decile 10 over Decile 1 in the M–V framework is to measure the expected utility corresponding to the investment in these two assets, respectively, as this calculation considers the whole distribution of returns corresponding to these two assets. Table 5.6 presents the expected utility for various commonly employed utility functions in economics and finance, and the expected value of the Prospect Theory function for the rates of returns (namely, the changes in returns as required by the Prospect Theory) corresponding to an $N = 10$ years' horizon.

As can see from Table 5.6, the expected utility of the relatively less risky assets (Decile 10) is larger than the expected utility of the relatively riskier assets (Decile 1), in cases with relatively large risk-aversion parameters. Specifically, the expected utility of Decile 10 is larger than the expected utility of Decile 1 for $b \geq 1$ with the exponential preference, and the same is intact for the myopic utility function with $\alpha \geq 2$ (recall that for $\alpha = 1$, the myopic function is reduced to the log-function). For the Prospect Theory value function, the preference is for Decile 1 rather than for Decile 10. Calculating

Table 5.6: The expected utility for the horizon $N = 10$ years for various utility functions.

$u(x) = -e^{-b(x)}$

	$b = 0.1$	$b = 0.5$	$b = 1$	$b = 5$	$b = 10$
Decile 1	-0.679	-0.273	-0.132	-0.008	-0.001
Decile 10	-0.757	-0.300	-0.119	-0.002	$-8E{-}05$

$u(x) = \frac{x^{1-\alpha}}{1-\alpha}$

	$\alpha = 0.1$	$\alpha = 0.5$	$\alpha = 2$	$\alpha = 5$	$\alpha = 10$
Decile 1	4.547	3.959	-0.510	-2.579	-387
Decile 10	2.868	3.286	-0.466	-0.086	-7.883

$u(x) = log(x)$

Decile 1	1.126
Decile 10	0.917

$$PT\ utility:\ u(x) = \begin{cases} -2.25(-x)^{0.88} & if\ x < 0 \\ x^{0.88} & if\ x \geq 0 \end{cases}$$

Decile 1	3.0678
Decile 10	1.683

the expected utility for a horizon of $N = 20$ years reveals very similar results.

Thus, for commonly accepted risk-aversion parameters (see the following discussion for the relevant parameters) and for the Prospect Theory value function, Decile 1 reveals a larger expected utility than Decile 10. These results are in contrast to the M–V results revealing a preference for Decile 10 (the less risky stocks) over Decile 1, particularly for relatively long investment horizons. This contrast between the M–V results and the expected utility results is enhanced when we compare stocks and bonds and also stock–bond diversified portfolios — an analysis to which we turn next.

From the investors' point of view, the more interesting issue is the changes in the stock–bond asset allocation with the horizon.

With stocks and bonds, we have similar results to those reported in Figures 5.11–5.13. Covering the period 1928–2019, the annual rates of returns on the S&P 500 stock index and 10-year Treasury bonds are employed to derive the cumulative distributions of returns (see footnote 5). The two cumulative distributions of annual returns of stocks and bonds cross only once, and the range over which bonds outperform stocks (the left tails of the distributions) shrinks with the horizon, indicating that stocks have an advantage over bonds that increases with the horizon (as these figures are very similar to those reported with the two deciles of stocks, they are not reported here).

Tables 5.7 and 5.8 report the expected utility of stocks (the S&P 500 stock index) and bonds (10-year Treasury bonds) for two horizons, $N = 10$ and $N = 20$ years.

Table 5.7: Expected utility for the horizon $N = 10$ years.

$u(x) = -e^{-b(x)}$

	$b = 0.1$	$b = 0.5$	$b = 1$	$b = 10$
S&P 500	-0.753	-0.298	-0.123	-0.000
Bonds	-0.849	-0.446	-0.205	$-2.9\mathrm{E}{-06}$

$u(x) = \frac{x^{1-\alpha}}{1-\alpha}$

	$\alpha = 0.1$	$\alpha = 0.5$	$\alpha = 2$	$\alpha = 5$	$\alpha = 10$
S&P 500	2.932	3.317	-0.482	-0.290	-1265.75
Bonds	1.739	2.552	-0.637	-0.054	-0.009

$u(x) = log(x)$

S&P 500	0.924
Bonds	0.475

Prospect Value Function: $u(x) = \begin{cases} -2.25(-x)^{0.88} & if\ x < 0 \\ x^{0.88} & if\ x \geq 0 \end{cases}$

S&P 500	1.726
Bonds	0.670

                        Stocks, Bonds, and the Investment Horizon

Table 5.8: Expected utility for the horizon $N = 20$ years.

$u(x) = -e^{-b(x)}$

	$b = 0.1$	$b = 0.5$	$b = 1$	$b = 10$
S&P 500	−0.500	−0.111	−0.037	−0.000
Bonds	−0.764	−0.279	−0.089	−2.3E−07

$u(x) = \frac{x^{1-\alpha}}{1-\alpha}$

	$\alpha = 0.1$	$\alpha = 0.5$	$\alpha = 2$	$\alpha = 5$	$\alpha = 10$
S&P 500	7.749	5.511	−0.228	−0.715	−1461411
Bonds	2.727	3.260	−0.405	−0.012	−0.0001

$u(x) = \log(x)$

S&P 500	1.855
Bonds	0.952

Prospect Value Function: $u(x) = \begin{cases} -2.25(-x)^{0.88} & \text{if } x < 0 \\ x^{0.88} & \text{if } x \geq 0 \end{cases}$

S&P 500	5.914
Bonds	1.594

As we can see from Table 5.7, for $N = 10$ years, for all utility functions reported here and for a wide range of relevant risk-aversion parameters, stocks are preferred to bonds, despite the left tails of the distributions over which bonds outperform stocks. Table 5.8 reveals similar results for the longer horizon, $N = 20$ years. Only for very large and unaccepted utility functions ($b = 10$ with the exponential preference and relatively large α with the myopic preference) do bonds have a larger expected utility than stocks. Thus, considering the investment in either stocks or bonds, for relevant degrees of risk aversion, the results given in Tables 5.7 and 5.8 support the "stocks for the long run" strategy, which in the decile analysis reported in

Table 5.6 is translated to "risky and profitable stocks (Decile 1) for the long run."

From these results, we conclude that employing the M–V rule for portfolio selection for relatively long horizons, typically more than one year, may induce an economic loss for investors. The reason is that by the M–V rule, we obtain that one should increase the weight of the relatively safe asset in the portfolio with the horizon, while according to the expected utility paradigm, the relatively risky asset becomes more attractive with the horizon.

However, recall that these M–V economic distortions occur for relatively long horizons. For relatively short investment horizons, the distributions of returns are approximately elliptical; hence, the M–V rule coincides with the expected utility maximization for all risk averters. For relatively long horizons, the distributions of returns become positively skewed, and the M–V rule is no longer consistent with the expected utility maximization, perhaps leading to an economic distortion.

The above comparison of the attractiveness of stocks and bonds according to the M–V analysis and alternatively expected utility analysis is not complete, as with the M–V analysis we find the optimal stock–bond *diversified* portfolio and the change in this optimal portfolio with the horizon, whereas with expected utility maximization, we calculate the expected utility of stocks and bonds, but not the optimal diversified portfolio between these two assets. It is possible that with a comparison of diversified portfolios, the gap between the two approaches would decrease. However, if the proportion of stocks in the diversified portfolio which maximizes the expected utility is relatively large for relatively long horizons, this result would support the "stocks for the long run" strategy.

5.6. Diversification: The Optimal Stock–Bond Investment Weights for Various Utility Functions

To find the investment weights which maximize the expected utility, we employ the annual rates of returns on stocks (the S&P 500 stock index) and bonds (US 10-year Treasury bonds) covering the period

1928–2019 (see footnote 5). The simulation is conducted as follows: for a given N-years' horizon, N years are drawn from this historical annual data. For each sampled year, we obtain the return on stocks and bonds corresponding to the same year and calculate the return on a portfolio comprising a share of w_b in bonds and $1 - w_b$ in stocks. The N returns are then compounded to calculate the N-year return of the annually balanced portfolio. This is the first observation of the returns for the given share of bonds w_b and the horizon N. We repeat this sampling method 50,000 times for various horizons and values of w_b. Then, for a given utility function, we find the value of w_b which maximizes the expected utility for each horizon. Note that to demonstrate technically the changes in the optimal investment with the horizon, we also employ some unrealistic risk-aversion parameters, as reported in what follows.

Figure 5.14 provides the optimal stock–bond diversification for various utility functions for various risk-aversion parameters, as well as for various investment horizons.

First, let's look at the optimal diversification with exponential utility function. As expected, for a low risk-aversion parameter, it is optimal to invest 100% in stocks; see the declining expected utility curve as a function of the investment weight in bonds w_b. However, for a larger risk-aversion parameter, we obtain a diversified portfolio that maximizes expected utility. For example, for $\alpha = 2$ and for a horizon of $N = 10$ years, investing about 43% in bonds is optimal (see Figure 5.14(a)). Finally, with an unrealistic very large risk-aversion parameter, $\alpha = 10$ and $N = 10$ years, as expected, investing 100% in bonds for all horizons is optimal. We present these results even though it is well documented in the literature that such a large risk-aversion parameter is economically unaccepted.[7]

Turning to the myopic utility functions (see Figure 5.14(b)) reveals similar results: for a relatively low risk-aversion parameter, 100% investment weight in stocks is optimal, and the opposite is

---

[7]Levy, H. and H. M. Markowitz (1979). Approximating expected utility by a function of mean and variance. *The American Economic Review* 69(3), 308–317.

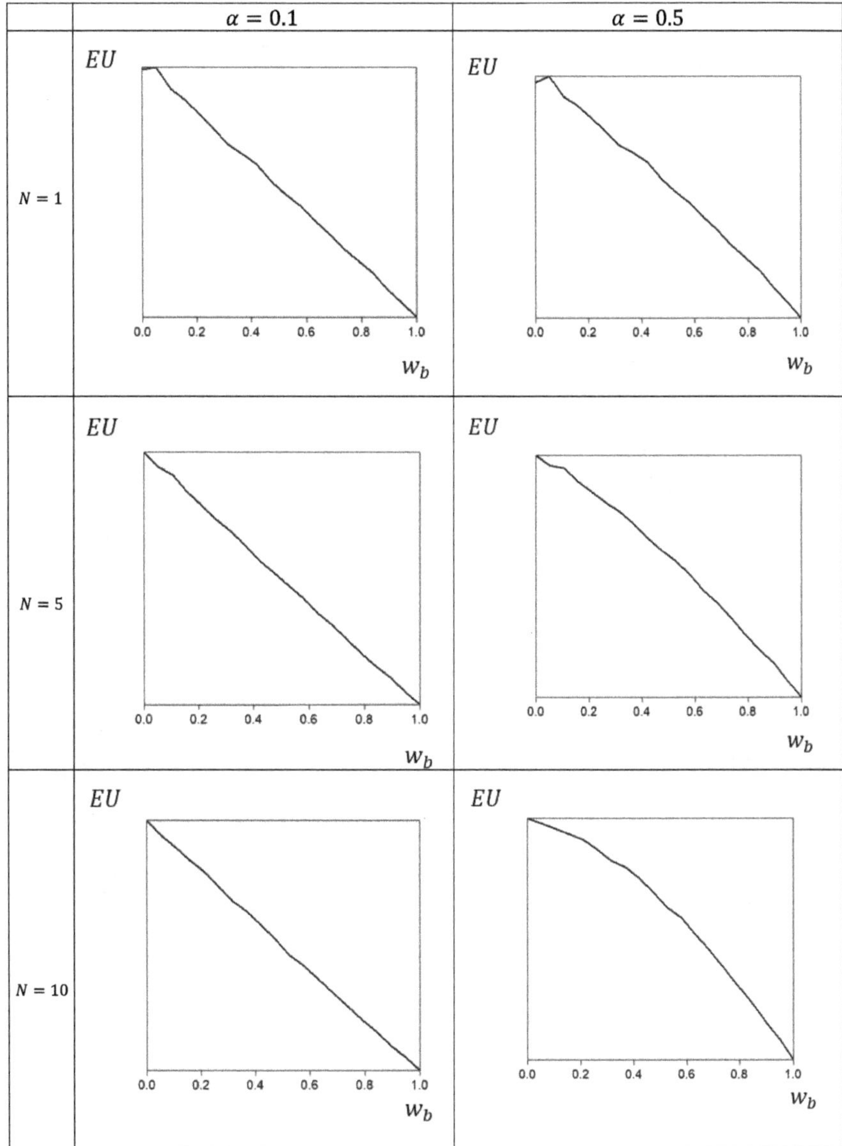

Figure 5.14: The optimal diversification between bonds and stocks for various horizons*: (a) D_i — the ith decile, $i = 1, 2, \ldots, 10$; (b) The utility function $u(x) = \frac{x^{1-\alpha}}{1-\alpha}$; (c) The utility function $u(x) = \log(x)$; (d) The utility function
$$u(x) = \begin{cases} -2.25(-x)^{0.88} & if \ x < 0 \\ x^{0.88} & if \ x \geq 0 \end{cases}.$$

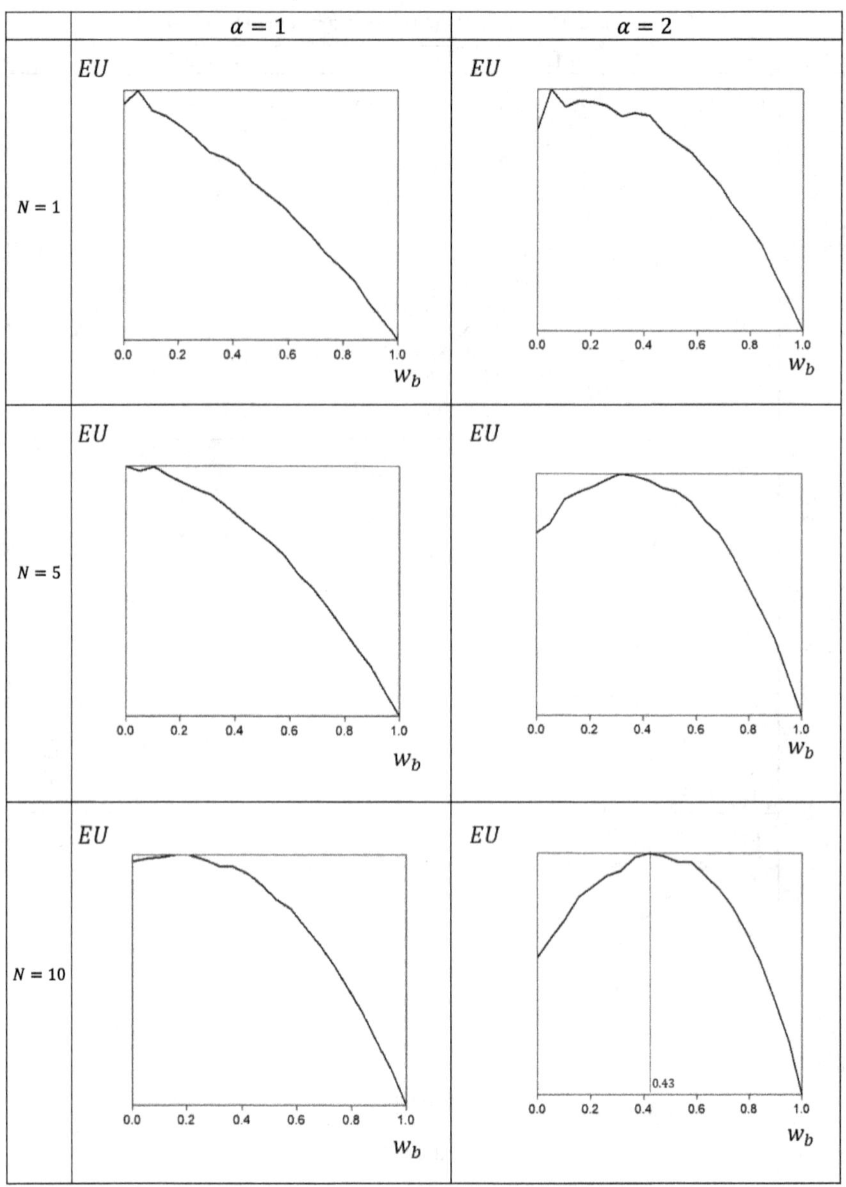

Figure 5.14: (*Continued*)

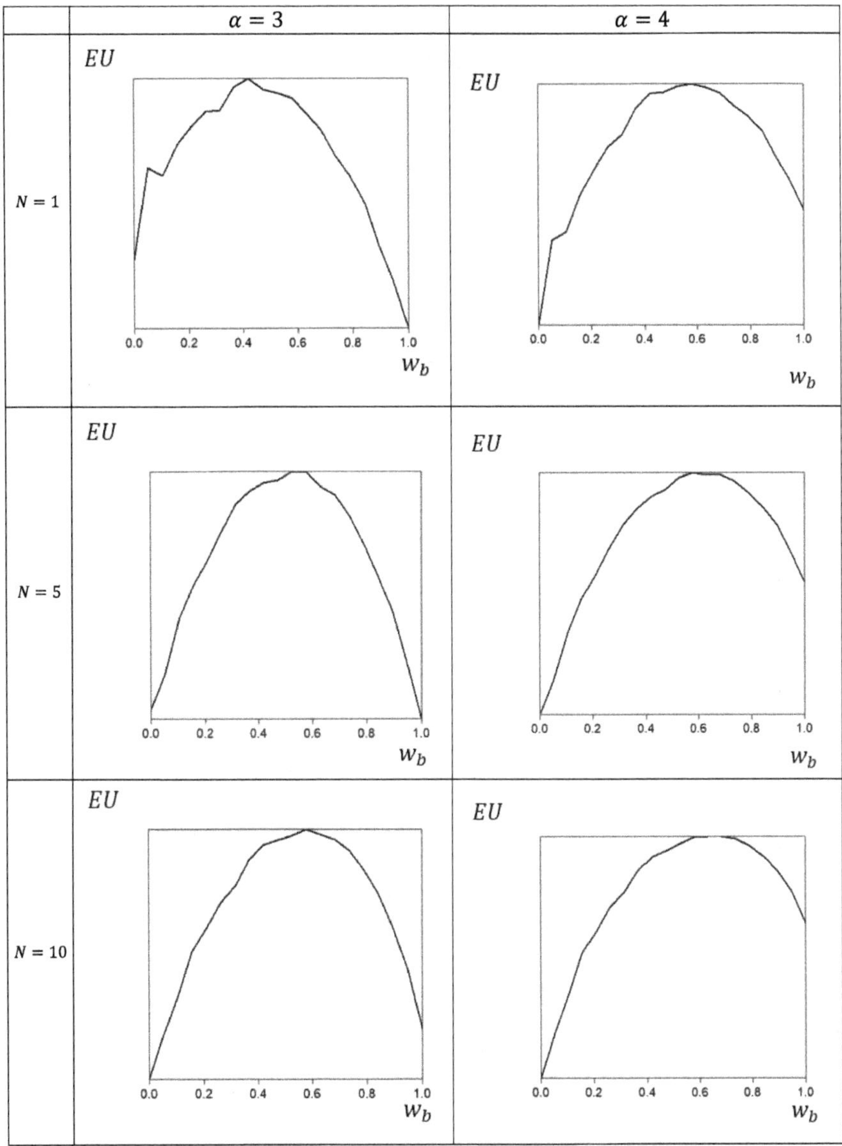

Figure 5.14: (*Continued*)

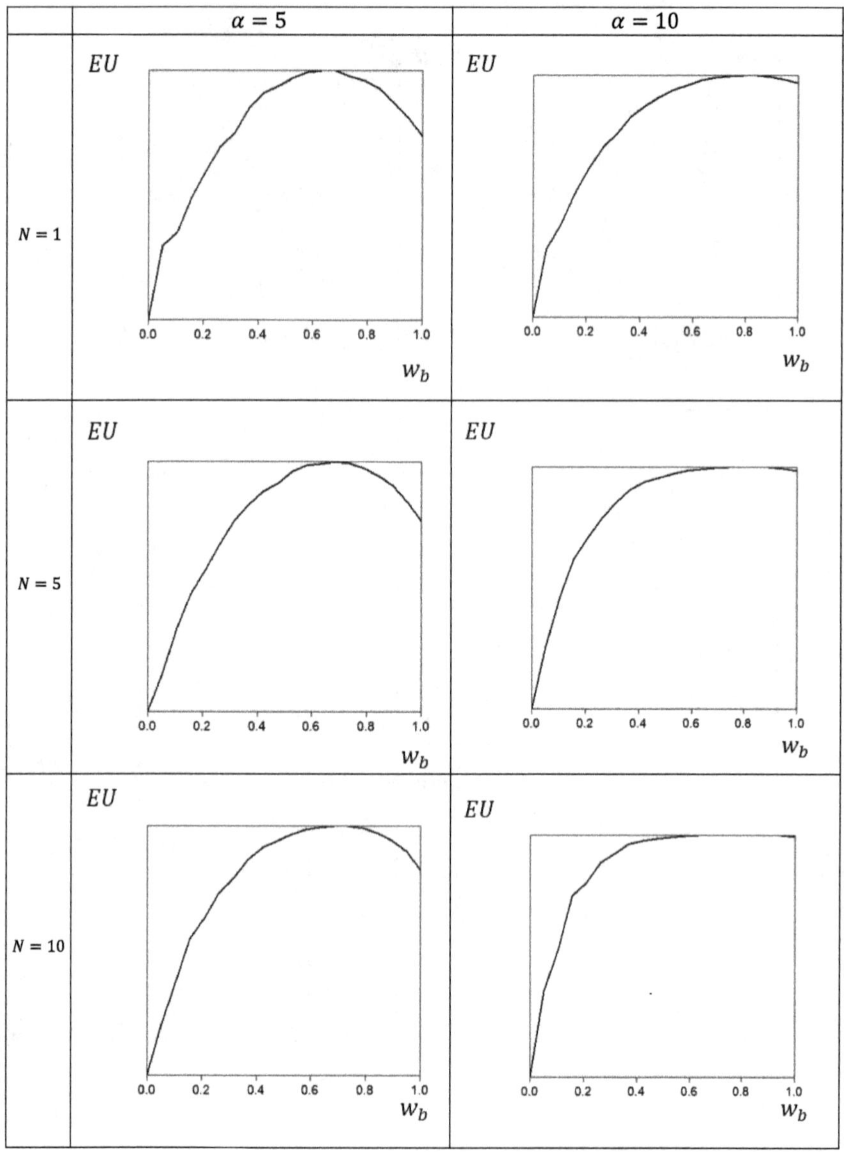

Figure 5.14: (*Continued*)

(b) Myopic utility function with risk aversion parameter α: $\frac{x^{1-\alpha}-1}{1-\alpha}$

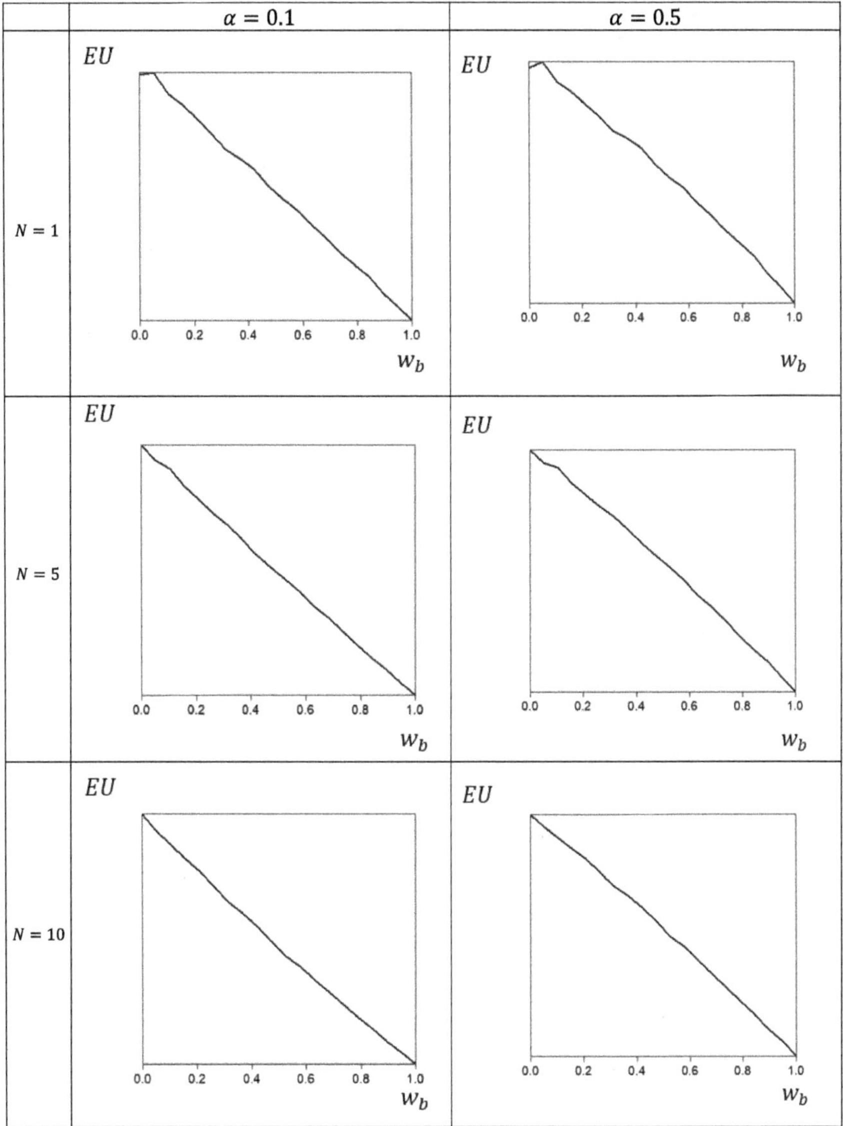

Figure 5.14: (*Continued*)

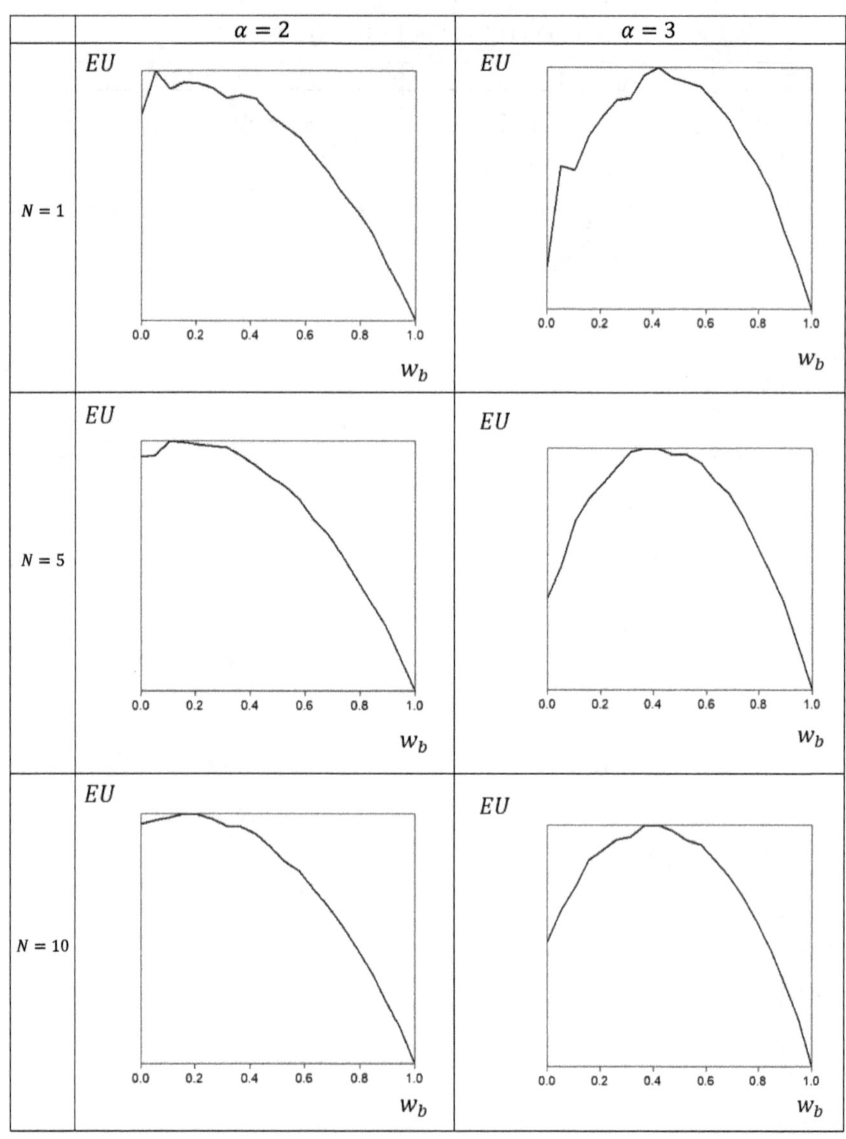

Figure 5.14: (*Continued*)

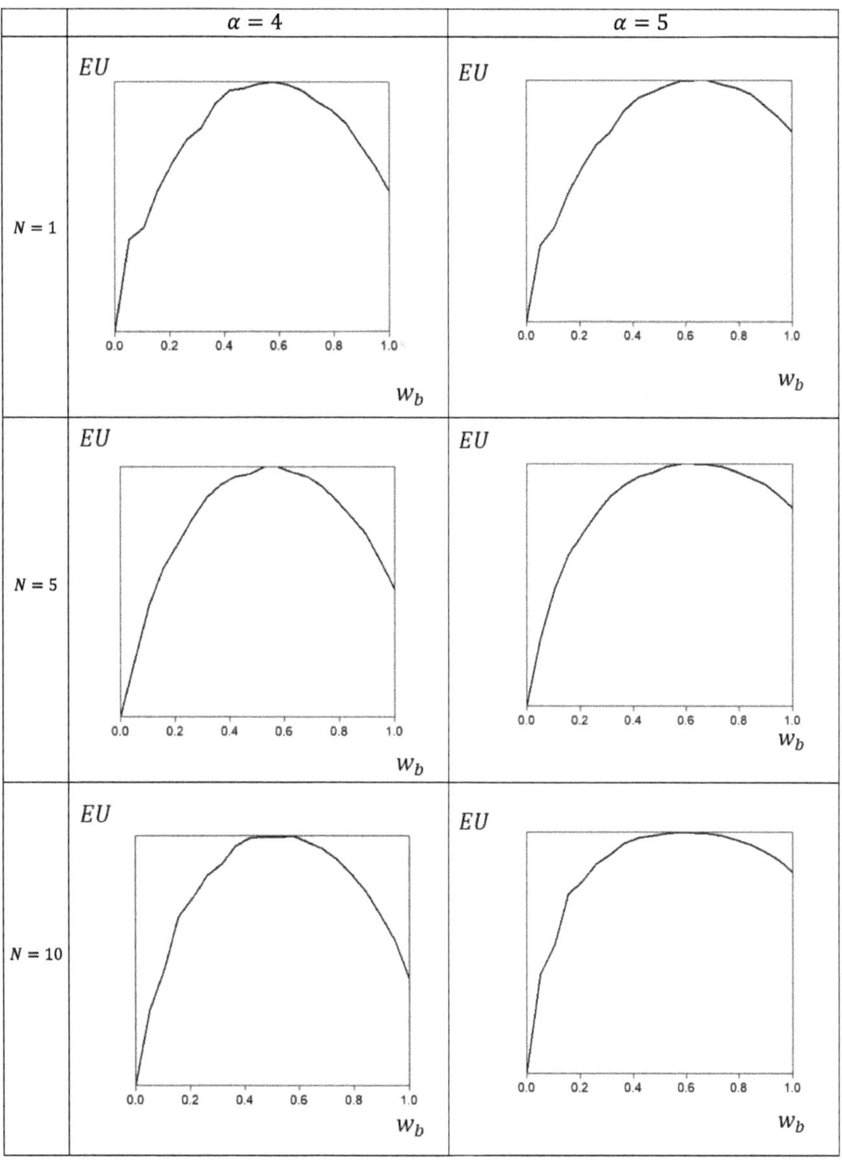

Figure 5.14: (*Continued*)

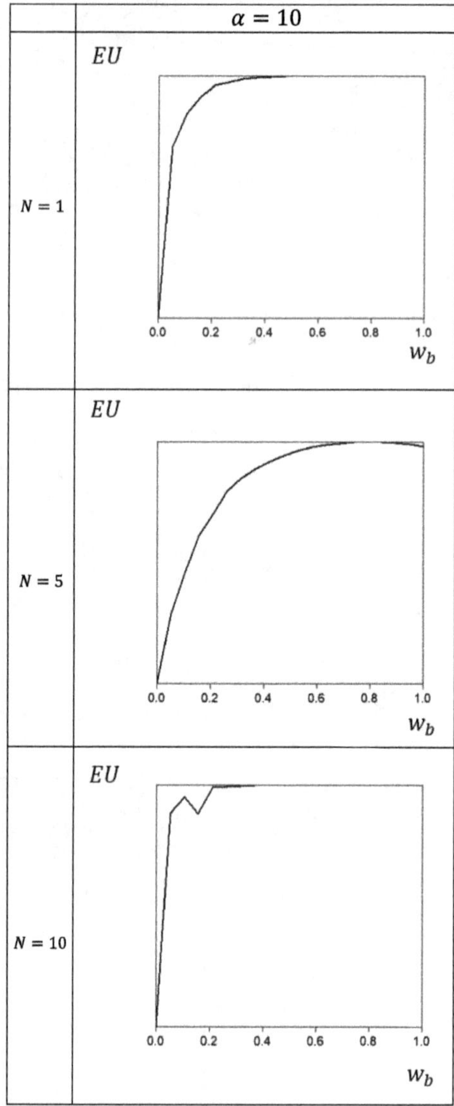

Figure 5.14: (*Continued*)

(c) $u(x) = log(x)$

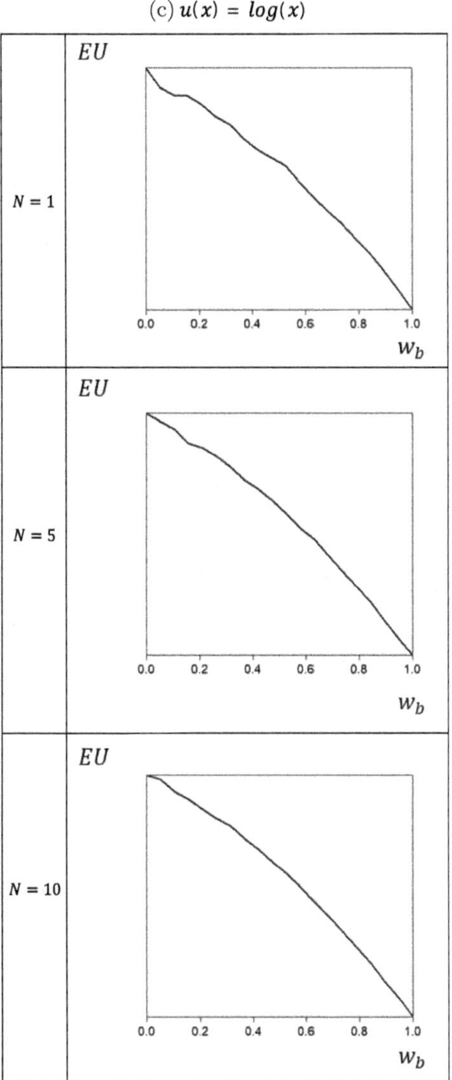

Figure 5.14: (*Continued*)

(d) Prospect theory value function $(x) = \begin{cases} -2.25(-x)^{0.88} & \textit{if } x < 0 \\ x^{0.88} & \textit{if } x \geq 0 \end{cases}$

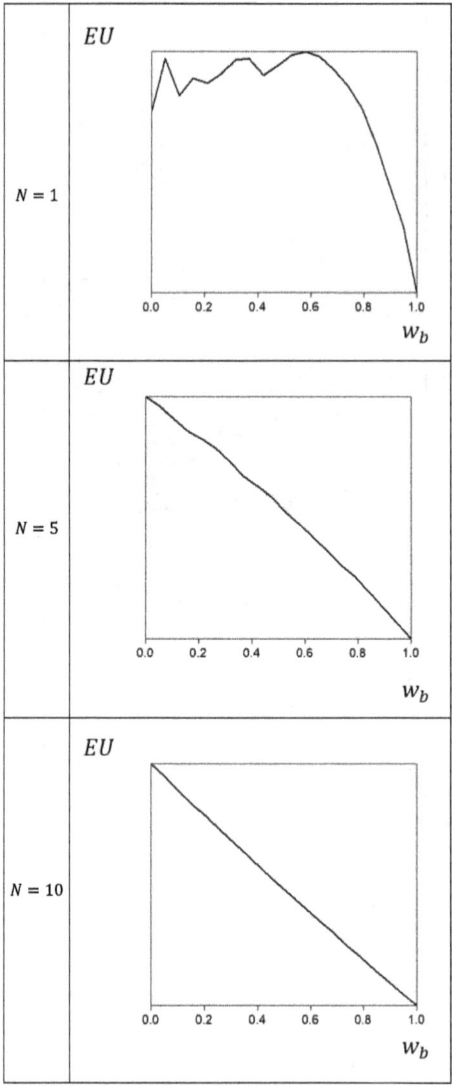

Figure 5.14: (*Continued*)

Note: *In all the figures given in 5.14, the horizontal axis stands for the optimal investment weight in bonds, w_b the vertical axis stands for the expected utility, and N stands for the horizon in years.

intact for a relatively large risk-aversion parameter. For a risk-aversion parameter of $\alpha = 3$, 4, and 5, we have an interior maximum. For $\alpha = 10$, the optimal investment in bonds is 100%. For the log-utility function (which is the myopic function where $\alpha \to 1$), 100% investment in stocks is optimal (see Figure 5.14(c)). Finally, Figure 5.14(d) provides the optimal portfolio corresponding to the Prospect Theory value function. Here, we have for $N = 1$ some fluctuations about the 100% optimal investment weights in stocks, and this stock preference for the larger horizon is more transparent: 100% investment in stocks is optimal. Although we present in Figure 5.14 the optimal stock–bond portfolios for various risk-aversion parameters, from an economic point of view, only a few of the results are economically relevant. Thus, for the exponential utility function, we obtain for the relevant risk-aversion parameters either that 100% investment weight in stocks is optimal or that diversification is optimal for the less accepted parameters ($\alpha \geq 2$).

With the more relevant myopic utility function, it is argued in the literature that the risk-aversion parameter is about 1,[8] and some argue that it is about 2.[9] For $\alpha \to 1$, the myopic function is reduced to the log-utility function, and as can be seen from Figure 5.14(c), 100% investment weight in stocks is optimal. Thus, for $\alpha \leq 1$, 100% investment in stocks is optimal. For $\alpha = 2$, some diversification with a large weight in stocks is optimal, where the optimal investment in bonds decreases with the horizon. For $\alpha = 3$, 4, 5, diversification is optimal, and for $\alpha = 10$, 100% investment weight in bonds is optimal.

Contrasting the M–V optimal diversification and the expected utility optimal diversification reveals that by the expected utility, for the relevant risk-averse parameters, there is a strong preference for stocks, and in most relevant cases, 100% investment in stocks is optimal. With the M–V methodology, we obtain a different result with a much stronger preference for bonds: for $N = 1$ year, only

---

[8]For a survey of the research concerning the risk-aversion parameter, see Mehra, R. and E. Prescott (1985). The equity premium: A puzzle. *Journal of Monetary Economics* 15(2), 145–161.

[9]Friend, I. and M. E. Blume (1975). The demand for risky assets. *The American Economic Review* 65(5), 900–922.

about 41% is invested in stocks, and for a longer horizon, this weight decreases dramatically. For $N = 10$ years, the optimal M–V investment weight in stocks is only about 22% (see Table 5.2(b)). A second discrepancy between the two investment paradigms is that while the assumed investment horizon has a strong effect on the optimal diversification by the M–V rule, its effect is only marginal with expected utility maximization (compare the results reported in Table 5.2(b) and in Figure 5.14).

5.7. Summary

The investment horizon affects the M–V rule, the M–V frontier, and the M–V efficient set, as well as the optimal M–V portfolio of risky assets, known as the market portfolio or the tangency portfolio. The three factors which affect the M–V choices are the individual's asset mean, variance, and all pairwise correlations. As all these parameters change dramatically with the assumed investment horizon, they affect the M–V optimal choices. Generally, the M–V frontier shifts upward and to the right with the horizon. While the mean and variance of each asset increases with the horizon, surprisingly, the correlations tend to zero with the horizon regardless of the one-period assumed correlation. Even if the one-period correlation is perfect $(+1)$, it decreases with the horizon and becomes equal to zero where the horizon increases indefinitely. Similarly, if the one-period correlation is negative, it increases and tends to zero as the horizon increases indefinitely. Thus, other things being equal, assets with positive one-period correlations become more attractive by the M–V rule with the horizon as the correlation decreases. An opposite phenomenon occurs with one-period negative correlations. Thus, as negative correlation decreases the selected portfolio risk, the advantage of the negative correlation slowly vanishes with the horizon as the correlation increases and tends to zero for a very long horizon. By the same token, the disadvantage of a positive correlation diminishes with the horizon. The importance of these changes in the correlations is important not only for the capital market but also for economic research investigating the correlation between two variables that are not additive with time, e.g., inflation, interest rates, growth rate in the population, and growth rate in the GDP.

In a portfolio composed of stocks and bonds, as the horizon increases, the optimal M–V weight invested in stocks decreases; hence, stocks seemingly become less attractive than bonds with the horizon. More generally, according to the M–V rule, assets with relatively high mean and high variance become less attractive than relatively safer assets with the horizon. For example, "small stocks" become less attractive than "large stocks" by this rule as the horizon increases. Similarly, bonds become more attractive than stocks with the horizon. These M–V results contradict the "stocks for the long run" paradigm, as well as the investment strategy of life cycle mutual funds, which invest more in stocks and less in bonds for long horizon investors.

Are relatively risky assets (the S&P 500 stock index, or "small stocks") really less attractive than less risky assets (bonds or "large stocks") in the long run? Calculating the expected utility of various commonly employed utility functions, as well as by the Prospect Theory value functions, reveals that the attractiveness of relatively risky assets relative to that of less risky assets isn't sensitive to the horizon, which is in contradiction to the M–V results. These findings indicate that employing the M–V rule for the long run is economically unjustified (particularly because the built-up positive skewness with the horizon is ignored by the M–V rule), and may induce an economic distortion.

In sum, for relatively short horizons (one year or less), the distributions of returns are close to elliptical (e.g., normal or logistic); hence, the M–V rule can be safely employed as it yields results that are consistent with expected utility results. Also, the M–V rule can be employed for short horizons as an approximation to the expected utility even in the case where normality of the distribution does not exist. However, for long horizons, the distributions of returns become positively skewed, and the approximation to expected utility is not intact. Therefore, employing the M–V rule leads to the wrong conclusions, asserting that bonds become more attractive than stocks in the long run.

Chapter 6

Risk and the Horizon: The Discounting Cash-Flows Approach with Rothschild and Stiglitz's Definition of Risk

In Chapter 5, we analyzed changes in the relative attractiveness of stocks and bonds with the horizon. More generally, we analyzed the changes in the relative attractiveness of various risky assets (not necessarily stocks and bonds) with different risk-return profiles with the horizon. We also showed, based on historical rates of returns, that bonds outperform stocks when one looks solely at the left tails of the cumulative distributions of the returns on stocks and bonds, which in practice are located to the left of the intersection point of the two cumulative distributions under consideration. The opposite result is intact for the right tails of the cumulative distributions of returns. Since the empirical cumulative distributions of stocks and bonds typically intersect only once, in this specific case, we have only two ranges of returns: one where bonds outperform stocks (left of the intersection point of the two cumulative distributions), and one where stocks outperform bonds (right of the intersection point of the cumulative distributions). When the two tails of the cumulative distributions are considered simultaneously (namely, the whole distributions of the returns on stocks and bonds are considered), the superiority of stocks over bonds for long horizons emerges, as for most relevant utility functions (and for most economically relevant risk-aversion parameters), the expected utility of the return on stocks is larger than that of the return on bonds. When diversified portfolios, rather than stocks and bonds in isolation, are considered, once again, a relatively large investment weight in stocks is optimal for most expected utility maximizers (and in some relevant cases, even 100% weight in stocks is optimal). When the mean–variance (M–V) rule is employed, just the opposite results are obtained — bonds are superior to stocks for long investment horizons. We argue that the M–V results approximately conform with the expected utility paradigm for relatively short investment horizons (roughly up to 1-year horizons), and that they are economically meaningless for relatively long investment horizons.

Notwithstanding, the reservation regarding these results (both in the M–V and expected utility frameworks), which is often argued in the literature, is that in the common empirical risk analysis, it is assumed that historical distributions of rates of returns serve as the best estimates of the future distributions; hence, the *ex-post* risk is a good proxy to *ex-ante* risk, an assumption that not all researchers agree with (see, for example, Pástor and Stambaugh[1] and Markowitz).[2] In this chapter, we solely rely on *ex-post* distributions of returns. In the next chapter, we relate to the concern about the difference between *ex-post* and *ex-ante* risk. Specifically, we discuss the effect of an unforeseen future risk of stocks not reflected in the *ex-post* data on choices.

With *ex-post* as well as *ex-ante* distributions of returns, it is accepted by most academic researchers and professional investors that, on average, stocks are more profitable than bonds — an assumption that is supported by empirical evidence as well as by theoretical argument, asserting that the required risk premium on stocks by risk averters is positive. Thus, there is no dispute among academic researchers and professional investors that the *expected* return of stocks is larger than the expected return on bonds. However, there is

---

[1]Pástor, L. and R. F. Stambaugh (2012). Are stocks really less volatile in the long run? *The Journal of Finance* 67(2), 431–478.

[2]Markowitz, H. M. (2020). *Risk–Return Analysis: The Theory and Practice of Rational Investing,* Vol. 3, McGraw Hill, New York.

ongoing dispute regarding the risk of stocks and bonds, particularly regarding the change in the risk of stocks with the horizon.

Thus, agreeing that the expected return on stocks is larger than the expected return on bonds, some researchers who investigate the relative attractiveness of stocks and bonds for the long run focus solely on the changes of the risk of stocks with the horizon. Some argue that stocks become riskier with the horizon, and some argue that they become safer. If indeed the risk of stocks decreases with the horizon, then by this approach, stocks become more attractive than bonds with the horizon as their mean is larger than the mean return of bonds, and the risk is lower than the risk of bonds. Of course, this approach assumes a two-parameter model and that there is a well-defined risk measure for all horizons — an issue which, as we shall see in this chapter, in itself is questionable.

Siegel[3] argues that stocks which are, on average, more profitable than bonds become also less risky with the horizon; hence, he advocates that stocks are a better investment than bonds for the long run. Moreover, he even claims that stocks become riskless for a horizon of 10 years or longer. Barberis[4] also advocates that stocks become more attractive with the horizon, but Avramov *et al.*[5] find inconclusive results in this respect. An opposite view to the one advocated by Siegel is advocated by Pástor and Stambaugh (see footnote 1), who claim that stocks become riskier with the horizon, as history will not necessarily repeat itself; hence, they cast doubt on Siegel's conclusion advocating that "stocks for the long run" is the best investment strategy. Specifically, Pástor and Stambaugh claim that stocks which are, on average, more profitable than bonds also become riskier with the horizon; hence, it is not clear which of these two investments, stocks or bonds, is superior in the long

---

[3]Siegel, J. J. (2014). *Stocks for the Long Run: The Definitive Guide to Financial Market Returns and Long-Term Investment Strategies*, McGraw-Hill, New York.
[4]Barberis, N. (2000). Investing for the long run when returns are predictable. *The Journal of Finance* 55(1), 225–264.
[5]Avramov, D., D. Cederburg and K. Lučivjanská (2017). Are stocks riskier over the long run? Taking cues from economic theory. *The Review of Financial Studies* 31(2), 556–594.

run. Markowitz (see footnote 2) also advocates that even a long history of rates of returns does not reveal all potential future risks, particularly of stocks. Despite this disagreement regarding future risk, in this chapter, we employ *ex-post* distributions of returns. Yet, we discuss some methodical issues that are also relevant to the *ex-ante* distributions which will be discussed in the next chapter.

The following issues related to the change of risk with the horizon are discussed in this chapter:

(a) How do we measure risk for various horizons? Does risk coincide with volatility, namely with the variance of returns, as suggested by both Siegel and Pástor and Stambaugh? If the answer is positive, is the variance the correct measure for risks for all investment horizons, which for some investors may be very short (months or years) and for other investors very long (20 or 30 years)?

(b) Suppose that the variance is the correct measure of risk for all horizons. How should one compare the risks of the returns on stocks faced on different dates, say the distributions returns which are obtained once after 1 year and once after 5 years? As it is realized that such comparison is invalid, it is suggested in the literature to calculate the *annualized* variance, which has the same time dimension for all horizons. Is this a correct procedure for comparing risks obtained in different horizons? Can it be defended economically?

(c) In calculating the variance and the annualized variance, it is common to calculate these parameters with the log-return, rather than the returns. However, the expected utility is defined on the return (or wealth) and not log-returns. Is there an economic justification for shifting from the return (or wealth) to the log-return (or log-wealth)? Note that with log-returns, it is technically easier to calculate the variance of the terminal wealth, as with the log-return, it becomes an additive random variable rather than a multiplicative variable.

(d) Is there a better way, which can be defended economically, to compare the risk faced on various dates?

(e) Is there a difference between the historical risks (even when measured by about a century of rates of returns) and future risks? Are there hidden risks like the October 19, 1987 Black Monday, where a stock market crash of about 25% in one day was recorded? Markowitz argues that such future hidden risks that are not reflected in the historical data exist (see footnote 2).

In this chapter, we analyze issues (a)–(d) above, while issue (e) is analyzed in detail in the next chapter. However, we would like to emphasize once again that all the issues analyzed in this chapter are relevant for both *ex*-post and *ex-ante* data.

6.1. The Annualized Volatility and the Horizon

First, we technically compare the annualized parameters of wealth and log-wealth, and then discuss the economic meaning of these two variables. Of course, the most interesting issue involves the *changes* in the volatility and annualized volatility of returns and of log-returns of stocks with the horizon. As it is common in the literature to employ the terms variance and volatility to measure the same phenomenon, we also employ these two terms interchangeably.

Employing the annualized volatility for a comparison of risks faced on different dates implies that if one wishes to compare the risk of, say, a 1-year investment and, say, a 5-year investment, it is suggested in the financial literature to compare the annualized volatility for these two horizons. Thus, it is suggested first to calculate the variance of the return on the 5-year investment, then to divide the obtained figure by five, and finally to compare the obtained result with the 1-year variance. Although there is no theoretical justification for using the annualized volatility, this procedure is employed in comparing risks faced on different dates; hence, it deserves special attention. Therefore, we elaborate on the calculation of the annualized variance with returns and log-returns, where the log-return is the method employed in the literature (see the cited studies in footnotes 1 and 3).

Suppose that one invests W_0 for N periods (say, N years) in an asset whose rates of return is r_i in the ith period (say, the ith year), where $i = 1, 2, \ldots, N$. Denoting the return (rather than the rate of return) in period i by $R_i \equiv 1 + r_i$, the terminal wealth after N periods is given by

$$W_N = W_0 \prod_{i=1}^{N} R_i. \tag{6.1}$$

For simplicity, and without loss of generalization, assume a \$1 investment, namely $W_0 = 1$. Thus, the return for N-periods is given by

$$W_N = \prod_{i=1}^{N} R_i. \tag{6.2}$$

Obviously, as R_i $(i = 1, 2, \ldots, N)$ are random variables, W_N is also a random variable, which is given by the terminal wealth distribution per one dollar of investment. With log-wealth we have

$$logW_N = \sum_{i=1}^{N} logR_i. \tag{6.3}$$

The end-of-period mean and variance depend on the assumption made on the return-generating process. Assuming identical independent distribution (*i.i.d.*) over time, we have that for all periods $R_i = R$, that is, the index i can be omitted. It is easy to show that with an *i.i.d.* assumption, the expected value of W_N is given by

$$E(W_N) = [E(R)]^N \tag{6.4}$$

with a *rate of return* for the whole period of

$$[E(R)]^N - 1. \tag{6.4'}$$

The variance of terminal wealth is given by

$$\sigma^2(W_N) = [\sigma^2(R) + (E(R))^2]^N - [E(R)]^{2N} \tag{6.5}$$

where R is the one-period return, which is identical for all such periods (see Tobin,[6] Levy,[7] and Levy,[8] and Eq. (3.6) given in Chapter 3).

Similarly, the mean of $logW_N$ is given by

$$ElogW_N = NElog(R)$$

and the variance of the log-wealth is

$$\sigma^2(logW_N) = \text{Variance}\left(\sum_{i=1}^{N} logR_i\right),$$

which with the *i.i.d.* assumption becomes

$$\sigma^2(logW_N) = N[Var(logR)]$$

where $Var(logR)$ stands for the one-period variance of log-returns. For simplicity in the following discussion, we assume that the one-period horizon is 1 year; hence, N denotes the N-year horizon. Thus, we refer in what follows to the variance and the annualized variance.

Shifting from the multi-period parameters to the annualized parameters, as done by Siegel (see footnote 3) and Pástor and Stambaugh (see footnote 1), it is easy to see that with log-wealth, the horizon does not matter as long as *i.i.d.* is assumed. More specifically, we have in this case

$$E_A(W_N) = NElog(R)/N = Elog(R)$$

and

$$\sigma_A^2(logW_N) = NVar(logR)/N = Var(logR)$$

where the added subscript A stands for the annualized parameters.

---

[6]Tobin, J. (1965). The theory of portfolio selection, in Hahn F. Y. and F. P. Brechling (eds.), *The Theory of Interest Rates*, London.

[7]Levy, H. (1972). Portfolio performance and the investment horizon. *Management Science* 18(12), B-635–B-749.

[8]Levy, H. (2016). *Stochastic Dominance: Investment Decision Making Under Uncertainty*, Springer, New York.

The effect of the horizon on the annualized mean return, and particularly on the annualized variance with the return rather than the log-return, is less transparent, and some algebraic manipulations are required to see that the annualized mean and variance of the return increase (as opposed to being constant as with the log-return) with the horizon.

Let us look first at the annualized mean rate of return. Recall that the annualized return (annualized 1 + rate of return) generally technically decreases with the horizon (as we divide the N-period return by N, we also divide the principle, namely the initial investment, in our case \$1, by N). Therefore, aiming to investigate the horizon's effect on profitability rather than on terminal wealth, we should subtract the principle (\$1) before the analyzation processes are done; hence, we need to analyze the following annualized term:

$$E_A(W_N - 1) = \{[E(R)]^N - 1\}/\, N\}.$$

While it is almost trivial that this term increases with the horizon for profitable investment, namely $E(R) > 1$, we present in the following a formal proof that paves the way for the calculation of the changes in the annualized variance of return, which is neither trivial nor intuitive.

Define

$$Z(N) = \{[E(R)]^N - 1\}/\, N\}.$$

Take the derivative of $Z(N)$ with respect to N to obtain

$$\partial Z(N)/\partial N = 1/N^2\{N\partial[E(R)]^N/\partial N - [E(R)]^N + 1\}. \qquad (6.6)$$

We show in what follows that the term in brackets is positive for $E(R) > 1$ (a positive expected rate of return), implying, as intuitively expected, that the longer the horizon, the larger the annualized expected return. Let us focus first on the term appearing in Eq. (6.6),

$$Y(N) \equiv [E(R)]^N.$$

Taking the log of both sides yields,

$$logY(N) = N\, logE(R).$$

Taking the derivative of both sides with respect to N, we have

$$Y'(N)/Y(N) = log E(R); \text{ hence,}$$
$$Y'(N) = [E(R)]^N log E(R). \quad (6.7)$$

Plugging (6.7) into (6.6), we obtain

$$\partial Z(N)/\partial N = 1/N^2 \{[N\partial[E(R)]^N/\partial N - [E(R)]^N + 1\}$$
$$= 1/N^2 \{N[E(R)]^N log E(R) - [E(R)]^N + 1]\}.$$

And the sign of the derivative is equal to the sign of the term in the square brackets which can be rewritten as

$$[E(R)]^N [N log E(R) - 1] + 1. \quad (6.8)$$

For $E(R) = 1$ (implying a zero expected rate of return), Eq. (6.8) becomes

$$[E(R)]^N (N log E(R) - 1) + 1 = 1(0 - 1) + 1 = 0. \quad (6.8')$$

Although it is not transparent from Eq. (6.8) that the derivative is positive for all $E(R)$, it can be easily shown (by taking the derivative of this equation with respect to $E(R)$ for a given N) that for all $E(R)$ (smaller or larger than 1), Eq. (6.8) is non-negative, and for most common values, it is positive, and therefore for the relevant range $\partial Z/\partial N > 0$. Thus, as intuition indicates, we also formally have shown that the annualized expected rate of return for all the relevant values $E(R)$ increases with the horizon, in contrast to the annualized expected log-return, which remains constant for all horizons.

We turn now to investigate the annualized variance of returns, claiming that it also increases with the horizon, in contrast to the results obtained with the log-return. Thus, we need to prove that the annualized variance of returns increases with N, that is,

$$\partial[\sigma^2(W_N)/N]/\partial N > 0. \quad (6.9)$$

By Eq. (6.5), we have

$$\sigma^2(W_N) = [\sigma^2(R) + (E(R))^2]^N - [E(R)]^{2N}.$$

And employing the binomial expansion of the first term yields

$$\sigma^2(W_N) = \sum_{i=0}^{N} \binom{N}{i} (\sigma^2(R))^i (E(R)^2)^{N-i} - [E(R)]^{2N} \qquad (6.10)$$

as for $i = 0$, the corresponding term given in Eq. (6.10) is $[E(R)]^{2N}$, and we can rewrite the multi-period variance as follows (note that the summation is from $i = 1$, rather than $i = 0$):

$$\sigma^2(W_N) = \left(\sum_{i=1}^{N} \binom{N}{i} (\sigma^2(R))^i (E(R)^2)^{N-i} + [E(R)]^{2N} \right) - [E(R)]^{2N}$$

canceling the last two terms, we obtain

$$\sigma^2(W_N) = \sum_{i=1}^{N} \binom{N}{i} (\sigma^2(R))^i (E(R)^2)^{N-i}.$$

Similarly, the variance corresponding to the $N + 1$-year investment horizon is equal to

$$\sigma^2(W_{N+1}) = \sum_{i=1}^{N+1} \binom{N+1}{i} (\sigma^2(R))^i (E(R)^2)^{N+1-i}.$$

We turn now to show that the annualized variance of return increases with N.

Writing explicitly the term $\binom{N}{i}$, the N-years variance can be rewritten as

$$\sigma^2(W_N) = \sum_{i=1}^{N} \frac{N(N-1)(N-2)\cdots(N-i+1)}{i(i-1)(i-2)\cdots 1} (\sigma^2(R))^i (E(R)^2)^{N-i}.$$

Dividing this multi-period variance by N, we obtain the annualized variance. Thus, the annualized variance is given by

$$\sigma^2(W_N)/N = \sum_{i=1}^{N} \frac{(N-1)(N-2)\cdots(N-i+1)}{i(i-1)(i-2)\cdots 1} (\sigma^2(R))^i [E(R)^2]^{N-i}.$$

$$(6.11)$$

By a similar argument, the $N + 1$-year horizon's annualized variance is given by

$$\sigma^2(W_{N+1})/(N+1) = \sum_{i=1}^{N+1} \frac{N(N-1)(N-2)\cdots(N+1-i+1)}{i(i-1)(i-2)\cdots 1}$$
$$\times (\sigma^2(R))^i [E(R)^2]^{N+1-i}. \tag{6.12}$$

We employ Eqs. (6.11) and (6.12) to show that by increasing the horizon from N to $N + 1$, the annualized variance increases. To see this, let us focus first on a given year i which can take any of the values $1, 2, 3, \ldots, N$ in the case of Eq. (6.11) and any value $i = 1,\, 2,\, 3, \ldots,\, N + 1$ in the case of Eq. (6.12). For any value i, we have

$$(\sigma^2(R))^i[(E(R))^2]^{N+1-i} > (\sigma^2(R))^i[E(R)]^2)^{N-i}, \text{ as } E(R) > 1.$$

We also have $\frac{N(N-1)(N-2)\cdots(N-i+1)}{i(i-1)(i-2)\cdots 1} > \frac{(N-1)(N-2)\cdots(N-i+1)}{i(i-1)(i-2)\cdots 1}$, as $N > 1$.

Therefore, for each value i we have

$$\frac{N(N-1)(N-2)\cdots(N-i+1)}{i(i-1)(i-2)\cdots 1}[(\sigma^2(R))^i(E(R)^2)^{N+1-i}]$$
$$> \frac{(N-1)(N-2)\cdots(N-i+1)}{i(i-1)(i-2)\cdots 1}[(\sigma^2(R))^i(E(R)^2)^{N-i}].$$

And by shifting from N to $N + 1$, we also add one positive term (the summation is $\sum_{i=1}^{N+1} \binom{N}{i}$ rather than $\sum_{i=1}^{N} \binom{N}{i}$). This factor enhances the increase in the annualized variance as the horizon increases. Thus, we finally conclude that by shifting from N to $N+1$, the annualized variance of return increases, that is,

$$\partial[\sigma^2(W_N)/N]/\partial N > 0 \text{ is intact.}$$

To illustrate the above results, and to show why the expected return must be greater than 1 to obtain the above results, consider the simple case of shifting from a 1-year horizon to a 2-year horizon.

With $N = 2$, we have

$$\sigma^2(W_2)/2 = [\sigma^2(R) + (E(R))^2]^2 - [E(R)]^4/2$$

(see Eq. (6.11) for the case $N = 2$).

Hence, given that the expected rate of return is positive $(E(R) > 1)$, we have

$$\sigma^2(W_2)/2 = [\sigma^4(R) + 2\sigma^2(R)(E(R))^2]/2$$
$$= [\sigma^2(R)(E(R))^2] + \sigma^4(R)/2 > \sigma^2(R).$$

Thus, by shifting from $N = 1$ to $N = 2$, the annualized variance increases, as long as the expected return is larger than 1.

Figure 6.1 provides the annualized variance of the log-return calculated in two alternative ways: the theoretical average, which is constant for all horizons (see the horizontal blue line that is parallel to the horizontal axis), and the simulated average with the *i.i.d.* assumption (see the black curve with fluctuations about the blue line) which is close to the theoretical horizontal line.

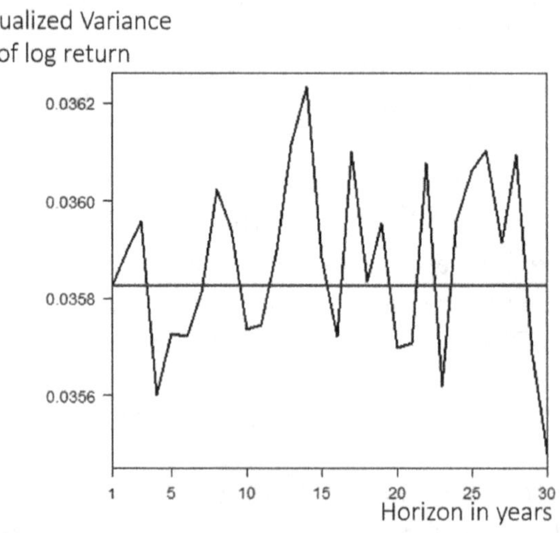

Figure 6.1: Annual volatility with log-return with *i.i.d.* assumption.

The data correspond to the annual rates of returns on the S&P 500 stock index for the period 1928–2019.[9] As the annual variance of the log-return with this data is 0.03582, the horizontal line is drawn at this height. The *i.i.d.* simulation is done with 100,000 observations, as done and explained in previous chapters. As with the simulation, we have many observations, one can extend the analysis for relatively long horizons, in our case, even to $N = 30$ years — a procedure that cannot be done without the simulations. As we can see from Figure 6.1, the simulated and precise theoretical annualized variance of the log-return almost coincide (note that the scale is very wide; hence, seemingly, we have large fluctuations, but the numerical fluctuations are very small). The small fluctuations of the simulated curve about the theoretical horizontal line would vanish were we to increase the sample size indefinitely.

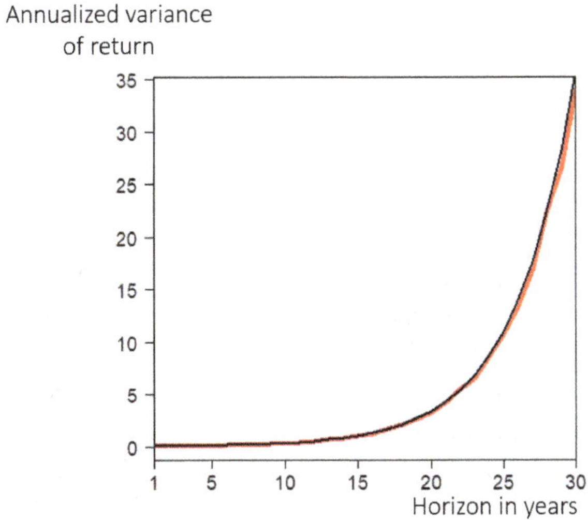

Figure 6.2: Annualized volatility with return calculated by dividing Eq. (6.5) by N.

---

[9]http://www.stern.nyu.edu/~adamodar/pc/datasets/histretSP.xls

     Stocks, Bonds, and the Investment Horizon

Table 6.1: The changes of the annualized variance with log-return and return with the horizon.

Horizon (Years)	With Log-Return	With Return
1	0.0358	0.0379
2	0.0359	0.0479
3	0.0360	0.0604
4	0.0356	0.0762
5	0.0357	0.0971
10	0.0357	0.3145
15	0.0359	1.0272
20	0.0357	3.1886
30	0.0355	33.9514

Figure 6.2 is similar to Figure 6.1, with the exception that the annualized annualized variance dividing Eq. (6.5) by N corresponds to the return and not log-return. We have two curves: one calculated by the theoretical multi-period annualized variance (dividing Eq. (6.5) by N) shown in black, and one calculated with the simulation, shown in red. As we can see, the annualized variance of return increases sharply with the horizon, which conforms with the mathematical analysis. Also, the two figures, as expected with 100,000 observations, almost coincide.

Table 6.1 provides the annualized variance of the return and log-return, corresponding to the simulation with 100,000 observations for some selected horizons. Consistent with the mathematical analysis with $i.i.d.$, the annualized variance of the log-return is almost invariant to the assumed horizon, and it is about 0.0358 for all horizons. However, the annualized variance of return increases sharply with the horizon, from 0.0379 for $N = 1$ year to 0.3145 for $N = 10$ years and increases exponentially to 33.9514 for an $N = 30$-year horizon.

6.2. Discussion

First, we have seen that even when one adheres to the annualized volatility principle, theoretically, there is a contrasting result with the annualized volatility of return and the annualized volatility of the log-return. With $i.i.d.$, the annualized volatility with the log-return is constant, while with returns rather than the log-return, the annualized volatility increases with the horizon. Thus, the following two questions arise:

1. The first question is in regard to the variable that should be employed in the calculation of the annualized volatility. Should one employ a return or log-return? This is an important question from a practical point of view due to the obtained contrasting results with these two variables.
2. The second question concerns the legitimacy of the *annualized* volatility method employed to compare volatility faced in different horizons. Can one defend the annualized approach economically? Is there a better approach to compare the risk faced on different dates?

Regarding the first question, recall that the von-Neumann and Morgenstern[10] expected utility is defined on wealth and not on log-wealth. Hence, in the most general case, expanding the expected utility Taylor series we have,[11]

$$EU(W + x) = f(Ex, \, \sigma^2(x), \, \mu_3(x) \cdots)$$

where W stands for wealth, x stands for the return on the risky asset, $\sigma^2(x)$ is the variance, and $\mu_3(x)$ is the third central moment (skewness), and as we can see from the above formula, also all other central moments determine the expected utility. From this formulation, it is clear that the variance is only one factor out of many economically meaningful factors affecting the expected utility. However, if the variance is the relevant measure for risk, in the most general case, one should employ the variance of return, W, and not the variance of $log(W)$. Notwithstanding, the most interesting question is whether there are specific conditions under which the variance of return, or alternatively the variance of log-return, provides a risk index that is consistent with the expected

---

[10]von-Neumann, J. and O. Morgenstern (1947). *Theory of Games and Economic Behavior, 2nd ed.*, Princeton University Press, Princeton, NJ.

[11]One can develop the expected utility $EU(W + x)$ about $(W + Ex)$, $EU(W+x) = U(W+Ex) + U''(W+Ex)\sigma^2(x)/2! + U'''(W+Ex)\mu_3(x)/3! + \cdots$.

utility paradigm. Thus, are there situations where the mean and variance (of the return or log-return) are sufficient to represent all other moments appearing in the Taylor expansion? To investigate this issue, we state in the following two existing theorems in the financial literature.

Theorem 1. *Given that x and y are normally distributed (more generally elliptic distributions), then*

$$EU(x) \geq EU(y)$$

for all risk-averse utility functions U if and only if

$$E(x) \geq E(y) \quad \text{and} \quad \sigma^2(x) \leq \sigma^2(x)$$

and there is at least one strict inequality (for a proof, see Tobin,[12] Hanoch and Levy,[13] and Chamberlain[14]).

Thus, if the distributions are normal, the variance of x, and not the variance of $log(x)$, is the relevant measure of risk. Moreover, in the normal case, the mean and the variance are all that are needed to determine the expected utility of the prospects under consideration, and all other higher central moments are either equal to zero or are a function of the variance. Thus, if the annualized return can be justified (this issue will be discussed next), with normal distributions, one should employ the annualized variance of return and not of log-return.

We can justify the variance of log-return as a measure of risk in one case — the case where the distributions of returns of the prospects under consideration are log-normal. This case is summarized in the next theorem.

---

[12]Tobin, J. (1958). Liquidity preference as behavior toward risk. *The Review of Economic Studies* 25(2), 65–86.

[13] Hanoch, G. and H. Levy (1969). The efficiency analysis of choices involving risk. *The Review of Economic Studies* 36(3), 335–346.

[14]Chamberlain, G. (1983). A characterization of the distributions that imply mean–variance utility functions. *Journal of Economic Theory* 29(1), 185–201.

Theorem 2. *If x and y are log-normally distributed, then*

$$EU(x) \geq EU(y) \text{ for all risk-averse utility functions, } U, \text{ if and only if}$$

$$E(x) \geq E(y) \, and Var(logx) \leq Var(logx)$$

and there is at least one strict inequality (for a proof, see Levy[15]).

Thus, Theorem 2 provides an economic justification for employing the variance of log-return as a risk index. Therefore, if the annualized methodology is justified, and the distribution is log-normal, one should employ the annualized variance of the log-return rather than the annualized variance of returns.

Are the distributions of returns typically normal or log-normal? Theoretically, if one revises their portfolio continuously, Merton[16] has shown that at any finite horizon (even a one-day horizon), the obtained theoretical distribution is log-normal. Hence, in such a case, indeed, the variance of log-return is the correct measure of risk. The continuous mathematical model and the emerged log-normal distribution at the end of any finite time is mathematically undisputable. The continuous investment model is also employed in deriving the Black and Scholes[17] option model, ending up with a log-normal distribution of the stocks' return. However, in practice, even a minimal transaction cost needed to pay for the portfolio revisions would ruin this model, as the expected return on the portfolio net of transaction costs would be negative. Moreover, it is obvious that no investor revises their portfolio continuously. Thus, in practice, one cannot rely on the continuous model to justify the variance of log-return as the appropriate measure of stock risk.

Empirical evidence also does not support the log-normal distribution, at least not for relatively short horizons. We have seen

---

[15]Levy, H. (1973). Stochastic dominance among log-normal prospects. *International Economics Review* 14(3), 601–614.

[16] Merton, R. C. (1990). *Continuous-Time Finance*, Basil Blackwell, Cambridge.

[17]Black, F. and M. Scholes (1973). The pricing of options and corporate liabilities. *Journal of Political Economy* 81(3), 637–654.

in Chapter 2 that the distributions of returns on risky assets (the S&P 500 stock index) are approximately symmetrical (logistic) for relatively short horizons (say, up to 1 year), and for relatively long horizons (for 10 years or longer), the distributions become close to log-normal. For intermediate horizons, the distributions are neither normal nor log-normal. Let us analyze an extreme case where the distributions are either normal or log-normal. Specifically, suppose that for 1 year the distributions of returns are precisely normal, and for a longer horizon, say for 10 years or more, the distribution of returns is precisely log-normal. Furthermore, suppose that for comparing the risk for different horizons the annualized method can be economically defended. In this case, for a 10-year horizon, we employ the annualized variance of log-return, and we need to compare it with the annual variance, in our case, a 1-year variance, which with the normal distribution should be measured by the variance of return and not the variance of log-return. Thus, by the annualized variance approach, with the correct risk indices, we are comparing apples and oranges — an unacceptable methodology. Note that if the distributions were log-normal for all horizons (as implied by the continuous-time model suggested by Merton), indeed the variance of log-return would be the appropriate measure of risk, as advocated by Theorem 2. However, even in this case, employing the annualized methodology (or any other time-interval method, say daily variance) for risk comparison for various horizons is questionable. This issue is elaborated in the next section.

6.3. Does the Annualized Volatility Measure Risk?

Suppose that for all horizons we have a distribution of the same shape, normal or log-normal, or even a simple case where the variance is technically employed as a measure of risk, even in the case where it is theoretically not the appropriate measure of risk. Another possibility that might be considered is that the variance is a measure of risk where the distribution is neither normal nor log-normal, but the M–V rule can be employed, as it approximately coincides with the expected risk-averse utility, as suggested by Markowitz[18] and by Levy and Markowitz.[19]

Assuming that the variance is employed as a measure of risk, can one justify the employment of the annualized variance method to compare risks faced on different dates? Probably the best way to show the main drawback of the annualized volatility methodology for risk comparison faced on different dates is with a simple example. For simplicity's sake, suppose that we follow Markowitz's approach asserting that the choices by the M–V rule approximately maximize the expected utility; hence, neither normal nor log-normal distribution is assumed. Thus, we can employ a simple example with discrete random variables that is easy to follow.

An example: Suppose that one employs the annualized variance to compare the risk faced 1 year ahead and the risk faced 2 years ahead (the discussion with years is for illustration only. It could be one week and two weeks, or any two time intervals). Thus, we have in this simple case only two horizons, $N = 1$ and $N = 2$. Furthermore, suppose that with a 1-year horizon the returns are 1 or 3 (again, we choose rounded figures that are easy to follow, but the same principle is also intact for more realistic figures) with an equal probability, and with a 2-year horizon, the returns are 1 or 9 with an equal probability. These two cash flows can represent the cash flows of the same prospects faced in different horizons or, for risk comparison, of any two cash flows of two different prospects faced on different dates.

A simple calculation reveals that the variance for a 1-year investment is equal to 1, and for a 2-year investment, the variance is equal to 16. The annualized variance in the 2-year investment is given by $16/2 = 8$. Thus, based on the annualized variance method, we reach the paradoxical result advocating that the risk of the cash flow obtained in the second year is larger than the risk of the cash flow obtained at the end of the first year. A simple glance at these two cash

---

[18]Markowitz, H. M. (1959). *Portfolio Selection*, John Wiley & Sons, New York.

[19]Levy, H. and H. M. Markowitz (1979). Approximating expected utility by a function of mean and variance. *The American Economic Review* 69(3), 308–317.

flow distributions reveals that with no discounting (as done by the annualized variance methodology; we later also introduce discounting to the risk comparison procedure), the 2-year return dominates the 1-year return by first-degree stochastic dominance (FSD); hence, the risk corresponding to the second-year cash flow cannot be larger than the risk corresponding to the first-year cash flow. Thus, every investor with increasing utility in wealth, regardless of their specific preference, would prefer the second-year cash flow over the first-year cash flow.

This example pinpoints the need to define risk in a more coherent way. The risk of any prospect is always subjective; for one investor an outcome of 5% may be considered as a bad result; hence, the prospect may be classified as risky, whereas for another investor, only if a negative result is possible is the prospect classified as risky. The certainty equivalent of the prospect may be an indication of the risk involved; however, this is a subjective measure.[20] When one wishes to consider the riskiness of two prospects or to determine whether stocks become riskier or safer with the horizon, namely to compare the risk of two cash flows of stocks obtained on two different dates, as with the certainty equivalent, here also, the whole distributions should be compared and not only the variance, as emerges in the example given in this section. This is exactly what is done by the discounting cash flow (DCF) approach, accompanied by Rothschild and Stiglitz's definition of risk. Note also that with the DCF approach, risk remains subjective. However, by employing this approach, we can find situations where we can determine whether the risk of one prospect is larger than that of another prospect, or whether the stocks' risk increases or decreases with the horizon. The DCF approach, along with Rothschild and Stiglitz's definition of risk, can identify situations where one can tell whether stocks become riskier or safer with the horizon without relying on annualized risk. If

---

[20]The certainty equivalent (CE) is given by solving the equation $EU(W + x) = U(W + Ex - \pi) = U(CE)$, where W stands for wealth, x for the return on the risky asset with expected value Ex, π stands for the risk premium, and CE is the certainty equivalent. CE is subjective as it depends on U.

such a situation exists, the determination that one cash flow is riskier than another is common *for all risk averters*; hence, the "increasing risk" determination is no longer subjective. This argument, as well as the numerical example given in this section, illustrates that the annualized volatility cannot measure risk in isolation of the other parameters of a distribution. Specifically, in this extreme example, based solely on the annualized volatility, we find that the cash flow obtained in the second year is riskier than the cash flow obtained in the first year — a result that contradicts the FSD rule; hence, it also contradicts the expected utility paradigm.

Indeed, as early as 1963, Baumol[21] realized that the variance (annualized or not annualized) typically cannot measure risk in isolation of the other parameters of a distribution. He suggested another risk index that considers the mean return as well as the variance.[22] More generally, the FSD is a rule which considers the whole distribution of returns to determine whether one cash flow is riskier than another. Thus, Baumol's suggestion is in the right direction of refining the risk index, and the FSD rule goes one step further as it completely conforms with the expected utility paradigm by considering all of the distribution's parameters rather than only the mean and the variance. Finally, if risk aversion is assumed, the second-degree stochastic dominance (SSD) rule is the relevant criterion to determine whether one cash flow is riskier than the other.

In sum, one cannot measure risk by ignoring some of the parameters of the distribution, unless the distribution is normal or alternatively log-normal as stated in Theorems 1 and 2, respectively. However, even if the distributions are normal for short horizons and log-normal for long horizons, one cannot compare risks in this situation, and *a fortiori*, one cannot use the annualized variance to compare risks faced on various dates. We next suggest a method for risk comparison faced on various dates — the discounted cash flow

---

[21]Baumol, W. J. (1963). An expected gain-confidence limit criterion for portfolio selection. *Management Science* 10(1), 174–182.

[22] Baumol suggests the risk index E-$k\sigma$, where E is the mean return and k is the selected number of standard deviations.

method (DCM). Adding the SSD rule, we can employ Rothschild and Stiglitz's approach to examine whether one cash flow is riskier than the other.

6.4. The DCM with Rothschild and Stiglitz's[23] Definition of Risk

6.4.1. *The suggested three stages for risk comparison faced on different dates*

We have seen that the distribution of returns may change with the horizon (see Chapter 2); therefore, we need a distribution-free method for a risk comparison faced on various dates. Suppose that one wishes to find which of the two prospects under consideration is riskier when the cash flows of one prospect occur at t_0 and the cash flows of the other prospect occur at t_1. Or consider even the cash flows obtained from the same asset, say stocks, on these two dates are compared, aiming to know whether stocks become riskier or safer with the horizon, an issue which is in a dispute in the literature (see Siegel (see footnote 3) and Pástor and Stambaugh (see footnote 1)). In such a risk comparison faced on various dates, we suggest the following three-stage procedure that generally leads to different risk ranking as obtained by the annualized volatility:

Stage 1: In the first stage, we suggest to bring all the cash flows of the two prospects under consideration (of the stocks' cash flows obtained on different dates) to a common date by discounting or investing all the cash flows at the riskless interest rate. The common date selected for such risk comparison does not affect the risk ranking. Let us demonstrate this procedure with two cash flows, one obtained at the end of the first year and the other obtained at the end of the second year. In this example, we bring all cash flows to the end of the second year simply by investing the cash flows of the first year for 1 year at the riskless interest rate. Suppose that one of the cash flows obtained

---

[23]Rothschild, M. and J. Stiglitz (1970). Increasing risk, I: A definition. *Journal of Economic Theory* 2(3), 225–243.

at the end of the first period is \$10, and the riskless interest rate is 5%. The investor is indifferent about obtaining \$10 at the end of the first period or \$10.50 at the end of the second period because they can borrow and lend at this riskless interest rate. Thus, \$10 at the end of the first year or \$10.50 at the end of the second year are equivalent. By the same token, we can invest all first-year cash flows at the riskless interest rate, obtaining a new cash flow, where each investor is indifferent about accepting either of these two cash flows. This investor "indifference property" is the economic justification of the suggested DCM. Likewise, one can bring the second-year cash flow to the first year by discounting all cash flows at the riskless interest rate. Also, in this case, the indifference property is intact. This first stage financial transaction allows us to shift from the situation where we compare "apples and oranges," to a comparison of "apples and apples" (in the case of investing) or "oranges with oranges" (in the case of discounting).

Stage 2: By bringing all cash flows to a common date, we now face new cash flows which generally have two different means. We have seen in the example given previously that one cannot compare the risks of two prospects with different means. The variance by itself generally does not measure risk. Therefore, Rothschild and Stiglitz suggest to compare only the risks of prospects with equal means, or to see whether one prospect differs from the other by a "mean preserving spread," namely a case where the mean is kept unchanged. As, in practice, it is rare to find two cash flows with the same mean, we suggest equating the means by borrowing or lending at the riskless interest rate. Thus, following Rothschild and Stiglitz's risk definition, in the second stage, we equate the means of the two cash flows under consideration. To equate the means of these two cash flows, we suggest to borrow or lend money at the riskless interest rate, and invest the available funds in a portfolio of one of the cash flows. The purpose of the procedure given in Stage two is to borrow or lend until the two cash flows (one with borrowing and lending and without borrowing and lending) have equal mean returns. One can leverage the cash flow with the lower mean, or alternatively, diversify between the riskless asset and the cash flow with the larger mean. As we shall later see, the determination of which cash flow is riskier is invariant to the selected procedure.

Stage 3: Finally, in the third stage, we employ Rothschild and Stiglitz's definition of "riskier than" to find which prospect, or cash flow, of the two prospects obtained on different dates is riskier. Cash flow G (representing one of the cash flows) is riskier than cash flow F (representing the other cash flows) if the two prospects have an equal mean and the following integral condition holds,

$$\int_a^x [G(t) - F(t)]dt \geq 0$$

for all values x, and there is at least one strict inequality, where F and G stand for the cumulative distributions of return of the two cash flows under consideration, and a stands for the lower bound of the returns.

Similarly, F is riskier than G if the following holds,

$$\int_a^x [F(t) - G(t)]dt \geq 0$$

for all values x, and there is at least one strict inequality.

If neither of the above inequalities holds for all x, by Rothschild and Stiglitz's definition of "riskier than," we cannot rank the two cash flows by their risk.

Note that this integral condition defines the case where F dominates G by SSD for the special case of equal means prospects. Hence, with this special equal mean case, we can employ the terms "riskier than" or SSD dominance interchangeably. This means that if G is riskier than F, there is also SSD dominance of F over G, implying that every risk averter would be better off investing in a combination of F with the riskless asset than in a combination of G with the riskless asset.

Before we generalize this claim, let us illustrate the suggested risk comparison procedure with a numerical example.

6.4.2. *Example: The discounting methods with Rothschild and Stiglitz's definition of risks*

In this example, we first present mechanically the three stages discussed above and then explain how the borrowing–lending transactions can be done in practice.

Suppose that one faces two prospects, F and G, where the cash flows of F will be obtained 2 years from now, and the cash flows of prospect G will be obtained 1 year from now. F and G can also represent the cash flows corresponding to two assets, or the cash flows on the same asset on two different dates.

Assume that the cash flows (the returns) of prospect F are 1 or 2 (namely 0% or 100% rates of return) with an equal probability of 0.5 (hence, the expected terminal wealth for a \$1 investment is \$1.50), and the cash flows of prospect G are 0.9 or 1.8 (namely, −10% or 80%) with equal probability (hence, the expected terminal wealth for a \$1 investment is \$1.35, namely a 35% rate of return). Assume an interest rate of 5%. With this example, we employ the three stages in the process of the risk comparison of the two cash flows obtained on these two different dates. In Stage 1, we reinvest the cash flows of prospect G obtained at the end of the first year at the interest rate of 5% for 1 year, bringing all cash flows to a common date, which, in this example, is the end of the second year. Thus, the adjusted cash flows of prospect G are

$$\text{either } 0.9 \times 1.05 = .945 \text{ or } 1.8 \times 1.05 = 1.890 \text{ with}$$

$$\text{equal probability of } 0.5.$$

Therefore, the expected cash flow of project G at the end of period 2 is

$$0.5 \times 0.945 + 0.5 \times 1.890 = 1.4175, \text{ namely } \$1.4175$$

$$\text{for each } \$1 \text{ initial investment.}$$

Knowing the two expected cash flows of F and G, in Stage 2, we leverage prospect G (the prospect with the lower mean) by borrowing (where the borrowing takes place at the end of the first year) at the interest rate of 5%, and the chosen leverage guarantees that the means of the two prospects at the end of the second year are equal. Thus, the leverage parameter α is selected such that the following equality holds:

$$(1 - \alpha) \times 1.05 + \alpha \times 1.4175 = 1.50$$

where 1.4175 is the mean return of prospect G (in terms of the second-year cash flows) and 1.50 is the mean return of prospect F where both cash flows are faced in Year 2.

Solving for the leverage parameter, we find that α, which equates the two means, is $\alpha = 1.2245$; hence, $1 - \alpha \cong -0.2245$. This means that for each \$1 initial investment, one needs to borrow 0.2245 dollars and invest in prospect G 1.2245 dollars. With this leverage, the distribution of the leveraged prospect G_α becomes

$$-0.2245 \times 1.05 + (1 - (-0.2245)) \times 0.945 = 0.9214$$

with a probability of 0.5, and

$$-0.2245 \times 1.05 + (1 - (-0.2245)) \times 1890 = 2.07858$$

with a probability of 0.5.

Note that the mean return on the leveraged twice prospect G is 1.5, as required (the small difference is due to numerical rounding). Equalizing the means of the two prospects when the cash flows are obtained on the same date, one can finally employ the definition of risk suggested by Rothschild and Stiglitz to find which prospect (or which cash flow) is riskier, or alternatively to declare that it is impossible to assert which prospect is riskier. Denoting the leveraged prospect G by G_α, we can compare the risk of F and G_α as these two prospects with cash flows obtained on the same date also have equal means. Thus, we turn to illustrate Stage 3:

Figure 6.3 presents the two cumulative distributions, F and G_α, corresponding to our example. These two cumulative distributions represent the cash flows obtained on the same date (in our example, at the end of the second year) and after leveraging prospect G such that the two distributions have an equal mean. Note that in Figure 6.3, G_α represents the time-adjusted and the mean-adjusted

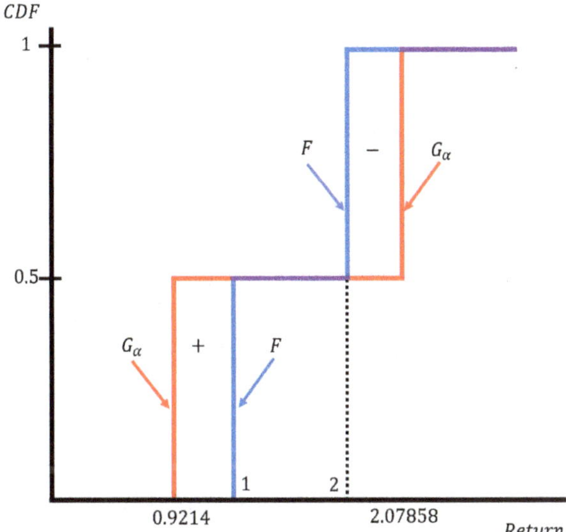

Figure 6.3: The cumulative distributions F and G_α corresponding to the numerical example.

cash flow. As can be seen, the "plus" area is equal to the "minus" area; hence,

$$\int_a^b [G_\alpha(t) - F(t)]dt = 0;$$

therefore, for all values of x smaller than b, we have

$$\int_a^x [G_\alpha(t) - F(t)]dt > 0$$

where a and b are the lower and upper bounds of the returns, respectively.

Hence, by Rothschild and Stiglitz's definition of risk, the cash flow corresponding to G_α is riskier than the cash flow corresponding to F, as long as the riskless asset is available.

In sum, the three stages of risk comparison are: bring all cash flows to a common date, equate the means, and then employ Rothschild and Stiglitz's definition of risk, or more precisely, the "riskier than" concept.

Note, however, that if the riskless asset is not available, there is no one risk index that tells us which cash flow is riskier. Thus, investigating the change in the riskiness of stocks with the horizon, we typically cannot assert whether stocks become riskier or safer with the horizon in the absence of the riskless asset. Moreover, even in the presence of the riskless asset, if the integral condition does not hold, we cannot determine if one cash flow is riskier than the other. Later in this chapter, we shall examine the integral condition empirically with the cash flows of stocks obtained on different dates with various alternative assumed riskless interest rates.

6.4.3. *Discussion*

With the example given in the previous subsection, we illustrate the three stages of the procedure to compare the risk of cash flows obtained at the end of the first year with the risk of a cash flow obtained in the second year. But how can this procedure be carried out in practice? The 2-year investment is simple, as there we do not mix the cash flow obtained in the second year with the riskless asset. However, with the cash flow obtained in the first year, the riskless asset is involved in two ways: firstly, by investing the first-year cash flow from the investment in the riskless interest rate for 1 year, and secondly, by mixing this invested cash flow with the riskless asset to equate the means of the two cash flows under comparison. Although we assume investing in the first year in the risky prospect and in the second year in the riskless asset, one can change the investment order and invest in the first year in the riskless asset and only in the second year in the risky prospect, as in both cases the cash flow at the end of the second year is identical, namely $(1 + r)x = x(1 + r)$, where x is the cash flow of the risky prospect. By this procedure the role of the riskless asset in the two stages is more transparent. Thus, by this investment procedure, at the end of the first year, for each $1 of initial wealth, the investor has $(1 + r)$ to invest in the risky prospect for the second year. Knowing the expected return on the two prospects, at the end of the first year, the investor leverages the 1-year investment in the risky prospect such that the two means at the end of the second year will be equal. With our specific example, we have

$$(1 - \alpha)(1.05) + \alpha(1 + r)(1.35) = 1.50.$$

Therefore, as obtained before, $\alpha \cong 1.2245$, where $\$(1 + r)$ is invested for 1 year in stocks whose mean rate of return is 35% with a leverage of α.

This more transparent procedure for equating the means is particularly important for investigating the change in the riskiness of stocks with the horizon. For example, suppose that we wish to compare the risk of a 1-year investment in stocks to a 2-year investment. For the 1-year investment in stocks and 1-year investment in the riskless asset, we suggest to invest the first year in the riskless asset, and in the second year to invest in stocks with a leverage, guaranteeing that the two means are equal, allowing us to apply the increasing risk definition of Rothschild and Stiglitz. Recall that with *i.i.d.* assumption of the return on stocks, the cash flow from investing the first year in the riskless asset and in the second year in stocks is $(1 + r)x$, and by investing in the first year in stocks and the second year in the riskless asset, we obtain identical cash flow $x(1+r)$, where x is the 1-year cash flow, which is identical for all 1-year periods. By the same token, when we compare investing for N years in stocks to investing for n years in stocks and $N - n$ in the riskless asset, we assume investing first the \$1 initial investment in the riskless asset for $N - n$ years, and only then to invest the accumulated wealth in the stocks for n years. Changing the order of the investment in stocks and the riskless asset would not change the analysis or the final results.

6.4.4. *Generalization of Rothschild and Stiglitz's approach*

Suppose that two cash flows are faced in periods t_1 and t_2, respectively. Bringing the two cash flows to a common date implies that we look instead of at the cash flows x_{t_1} and x_{t_2} at the cash flows ax_{t_1} and x_{t_2}, where a is a constant reflecting the compounding factor (or the discounting factor) at the riskless interest rate. Next, by equating the means by leveraging the cash flow with the lower mean, we create a new random variable denoted by $ax_{t_1,\alpha}$, where α is the leverage parameter that equates the means of cash flows, creating the cumulative distributions, F and G. Then we employ Rothschild and Stiglitz's definition of "riskier than" to figure out which cash flow is riskier, or to conclude that this is impossible to determine. The selected common date to which all cash flows are brought does not affect the SSD relationship (see the following). Notwithstanding, one should be careful regarding the number of years of the investment at the riskless asset, as well as by selecting the leverage level which equates the means. This crucial point is illustrated in what follows.

Suppose that one wishes to compare the riskiness of two cash flows, e.g., cash flows from investing in stocks for different horizons: one cash flow is obtained at the end of the first year and one cash flow is obtained 10 years ahead. Denoting these two cash flows by x_1 and x_{10} (both are random variables), with this specific case, we illustrate the following three stages:

Stage 1: Invest the \$1 initial wealth at the riskless interest rate, r, for 9 years, and then invest the accumulated wealth at the end of the 9th year for 1 year in the stocks. (Note that with *i.i.d.*, the same return is obtained by investing in stocks for 1 year and then investing the obtained cash flow at the riskless interest rate for 9 years.) Thus, we create a new random variable, which we denote as $x_1(10)$,

$$x_1(10) = (1 + r)^9 x_1$$

where $x_1(10)$ is the return obtained at the end of the 10th year, and x_1 is the return on the investment in stocks for 1 year. Note that the above formula is stated in terms of terminal wealth.

Thus, comparing risks faced at $N = 1$ and $N = 10$, the investment in the riskless asset is only for 9 years.

Stage 2: Equate the two means by employing the following leverage, where this equation is written in terms of rates of returns (recall that x_1 is the cash flow which is also equal to the return per \$1 investment)

$$(1 - \alpha)r + \alpha(1 + r)^9(Ex_1 - 1) = E(x_{10} - 1).$$

Note that $(1 + r)^9$ is the dollar investment in stocks at the beginning of the 10th year, and $(Ex_1 - 1)$ is the *rate* of returns on stocks for 1 year, $E(x_{10} - 1)$ is the *rate* of returns on stocks for a 10-year investment period, and r is the interest rate. For example, if the \$1 invested in the riskless asset of 5% for 9 years accumulates to about \$1.55 at the end of the 9th year, and the rate of returns on stocks for 1 year $(Ex_1 - 1)$ is 10%, the above equation becomes

$$(1 - \alpha)5\% + \alpha 1.55(10\%) = E(x_{10} - 1) = (1.1)^{10}(100\%) - 100\%.$$

Therefore,

$$5\% - \alpha 5\% + \alpha 15.5\% \cong 159\%; \text{ hence,}$$

$$\alpha = (159\% - 5\%)/10.5\% \cong 14.7.$$

Note that all values are written above in percentage terms; hence, the return on stocks for 10 years is written as $(1.1)^{10}(100\%) - 100\%$.

Thus, to draw the two distributions for the relevant "riskier than" comparison, we need first to solve for α which equates the means, and then employ this solved leverage parameter with each observation $x_1(1 + r)^9$, and only then compare Rothschild and Stiglitz's integral condition to figure out whether one distribution is riskier than the other.

One may suspect that the "riskier than" results may be a function of the discounting process and the employed leverage α. Regarding the discounting factor, it was proven in the literature that the common date selected to bring all cash flows does not affect the SSD relationship. Namely, if ax dominates y by SSD, also $(ba)x$ dominates $(b)y$ by SSD, where a and b are constants reflecting the interest rate employed to discount or invest the cash flows, bringing them to a common date. Thus, if we shift all the cash flows by a factor of b, it does not change the dominance relationships.

What about the process of equating the means? Does the selected level of equating the means affect the SSD relationship? Suppose that cash flow $ax_{t_{1,\alpha}}$ is found to be riskier (or less risky) than cash flow y. Is it possible that cash flow $ax_{t_1,\alpha}$ may not be riskier (or less risky) than the other cash flow if the last cash flow is also leveraged and shifts to another mean return? In short, one may suspect that the SSD dominance (hence, the risk ranking) may be a function of the selected date to which the two cash flows are brought and the employed leverage for equating the two means. This argument, although intuitively appealing, is not valid; hence, the procedure suggested previously is intact. Specifically, Levy[24] has shown that if the integral condition of Rothschild and Stiglitz (or the SSD condition) is valid for $ax_{t_1,\alpha}$ and x_{t_2}, it is also valid for all other possible levels of leverage. Namely, if there is SSD dominance of $ax_{t_1,\alpha}$ on x_{t_2}, then for each combination of the riskless asset and x_{t_2}, there is another combination of ax_{t_1} and the riskless asset which dominates it by SSD. Thus, if the integral condition holds for one degree of leverage, then the integral condition asserting "riskier than" (or SSD dominance) is intact for all arbitrary selected degrees of leverage. This claim about the selected leverage is summarized by the following theorem:

Theorem 3. *Let F and G be two prospects with two different means, E_F and E_G. Diversify between G and the riskless asset to create a prospect E_{G_α} such that $E_{G_\alpha} = E_F$. If G_α is riskier than F by Rothschild and Stiglitz's "riskier than" definition (namely, F dominates G_α by SSD), then for any other arbitrary combination G_α and the riskless asset, say, G_β, there is a another combination of F with the riskless asset, say, F_δ, such that the two new prospects have equal means, and G_β is riskier than F_δ. Thus, the two means can be shifted to any arbitrary level without affecting the SSD, if it exists.*

Thus, one can select any arbitrary level for comparing the means. It is sufficient to find one combination of one of the assets that dominates the other asset by SSD to conclude that such dominance exists for all possible levels of selected means.

---

[24]Levy, H. (1977). The definition of risk: An extension. *Journal of Economic Theory* 14(1), 232–234.

6.5. Are Stocks Riskier or Safer with the Horizon? The Empirical Evidence

Having this definition of "riskier than," we can turn to the question in dispute, namely whether stocks become safer or riskier *with* the horizon. In this section, we rely on historical rates of returns in the S&P 500 stock index, and in the next chapter, we discuss whether the *ex-post* volatility reflects the future volatility. Specifically, we add to the stock distribution of return risks that have not occurred even in the last century.

In line with the theoretical analysis given previously and the "riskier than" definition of Rothschild and Stiglitz, we discuss and compare three distributions of returns as follows:

F_N, which denotes the distribution of return on the investment in the S&P 500 index for N years.

$G_{n,r}$, which denotes the distribution of return on the investment in the S&P stock index for $n < N$ years and investing the obtained cash flows for $N - n$ years at the riskless interest rate. Hence, the above two cash flows are obtained on the same date — the end of the Nth year.

$G_{n,r,\alpha}$, which denotes the distribution of the return of $G_{n,r}$ after equating the means. In other words, we mix $G_{n,r}$ with the riskless asset, guaranteeing that the expected returns of F_N and $G_{n,r}$ are identical.

Having the 1928–2019 annual rates of returns in the S&P 500 stock index, we derive each of these three distributions by randomly drawing a large number of observations from the historical series corresponding to these years. For example, to derive F_N (which is the distribution of compounded returns for an N-years investment in stocks), we draw N observations from the historical series, and calculate the compounded return for this period. We repeat this procedure 100,000 times to obtain F_N. To obtain $G_{n,r}$, we draw n observations, calculate the compounded return and the accumulated return of each n-year investment, and invest the cash flows from the stocks at the riskless asset for $N - n$ years, yielding $G_{n,r}$, which corresponds to the N-year investment, n in the stocks, and $N - n$ in the riskless asset (lending or borrowing). In the last stage, we mix the distribution $G_{n,r}$ with the riskless asset, as explained beforehand to obtain $G_{n,r,\alpha}$.

We conduct the above calculation for various values, N, n, and r. We present in what follows a sample of these density functions, as well as a sample of the cumulative distribution functions. Then we present a table which summarizes the "riskier than" results for all values of N and n, and various riskless interest rates.

Figure 6.4(a) compares the density functions of the rates of returns of three investments for two horizons: $N = 10$ and $n = 1$. Comparing these two horizons, do stocks become riskier or safer with the horizon? As we can see from Figure 6.4(a), for the average interest rate prevailing in the period 1928–2019 (about 3.4%), the density function of F_N is located in most of the range of returns to the right of the density function of $G_{n,r}$, a result stemming from the fact that the interest rate at which we invest the funds obtained from a 1-year investment in stocks is invested for the next 9 years at a relatively low interest rate (at least compared to the returns on stocks). However, as we equate the means, the density function corresponding to $G_{n,r}$ is shifted to the right — compare the density functions corresponding to $G_{n,r}$ and $G_{n,r,\alpha}$ in Figure 6.4(a).

Figure 6.4(b) presents the density function with a hypothetical unrealistic high interest rate. We show this density function for this unrealistic rate simply to shed more light on the role of the riskless interest rate in defining "riskier than" between investment strategies. As can be seen from Figure 6.4(b), in most of the range of returns, $G_{n,r}$ is located to the right of F_N due to the high interest rate employed in investing the funds obtained at the end of the first year for the next 9 years. When we equate the means, this density function shifts to the left (compare $G_{n,r}$ and $G_{n,r,\alpha}$). This is the opposite of what we obtained with the low interest rate — compare Figures 6.4(a) and 6.4(b).

In order to determine whether stocks become riskier or safer with the horizon, we need to analyze the two cumulative distributions under consideration rather than the density functions. We can see

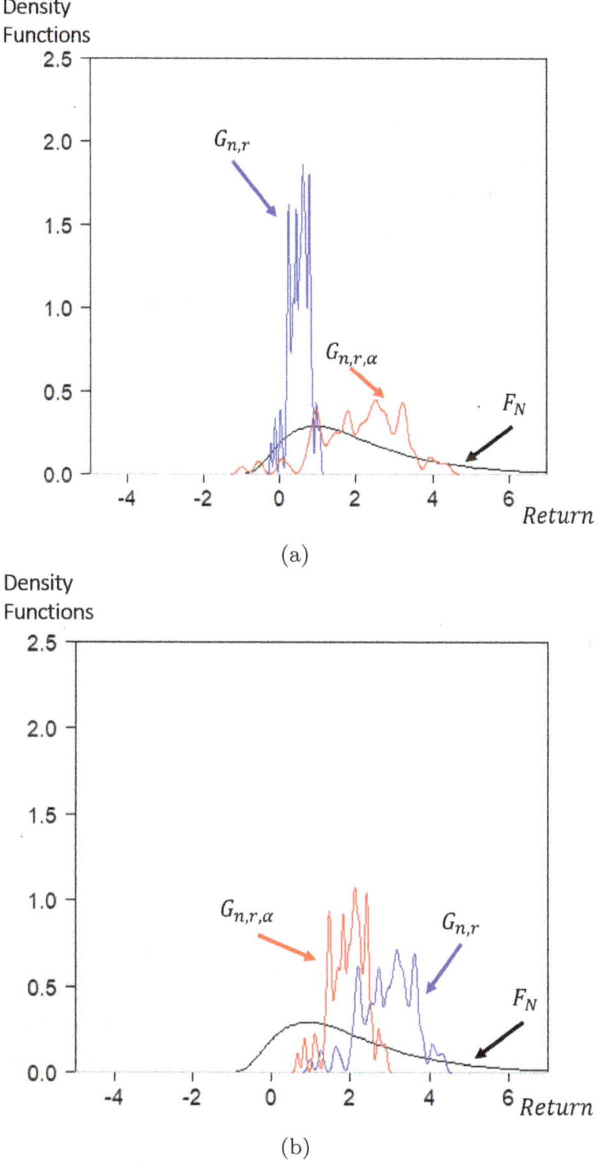

Figure 6.4: The density functions of F_N, $G_{N,r}$, and $G_{n,r,\alpha}$ for the two alternative interest rates: $r = 0.034$ and, alternatively, $r = 0.15$: (a) $r = 0.034$; (b) $r = 0.15$.

from Figure 6.5(a) that the cumulative distribution of F_N (where $n = 10$ years) is located mostly to the right of $G_{n,r}$ (where $n = 1$), as we reinvest the cash flows obtained from stocks after 1 year for the next 9 years at a relatively low interest rate. When we equate the means, we obtain the cumulative distributions, as presented in Figure 6.5(b). As the total area enclosed between the two cumulative distributions is by construction equal to zero (as the means are equal), the "$-$" area must be equal to the two "$+$" areas (see Figure 6.5(b)); hence, it is larger, in absolute terms, than the first "$+$" area.

Thus, we have the following results presented in Figure 6.5(b):

$$\int_a^b [G_{n,r,\alpha}(x) - F_N(x)]dx = 0$$

where a and b are the lower and upper bounds of the returns, respectively, implying that

$$\int_a^{a_2} [G_{n,r,\alpha}(x) - F_N(x)]dx < 0;$$

hence, $F_N(x)$ does not dominate $G_{n,r,\alpha}(x)$ by SSD. Similarly, we have

$$\int_a^{a_1} [F_N(x) - G_{n,r,\alpha}(x)]dx < 0$$

(see Figure 6.5(b)); hence, $G_{n,r,\alpha}(x)$ also does not dominate $F_N(x)$ by SSD.

Two implications emerge from the above analysis corresponding to the $N = 10$ and $n = 1$ horizons. The first result is that, for these two horizons, we cannot determine whether stocks become riskier or safer with the horizon. The second implication, which directly emerges from the first, is that when we compare investing in stocks for 10 years or for 1 year, and in the riskless asset for 9 years, there is no SSD dominance, as some risk-averters may be better off by investing in stocks for 10 years and others may be better off by investing in stocks for 1 year and investing in the riskless asset for 9 years. Obviously, these empirical results are intact for an interest rate of about 3.4% and may change with the assumed riskless interest rate.

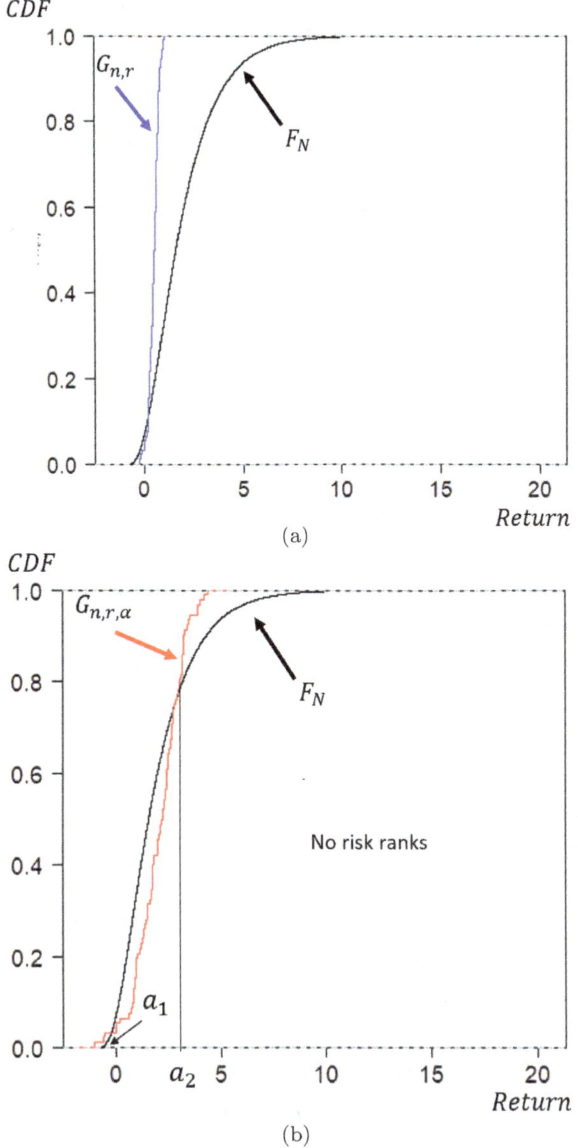

Figure 6.5: The cumulative distributions F_N, $G_{n,r}$, and of F_N and $G_{n,r,\alpha}$ for an interest rate of $r = 0.034$ and horizon $N = 10$: (a) $G_{n,r}$ and F_N; (b) $G_{n,r,\alpha}$ and F_N.

Table 6.2: The SSD dominance for various pairs of horizons and for various interest rates* SSD (or "increasing risk") table for leveraged CDFS.

	$r_1 = 0$	$r_2 = 0.005$	$r_3 = 0.01$	$r_4 = 0.02$	$r_5 = 0.034$	$r_6 = 0.15$	$r_7 = 0.3$
1 SSD 2	No	No	No	No	No	Yes	Yes
2 SSD 1	Yes	Yes	Yes	Yes	Yes	No	No
1 SSD 5	No	No	No	No	No	Yes	Yes
5 SSD 1	Yes	Yes	Yes	No	No	No	No
1 SSD 10	No	No	No	No	No	Yes	Yes
10 SSD 1	Yes	No	No	No	No	No	No
2 SSD 5	No	No	No	No	No	Yes	Yes
5 SSD 2	Yes	Yes	Yes	Yes	No	No	No
2 SSD 10	No	No	No	No	No	Yes	Yes
10 SSD 2	Yes	No	No	No	No	No	No
5 SSD 10	No	No	No	No	No	Yes	Yes
10 SSD 5	Yes	No	No	No	No	No	No

Note: *In the table, the CDF for the short horizon investment in stocks is $G_{n,r,\alpha}(x)$, and for the long horizon investment in stocks is $F_N(x)$. The number in the first column is the number of years invested in stocks, the distribution that is dominated by SSD is the riskier one.

Table 6.2 summarizes the SSD results regarding the changes in the stocks' risk with the horizon for various pairwise comparisons of n and N, as well as for various assumed riskless interest rates. In this table, "No" stands for no SSD dominance and "Yes" stands for the existence of SSD dominance. For example, when we compare $n = 1$ with $N = 10$ for $r = 3.4\%$, the table twice reports "No," implying that we cannot determine whether stocks become riskier or safer with the horizon, a result that conforms with the graphical analysis presented before, corresponding to these two horizons (see Figure 6.5(b)). From this table, it is interesting to see that with very low interest rates, we conclude that stocks become safer with the horizon (as reinvesting is at a very low interest rate, which decreases the attractiveness of a bond investment strategy), and for relatively large and unrealistic interest rates, just the opposite occurs (see the right-hand side of the table). Specifically, for an interest rate of 15% or more, using our approach, we can safely conclude that stocks become riskier with the horizon. For a zero-interest rate, we can assert that stocks become safer with the horizon. For interest rates between these two values, inconclusive results are obtained. For example, for a 2% interest rate, we obtain that stocks become safer when we increase the horizon from one to two years, and by increasing the horizon from two to five years, but for all other comparisons, with a 2% interest rate, we cannot determine whether the risk of stocks increases or decreases with the horizon. Nevertheless, the main conclusion from this table is that for the most reasonable riskless interest rates, we obtain that we cannot determine whether stocks become riskier or safer with the horizon (see the interest rate in the range of 0.02–0.034, a range for which the "No" result dominates the table).

6.6. Summary

Regarding the investment in financial assets, mainly in stocks and bonds, two important questions arise. Both are important from theoretical and practical points of view:

(a) Do stocks become more or less attractive than bonds with the investment horizon?
(b) Do stocks become riskier or safer with the horizon?

As there is no dispute that stocks are, on average, more profitable than bonds, some researchers focus on the second issue — the change in the riskiness of stocks with the horizon — an issue to which we devote this chapter. If stocks, which are more profitable than bonds, also become safer with the horizon, then one is tempted to conclude that stocks also become more attractive than bonds with the horizon.

It is suggested in the literature to calculate the risk either by the variance of returns or by the variance of log-returns. Moreover, to compare risk faced on different dates, it is suggested to calculate the annualized volatility corresponding to various investment horizons. Siegel advocates that the risk of stocks decreases with the horizon, while Pástor and Stambaugh reach just the opposite conclusion.

We first show that neither the variance of return nor the variance of log-return measure the economic risk properly, unless the distributions of returns are normal or log-normal, respectively. Secondly, if the variance indeed measures the risk involved, the annualized methodology is inappropriate, and hence may lead to wrong conclusions. Facing risks on different dates, with borrowing and lending, we suggest first to bring all cash flows to a common arbitrary date (the selected date does not affect the results), equate the means by mixing one of the cash flows with the riskless asset, and finally employ Rothschild and Stiglitz's "riskier than" definition to determine whether one of the cash flows is riskier than the other. Unlike the risk comparison with annualized volatility, with our approach, we may maintain either that one cash flow is riskier than the other or that it is impossible to determine which cash flow is riskier. Thus, "riskier than" and SSD dominance imply each other. For example, if investing for 1 year in stocks and 9 years in the riskless asset is safer than investing for 10 years in stocks, it implies that the safer investment dominates the other one by SSD.

Employing the 1928–2019 annual rates of returns corresponding to the S&P 500 stock index, we find that with zero interest rate stocks become safer with the horizon; for very high riskless interest rates, stocks become riskier with the horizon; and for a wide range of relevant riskless interest rates, it is impossible to determine whether stocks become riskier or safer with the horizon. The implication is that comparing investment in stocks for n years and in bonds for $N - n$ years to the investment in stocks for N years, there is no SSD dominance. Some investors are better off with one strategy and other more risk-averse investors are better off with the other strategy.

Chapter 7

Stock Risk: Do Historical Crashes Tell the Whole Story? The Black Swan Hypothesis[1]

In making investment decisions, and particularly for selecting the optimal diversified portfolio of risky assets, one needs to employ some inputs, e.g., the distribution of rates of returns, on various assets. In some cases, this input is needed for calculating the various parameters (e.g., expected returns, variances, and correlations), which, in turn, determine a portfolio's risk and the optimal diversification among the risky assets under consideration. Generally, historical rates of returns are employed in calculating the various needed parameters. In employing historical rates of returns, it is implicitly assumed that historical risk is the best estimate of future risk. However, one does not need to rely solely on historical rates of returns. Specifically, based on historical data, the employed rates of returns can be objective, subjective, or even a mix of the two. For example, one can employ the *ex-post* objective series of rates of returns and adjust the observed distribution to reflect an investor's subjective beliefs, e.g., assigning a larger probability weight to the last observation or employing a sophisticated statistical approach to estimate the *ex-ante* distribution of returns based on the information provided by the historical distribution and other available information, where the *ex-ante* estimated distribution generally differs from the *ex-post* distribution. For example, when President Trump was elected, some

---

[1]Nassim, N. T. (2007). *The Black Swan: The Impact of the Highly Improbable.* Random House, New York.

investors could adjust the historical rates of returns to reflect the new economic and international policy declared by the new president. The same argument can be attributed to changes in the economic policy that are occurring since the election of President Biden. If such a subjective approach is adopted, it implies that the investor believes that history will not repeat itself. Indeed, the experimental evidence is that, generally, some subjective beliefs are employed. For example, a study dealing with choice among risky prospects reveals that investors do not rely solely on historical rates of returns and that they make some subjective adjustments. In an experiment of choosing between uncertain investments, faced with, say, prospects with the last 5 years' rates of return, it is found that subjects, on average, assign more than 0.2 probability to the last observation, hence relying on *ex-post* data with some subjective modifications.[2]

Notwithstanding, it is common for academic researchers and professional investors to employ *ex-post* data where for each year (or month), an equal probability is assigned. For example, this is the procedure employed in calculating and reporting the periodical Sharpe performance index of mutual funds, and in calculating the beta of an asset and the variance of the return on an asset, or in testing empirically the capital asset pricing model (CAPM). Obviously, when one employs *ex-post* rates of returns, the time series must be long enough to provide statistical reliability. Yet, some researchers argue that even very long time series of rates of returns (one or two centuries of data), particularly regarding the returns of stocks, does not fully reflect all future hidden and unexpected risks of stock crashes; in the future, we may face new unwitnessed black swan events (see footnote 1). Hence, it is claimed that the future risk of stocks is different from the historical risk. This view is advocated by several researchers cited in the previous chapter.

In this chapter, we first elaborate on these contrasting views regarding the association between *ex-post* and *ex-ante* risk of stocks, and then incorporate the future risk of stocks into the

---

[2]Levy, H. and M. Levy (2005). Overweighing recent observations: Experimental results and economic implications, in Zwick, R. and A. Rapoport (eds.), *Experimental Research*, 155–183.

decision-making process in several alternate ways. As we shall see in what follows, these added future risks are relatively large, not seen in history. We first add future annual crashes in the stock market never seen in history to the distributions of the rates of returns, with some assigned probabilities to these crashes, and analyze the sensitivity of the stock–bond optimal portfolio to these added crashes. Next, we change the economic regime, a change which makes stocks permanently less attractive than bonds relative to the attractiveness that is fully based on historical rates of returns. With the changes in the economic regime, no crashes are involved, but the whole distribution of the returns on stocks is shifted to the left.

We conduct each of the above two analyses in two frameworks: the mean–variance (M–V) and expected utility frameworks. While the expected utility is the correct framework in which to analyze these issues, particularly for long horizons, we also employ the M–V framework, which is still the most popular among researchers and professional investors.

Finally, note that though some crashes never seen before may occur in the future, no one can tell the magnitude or probability of these potential crashes occurring. Therefore, in this chapter, we analyze a wide spectrum of negative events in the stock market and the sensitivity of the optimal diversification between stocks and bonds to these events, but we obviously cannot tell which of them may actually occur. We want the reader to be aware of such future risks so that each investor may look at the results and adopt the event that they subjectively believe in. Note, however, that assuming such crashes also has an economic price because if the negative events in the stock market do not occur, there is a deviation from optimal diversification, exacting an economic price from the investor.

7.1. Contrasting Views Regarding the Association Between Historical and Future Stock Risk

In his empirical analysis of the changes in the relative attractiveness of stocks and bonds with the horizon, Siegel[3] implicitly assumes that

---

[3]Siegel, J. J. (2014). *Stocks for the Long Run: The Definitive Guide to Financial Market Returns and Long-Term Investment Strategies*, McGraw-Hill, New York.

if one considers a very long series of rates of returns on stocks, it is sufficient for estimating the future parameters and future risk; hence, it is implicitly assumed that history best predicts the future, namely history approximately will repeat itself. Thus, the implicit assumption is that a long enough history of rates of returns on stocks, which includes historical stock market crashes, reflects all future possible crashes in the stock market. Relying on 206 years of historical rates of returns on stocks that include several severe stock market crashes, Siegel concludes that the relative attractiveness of stocks increases with the investment horizon. Specifically, by his approach, stocks which are relatively risky for a 1-year investment become almost completely safe for investors with a 10-year or longer investment horizon. By his approach, investors for pension should allocate the lion's share of their portfolio to stocks.

While the historical facts are undeniable, the crucial issue in dispute in the literature is whether the historical data, even covering two centuries, properly reflects all possible future stock risks. Several researchers cast doubts on the perfect association between *ex-post* risk and *ex-ante* risk. The argument of those who disagree with Siegel's approach is that even a two-centuries-long series of rates of returns does not reflect all potential future risks of stocks due to potential changes in the economy or the occurrence of specific events that have not occurred in the past; hence, future risk is not reflected in the distribution of past rates of returns. And if there are hidden risks not observed in the past, it casts doubts on Siegel's conclusion of "stocks for the long run" and the investment strategy employed by life cycle mutual funds. Let us elaborate on the argument raised by those who believe that there are future risks of stocks not observed in the past.

Pástor and Stambaugh,[4] who strongly disagree with Siegel's conclusion, advocate that relying on historical fluctuations in stock prices is insufficient for discovering all future possible stock risks. Employing sophisticated statistical methodology to estimate the

---

[4]Pástor, L. and R. F. Stambaugh (2012). Are stocks really less volatile in the long run? *The Journal of Finance* 67(2), 431–478.

future risk of stocks, they conclude:

> *"We find that stocks are actually more volatile over long horizons from an investor's perspective. Investors condition on available information but realize their knowledge is limited in two key respects. First, even after observing 206 years of data (1802–2007, years employed by Siegel), investors do not know the values of the parameters of the return-generating process, especially the parameters to the conditional expected return. Second, investors recognize that the observable "predictors" used to forecast returns deliver only an imperfect proxy for the conditional expected return, whether or not the parameter values are known"*(see pp. 431–432).

Pástor and Stombaugh are not alone in this view. Markowitz[5] argues that there are hidden *ex-ante* risks of stocks not reflected in the *ex-post* data. He argues that beliefs regarding well-documented financial relationships can be (a) temporarily violated or (b) changed permanently, until some event occurs and they change permanently again. We focus below on the examples Markowitz provides — examples regarding temporary extreme fluctuations in stock prices that have never historically occurred. Thus, he argues that there are future risks of stocks that are not reflected in the historical data. Markowitz illustrates the potential future risks not reflected historically with two examples of temporary but sharp changes in the stock market that cannot be predicted by standard statistical tools.

(1) "Black Monday" of October 19, 1987: With this example, Markowitz focuses on daily fluctuations in the stock market which have not been observed since 1926. Based on historical fluctuations in stock prices since that time, the daily standard deviation of the large-cap stock index is about 1%. However, on October 19, 1987, the stock index dropped about 25% in one day, implying that we observed a 25-standard-deviation shift in the rate of return from the mean daily rate of return. Thus, an investor with a one-day investment horizon faced a

---

[5]Markowitz, H. M. (2020). *Risk–Return Analysis: The Theory and Practice of Rational Investing*, Vol. 3, McGraw Hill, New York.

daily fluctuation never seen before, indicating that, in the stock market, one may face a sudden unpredicted risk that is not reflected in the historical daily fluctuations, even with a very long series of data (since 1926). In other words, just because an extreme outlier has not occurred before does not prove it cannot happen in the future. In sum, in relying on an *ex-post* distribution, the probability of 25-standard-deviation shifts in the rate of return to the left is close to zero . . . but it occurred in 1987. Thus, it is possible that the whole distribution of returns on stocks has been shifted to the left, that is, the *ex-post* distribution is not necessarily identical to the *ex-ante* distribution.

(2) The Long-Term Capital Management (LTCM) case: LTCM was a hedge fund established in 1994. LTCM had a strategy which took on very high leverage and assumed that the extreme event of a spike in demand for liquid assets, which has never occurred in the past, won't occur in the future. In 1998, due to several global events, there was a sudden "flight to quality" and the demand for liquid assets, rather than illiquid assets, spiked. This event, which hasn't happened before and LTCM assumed won't happen at all, induced to LTCM a loss of $4.6 billion, leading to the eventual shutdown in 2000. Thus, though the event of a spike in demand for liquid assets is unlikely to happen again, Markowitz advocates that historical data does not tell us the whole story regarding future risk.

Suppose that one accepts this approach, and believes that there are future potential risks in the stock market at a magnitude never seen before. A natural question following this argument is: What are empirically reasonable values for a future disaster's probability and its magnitude? Rietz[6] and Barro[7] address this issue. Specifically, it is suggested that there are future risks of stocks not captured by the historical rates of returns, and these future potential large risks may

---

[6]Rietz, T. A. (1988). The equity risk premium: A solution. *Journal of Monetary Economics* 22(1), 117–131.

[7]Barro, R. J. (2006). Rare disasters and asset markets in the 20th century. *The Quarterly Journal of Economics* 121(3), 823–866.

explain the risk premium puzzle of Mehra and Prescott.[8] Studying crashes in the gross domestic product (GDP) of 35 countries in the last century, Barro estimates that the probability of a crash is 1.7% per year, and the average magnitude of that crash is -29% (2006, pp. 826–829). For the United States (US) market, Barro estimates an annual crash probability of 2%, and a crash magnitude of 29.5% (see Barro, 2006, p. 831 and Table I).

What can one conclude from Barro's empirical findings? Should one overlook historical rates of returns for future investment decision-making? Absolutely not! Even Markowitz who provides two extreme examples of future hidden risk does not recommend ignoring historical information. Recall that there is theoretical and empirical evidence that stocks (held in a portfolio and not individual stocks) are, on average, more profitable than bonds, and that small stocks, once again on average, are more profitable than large stocks. Moreover, the fluctuations in the rates of returns on small stocks are more intensive than the fluctuations in the returns of large stocks, which, in turn, are more intensive than the fluctuations in the rates of returns on bonds. These historical facts are important and should be employed in constructing the optimal investment strategy. For example, an investor who is extremely risk-averse should invest in bonds, and if stocks are included in the portfolio, only small weight should be allocated to them. Just the opposite is recommended for an investor with a high tolerance for risk. Thus, historical characteristics of these alternative assets are very likely to be with us also in the future and, therefore, should serve investors as input for investment decision-making. However, these facts are not in contradiction to the possibilities of a sudden sharp fall in stock prices never seen before — a possibility that should be considered with the historical data in the portfolio construction process. Thus, one should rely on some characteristics of assets observed in the past, and also incorporate future risks not observed before.

---

[8]Mehra, R. and E. C. Prescott (1985). The equity premium: A puzzle. *Journal of Monetary Economics* 15(2), 145–161.

Future risk in the stock market, not observed in history, may occur in the following two main forms:

A. An unexpected temporary crash in the stock market without a change in the economic regime. This may occur due to a 1-year drought, nuclear disaster, war, pandemic, etc. This stock market crash may last for one or two years, and recovery generally occurs after this bad period has elapsed.

B. A change in the economic regime, e.g., changes in the corporate tax system, regulations, or international trade system that may be induced by relatively large customs and other trade barriers inducing a shrinkage in the volume of international trade, the world climate which reduces the profitability of virtually all firms, a political regime, etc. In this scenario, the whole distribution of returns is shifted to the left; hence, the mean annual rate of returns on stocks drops from, say, about 11.6%, as observed in the period 1928–2019, to 11.6%–Δ%, where the more severe the negative change in the economy, the larger the Δ.

In analyzing the effect of the above two changes in the relative attractiveness of stocks and bonds, one needs to employ different techniques. In Case A, given above, there is a crash followed by a recovery; therefore, one needs to add some extreme negative annual rates of returns that have never occurred in the past to the historical series of rates of returns. Although, after the crash, investors once again face the historical distribution of rates of returns, recall that the investor who invests in the year of the crash suffers a big loss, and sometimes in selling the stocks, does not enjoy the recovery. Specifically, when stock–bond portfolios are considered, it is suggested in Case A to add the pair $(x, p(x))$ to the historical rates of returns on stocks, where x is a negative rate of return that has never occurred in the past and $p(x)$ is the probability of such an event. We examine the sensitivity of the optimal stock–bond diversification to the addition of these negative events, and particularly analyze the effect of the added extreme negative return on the optimal diversification between stocks and bonds corresponding to various investment horizons. Of course, various pairs $(x, p(x))$ can be examined, reflecting the subjective beliefs and the risk tolerance of the investor under consideration.

In the case of an economic regime change described in Case B, this is not one event followed by a recovery. Here, the mean rate of return on stocks is reduced permanently, or at least is reduced for a long time period by a $\Delta\%$.

Obviously, the investment horizon, which is the core of this book, also plays a central role in the risk analysis in the case where extreme cases not observed in history are incorporated. Specifically, if one invests for one day, they may suffer a 25% loss, like the one that occurred on October 19, 1987. However, if one invests for pension, say for 30 years, the financial damage of such a negative strong event on the total accumulated wealth diminishes drastically. For example, suppose that a year with an annual rate of return of -70%, which has never occurred in history, suddenly occurs. Note that the worst year for investors in the stock market during the period 1928–2019 was 1931, with rate of return of -43.84%. Thus, -70% is indeed an extreme annual negative rate of return never before seen in the history of the stock market. For an investor for 30 years, this is only one outlier out of 30 years included in the investment horizon; hence, its negative effect may be diluted. Thus, it is very unpleasant to experience such a loss, but it does not necessarily spell disaster for long-horizon investors. Similarly, losing 25% in one day on October 19, 1987 would not be a disaster for an investor with a very long investment horizon, nor even to an investor who invested for the whole year in 1987, ending with a positive rate of return for the year of 5.81%, despite the -25% loss in one day.[9]

In a nutshell, future losses not being recorded in history should be considered, particularly losses of risky assets (stocks). However, the longer the investment horizon, the more this unpredicted risk is allegedly mitigated and, in some cases, completely washed out. These potential risks not observed before are very crucial for short-term investors who do not have the across-time diversification element.

---

[9]http://www.stern.nyu.edu/~adamodar/pc/datasets/histretSP.xls.

As this potential future risk is crucial, and pillars of the financial profession advocate that such risks prevail, history does not repeat itself and investors should be aware of unknown risks. In this chapter, we address all these issues: the effect of outliers (crashes and the effect of changes in the economic regime on optimal stock–bond diversifications) for various investment horizons.

7.2. Case A: Adding to the Historical Distribution an Event with a −70% Annual Rate of Return with a Probability $P(X)$

Covering the period 1928–2019, we have 92 annual historical rates of returns on stocks and bonds.[10] We add to the annual rates of returns of stock series, n-years with a negative annual rate of return of −70% each, that is, an extreme negative rate of return which has never before occurred. We incorporate this large loss for n-years where we employ alternatively $n = 1, 2, \ldots 5$. This implies that with $n = 1$, the probability of such an annual crash in the stock market in the future is $1/93 = 1.07\%$ (note as we add 1 year, we shift from 92 to 93 years), with $n = 2$, it is $2/94 = 2.12\%$, with $n = 3$, it is $3/95 = 3.15\%$, with $n = 4$, it is $\cong 4.2\%$, and finally with $n = 5$, it is $\cong 5.2\%$. Obviously, we do not suggest that 1-year investors assume that such a crash will occur in the future with such a relatively large probability, but analyze the optimal stock–bond allocation for such potential events. Note that Barro (see footnote 7) estimates the probability of an annual crash at about 2%, less than half of the 5.2% probability we employ here. Thus, it seems that even adding two crashes of −70% each represents an extreme pessimistic approach. Also, note that by adding a −70% crash, this is on top of the crashes that have occurred in the past, including the negative rates of returns in the Great Depression, the 2008 crash in the stock market, etc. We analyze the effect of the added crashes on stock–bond diversification corresponding to various investment horizons in what follows, first by employing the M–V rule and then by the expected utility maximization.

---

[10] *Ibid.*

7.2.1. *The M–V optimal portfolio with −70% crashes in the stock market*

We employ the M–V optimization technique for solving the optimal stock–bond portfolio. We first employ the historical rates of returns of stocks and bonds with no additional crashes in the stock market. When we add n-crashes of -70% each to the stock market, we assume no crash in the bond market; hence, we analyze the worst-case scenario from the stockholders' point of view. As we sample years with rates of returns on stocks and bonds simultaneously (hence, consider the possible correlations between these two assets), when we consider one crash, we add a year with this negative rate of return on stocks, and to the bonds, we add in the same year the average rate of return on bonds, which was in the period under consideration 5.14%; hence, it is assumed that no crash in the bond market accompanies the crash in the stock market. Similarly, when we add n years of crash in the stock market, we add n years with this average return on bonds to the bond rates of return series.

Figure 7.1 presents the M–V efficient frontier composed of stocks and bonds without the crash and with 1, and alternatively 5 annual crashes of –70% each in the stock market for various investment horizons, N. The point TP stands for the tangency portfolio with a riskless annual interest rate of 3.4%, which is the average riskless interest rate prevailing in the period 1928–2019. Thus, the point TP provides the optimal stock–bond portfolio in the M–V framework. For a large horizon N, a simulation is needed; otherwise, we will have very few observations. Thus, when we have an N-year investment horizon, we draw N observations, calculate the compounded return for this horizon, and repeat this procedure 100,000 times. Thus, the M–V frontiers with 100,000 observations are drawn twice, once with historical data, namely with no crash added (see stocks with no-event curve), and once with 100,000 observations employed with the added n-crashes. Of course, the riskless interest rate is also compounded to reflect the assumed investment horizon.

Let us first glance at Figure 7.1(a), corresponding to an $N = 1$-year investment horizon. For an $n = 1$ crash, as well as for $n = 5$ crashes added, the M–V frontier shifts downward and to the right

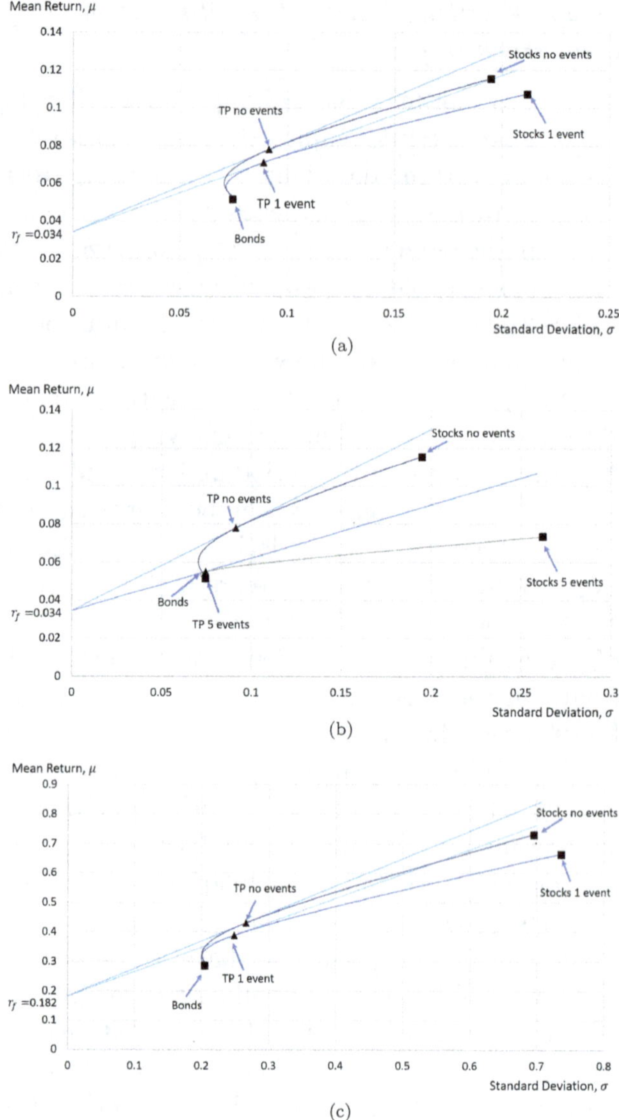

Figure 7.1: The M–V frontier with n events, each with a -70% rate of return for various horizons, N: (a) $N = 1$ year with no crash added and with $n = 1$ (crash), a -70% rate of return is added; (b) $N = 1$ year with no crash added and with $n = 5$ events added with a -70% rate of return for each; (c) $N = 5$ years with no crash added and when an $n = 1$ event (crash) with a -70% rate of return is added; (d) $N = 5$ years with no crash added and with $n = 5$ events added with a -70% rate of return for each.

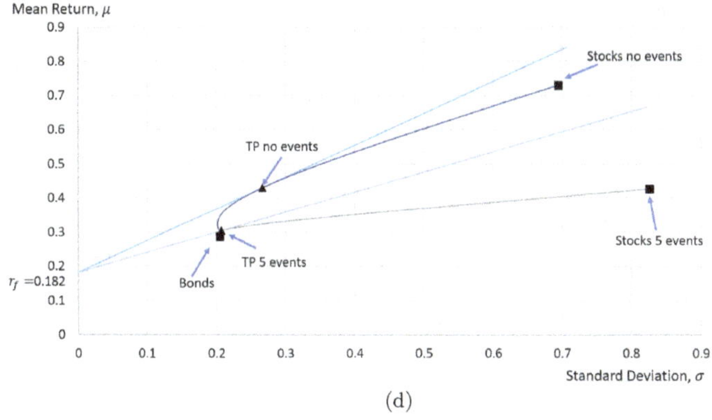

Figure 7.1: (*Continued*)

relative to the efficient frontier derived with historical data. The shifts downward are obvious as the mean stock rate of return declines by adding the -70% events. The shifts to the right occur because adding such an extreme event increases the variance of the rate of return on stocks (compare the point labeled by stocks corresponding to the two curves given in Figure 7.1(a)). Obviously, with $n = 5$ crashes, the shift downward and to the right is more intensive than with the case $n = 1$ crash (compare Figures 7.1(a) and (b), note that the scale of these two figures differs). When we increase the horizon, the results in principle are very similar (see Figures 7.1(c) and (d) for the $N = 5$-year horizon). We drive the M–V frontiers also for $N = 10$ and $N = 20$ years, but as the shifts in the curves are very similar, we do not present them here. However, the optimal diversifications corresponding to the TG point for all horizons are reported in what follows.

Table 7.1 presents the optimal stock–bond M–V diversification corresponding to various horizons, N, and $n = 0, 1$, and 5 alternative crashes of -70%.

Let's look first at the case of $n = 0$ crashes with various horizons, N. Thus, these results correspond to the optimal M–V diversification that relies solely on historical rates of returns. We see that with historical data, the optimal investment weight in stocks decreases from 41.4% for $N = 1$ to only about 10.3% for an $N = 20$-year

Table 7.1: The optimal investment weight by the M–V rule for various horizons, N, and for $n = 0, 1$, and 5 events of -70% annual stock market crashes.

Horizon (years)	Number of Events	S&P500 Weight in the TP*	Bonds Weight the TP*	Mean of TP*	SD of TP*
1	0	0.414	0.586	0.078	0.091
	1	0.352	0.648	0.071	0.089
	5	0.156	0.844	0.055	0.075
5	0	0.326	0.674	0.430	0.266
	1	0.272	0.728	0.388	0.249
	5	0.127	0.873	0.304	0.207
10	0	0.226	0.774	0.954	0.493
	1	0.193	0.807	0.866	0.462
	5	0.098	0.902	0.689	0.377
20	0	0.103	0.897	2.367	1.153
	1	0.091	0.909	2.174	1.082
	5	0.058	0.942	1.810	0.906

Note: *TP: tangency portfolio.

horizon. Thus, even without adding future crashes to the stock market, by the M–V rule, we find that the "bonds for the long run" investment strategy better fits the characteristics of the historical stock–bond data than the conventional view asserting "stocks for the long run." This result stems from the fast increase in the variance of stocks with the horizon — a disadvantage of stocks, at least in the M–V framework. However, recall that this conclusion is based on the M–V rule, which is widely employed in practice, but may be non-optimal, particularly for long horizons.

When we add one -70% annual crash, the optimal M–V weight in stocks drops from 35.2% for an $N = 1$-year horizon to 9.1% for an $N = 20$-year horizon. Similar results are obtained for $n = 5$ crashes added, as the investment weight in stocks drops from 15.6% for $N = 1$ to only 5.8% for $N = 20$ years. Thus, by the M–V choices, with and without added crashes in the stock market, we obtain the surprising result that the "bonds for the long run" investment strategy is the best strategy.

We stress at the outset that these are M–V optimal investment weights. However, these are merely technical results of the M–V rule that may be misleading, particularly for long investment horizons where the distributions of returns are positively skewed. We turn now to the expected utility analysis.

7.2.2. *The expected utility optimal investment weights with additional annual − 70% crashes*

While the M–V rule is widely used, it has drawbacks as it is non-optimal for long horizons; hence, the implied result "bonds for the long run" which is technically correct may be economically misleading. Therefore, we conduct the same exercise as done with the M–V rule, but this time with expected utility, where the utility function is assumed to be myopic, with risk-aversion parameter α. Figure 7.2 presents the optimal investment in stocks as determined by expected utility maximization, where on the vertical axis we have the optimal weight in stocks and on the horizontal axis we have the number of −70% annual crashes added to the historical rates of returns on stocks. In all four figures, we obtain a very similar pattern: for very low risk-aversion parameters, the investment weight in stocks is very high, and with up to three crashes added, it remains 100%. Even with five annual crashes of −70% each, the investment weight in stocks is relatively large with the low risk-aversion parameter. However, as expected, the larger the risk aversion parameter, the smaller the investment weight in stocks, and this result is valid for all horizons, N. For the most relevant range of risk-aversion parameters, $1 \leq \alpha \leq 2$, the investment weight in stocks is about 75% with no added crash, and it drops sharply with the added number of crashes, ending up with about 20% investment weight in stocks for five added crashes.

As the advantage of bonds increases with the number of crashes added, and with the increase in the risk-aversion parameter of the myopic utility function, one wonders if with the extreme number of added crashes, compared in isolation and not in portfolio contexts, bonds dominate stocks for all investors, or only for risk averters. Specifically, do bonds dominate stocks by first-degree stochastic dominance (FSD) or second-degree stochastic dominance (SSD) with

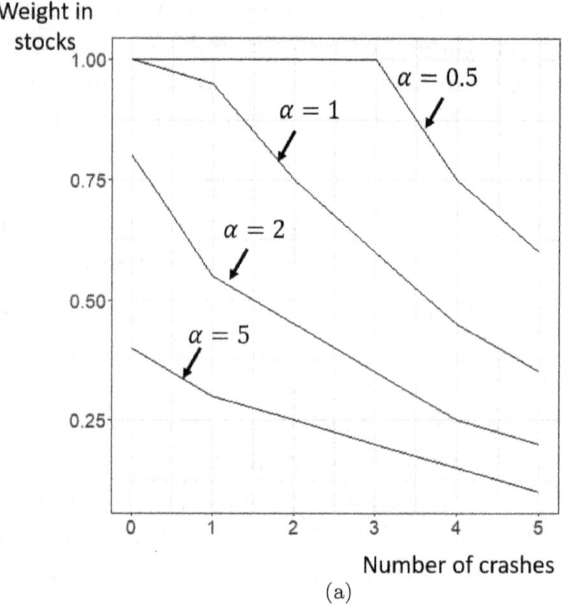

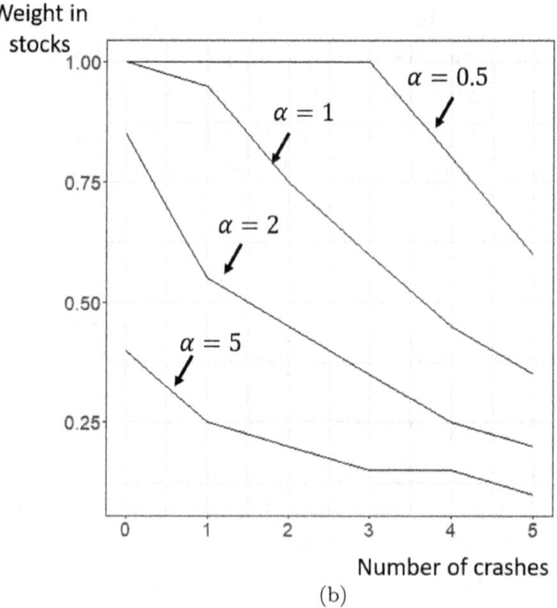

Figure 7.2: The optimal investment weight in stocks with myopic utility function $u(x) = \frac{x^{1-\alpha}}{1-\alpha}$ for various α and various added numbers of annual crashes, each of -70%: (a) $N = 1$ year; (b) $N = 5$ years; (c) $N = 10$ years; (d) $N = 20$ years.

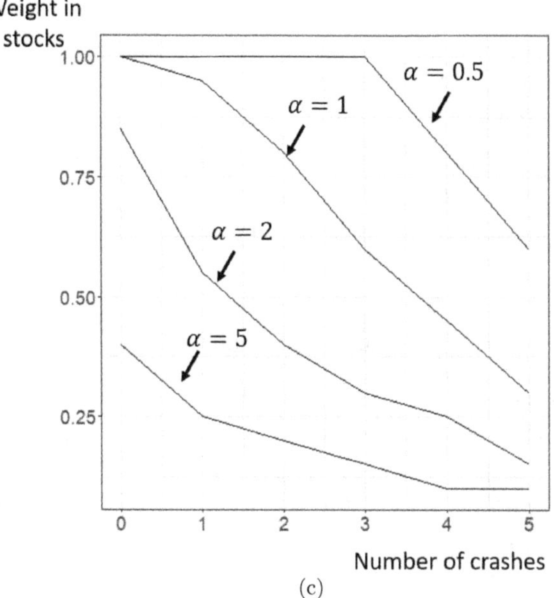

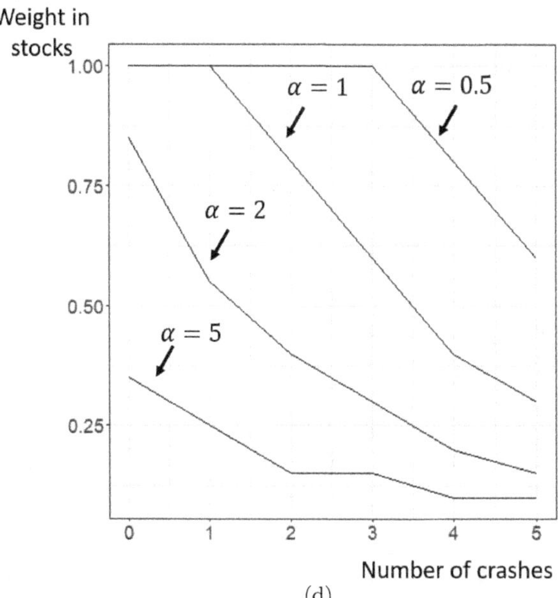

Figure 7.2: (*Continued*)

five crashes added? Figure 7.3 reveals that despite the dramatic reduction in the mean rate of return on stocks, bonds still do not dominate stocks, either by FSD or by SSD. In Figure 7.3(b), we zoom in on the left tails of the distributions. Note that with historical returns, the lowest rate of return on stocks is about -44%, while with crashes, the lowest rate of return is -70%. The difference of all the distributions with crashes regards the probability of -70% occurring (with one up to five possible crashes).

From the cumulative distribution functions (CDFs) given in Figure 7.3, we draw the following conclusions:

1. As expected, the cumulative distributions of stocks shift to the left with the additional -70% crashes, and the larger the number of added crashes, the more intensive is the shift to the left.
2. The cumulative distributions of bonds and stocks always intersect; hence, there is no FSD dominance.
3. The cumulative distributions of bonds intersect the cumulative distribution of stocks from below; hence, stocks cannot dominate bonds by SSD. Even with five added crashes of -70%, the "+" area is smaller than the "−" area; hence, bonds also do not dominate stocks by SSD.[11]
4. As we add annual crashes and do not reduce each return on stocks, the steepness of the CDF of stocks decreases. Namely, -70% rates of returns are added to the left side of the CDF, but the large positive rates of returns on stocks that occurred in history remain unchanged, although the probability of these positive returns slightly decreases as we add more observations with negative returns.

Thus, if one has to choose between stocks and bonds (and not a portfolio of the two), the choice still depends on preferences, despite the five large crashes added to the stock market. Of course, if we add

---

[11]Note that prospect F (bonds) dominates prospect G (stocks) by SSD if and only if $\int_a^x [G(t) - F(t)]dt \geq 0$ for all x, and there is at least one inequality. As the negative area is larger than the positive area (in absolute terms), see Figure 7.3, bonds do not dominate stocks by SSD as there is at least one value x for which this integral is negative. By the same integral condition, stocks also cannot dominate bonds by SSD.

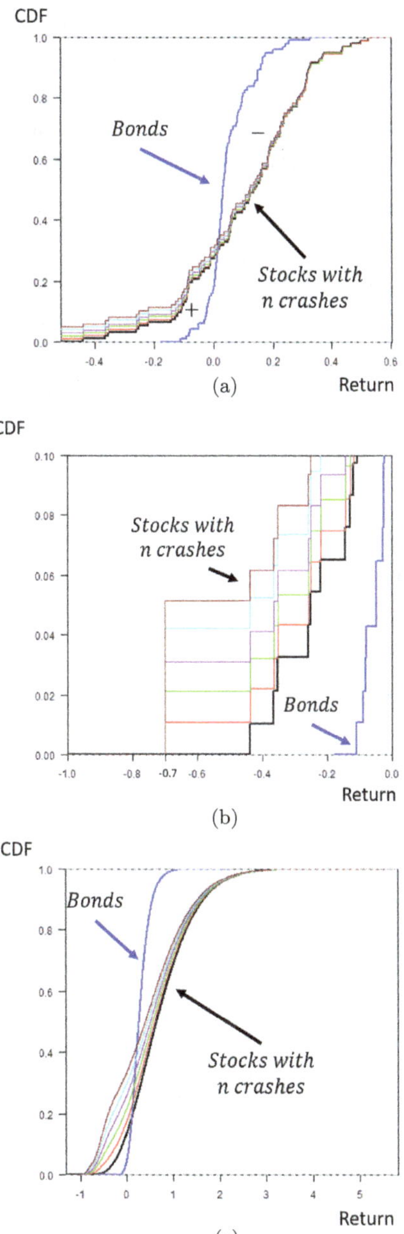

Figure 7.3: The cumulative distributions of bonds and stocks with n stocks crashes of -70% each, when $n = 0, 1, \ldots, 5$: (a) With $N = 1$ year; (b) Left tail with $N = 1$ year; (c) With $N = 5$ years.

more crashes, say 10 crashes, bonds will dominate stocks by SSD as the "+" area depicted in Figure 7.3 will be larger than the "−" area (see Figure 7.3(a)). However, it seems that adding five crashes of −70% each is very pessimistic and unrealistic, let alone a larger number of crashes. Therefore, we conclude that even by adding a quite pessimistic future risk, neither stocks nor bonds dominate each other by SSD. Yet, as expected, in a portfolio context, the optimal weight of bonds increases with the number of crashes added.

We turn now to the analysis of the changes in the expected utility optimal diversification between stocks and bonds with the horizon. The most interesting issue is contrasting the change in the optimal diversification between stocks and bonds with the horizon in the expected utility framework with these changes in the M–V framework. Figure 7.4 provides these results. The results correspond to the myopic utility function with the risk-aversion parameter $\alpha = 2$, but the results are very similar for the range $0.5 \leq \alpha \leq 5$, hence for all relevant risk-aversion parameters. The astonishing result is that the optimal diversification curves in most cases are almost horizontal, implying that the horizon almost does not affect the

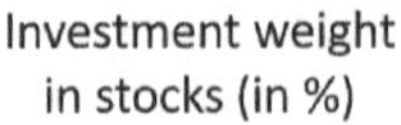

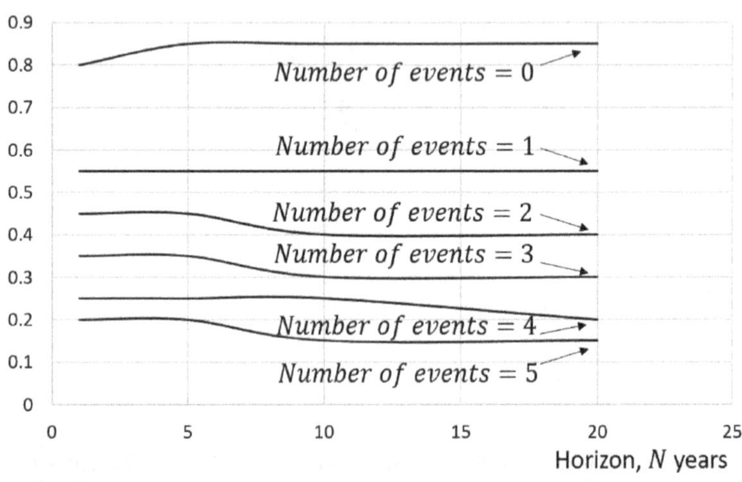

Figure 7.4: The optimal investment weight in stocks for various number of crashes, n, for various horizons, N, with the myopic utility function with $\alpha = 2$.

Table 7.2: The optimal investment in stocks for various numbers of crashes and for various horizons (with myopic utility function with $0.5 \leq \alpha \leq 5$).

Horizon (Years)	Number of Added Events	$\alpha = 0.5$	$\alpha = 1$	$\alpha = 2$	$\alpha = 5$
$N = 1$	0	1.00	1.00	0.80	0.40
	1	1.00	0.95	0.55	0.30
	2	1.00	0.75	0.45	0.25
	3	1.00	0.60	0.35	0.20
	4	0.75	0.45	0.25	0.15
	5	0.60	0.35	0.20	0.10
$N = 5$	0	1.00	1.00	0.85	0.40
	1	1.00	0.95	0.55	0.25
	2	1.00	0.75	0.45	0.20
	3	1.00	0.60	0.35	0.15
	4	0.80	0.45	0.25	0.15
	5	0.60	0.35	0.20	0.10
$N = 10$	0	1.00	1.00	0.85	0.40
	1	1.00	0.95	0.55	0.25
	2	1.00	0.80	0.40	0.20
	3	1.00	0.60	0.30	0.15
	4	0.80	0.45	0.25	0.10
	5	0.60	0.30	0.15	0.10
$N = 20$	0	1.00	1.00	0.85	0.35
	1	1.00	1.00	0.55	0.25
	2	1.00	0.80	0.40	0.15
	3	1.00	0.60	0.30	0.15
	4	0.80	0.40	0.20	0.10
	5	0.60	0.30	0.15	0.10

optimal allocation to stocks and bonds. While, as expected, the larger the number of assumed crashes, the lower the horizontal curve, implying that a smaller weight is invested in stocks, and increasing the horizon for a given number of crashes almost does not affect this optimal allocation.

Table 7.2 summarizes the optimal stock–bond diversification for a risk-aversion parameter, α, for various horizons, N, and for the number of added events, where each event denotes adding 1 year with a rate of return of -70%. As expected, the larger the risk-version parameter, and the larger the number of added crashes, the smaller the optimal investment weight in stocks. However, consistent with Figure 7.4, for a given risk-averse parameter and for a given number of crashes, the optimal expected utility allocation to stocks is almost invariant to the assumed investment horizon. For example, for $\alpha = 2$ and $n = 1$ added crashes, the allocation to stocks is 55% for all horizons from $N = 1$ year to $N = 20$ years. For more crashes, we have some change in the investment weight in stocks, but it is not very drastic. For example, for four crashes, it is 25% up to $N = 10$ years, and it drops to 20% for $N = 20$ years.

7.2.3. *Discussion*

1. First, it is well known that with a myopic utility function with periodical revisions and with identical independent distribution (*i.i.d.*), the optimal diversification is invariant to the assumed investment horizon, as shown by Merton and Samuelson.[12] Therefore, one may suspect that the results reported in Table 7.2 are not surprising. This argument is not intact in our analysis as we assume maximizing expected utility defined on terminal wealth with no annual portfolio revisions. For example, for a 1-year horizon, one maximizes

$$EU[w_1(x_1) + (1 - w_1)y_1]$$

where w_1 is denotes the optimal investment in stocks for 1-period investors, where the 1-period return on stocks is x_1 and $(1 - w_1)$ is the optimal investment in bonds whose 1-period return is y_1. Thus, for the 1-period investment, we solve for w_1 which maximizes the above expected utility. For a 2-period horizon, we need to solve for the optimal investment in stocks which maximizes the following

---

[12]Merton, R. C. and P. A. Samuelson (1974). Fallacy of the log-normal approximation to optimal portfolio decision-making over many periods. *Journal of Financial Economics* 1(1), 67–94.

expected utility:

$$EU[w_2(x_1 x_2) + (1 - w_2)y_1 y_2]$$

where w_2 denotes the optimal investment in stocks for the 2-period horizon, and as the 2-period distributions of returns (of stocks and bonds, respectively) are not identical to the 1-period distribution of returns (of stocks and bonds, respectively), generally $w_2 \neq w_1$. Indeed, we do not obtain identical optimal investment weights for all horizons. However, surprisingly, for most cases, we obtain either no change in the investment weights with the horizon or relatively very small changes, even with no portfolio revisions.

2. The M–V and the expected utility frameworks provide much different results. While with the M–V rule, we conclude "bonds for the long run," with the expected utility framework, we conclude approximately "constant stock–bond diversification for all horizons." As the M–V analysis is invalid for relatively long horizons and the expected utility is intact for all horizons, the constant allocation for all horizons is the correct economic result. Yet, although we solve for the optimal diversification with the myopic function, different results may emerge with other preferences.

3. Adding two annual crashes and with a risk-aversion parameter equal to 2, we obtain a balanced portfolio of stocks and bonds, with some advantage to bonds.

7.3.　Change in the Economic Regime: A Reduction of a Constant From All Rates of Returns

We turn now to a possible change in the economic regime, a case where there is a permanent reduction in the profitability of stocks. We reduce each of the returns on stocks by $x\%$, where $x = 1\%, 2\%, 3\%, 4\%$, and 5%. Note that with a 5% reduction in the returns of all observations, the mean rate of return is also reduced by 5%. For the whole period covered in this study, the mean returns on stocks and bonds are 11.57% and 5.14%, respectively. By reducing the mean of stocks by 5%, the adjusted mean rate of return on stocks is 6.57%; hence, even in this extreme case, the mean return on stocks is larger than the mean return on bonds by 1.43%. Therefore, bonds cannot dominate stocks by FSD or SSD even in such an extreme change in the economy against stocks.[13]

Figure 7.5 presents the M–V frontiers with no drop in the returns and, alternatively, with 1% and 5% reductions in all the stocks' rates of returns for various horizons, N. Note that with a constant reduction in all returns, for $N = 1$, the point on the graph corresponding to stocks with reductions in the returns is located exactly below this point with no reduction. The technical explanation for this result is that the mean is reduced without affecting the variance (see Figures 7.5(a) and (b)). A different picture is obtained for all horizons, $N > 1$. In these cases, the point corresponding to stocks is shifted below and to the left, relative to the point with no reduction in the returns (see Figures 7.5(c) and 7.5(d)). The reason for shifting below this point is obvious. The explanation for the shift to the left is because the multi-period variance is an increasing monotonic function of the 1-period variance and 1-period mean (see Chapter 2). As by reducing the mean, we also decrease the multi-period variance, we obtain the shift to the left of the point corresponding to stocks.[14]

Table 7.3 provides the optimal M–V diversifications for various horizons for 1% and 5% reductions in the mean rates of returns on stocks. As before, the M–V investment weight in stocks decreases sharply with the horizon, even in the case where historical rates of

---

[13]A necessary condition for SSD dominance is that the dominating prospect will have a higher or equal mean return than the dominated one. As bonds have a lower mean than the mean of stocks, even after the 5% reduction in returns, bonds cannot dominate stocks by SSD.

[14]See Eq. (6.5) in Chapter 6 for the relationship between the multi-period variance and the 1-period mean return.

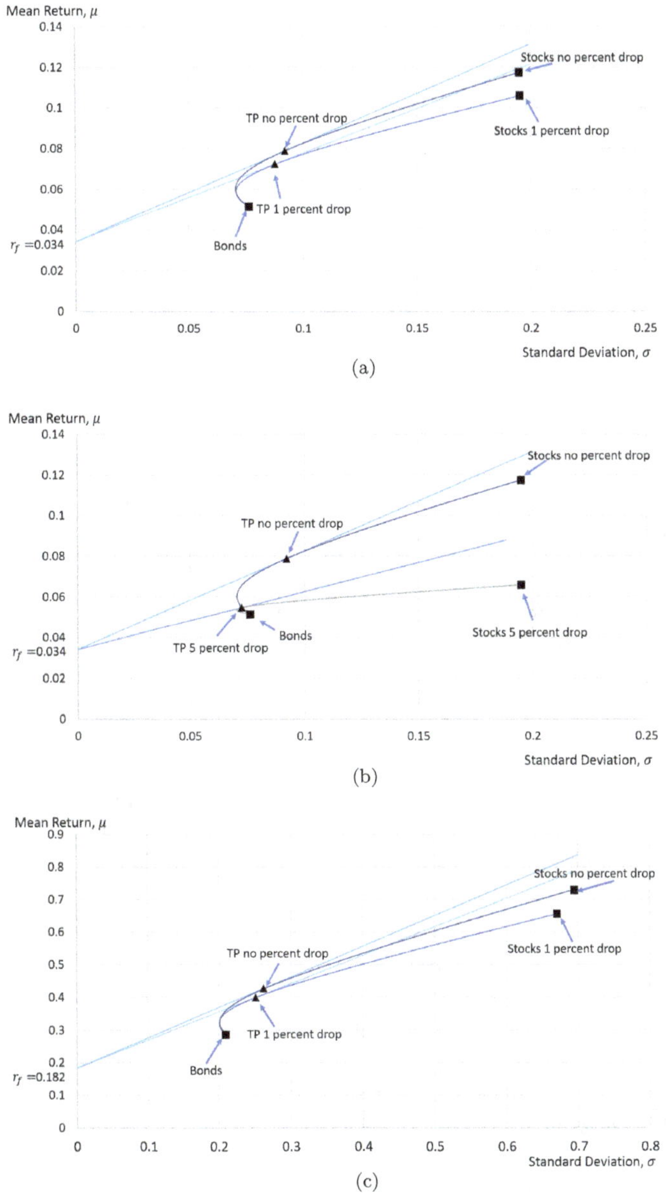

Figure 7.5: The M–V frontier with n events of -1% each in all stock returns for various horizons, N: (a) $N = 1$ year, with a -1% reduction in the rate of return on stocks; (b) $N = 1$ year, with a -5% reduction in the rate of return on stocks; (c) $N = 5$ years, with a -1% reduction in the rate of return on stocks; (d) $N = 5$ years, with a -5% reduction in the rate of return on stocks.

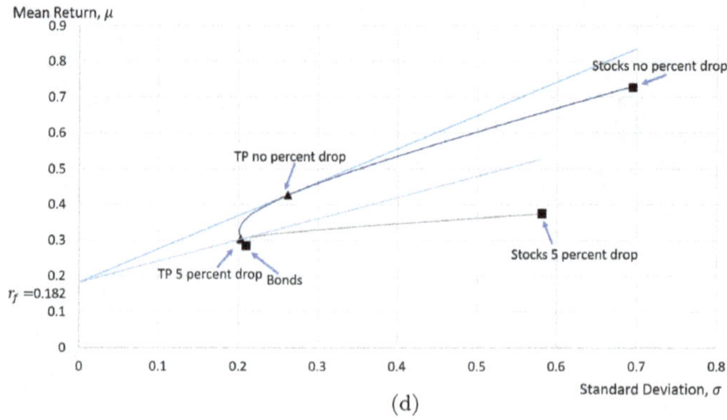

Figure 7.5: (*Continued*)

Table 7.3: The optimal M–V investment weights in stocks and bonds for various horizons for 1% and alternatively 5% reductions in the rate of returns on stocks.

Horizon	Percent Drop	S&P500 Weight in the TP*	Bonds Weight the TP*	Mean of TP*	SD of TP*
1	0	0.419	0.581	0.079	0.092
	1	0.382	0.618	0.072	0.088
	5	0.221	0.779	0.055	0.072
5	0	0.321	0.679	0.427	0.262
	1	0.308	0.692	0.400	0.251
	5	0.196	0.804	0.303	0.203
10	0	0.225	0.775	0.955	0.494
	1	0.221	0.779	0.892	0.466
	5	0.169	0.831	0.691	0.373
20	0	0.102	0.898	2.366	1.153
	1	0.111	0.889	2.251	1.102
	5	0.129	0.871	1.833	0.894

Note: *TP: tangency portfolio.

returns are employed: it decreases from 41.9% for $N = 1$ to 10.2% for $N = 20$ years. The reduction in the M–V optimal weight in stocks is relatively smaller for relatively long horizons. Even more surprising is that for $N = 20$ years, the optimal investment in stocks with a 5% reduction in returns is 12.9% — larger than the investment weight with no return reduction (compared to 10.2%). This counterintuitive result is explained, once again, by the relation between the multi-period variance and the mean: the smaller the mean return, the slower the increases in the multi-period variance with the horizon. Thus, for $N = 20$ years, the multi-period variance of stocks is smaller with the return reduction than with the variance with the no-return reduction.[15]

So far, we analyzed the M–V results with a percent reduction from all rates of returns on stocks. As before, we complete the analysis by examining the expected utility optimal diversification with a reduction in the rates of returns on stocks. Figure 7.6 presents the results. As before, for a low risk-aversion parameter, investing in stocks 100% is optimal for all horizons, even with a -4% reduction in returns. However, the optimal investment in stocks is sharply reduced with the risk-averse parameter.

Despite the decrease in the attractiveness of stocks in the stock–bond portfolio with the reduction in the stock returns, as before, bonds do not dominate stocks either by FSD or by SSD. Figure 7.7 reveals that the cumulative distributions of stocks and bonds intersect, and once again, the "−" area is larger (in absolute terms) than the "+" area, which explains the no dominance findings. Note that unlike the case of the added -70% crash, here, the whole distribution of stocks shifts to the left as we reduce each rate of return on stocks by the same percentage. In Figure 7.3(b), we zoom

---

[15]On the relationship between the multi-period variance and the 1-period mean, see Eq. (6.5) in Chapter 6.

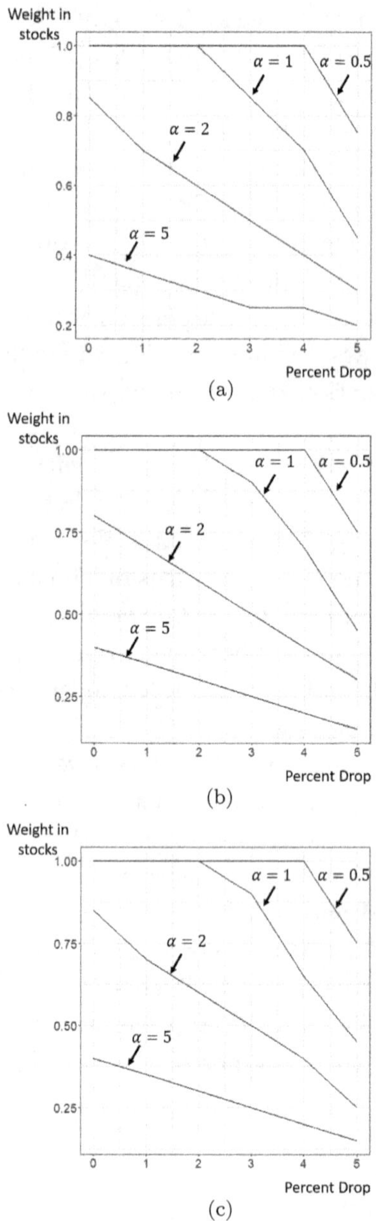

Figure 7.6: The optimal investment weights in stocks with myopic utility function $u(x) = \frac{x^{1-\alpha}}{1-\alpha}$ for various α, as a function of the percent drops with -1%, -2%, $\ldots$, -5% in the returns on stocks: (a) $N = 1$ year; (b) $N = 5$ years; (c) $N = 10$ years; (d) $N = 20$ years.

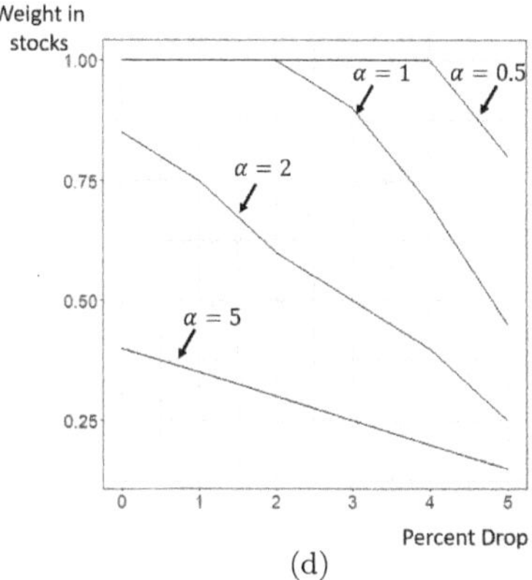

Figure 7.6: (*Continued*)

in on the left tails of the distributions. As we can see, the lowest
rate of return with historical data is about -44%, and for the other
distributions, the lowest rate of return is reduced by 1%, 2%, 3%,
4%, and 5%, respectively.

We turn now to analyze the optimal expected utility diversification as a function of the assumed horizon, N. Figure 7.8 reveals,
once again, almost horizontal curves, indicating that the optimal
investment in stocks is almost invariant to the assumed investment
horizon. Indeed, Table 7.4 reveals that for a given reduction in the
rates of returns, the optimal investment in stocks is almost invariant
to the assumed horizon. A slight reduction is observed by increasing
the horizon beyond $N = 5$ years, from 30% to 25%.

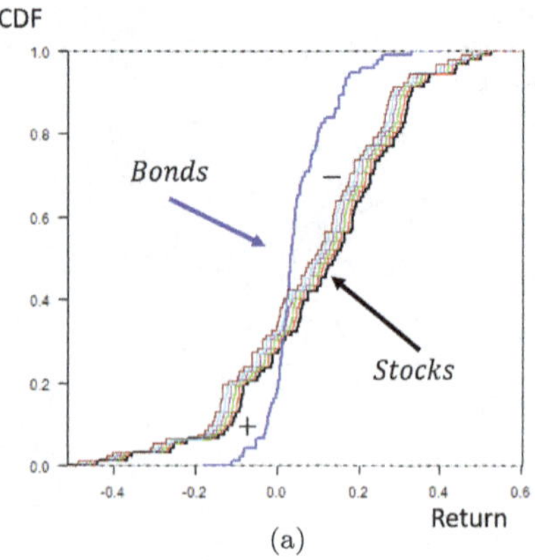

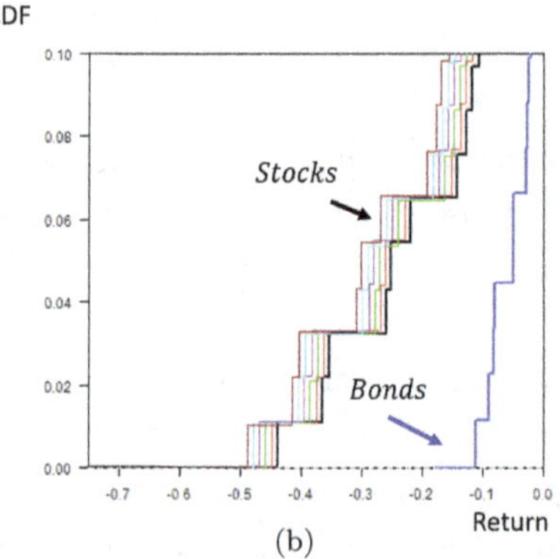

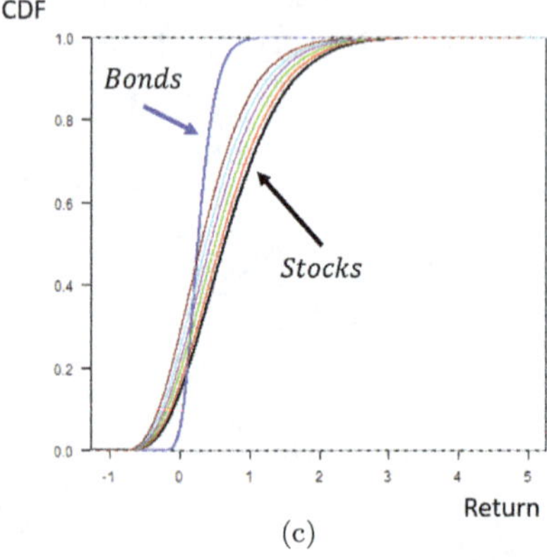

Figure 7.7: The CDF of bonds and stocks with reductions in the rate of return of stocks of $-1\%, -2\%, \ldots, -5\%$: (a) With $N = 1$ year; (b) Left tail with $N = 1$ year; (c) $N = 5$ years.

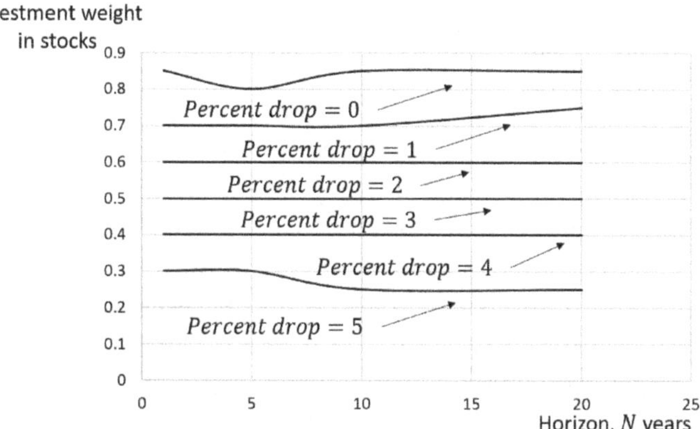

Figure 7.8: The change in the optimal investment weight in stocks with the horizon, N, for various percentage reductions in the rate of return on stocks for $\alpha = 2$.

Table 7.4: The optimal investment in stocks for various α s, various reductions in the rate of return on stocks, and for various horizons.

Horizon (Years)	Percentage Drop	$\alpha = 0.5$	$\alpha = 1$	$\alpha = 2$	$\alpha = 5$
$N = 1$	0	1.00	1.00	0.85	0.40
	-1%	1.00	1.00	0.70	0.35
	-2%	1.00	1.00	0.60	0.30
	-3%	1.00	0.85	0.50	0.25
	-4%	1.00	0.70	0.40	0.25
	-5%	0.75	0.45	0.30	0.20
$N = 5$	0	1.00	1.00	0.80	0.40
	-1%	1.00	1.00	0.70	0.35
	-2%	1.00	1.00	0.60	0.30
	-3%	1.00	0.90	0.50	0.25
	-4%	1.00	0.70	0.40	0.20
	-5%	0.75	0.45	0.30	0.15
$N = 10$	0	1.00	1.00	0.85	0.40
	-1%	1.00	1.00	0.70	0.35
	-2%	1.00	1.00	0.60	0.30
	-3%	1.00	0.90	0.50	0.25
	-4%	1.00	0.65	0.40	0.20
	-5%	0.75	0.45	0.25	0.15
$N = 20$	0	1.00	1.00	0.85	0.40
	-1%	1.00	1.00	0.75	0.35
	-2%	1.00	1.00	0.60	0.30
	-3%	1.00	0.90	0.50	0.25
	-4%	1.00	0.70	0.40	0.20
	-5%	0.80	0.45	0.25	0.15

7.4. Summary

In this chapter, we analyze the change in the relative attractiveness of stocks and bonds when future potential risks not observed in history are added to the historical rates of returns on stocks with no increase in the risk of bonds. We analyze two scenarios: with several events of -70% annual crashes added to the stock market and changes in the economic regime where the whole distribution of returns on stocks is shifted to the left permanently by a given percentage.

Examining the changes in stock–bond diversification with the horizon, we obtain contrasting results with the M–V analysis and the expected utility analysis. While the M–V analysis, which is widely employed in economics and finance, reveals that "bonds for the long run" is an optimal investment strategy with and without the added crashes, by the expected utility analysis we find that approximately a "constant stock–bond mix" is optimal for all horizons. This optimal investment strategy prevails in both scenarios: when one does not consider future crashes in the stock market as well as when one adds crashes.

The M–V analysis does not conform with the expected utility paradigm, particularly for long investment horizons where the distributions of the rates of returns are positively skewed (a fact that the M–V rule ignores). In contrast, the expected utility results, that the optimal investment proportions do not change much with the horizon, are economically relevant for all horizons, and these results are intact for a wide range of risk-averse parameters. However, note that these results are valid for the myopic utility function, which is widely employed in economics and finance, but may not be valid for other preferences.

Finally, we consider also possible appearances of black swan events (see footnote 1). Adding several annual crashes of -70% each, or reducing all the rates of returns on stocks yields similar stock–bond diversification results. However, the effect on the cumulative distribution of these two types of reductions in the returns on stocks is different; when crashes of -70% are added, the cumulative distribution of stocks becomes flatter, as negative returns are added without affecting the historical positive returns. However, when some percentage is reduced from all historical rates of returns, the whole distribution is simply shifted to the left. Yet, this basic different effect on the cumulative distributions does not much affect the changes in the optimal diversification with the horizon.

Chapter 8

Discrete and Continuous Returns and the Investment Horizon

The rate of return and the expected rate of return on assets with uncertain cash flows are commonly employed for prospect ranking, risk measurement, analysis of the risk–return relationship of various assets, beta measurement, and testing the Sharpe–Lintner capital asset pricing model (CAPM) and the Fama–French three-factor model. Rates of returns used in economics and finance are commonly measured in two alternative forms: the continuous rate of return and the discrete rate of return. In calculating the continuous rate of return with the annual rate of return, r, it is assumed that the return is compounded continuously or at n times during the year at a rate of return r/n, where n approaches infinity. In contrast, in the discrete calculation of the rate of return, R, say for one year, no compounding takes place. However, a problem arises even when using the same dataset as there is a gap between the continuous rate of return and the discrete rate of return — a gap which rapidly increases with the investment horizon. We find that the employed method for calculating the return may affect prospect ranking and the optimal choices in the expected utility framework. Moreover, the longer the investment horizon, the larger the gap between the continuous and discrete rates of returns, and hence, the larger the difference may be in prospect ranking by these two methods.

359

In this chapter, we present the two rates of returns mentioned above and analyze the advantages and disadvantages of each. We show that the continuous rate of return has some technical advantages over the discrete rate of return mainly because the multi-period continuous return is additive rather than multiplicative. However, we advocate that only the discrete rate of return conforms with the expected utility paradigm, as utility is defined on wealth and not on *log-wealth*. Therefore, employing the continuous rate of return, particularly for prospect ranking, may induce economic distortion. Note that in the rest of the chapter, *log* is used to denote natural logarithms.

At the outset, we would like to stress that the way the rate of return is calculated is only indirectly related to the horizon issue which is the core of this book. Specifically, the investor may have a given horizon, say of N years, and for this horizon, say for prospect ranking and risk analysis, they may employ either the continuous rate of return or the discrete rate of return. Thus, even though the horizon is fixed, the two calculation methods of the rates of returns may create a gap, and perhaps an economic distortion, that grows with the length of a predetermined horizon.

For relatively short horizons and for relatively low rates of returns, we advocate using the continuous or discrete rates of returns interchangeably as the chance of economic distortion induced by employing the continuous rate of return is relatively small. However, this is no longer true when it comes to long horizons. Because of the compounding effect, for given annual rates of returns (continuous and discrete), the gap between the multi-period continuous and multi-period discrete rates of returns increases rapidly with the horizon. For relatively long horizons, because the distributions of continuous and discrete returns are quite different, the prospect ranking may depend on the type of rate of return employed. As we shall see in what follows, only the discrete rate of return conforms with the expected utility paradigm. Therefore, the longer the horizon, the greater the chance that an economic loss may occur if the continuous rate of return is employed rather than the discrete rate of return.

8.1. The Continuous and Discrete Rates of Returns and the Investment Horizon

First, let us present the continuous and discrete rates of returns. For the one-period horizon (for simplicity, assume that this period is one year), the discrete annual return $1 + R$, with R as the rate of return, is given by

$$1 + R = P_1/P_0 \tag{8.1}$$

where P_1 and P_0 stand for the asset value (or stock price when we deal in an investment in stocks) at the end of the year and at the beginning of the year, respectively. If an investment in stocks is under consideration, the stock price P_1 is adjusted for dividends, stock dividends, splits, etc.

The continuous annual rate of return is the value r, which solves the following equation:

$$P_1 = P_0 \lim_{n \to \infty} (1 + r/n)^n = P_0 e^r \tag{8.2}$$

where n, the number of times that the return is compounded, approaches infinity.

Equation (8.2) can be rewritten as,

$$\frac{P_1}{P_0} = \lim_{n \to \infty} (1 + r/n)^n = e^r.$$

Hence, the relation between the discrete rate of return, R, and the continuous rate of return, r, is given by

$$log(P_1/P_0) = log(1 + R) = log(e^r) = r. \tag{8.3}$$

Thus, we have the following relation between the two rates of returns:

$$log(1 + R) = r. \tag{8.3'}$$

For example, if $P_0 = \$100$ and $P_1 = \$115$, the discrete rate of return is $R = 15\%$, and the continuous rate of return is $log(P_1/P_0) = log1.15 \cong 14\%$. In this specific example, there is a gap of about 1% between the rates of returns obtained by the two alternative calculation methods. This gap increases with the rate of return, R, and as a consequence, also with the investment horizon because, for a given annual rate of return, the longer the horizon, the larger the accumulated multi-period gap is between these two rates of returns. To illustrate the horizon effect on this gap between the two rates of returns, suppose that the annual rate of return on common stocks is 10%. With an $N = 1$-year horizon, the continuous rate of return is $log(1.1) \cong 0.0953$ or about 9.53%; hence, the gap between the two rates of returns is relatively small. However, suppose now that the investment horizon is 10 years. In this case, with the same annual rate of return, the discrete return for the whole period is $(1.1)^{10} \cong 2.59$, and the discrete rate of return is 159%, while the continuous rate of return is $log(1 + R) = log(2.59) \cong 95.17\%$ (for more comparisons of the two interest rates, see Tables 8.1 and 8.2 that follow). Thus, while for a 1-year horizon, the gap between the two rates of returns is relatively small, for a longer horizon, the gap between these two rates of returns is quite large. This implies that the chance of making a poor economic choice by employing r rather than R increases with the horizon. For example, suppose that an investor wishes to select one prospect from two available prospects whose cash flows will be obtained one year in the future. As for a 1-year investment, the returns are presumably rather small, one can employ the distributions of the discrete or alternatively the continuous rates of returns of the two prospects under consideration, and probably the distributions; hence, the prospect ranking will not be affected much by the rate of return-type employed. However, if these cash flows are faced N years from now, and the profit on an annual basis is unchanged, the gap between the N-years' two distributions corresponding to the two ways of calculating the returns could be substantial. Therefore, relying on the multi-period continuous rate of return rather than on the correct discrete multi-period rate of return may induce wrong choices and significant economic distortion. Specifically, with the distributions of the continuous rates of returns, the inferior prospect by expected utility may be chosen. Let us elaborate.

Table 8.1: The multi-period continuous return as a function of the 1-period discrete return, R, and the horizon N.

Horizon, N	Annual Discrete Rate of Return, R												
	-0.2	-0.15	-0.1	-0.05	0	0.05	0.1	0.15	0.2	0.25	0.3	0.35	0.4
1	-0.2231	-0.1625	-0.1054	-0.0513	0.0000	0.0488	0.0953	0.1398	0.1823	0.2231	0.2624	0.3001	0.3365
2	-0.4463	-0.3250	-0.2107	-0.1026	0.0000	0.0976	0.1906	0.2795	0.3646	0.4463	0.5247	0.6002	0.6729
3	-0.6694	-0.4876	-0.3161	-0.1539	0.0000	0.1464	0.2859	0.4193	0.5470	0.6694	0.7871	0.9003	1.0094
4	-0.8926	-0.6501	-0.4214	-0.2052	0.0000	0.1952	0.3812	0.5590	0.7293	0.8926	1.0495	1.2004	1.3459
5	-1.1157	-0.8126	-0.5268	-0.2565	0.0000	0.2440	0.4766	0.6988	0.9116	1.1157	1.3118	1.5005	1.6824
6	-1.3389	-0.9751	-0.6322	-0.3078	0.0000	0.2927	0.5719	0.8386	1.0939	1.3389	1.5742	1.8006	2.0188
7	-1.5620	-1.1376	-0.7375	-0.3591	0.0000	0.3415	0.6672	0.9783	1.2763	1.5620	1.8365	2.1007	2.3553
8	-1.7851	-1.3002	-0.8429	-0.4103	0.0000	0.3903	0.7625	1.1181	1.4586	1.7851	2.0989	2.4008	2.6918
9	-2.0083	-1.4627	-0.9482	-0.4616	0.0000	0.4391	0.8578	1.2579	1.6409	2.0083	2.3613	2.7009	3.0283
10	-2.2314	-1.6252	-1.0536	-0.5129	0.0000	0.4879	0.9531	1.3976	1.8232	2.2314	2.6236	3.0010	3.3647
11	-2.4546	-1.7877	-1.1590	-0.5642	0.0000	0.5367	1.0484	1.5374	2.0055	2.4546	2.8860	3.3012	3.7012
12	-2.6777	-1.9502	-1.2643	-0.6155	0.0000	0.5855	1.1437	1.6771	2.1879	2.6777	3.1484	3.6013	4.0377
13	-2.9009	-2.1127	-1.3697	-0.6668	0.0000	0.6343	1.2390	1.8169	2.3702	2.9009	3.4107	3.9014	4.3741
14	-3.1240	-2.2753	-1.4750	-0.7181	0.0000	0.6831	1.3343	1.9567	2.5525	3.1240	3.6731	4.2015	4.7106
15	-3.3472	-2.4378	-1.5804	-0.7694	0.0000	0.7319	1.4297	2.0964	2.7348	3.3472	3.9355	4.5016	5.0471
16	-3.5703	-2.6003	-1.6858	-0.8207	0.0000	0.7806	1.5250	2.2362	2.9171	3.5703	4.1978	4.8017	5.3836
17	-3.7934	-2.7628	-1.7911	-0.8720	0.0000	0.8294	1.6203	2.3760	3.0995	3.7934	4.4602	5.1018	5.7200
18	-4.0166	-2.9253	-1.8965	-0.9233	0.0000	0.8782	1.7156	2.5157	3.2818	4.0166	4.7226	5.4019	6.0565
19	-4.2397	-3.0879	-2.0018	-0.9746	0.0000	0.9270	1.8109	2.6555	3.4641	4.2397	4.9849	5.7020	6.3930
20	-4.4629	-3.2504	-2.1072	-1.0259	0.0000	0.9758	1.9062	2.7952	3.6464	4.4629	5.2473	6.0021	6.7294

Table 8.2: The values of R_N and r_N for various horizons (in %).

	Annual $R = 5\%$		Annual $R = 10\%$	
Horizon, N	R_N	r_N	R_N	r_N
1	5.00	4.88	10.00	9.53
2	10.25	9.76	21.00	19.06
3	15.76	14.64	33.10	28.59
4	21.55	19.52	46.41	38.12
5	27.63	24.40	61.05	47.66
10	62.89	48.79	159.37	95.31
20	165.33	97.58	572.75	190.62

For an N-years horizon, the discrete rate of return denoted by R_N is given by

$$P_N/P_0 \equiv R_N = (1 + R)^N - 1 \tag{8.4}$$

where P_0 is the current asset price, P_N is the asset price N years from now, and R_N is the discrete rate of return for the whole investment period of N years.

Similarly, with the same observed asset values, the N-period continuous rate of return is given by

$$\frac{P_N}{P_0} = \lim_{n \to \infty} (1 + r/n)^{nN} = e^{rN}. \tag{8.5}$$

Hence, the N-years continuous rate of return denoted by r_N is given by

$$log\left(\frac{P_N}{P_0}\right) \equiv r_N = log \lim_{n \to \infty} (1 + r/n)^{nN} = log(e^{rN}) = rN. \tag{8.6}$$

Although the gap between R and r may be relatively small, it may be very large between R_N and r_N as the continuous rate of return increases additively with N, and the discrete rate of return increases faster due to the compounded effect.

Table 8.1 presents the difference between the continuous rate of return for various discrete rates of return as a function of the horizon.

The table presents the multi-period continuous rate of return r_N corresponding to cash flows obtained N years in the future as a function of the annual discrete annual rate of return R and as a function of the horizon, N. For example, as previously shown, for $R = 0.1$ (that is, 10% a year) for $N = 1$ year, the continuous rate of return is .0953 (that is, 9.53%). However, for a horizon of $N = 10$ years, the continuous 10-year return is .9531 (95.31%). However, as shown before, the discrete rate of return for 10 years in this case (not shown in Table 8.1) is $(1.1)^{10} - 1 = 1.5931\,(159.31\%)$.

Table 8.2 presents the difference between the two rates of returns, continuous and discrete, for two selected annual values of $R = 5\%$ and 10% in a more transparent way, where both rates of returns are presented in multi period terms.

Thus, the table presents the multi-period values of r_N and R_N, respectively. For example, for $R = 5\%$ for an $N = 1$-year horizon, the continuous rate of return is very close to 5% (4.88%). In comparison, for $N = 10$ years, the multi-period discrete rate of return is 62.89%, while the continuous multi-period rate of return is only 48.79%. Thus, even for a relatively low 1-period return of 5%, a large difference between the two rates of returns grows with the horizon.

Taking a closer look at the definitions of the continuous and discrete rates of returns, note that employing $(1 + R)$ or e^r (rather than r) yields the same result because these two values are identical:

$$P_{t+1}/P_t = (1 + R) = e^r.$$

Thus, there are two mathematical ways to present the same rate of return. For example, if $P_{t+1} = \$110$ and $P_t = \$100$, we have $(1 + R) = 1.10$, that is, $R = 10\%$, $r = log(1.10) = 0.09531$, and $e^r = 10\%$. Therefore, no economic distortion occurs with these two ways of presenting the same profit on the investment as long as the employed continuous profit is e^r and not r. The same conclusion also holds for multi-period comparisons. However, in economic and financial research, the continuous rate of return, r, and not e^r, is commonly employed, that is, $r = log(1 + R)$ is employed; hence, a difference between the two calculation methods emerges, as presented in Tables 8.1 and 8.2. As $r \neq R$, this difference may affect prospect ranking and the choices under uncertainty. Employing the continuous rather than the discrete rate of return may also substantially affect the results of empirical studies that test the relation between risk and return and those that analyze the change in the distribution of stock returns with the horizon.

As shown in Tables 8.1 and 8.2, employing R or r has a negligible effect in the specific case where the rates of returns are relatively small. In this case, it is well known that $R \cong r$. Therefore, if the rate of return is small, which virtually characterizes all cases with very short investment horizons, the difference between the two rates of returns is negligible. For example, empirical studies of stock market behavior that employ daily, or weekly, or even monthly returns, which are commonly very small, find that returns are generally less affected by the employment of R or alternatively r than studies employing, say, annual or longer horizons' rates of returns.

Despite the possible economic distortion induced by employing r instead of R, it seems that there is no agreement in the literature whether r or R should be employed in economic research. Indeed, numerous studies employ R, while others employ r, and even some employ both R and r in different studies. We cite here only a few empirical examples out of numerous studies that employ r or R. For example, Fama and MacBeth[1] and Fama and French[2] test the validity of the CAPM with R as the dependent variable. However, Fama, in his earlier studies of the behavior of stock market prices[3] and of market efficiency[4] employs the continuously compounded return, r. Fama, who is aware of the differences of the two calculating methods of the rates of returns, and their effect on the obtained

---

[1]Fama, F. E. and J. D. MacBeth (1973). Risk, return and equilibrium: Empirical tests. *Journal of Political Economy* 81(3), 607–636.

[2]Fama, F. E and K. R. French (1992). The cross section of expected stock return. *The Journal of Finance* 47(2), 427–465.

[3]Fama, F. E. (1965). The behavior of stock-market prices. *Journal of Business* 38(1), 34–105.

[4]Fama, E. F. (1970). Efficient capital markets: A review of theory and empirical work. *The Journal of Finance* 25(2), 383–417.

results, correctly argues in his 1965 study that employing r is mathematically more convenient than employing R, although from an economic point of view, R should be employed. Moreover, he advocates that there are three main reasons for employing r rather than R:

(a) *First, the change in log price is the yield, with continuous compounding, from holding the security for that day.*
(b) *Second, Moore [41, pp. 13–15] has shown that the variability of simple price changes for a given stock is an increasing function of the price level of the stock. His work indicates that taking the logarithms seems to neutralize most of this price level effect.*
(c) *Third, for changes less than ±15 per cent, the change in log price is very close to the percentage price change, and for many purposes, it is convenient to look at the data in terms of percentage price changes. (See footnote 4.)*

Point c, in our view, is the most convincing. For a 15% discrete rate of return, the corresponding continuous rate of return is $log(1.15) \cong 14\%$.

Indeed, in Table 8.1, we have seen that the gap between R and r is relatively small for an annual rate of return below 15%, so long as the horizon is one year. For monthly rates of returns which are relatively low, the difference between the two rates of returns is even smaller than those reported in Table 8.1 for $N = 1$ year. Thus, for daily, weekly, or even monthly horizons, the two rates of returns are relatively close. However, presumably a large segment of investors makes their choice based on the distributions of returns corresponding to longer horizons — one year or longer — where a large gap between the two rates of returns may emerge.

There is evidence showing that even long horizon investors (say, those saving for pension) tend to evaluate their portfolio frequently, mostly once a year. For this view, see Benartzi and Thaler.[5] Thus,

---

[5]Benartzi, S. and R. H. Thaler (1995). Myopic loss aversion and equity risk premium. *The Quarterly Journal of Economics* 110(1), 73–92.

this annual evaluation indicates that the investment horizon is typically about one year. One may suspect that with annual rates of returns on stocks, which is on average about 10%, there is only a negligible difference between the continuous and discrete rates of returns. However, this is not the case even with annual rates of returns. With empirical annual rates of returns, a substantial difference between R and r may exist. Hence, there may be important economic implications to the rate of return calculation method, even with annual data. To illustrate this point, we find that for the period 1928–2020 (93 years), there were 6 years with an annual rate of return larger than $\pm 40\%$, 21 years with an annual rate of return larger than $\pm 30\%$, 29 years with rates of returns larger than $\pm 25\%$, and 51 years with returns larger than $\pm 15\%$.[6] Thus, for almost 50% of this time period, the annual rates of returns do not stand the criterion for approximation of less that $\pm 15\%$, as suggested by Fama. With these actual annual rates of returns, the gap between R and r is relatively large. For example, with a 25% return, the continuous compounded return is 22.3%, and the difference between the two measurement methods is not negligible, let alone for a return of 40% where the corresponding continuous rate of return is only 33.6%. These differences are quite large and, therefore, once annual rates of returns are employed, making an investment decision based on R or r may lead to different choices.

Finally, as we cited so far, in older studies which employ R or r, one is tempted to believe that there is currently a consensus regarding the calculation method of the rate of return — but this is not the case. Some researchers still employ R and others employ r. For example, Fama and French (see footnote 2), in studying the CAPM and the three-factor model, employ the discrete return, R, as the dependent variable. Virtually all recent studies testing the risk–return relationships of various assets also employ R rather than r. However, some recent studies have gone against this trend, employing r rather than R, that is, $log(1 + R)$ rather than R. For example, in their argument as to whether stocks become riskier or safer with the

---

[6]http://www.stern.nyu.edu/~adamodar/pc/datasets/histretSP.xls.

investment horizon, both Siegal[7] (2014) and Pástor and Stambaugh[8] employ the continuously compounded rate of return, $log(1 + R) = r$.

8.2. Employing the Continuous Rate of Return to Mitigate the Positive Asymmetry of the Distribution

Justifying employment of the continuous rate of return, we may add to Fama's three points theoretical statistical reasoning. When uncertainty prevails, and one wishes to conduct some statistical significance tests corresponding to distributions that are positively skewed, switching from the discrete calculation to the continuous calculation has some statistical advantages. Specifically, empirical evidence reveals that the distributions of returns on stocks for relatively long horizons are positively skewed, as these distributions tend to be log-normal. Hence, by shifting from returns to log-returns (that is, switching from the discrete to the continuous calculation of the rates of returns), one obtains a normal distribution (or at least a symmetrical one), a property necessary for conducting various statistical tests. This existing empirical positive asymmetry is not confined to the stock market. The same positive skewness in the distribution characterizes many economic variables, e.g., income distribution; hence, when taking the *log* of these variables, this asymmetry partially or completely vanishes.

Figure 8.1 presents the distributions of returns on the S&P 500 stock index for $N = 1$ and alternatively $N = 10$ years. As can be seen from this figure, for an $N = 1$-year horizon, the density function is quite symmetrical, and for $N = 10$ years, the density function of the rates of returns, of course, shifts to the right. However, what is more interesting is that it becomes positively skewed. In various statistical testing, normality is essential, which obviously cannot hold

---

[7]Siegel, J. J. (2014). *Stocks for the Long Run: The Definitive Guide to Financial Market Returns and Long-Term Investment Strategies*, McGraw-Hill, New York.

[8] Pástor, Ĺ. and R. F. Stambaugh (2012). Are stocks really less volatile in the long run? *The Journal of Finance* 67(2), 431–478.

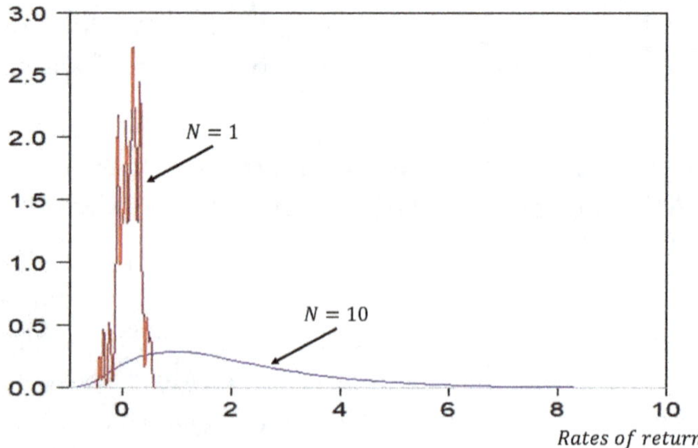

Figure 8.1: The density function of the rates of returns on the S&P 500 stock index for $N = 1$ and $N = 10$ years.

Note: In red, the return for $N = 1$ year; in blue, the return for $N = 10$ years.

with positive skewness. Therefore, it is common to take the *log* of the variables to avoid this.

Figure 8.2 presents the density function of $log(1 + R)$ for an $N = 1$-year and an $N = 10$-year investment horizon. As can be seen from the figure, the 10-year density function, which was positively skewed with R, becomes quite symmetrical with $log(1 + R)$, and the one-year density function, which was quite symmetrical with R, becomes negatively skewed with $log(1 + R)$. Thus, if one needs symmetry for statistical testing, for short horizons, employing the return is recommended, but for long horizons, it is recommended to employ $log(1 + R)$, that is, the continuous rate of return. Of course, these transformations of the returns have some statistical advantage, but as we shall see in what follows, there is no free lunch, as employing the continuous rate of return also has an economic disadvantage in that it may induce economic distortion.

Employing the continuous or the discrete rate of return may also affect regression analysis, widely employed in economic and financial research, for example, to calculate a stock's beta that is needed for testing equilibrium pricing models. Basically, employing $log(1 + R)$ rather than R shrinks the large returns more than the small returns;

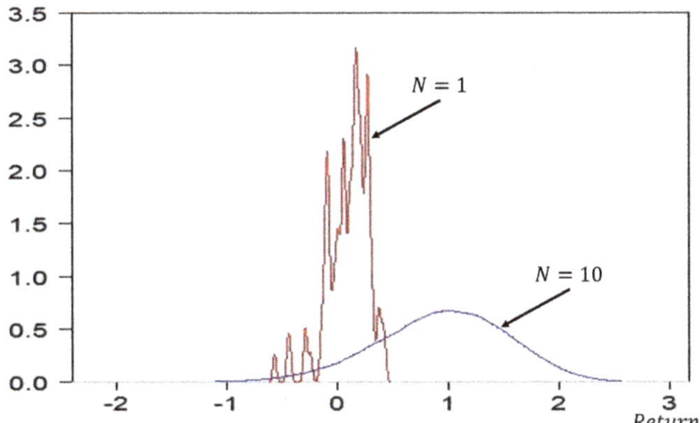

Figure 8.2: The density function of $log(1 + R)$ of the S&P 500 stock index for $N = 1$ and $N = 10$ years.

Note: In red, the return for $N = 1$ year; in blue, the return for $N = 10$ years.

Table 8.3: Beta of two stocks with R and $log(1 + R)$ with monthly rates of returns.

	β_{return}	$\beta_{\log(1 + return)}$
American Electric Power Company, Inc. (AEP)	0.2965	0.3091
Alphabet Inc. (Google) (AAL)	0.9371	0.9206

Note: Based on the 144 months between January 2009 and December 2020.

hence, the regression coefficient with continuous and discrete rates of returns may substantially differ. In measuring a stock's beta, we expect that for defensive stocks, the rate of return employed will have only a minor effect with short horizons (with daily, weekly, or even annual rates of returns), but for aggressive stocks, a large difference is expected with annual rates of returns, but probably not with monthly rates of returns.

Table 8.3 provides the beta of two stocks calculated both by R and $log(1 + R)$. The beta is calculated by running the regression of the return of the stock under consideration on the return of the market portfolio, in this specific case the S&P 500 stock index.

Table 8.4: Beta of defensive and aggressive stocks with R and $log(1+R)$ with annual rates of returns.[*]

	$\beta_{rate\ of\ return}$	$\beta_{\log(1+\ rate\ of\ return)}$
American Electric Power Company, Inc. (AEP)	0.2484	0.2383
Alphabet Inc. (Google) (AAL)	1.5305	1.2239

Note: [*]Yearly returns were calculated based on the 144 months between January 2009 and December 2020.

As can be seen from this table, betas calculated with the monthly rates of returns with R or with $log(1 + R)$ are very close to each other, and this phenomenon is intact for both stocks. These results are not surprising as we employ monthly rates of returns for which the continuous rates of returns are typically very close to the discrete rates of returns. However, Table 8.4 reveals that with annual rates of returns, a much different picture emerges. First, note that the defensive stock beta, once again, is almost identical when calculated by the continuous and discrete rates of returns. This result is not surprising as the returns from American Electric Power Company are typically low. However, for the aggressive stock (as measured with annual rates of returns), the beta of Alphabet Inc. with annual rates of returns is 1.5305 when calculated with return, R, and this reduces to 1.2239 when calculated with the continuous rates of return $log(1 + R)$.

Figure 8.3 presents the regression lines of the defensive and aggressive stocks calculated with annual data with R and $log(1+R)$, respectively. As can be seen, the large return with R typically shrinks when we switch to $log(1 + R)$; hence, the aggressive stock becomes much less aggressive when one shifts from R to $log(1 + R)$. Indeed, the beta is reduced from about 1.53 with discrete rates of returns to about 1.22 with continuous rates of returns.

In sum, the horizon plays a crucial role also with beta calculation: the longer the horizon, the larger the returns and the more skewed is the distribution of returns, and the larger is the effect of the employed rates of returns (continuous or discrete) on the beta.

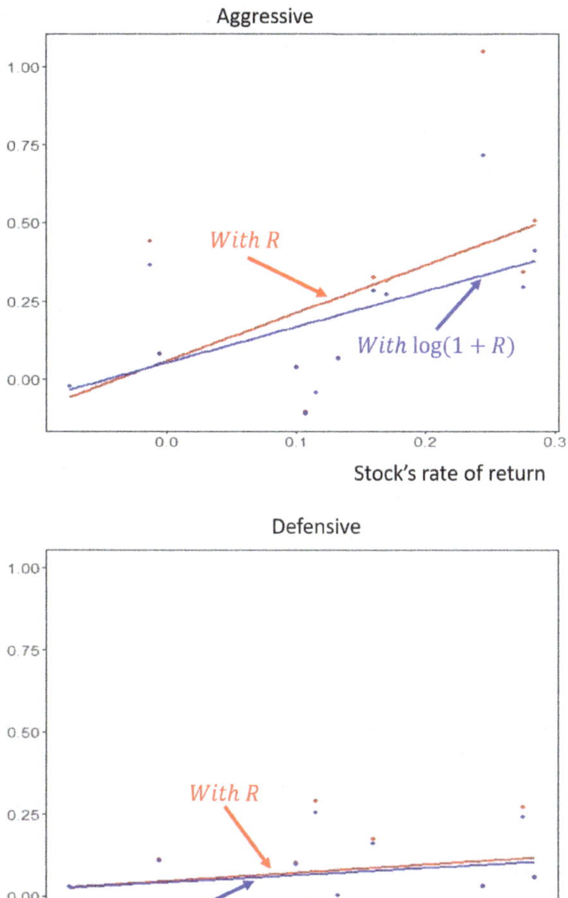

Figure 8.3: The regression lines with annual continuous and discrete rates of returns.

8.3. Ranking Prospects by the Continuous and Discrete Distributions of the Rate of Return

As with actual annual rates of return, in some years, the gaps between the continuous and discrete rates of returns are very large, so the next logical questions are: Does this matter? Does the method used to calculate the rate of return affect the empirical results, the economic conclusions, and the prospect ranking? Does the calculation method affect the choice between two uncertain prospects? Which of the two calculating methods is consistent with the expected utility paradigm? These questions are particularly important for relatively long horizons because, as shown in Tables 8.1 and 8.2, here the gap between the two rates of returns is very large.

Although employing the continuous rate of return is more convenient and easier to handle mathematically (particularly in multi-period analysis, see what follows), the theoretically correct method is to employ R rather than r, and any deviation from relying on R in decision-making may induce an economic cost.

First, let us elaborate why R and not r should be employed in investment decision-making. The two main paradigms of investment decision-making under uncertainty — expected utility and prospect theory — are defined in terms of wealth $U(w)$ (or change of wealth in the case of prospect theory) and not in *log-wealth* (or in terms of the change in *log-wealth*). Therefore, the discrete return calculation, which is a function of the end of period wealth, is the correct method to employ for decision-making. Specifically, suppose that for a \$1 investment (which is assumed to be the total wealth), the return is $(1 + R)$. Thus, the utility of this investment is $U(1 + R)$, and where the return is random, the expected utility is given by $EU(1 + R)$. However, when a continuous rate of return is employed, the utility of this investment is given by $U(r) = U(log(1 + R))$ with expected utility $EU(r) = EU(log(1 + R))$. As von-Neumann and Morgenstern's[9] expected utility is defined on wealth and not *log-wealth*, it is obvious that only the discrete return is relevant for decision-making and prospect ranking. Thus, the continuous rate of return should not be employed, even if it is mathematically more convenient to handle, particularly in a multi-period case.

Notwithstanding, as for each value R there is a corresponding value r, one is tempted to believe that in choosing between two

---

[9]von Neumann, J. and O. Morgenstern (1953). *Theory of Games and Economic Behavior*, 3rd ed., Princeton University Press, New Jersey.

alternative uncertain prospects, one can technically employ the distribution of either R or r interchangeably, without affecting choices despite the theoretical argument that only employing R conforms with expected utility. While this intuition is intact for comparing prospects by first-degree stochastic dominance (FSD), it is an invalid statement for higher degree stochastic dominance, e.g., for second-degree stochastic dominance (SSD). In other words, risk averters who employ r rather than the correct rate of return R may face an economic distortion as the optimal prospect may not be chosen. Specifically, suppose that there are two prospects, and an investor wishes to invest in one of them. Facing these two uncertain prospects, say A and B, employing the distributions of r to choose between them may yield a clear-cut result for all risk averters, recommending that each investor choose one of the two uncertain prospects under consideration, say prospect A (hence, prospect B is relegated to the inefficient set and, therefore, cannot be selected), while with the discrete rate of return, R, some risk averters may prefer prospect B. In brief, with the distributions of r, prospect A dominates prospect B by SSD, but with the distributions of R, such SSD dominance does not exist. In that case, the rejected prospect by r (prospect B) may be optimal for investors who employ the correct profitability measure, R. The economic distortion and utility loss stem from the fact that by r, prospect A is selected, while some risk averters may increase their expected utility by switching from prospect A to the seemingly inferior prospect, prospect B.

In the analysis given in what follows, we assume that R, which conforms with expected utility, is employed for prospect ranking, and we analyze whether that ranking may change with any monotonic transformation of the rate of return R. Then we use the $log(1+R) = r$ transformation as a specific case of such a monotonic transformation. In both the continuous and discrete calculations, it is assumed that $R : \Omega \to \mathbb{R}$ and also $\varphi(R) : \Omega \to \mathbb{R}$, where $\varphi(R)$ is some monotonic non-decreasing transformation of the random variable. In the following analysis, we have the following notations: Two prospects F and G are defined with the return $x = (1 + R)$. The same two prospects are analyzed again, but this time defined on the transformation of the return: $\varphi(x) = log(x)$, and the cumulative distributions of the transformed return of the two prospects under consideration are denoted by F^* and G^*, respectively.

First, let us analyze the FSD preference, namely an analysis for all monotonic non-decreasing utility functions — a case where, as shown in what follows, employing R and r yield the identical dominance relationship, hence an identical FSD efficient set.

Theorem 1. *Suppose that one faces two prospects with cumulative distributions F and G with the random variable return $x \equiv 1 + R$, where $x \geq 0$. Define a monotonic non-decreasing function of x denoted by $\varphi(x)$, namely $\varphi'(x) \geq 0$. Denote the cumulative distributions of the two prospects corresponding to $\varphi(x)$ by F^* and G^*. Then F dominates G by FSD if and only if F^* dominates G^* by FSD. Thus, a monotonic non-decreasing function of the return does not alter the FSD ranking.[10] Finally, as the cumulative prospect theory value functions are included in the set of all non-decreasing utility functions, the statement in this theorem applies to expected utility and prospect theory alike.[11]*

Proof. F dominates G by FSD if and only if $F(x) \leq G(x)$, and there is at least one strict inequality for some x_0.[12] This well-known dominance condition can also be stated in terms of the distribution quantiles as follows: F dominates G by FSD if and only if $Q_F(p) \geq Q_G(p)$ for all values p ($0 \leq p \leq 1$ with at least one strict inequality), where the quantile $Q(p)$ is given by the solution to the equation $p = p_r[x \leq Q(p)]$. Thus, the quantile of a given value p is given

---

[10]FSD asserts that $F(x) \leq G(x)$ for all x with at least one strict inequality if and only if, $E_F(U) \geq E_G(U)$ with at least one strict inequality for all non-decreasing utility functions U; see Levy, H. (2016). *Stochastic Dominance: Investment Decision Making Under Uncertainty,* 3rd Ed., Springer, New York.

[11]As the FSD rule is invariant to the initial wealth, it can be extended to prospect theory which is defined in terms of change of wealth.

[12]Note that the FSD dominance can be stated in terms of the returns or rates of returns, namely FSD is invariant to the initial wealth. In the theorem, we choose to state the FSD in terms of the returns, hence $x \geq 0$, allowing us to relate to the transformation $\varphi(x) = log(x)$.

by some specific value of the return x. To prove the claim given in Theorem 1, first note that as the transformation is a non-decreasing monotonic function, we have

$$p = p_r[Q_F(p) \geq Q_G(p)] = p_r[\varphi(Q_F(p))] \geq \varphi(Q_G(p))]. \tag{8.7}$$

Therefore,

$$Q_F(p) \geq Q_G(p) \Leftrightarrow \varphi[Q_F(p)] \geq \varphi[Q_G(p)] \tag{8.8}$$

so long as $\varphi'(x) \geq 0$ (recall that the quantiles are nothing but the values of the random variable x). As the *log* function is a monotonic non-decreasing function of x, one can employ return R or *log*-returns interchangeably without affecting the FSD relationships. This is an encouraging result, as employing R or r does not affect the FSD relationship of the two prospects under consideration.[13]

Discussion: We proved that the efficient FSD set is invariant to the rate of return calculation method. Notwithstanding, even in this case, an economic loss may occur as the *optimal* investment selected from the FSD efficient set by a specific utility function may not be the same with r and R. Figure 8.4 demonstrates this point. The FSD efficient sets determined by R and r are identical, but the optimal choice for a given utility function from the efficient set may depend on the rate of return calculation method; hence, also in this FSD case, a utility loss may occur. For example, with r, prospect A is selected, whereas with R, prospect B is selected, and as R is employed, a utility loss incurs even in the FSD case where the two efficient sets are identical.

Thus, the choice of the inefficient prospect does not occur, but the choice of the non-optimal prospect may. To illustrate this claim, suppose that one prospect, say prospect F, yields a return of 1 or 10 with equal probability, with *log-returns* of 0 and 2.30, respectively. The other prospect, prospect G, yields 5 with certainty with a *log-return* of 1.61. As the two cumulative distributions, with return and *log-return*, cross, the two prospects are included in the FSD efficient set, which conforms with Theorem 1. Suppose that only

---

[13]Note that employing R or $(1 + R)$ does not affect the dominance relationship.

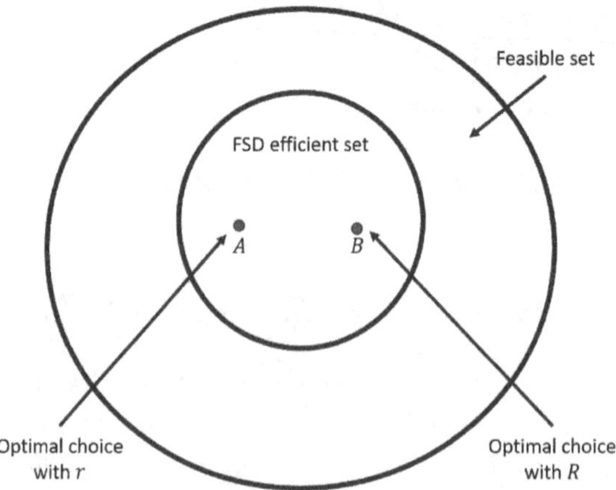

Figure 8.4: The FSD efficient set with R and r and the optimal choices from the efficient set.

these two prospects are included in the FSD efficient set and all other available prospects are FSD inefficient. Thus, the investor selects a prospect from one of these two FSD efficient prospects. Suppose that the utility function is linear $U(x) = x$. It is easy to see that with returns, prospect F with the larger mean is selected, but with *log-returns*, prospect G is selected. Thus, although the FSD efficient set is invariant to the way the return is calculated, the optimal prospect selected from the efficient set is affected. Therefore, even in the FSD case, employing the continuous rate of return may induce a utility loss.

From the FSD results given above, one is tempted to believe that the efficient sets are also invariant to the return calculation method with higher degree stochastic dominance rules. For example, if the transformation is monotonic and concave, it intuitively seems that using R or r would not affect the SSD efficient set. As we shall see in the following (*Theorem 2*), this intuition is misleading: when risk aversion is assumed, one cannot extend the results of *Theorem 1* even if the transformation of the return is a non-decreasing concave function like $\varphi(x) = log(x)$. As before, we denote the two cumulative distributions of $x = (1 + R)$ by F and G, and the cumulative distributions of $\varphi(x)$ by F^* and G^*.

Theorem 2. *Denote by F and G, as before, the cumulative distributions of two prospects under consideration corresponding to $x = (1 + R)$, and by F^* and G^*, the cumulative distributions of the transformed variables, $\varphi(x)$. Furthermore, assume that the transformation function, φ, is non-decreasing and concave, which fits the risk-aversion assumption, namely $\varphi' \geq 0$ and $\varphi'' \leq 0$. Then*

$$F \text{ dominates } G \text{ by } SSD \Rightarrow F^* \text{ dominates } G^* \text{ by } SSD.$$

However,

$$F^* \text{ dominates } G^* \text{ by } SSD \nRightarrow F \text{ dominates } G \text{ by } SSD.$$

Thus, unlike with FSD, with SSD, we have sufficiency, but not necessity. This implies that using $r = log(1 + R)$ rather than the correct return, $1 + R$, may induce elimination from the efficient set prospect G^*, which may be optimal for some risk averters when the correct return, $(1 + R)$, is employed.

Proof. Although the criterion for SSD is commonly stated in terms of the cumulative distributions,[14] here also, the proof is easier with the quantile approach. By the quantile approach, F dominates G by SSD if and only if

$$\int_0^p [Q_F(t) - Q_G(t)]dt \geq 0 \quad \text{for all } 0 \leq p \leq 1 \tag{8.9}$$

and there is at least one strict inequality.

Unlike the requirement of FSD, with SSD, the cumulative distributions of the two prospects under consideration may cross. However, to have SSD of F over G, the integral condition given by Eq. (8.9) implies that for each negative area, there must be a preceding positive area (which is *no smaller* than the negative area under consideration). This implies that with a dominance with the

---

[14]By the cumulative distribution approach, F dominates G by SSD if and only if $\int_0^x [G(t) - F(t)]dt \geq 0$ for all x, and there is at least one strict inequality; see Levy (2016).

concave transformation, the following must also hold:

$$\int_0^p \{\varphi[Q_F(t)] - \varphi[Q_G(t)]\}dt \geq 0 \quad \text{for all } 0 \leq p \leq 1. \qquad (8.10)$$

The explanation of Eq. (8.10) is that the assumption that $\varphi' \geq 0$ and $\varphi'' \leq 0$ implies that the negative area receives a smaller weight than the positive area preceding it; hence, with the concave monotonic non-decreasing transformation, $\varphi(x)$, if Eq. (8.9) holds, then the integral given by Eq. (8.10) is *a fortiori* non-negative. In sum, it is shown that SSD of F over G with $(1 + R)$ also implies SSD with $r = log(1 + R)$ (note that we have $x = (1 + R)$ and $log(x) = log(1 + R) = r$).

To complete the proof of *Theorem 2*, we need to show that SSD by $r = log(1+R)$ does not imply SSD by $(1+R)$. To show this claim, one counterexample is sufficient.

8.3.1. *Numerical counterexample*

We demonstrate that the necessity part of *Theorem 2* does not hold with a specific example. Suppose that prospect G yields either 1 or 16 and with an equal probability of $\frac{1}{2}$ and F yields 8 with a probability of 1. It is obvious from Figure 8.5(a) that neither F nor G dominates the other by SSD. F does not dominate G by SSD as it has a lower mean (the mean of F is 8 and for G, it is 8.5), and G does not dominate F by SSD as it starts from the left. Thus, by SSD, both F and G are efficient, namely some risk averters may choose F and others may choose G. This conclusion is correct as long as we employ $(1 + R)$, which conforms with the expected utility paradigm.

We turn now to analyze SSD with the transformation $r = log(1 + R)$. Figure 8.5(b) reveals that F^* dominates G^* by SSD as we have

$$\int_0^x [G^*(t) - F^*(t)]dt \geq 0 \quad \text{for all values } x.$$

Hence, F^* dominates G^* by SSD.

Thus, using r one would mistakenly recommend that every risk averter choose F^*, yet with actual rates of return R or with returns

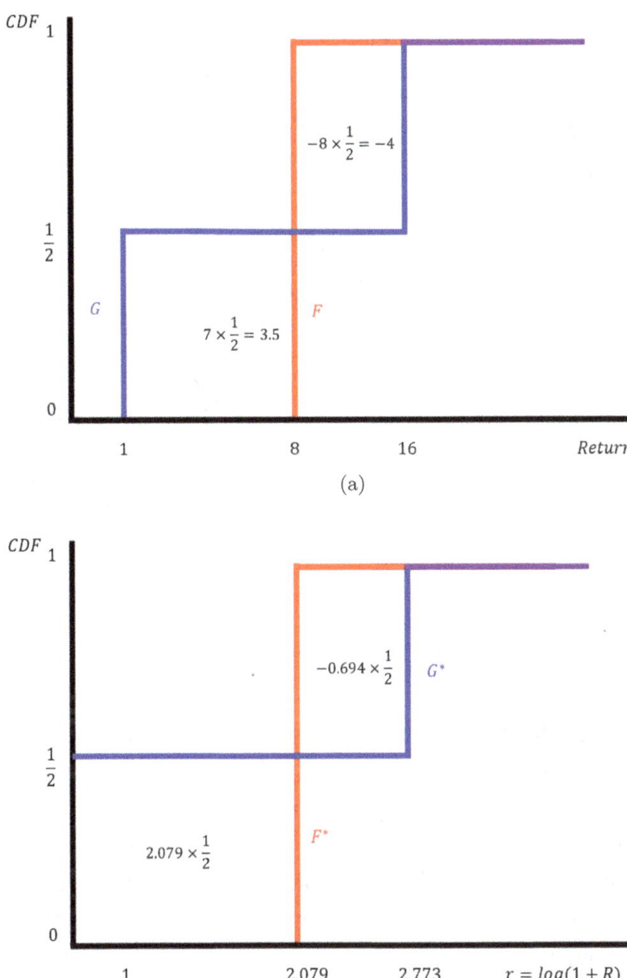

Figure 8.5: Numerical example showing that F^* dominates G^* by SSD, but that such dominance does not exist with F and G: (a) Return; (b) $log(1 + R)$.

$(1+R)$, some risk averters may prefer G^*. Specifically, with any risk-averse preference that is close to a linear function, G is preferred to F. For example, with the risk-averse function $U(z) = z^{0.9}$, we obtain

$$EU_G(1 + R) = (1/2)1^{.9} + (1/2)(16)^{.9} = 6.563$$

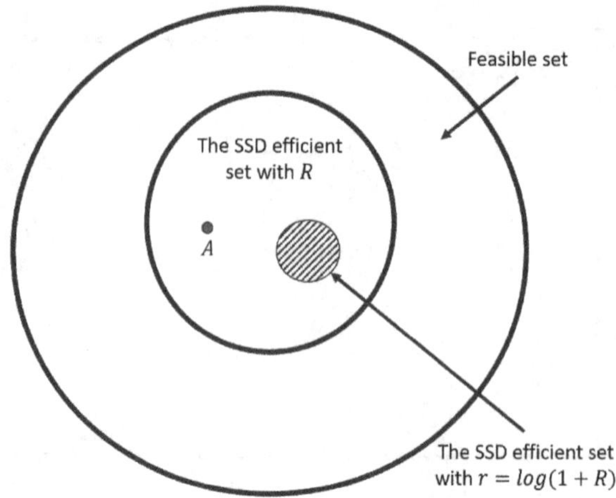

Figure 8.6: The SSD efficient set with R and $r = log(1 + R)$.

and

$$EU_F(x) = 8^{.9} = 6.498.$$

Hence, G is preferred to F by this risk averter, in contradiction to the SSD dominance of F over G with $log(x)$.

In sum, using $r = log(1 + R)$ to rank uncertain prospects for all risk averters may be misleading for some risk averters as it may relegate a prospect that is optimal to the SSD inefficient set. Figure 8.6 demonstrates the relationship between the SSD efficient set derived with r and R. According to *Theorem 2*, by employing $r = log(1+R)$, prospect A is relegated to the SSD inefficient set even though it may be optimal for some risk averters as it is included in the SSD efficient set with R. Thus, employing $r = log(1 + R)$ rather than R may induce relegating a prospect to the SSD inefficient set, though it is SSD efficient when using R.

We now turn to analyze the effect of the specific transformation of the return corresponding to the normal and lognormal distributions that are widely employed in the economic literature. This is of crucial importance in regard to investment in stocks for long horizons, as the distribution of returns tends be log-normally distributed.

8.4. The Log-Normal and Normal Distributions

While *Theorem 2* relates to any unrestricted distributions, we confine the SSD analysis in this section to log-normal distributions and to the log-transformation of the random variable, which by definition is normal. This situation is of particular interest regarding investment in risky assets for a very long horizon. Thus, we assume relatively long investment horizons where the return on stocks is assumed to be log-normally distributed, and the transformed random variable is normally distributed. We examine the SSD relationship of the two log-normal prospects under consideration and the two corresponding transformed normal prospects.

First, note that because the SSD dominance with return $(1+R) = x$ and with the transformation $\varphi(x) = log(1 + R)$ does not always coincide (see *Theorem 2*), this does not imply that for specific distributions, in our case the log-normal and normal distributions, such SSD equivalence cannot exist. In other words, the information that the distributions are log-normal and the transformed distributions are normal may change the results stated in *Theorem 2*, which are general and, therefore, relate to any two distributions and not to specific ones. As the log-normal distribution is of special importance to economics and finance, particularly because the distribution of stock returns tends to be log-normal for relatively long horizons, we investigate whether the SSD relationship of the return x on stocks, which is assumed to be log-normally distributed (for relatively long horizons), and SSD dominance with the specific transformation, $log(x)$, which by definition is normally distributed, coincide. In a nutshell, we assume that, for relatively long horizons, the distributions of the stocks' discrete returns are log-normal and investigate whether shifting to continuous rates of returns (as is widely done in economic research), $log(x)$, may induce a different efficient set than the one obtained with the log-normal distributions.

To determine if the two SSD efficient sets with log-normal and normal distributions are identical, we analyze mainly whether investors in stocks for the long run can safely shift from x to $log(x)$ without affecting the content of the SSD efficient set. Specifically, we assume that we compare two prospects F and G that are log-normally distributed, and alternatively, the two transformed prospects F^* and G^* that are normally distributed, as they are obtained from F and G using the *log* transformation. Are the SSD relationships with F and G and alternatively with F^* and G^* identical?

Before we investigate this SSD relationships for the log-normal and normal distributions, let us state the formulas for the first two moments of these distributions — formulas which will be employed in the following proofs.

We have the following relationship between the parameters of the normal and log-normal distributions[15]:

If x is log-normally distributed with parameters μ, σ^2, denoted by $\Lambda \sim (\mu, \sigma)$, then

$$E(x) = e^{\mu+(1/2)\sigma^2} \quad \text{and} \quad \sigma^2(x) = e^{2\mu+\sigma^2}[\sigma^2 - 1] \qquad (8.11)$$

where

$$\mu = E(log(x)) \quad \text{and} \quad \sigma^2 = Var(log(x)),$$

and $log(x)$, which is normally distributed, has the following parameters:

$$log(x) \sim N(\mu,\ \sigma^2)$$

where Λ and N denote the log-normal and the normal distributions, respectively. In our analysis, we have that $x = (1 + R)$, the discrete rate of return, is log-normally distributed and $r = log(1 + R)$, the continuous rate of return, is normally distributed.

Theorem 2, which is not limited to log-normal distributions, asserts that the sufficiency side of the proof holds for any distribution; hence, specifically, it also holds for the log-normal distributions. If for the log-normally distributed variables, $x = (1 + R)$, F dominates G by SSD, then the dominance also holds for F^* and G^*, which are obtained from F and G, respectively, using the *log* transformation.

---

[15]See Aitchison, J. and J. A. C. Brown (1963). *The Lognormal Distribution*, Cambridge University Press, Cambridge.

While we know that the converse does not hold for all distributions, we next check whether adding the information that the distributions are log-normal and normal, respectively, may change the necessity claim of *Theorem 2*. Specifically, we check whether the converse is also true with lognormal distributions: namely, we check whether with normal distributions, F^* dominates G^* by SSD also implies that with log-normal distributions, F dominates G by SSD. If the answer to this question is positive, the SSD efficient sets with the log-normal distributions and with the transformed normal distributions coincide, despite the fact that such identity does not generally exist for all unrestricted distributions.

Now, we turn to illustrate that the log transformation of x dominance with the continuous rate of return (namely, of $log(1+R)$) does not imply dominance with the discrete rate of return, $(1+R)$. Thus, the specific information that the distribution is log-normal does not change the results as stated in *Theorem 2*. To see this claim, suppose that with $log(x)$, namely with normal distributions, F^* dominates G^* by SSD. Furthermore, let us assume for simplicity and without loss of generality that

$$\mu_{F^*} = \mu_{G^*}, \sigma_{F^*} < \sigma_{G^*} \tag{8.12}$$

which is a specific case of the above SSD dominance with the assumed normal distributions.

With our previous notation, we assume that it is given that with the normal distributions, there is SSD dominance of F^* over G^*. Does this imply that with the discrete returns $(1+R)$, namely the log-normal distributions, F dominates G? The answer is negative. To see this, recall that with the log-normal distributions, we have

$$E(x) = e^{\mu+(1/2)\sigma^2}$$

where $E(x)$ is the mean return of the log-normal distribution. As by assumption $\mu_{F^*} = \mu_{G^*}$, $\sigma_{F^*} < \sigma_{G^*}$, with the log-normal distributions, we obtain that $E_F(x) < E_G(x)$. Recalling that a necessary condition for SSD dominance with log-normal distributions (actually for any two distributions) of F over G is that $E_F(x) \geq$

$E_G(x)$, we can safely conclude that the log-normal distribution F does not dominate the log-normal distribution G.

In sum, by *Theorem 2*, if F dominates G by SSD with discrete returns $(1 + R)$, shifting to the continuous rates of returns $r = log(1+R)$ will not change this SSD dominance. However, the opposite is generally not true. Dominance with continuous rates of returns does not necessarily guarantee dominance with the discrete return. In principle, adding information to the distributions of returns may change this opposite claim given in *Theorem 2*. However, we find that adding specific information that the distributions of $(1 + R)$ are log-normal does not change the opposite claim, as stated in this theorem.

8.5. Summary

In empirical studies, some researchers employ the discrete rate of return, R (or $(1+R)$), and some employ the continuous rate of return given by $r = log(1 + R)$. It is well known that r is easier to employ, particularly for multi-period analysis, as we have the relationship $log(1 + R)^N = Nlog(1 + R)$, and this additive return is much easier to handle mathematically. Thus, researchers are tempted to employ the continuous rate of return. Yet, as expected utility is defined on returns, $(1+R)$, and not on $log(1+R)$, employing the continuous rate of returns may affect the empirical results, the economic conclusion, and, even more importantly, it may lead to non-optimal choices, as prospect ranking may be affected by the employed rate of returns.

The longer the investment horizon, the more crucial the difference is between the continuous and discrete rates of returns. For a relatively short horizon and relatively low rates of returns, the gap between the discrete and the continuous rates of returns is negligible. However, even for relatively low annual rates of returns, when the investment horizon increases, e.g., in the case of investing for pension, the difference between the discrete and continuous rates of returns may be huge. Note, however, that even with a one-year horizon, namely with annual rates of returns on stocks, the difference between the two rates of returns may be very large for some years. For example, considering the annual rates of returns on the S&P 500 stock index in the period 1928–2020, there were several years with returns of 40% or more. For such rates of returns, the continuous rate of returns is $r = log(1.4) \cong 34\%$, which is substantially smaller than the discrete 40%. Thus, even with annual rates of returns (which is the typical investment horizon), employing the continuous rates of returns may lead to the wrong prospect choice and to economic loss. Of course, for longer horizons, the gap between the two rates of returns is even larger.

We find that prospect ranking may change with the calculation method of the rate of returns. The FSD efficient set is unaffected by the calculation method of the rate of returns, but the optimal choice from the efficient set may be affected; hence, a non-optimal prospect may be selected, even in the FSD case. With SSD, namely when risk aversion is assumed, the efficient set obtained with the continuous rate of returns is smaller (in the weak sense) than the set constructed with the discrete rate of returns; hence, a direct economic loss may occur. Specifically, an optimal portfolio for some risk averters may be relegated to the inefficient set by employing the continuous rate of returns. These general SSD results (with no constraints on the shape of the distributions of returns under consideration) are also intact when one examines only the analysis of the log-normal distribution and the transformed normal distribution, which are widely employed in economics and finance.

In sum, the longer the horizon, the larger the gap between the continuous and discrete rates of returns, and the greater the chance that a non-optimal prospect will be selected by employing a continuous rate of returns that does not conform with expected utility.

Chapter 9

Almost Stochastic Dominance Rules and the Horizon

Suppose that investors face the following two uncertain prospects: prospect F which yields 1% or alternatively 100% with an equal probability of 0.5, and prospect G which yields 2% with certainty. It is predicted that with these two alternative choices, virtually all investors would prefer prospect F over G.

However, suppose that a few, say, out of a group of each 100 investors under consideration, five investors, in contrast to our prediction, choose prospect G. Reducing the certain rate of return of prospect G from 2% to 1.1% (or even to 1.0001%), would they still stick to prospect G? Probably not. Thus, we have a hypothetical situation where all investors, or virtually all of them, would prefer prospect F over prospect G. Yet, employing first-degree stochastic dominance (FSD), second-degree stochastic dominance (SSD), as well as the mean–variance (M–V) rule reveals that neither F nor G dominates the other — a result that is paradoxical. The paradox stems from the fact that all investors, risk averters and risk seekers alike, prefer prospect F over prospect G, yet the standard investment decision rules are unable to reveal this preference. The explanation for this paradox is that the standard decision-making rules mentioned above apply to *all* utility functions in a given set of preferences, including some pathological utility functions, where a utility function is defined as pathological if, in practice, it does not fit the preference of any investor. Thus, pathological preferences technically exist, but they are economically irrelevant.

389

Drawing the cumulative distributions of the two prospects given in this example, there is small range of return where the cumulative distribution of prospect F is located to the left and above of the cumulative distribution of prospect G (see Figure 9.1). For utility functions assigning an extremely and unrealistically large utility weight to the negligible left tails of the distributions where G is above F, we obtain that prospect G is preferred; hence, F does not dominate G by FSD, as dominance implies that the expected utility of F is larger (or equal) to the expected utility of G for all possible utility functions. If the relative assigned utility weights on the left and right tails of the distributions (see area A and B in Figure 9.1) do not fit the preference of any investor, we define this utility function as pathological. To eliminate such paradoxes, we need to define a set of preferences which does not include these pathological preferences. Of course, identifying pathological and non-pathological preferences is not an easy task, and we address this issue in this chapter.

How does this issue relate to the assumed investment horizon, which is the core of this book? In this chapter, we show that with cumulative distributions of the return on stocks and bonds, typically there is only one intersection between the two cumulative distributions, where the left tail of the distribution of stocks is located to the left and above the left tail of the cumulative distribution of bonds, and this nagging location of the left tails avoids the dominance of stocks over bonds, exactly as in the example with F and G,

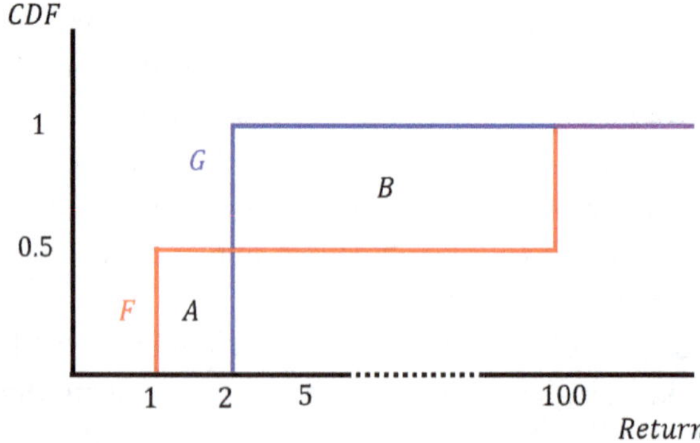

Figure 9.1: The cumulative distributions of F and G.

illustrated in Figure 9.1. However, with stocks and bonds, this FSD violation area of the left tails of the distributions shrinks with the horizon, which is the basis for the hypothesis that the longer the horizon, the larger the proportion of investors who prefers stocks over bonds. Thus, although the FSD rule does not support the investment strategy "stocks for the long run" (as the two cumulative distributions cross), the almost FSD rule (AFSD), which will be defined later in this chapter, may support it — if not for all investors, for "almost all investors." Hence, these investment rules are termed "almost stochastic dominance" (ASD) rules.

In a nutshell, we find empirically that stocks typically do not dominate bonds by FSD (or by the SSD and M–V rules) even for very long horizons, but such dominance for all non-pathological preferences may exist, and the longer the horizon, the smaller the FSD violation area (the ratio of area A divided by area B, in Figure 9.1 becomes close to zero as the horizon increases indefinitely), which intuitively hints, even though it does not prove, that the set of the non-pathological preferences may increase with the horizon. If this intuition is not misleading, it means that the proportion of investors who prefer stocks over bonds increases with the horizon.

Notwithstanding, recall that although the relative size of the FSD violation area corresponding to the return of stocks and bonds (such as area A in Figure 9.1) shrinks with the horizon, the multi-period *minimum* return, particularly of stocks, also decreases with the horizon;[1] hence, it is possible that the intuition mentioned previously is misleading, and for very long horizons, bonds are preferred to stocks, at least for some utility functions with a relatively large, but still acceptable, degree of risk aversion. Thus, we have two opposing forces which intensify with the horizon: the relative size of the FSD violation area shrinks, favoring stocks for the long run, whereas the negative lowest return, particularly of stocks, decreases with the horizon, favoring bonds for the long run. In this chapter, we will

---

[1] For example, if the one-period minimum rate of return is, say, -40%, the two-period minimum rate of return is $(1{-}0.4)^2 - 1 = -0.64$, that is, -64%.

elaborate on this issue and empirically examine these two opposing forces corresponding to the attractiveness of stocks and bonds with some commonly employed utility functions.

9.1. Almost First-Degree Stochastic Dominance

Just as there are stochastic dominance (SD) rules of various degrees, we can define ASD of various degrees. This chapter is devoted to AFSD, which makes the most general assumption that all researchers presumably agree upon, namely that the utility function is monotonically non-decreasing. Making assumptions regarding the higher derivatives of the utility function, one can similarly also derive higher degree ASD rules, but these will not be discussed in this book. For a detailed discussion of these rules, see Leshno and Levy[2] and Levy.[3]

In order to present the AFSD rule and the effect of the horizon on the choices it implies, which may avoid some paradoxes like the one given in Figure 9.1, let us first present the expected utility difference of two prospects under consideration, prospects F (stocks) and G (bonds). The expected utility of F and G are given by the following two equations:

$$E_F U(x) = \int_a^b f(x)U(x)dx$$

and

$$E_G U(x) = \int_a^b g(x)U(x)dx$$

where f and g are the density functions of the two prospects under consideration and U stands for the utility function. The values a and b are the lower and upper bounds on the values of x, respectively.

---

[2]Leshno, M. and H. Levy (2002). Preferred by 'all' and preferred by 'most' decision makers: Almost stochastic dominance. *Management Science* 48(8), 1074–1085.

[3]Levy, H. (2016). *Stochastic Dominance: Investment Decision Making Under Uncertainty*, 3rd ed., Springer, New York.

The difference between the expected utility of the two prospects is given by

$$\Delta \equiv E_F U(x) - E_G U(x) = \int_a^b [f(x) - g(x)]U(x)dx.$$

Integrating by parts, this term yields

$$\Delta \equiv E_F U(x) - E_G U(x) = [F(x) - G(x)] \, U(x)|_a^b$$

$$+ \int_a^b [G(x) - F(x)]U'(x)dx.$$

As with cumulative distributions, we have $F(b) = G(b) = 1$ and $F(a) = G(a) = 0$, the first term on the right-hand side is equal to zero, and we have the following relationship between the expected utility difference and the cumulative distributions:

$$\Delta \equiv E_F U(x) - E_G U(x) = \int_a^b [G(x) - F(x)]U'(x)dx. \qquad (9.1)$$

From this equation, we can see that if by assumption $U'(x) \geq 0$, then if $F(x) \leq G(x)$ for all values x (and there is at least one strict inequality), then F has a larger expected utility than G. Hence, for all utility functions that are monotonically non-decreasing (i.e., $U' \geq 0$), that is, for all $U \epsilon U_1$, where U_1 is the set of all the monotonic non-decreasing utility functions, prospect F has a greater expected utility than prospect G.

The advantage of the FSD rule is that it relates to all non-decreasing utility functions $U \epsilon U_1$. However, as we shall see in what follows, this is also the inherent basic drawback of the FSD rule, as the set U_1 also includes utility functions that do not fit any investor's preference, which is the source of the paradoxical results like the one given in the introduction. Thus, the fact that the FSD rule relates to all preferences is both a blessing and a curse. It is worth mentioning that the same drawback also exists with other decision rules, e.g., the SSD and M-V rules.

The task of the AFSD rule is to eliminate some preference from U_1, preferences known as "pathological preferences," and to establish investment decision rules corresponding to only non-pathological preferences. Thus, we suggest a new stochastic dominance rule, the AFSD rule (or ASSD rule for almost second-order stochastic dominance), by which the paradoxical choices are avoided. The AFSD rule may also shed light on the change in the relative attractiveness of stocks and bonds with the horizon — a task which the FSD rule cannot fulfill because as with FSD, there is no dominance between these two assets, regardless of the length of the assumed horizon.

9.1.1. *The change in the FSD violation area of stocks and bonds with the horizon*

Suppose that the cumulative distribution of prospect F (stocks) is located below the cumulative distribution of prospect G (bonds) in most, albeit not all, of the range of rates of return. When we examine whether F dominates G by FSD, all ranges of return where $G(x) < F(x)$ constitute the FSD-violation ranges of return (for an example, see area A given in Figure 9.1), and F does not dominate G by FSD because of these FSD violation areas. However, with cumulative distributions of return on stocks and bonds, we typically have cumulative distributions, as shown in Figure 9.2. The two cumulative distributions typically cross only once, where on the left-hand side, we have $G(x) < F(x)$, where F stands for the cumulative distribution of stocks and G stands for the cumulative distributions of bonds. The FSD violation area is given by area A, which we depicted in the figure with a minus sign, $-A$, emphasizing that we examine whether F dominates G by FSD (see Figure 9.2).

First, note that by choosing a linear utility function of the form $U(x) = x$, Eq. (9.1) becomes

$$\Delta \equiv E_F U(x) - E_G U(x) = \int_a^b [G(x) - F(x)]U'(x)dx$$

$$= E_F(x) - E_G(x) = \int_a^b [G(x) - F(x)]dx. \tag{9.2}$$

Therefore, the difference in the expected return is given by the area enclosed between the two cumulative distributions, namely $B - A$ (see Figure 9.2). As we can see from Figure 9.2, B increases with the

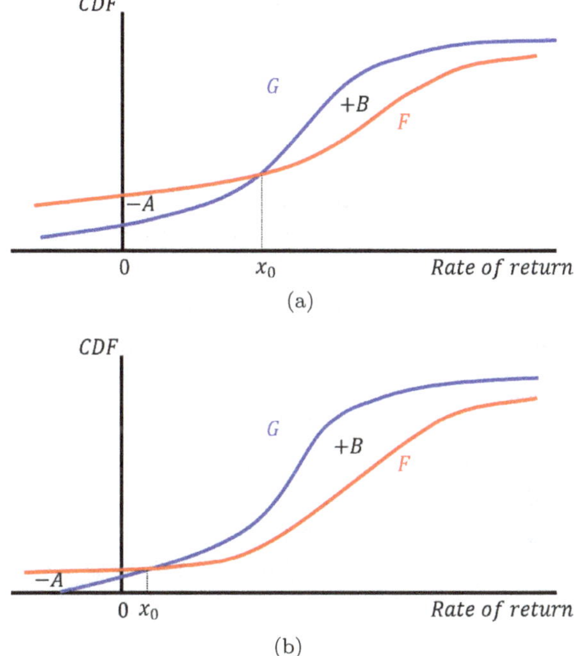

Figure 9.2: The cumulative distributions of stocks (F) and bonds (G) for $N = 1$ year and $N = 30$ years: (a) $N = 1$ year; (b) $N = 30$ years.

horizon and $-A$ increases (or decreases in absolute terms). Hence, as expected, the multi-period difference of the area enclosed between the CDFs of stocks and bonds, denoted by $B - A$, increases with the horizon. This favorite result of stocks is one of the main arguments employed by those advocating that "stocks for the long run" is the best investment strategy.

The areas B and $-A$ also determine the relative FSD-violation area. Specifically, for the establishment of the AFSD rule, we employ the relative FSD violation area given by

$$\epsilon_1(F) \equiv |-A|/(|-A| + B) \tag{9.3}$$

where we consider whether F dominates G by AFSD, and by

$$\epsilon_1(G) \equiv |-B|/(A + |-B|)$$

where we examine whether G dominates F by AFSD. Note that, with such examination of dominance of G over F, we replace the signs of A and B given in Figure 9.2. By these definitions, we have

$$\epsilon_1(F) + \epsilon_1(G) = 1 \tag{9.4}$$

where $\epsilon_1(F)$ is the FSD-violation area when we examine whether F dominates G by AFSD, and $\epsilon_1(G)$ is the FSD-violation area when we examine whether G dominates F by AFSD. As we are looking for the smallest possible FSD-violation area, in searching for dominance by the AFSD rule, we examine only the case $\epsilon_1 < 0.5$. In the rest of the chapter, we examine only whether F (stocks) dominates G (bonds) by AFSD, and denote the violation area simply by $\epsilon_1 \equiv \epsilon_1(F)$. The reason for this analysis is that in the comparison of stocks and bonds, typically $\epsilon_1 < 0.5$, that is, stocks may dominate bonds by AFSD, but the opposite can never occur (see Figure 9.2).

Finally, note that as we require by AFSD of F over G that $\epsilon_1 < 0.5$, this implies that a necessary condition for AFSD dominance of F over G is

$$E_F(x) > E_G(x).$$

To see this claim, recall that

$$\epsilon_1 = \frac{A}{A+B} < 1/2 \Rightarrow B - A > 0 \Rightarrow E_F(x) > E_G(x).$$

Finally, note that the FSD violation area is given in relative terms, e.g., 5% of the total area (in absolute terms) is enclosed between F and G. Figure 9.2(a) demonstrates the typical FSD violation area corresponding to stocks and bonds for a horizon of $N = 1$ year, and Figure 9.2(b) demonstrates this for a longer horizon of $N = 30$ years. Thus, as the horizon increases, with cumulative distributions of stocks and bonds, we find that the relative FSD violation area typically shrinks with the horizon, implying that the difference between the mean return of stocks and bonds increases with the horizon. Later in this chapter, we provide the violation area for various horizons corresponding to the actual empirical rates of return on stocks and bonds.

9.1.2. *An example of an FSD paradox and of a pathological preference*

Consider the *utility* function given by the following:

$$U_1(x) = \begin{cases} x & \text{if } \leq x_0 \\ x_0 & \text{if } x > x_0. \end{cases} \tag{9.5}$$

As this function is monotonically non-decreasing, mathematically it is included in the set U_1. Therefore, the FSD rule also relates to this utility function. Now, suppose that investors have to choose between prospects F and G given by the following:

F yields \$1 or \$1,000 with an equal probability of 0.5, and

G yields \$2 or \$3 with an equal probability of 0.5.

What should be the predicted choice between these options? We suspect that if we presented this question to a large sample of investors, 100% would choose prospect F. Despite this predicated choice of prospect F over G, neither F nor G dominates the other by the FSD rule (such dominance also does not exist with the SSD and M–V rules). As can be seen from Figure 9.3, the two cumulative distributions F and G intersect; hence, no FSD exists. But suppose that indeed, as expected, all investors in practice choose F even though there is no FSD of F over G. This is a paradoxical result that reveals the shortcomings of the existing investment decision rules —

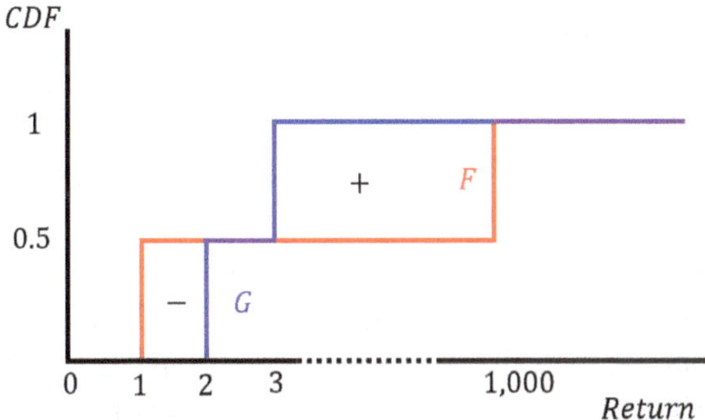

Figure 9.3: The cumulative distribution functions of F and G.

in the case analyzed in this chapter, it is a shortcoming of the FSD rule. Finally, for those readers who are skeptical about the choice of prospect F by all investors, let us increase the \$1,000 outcome of F to a million dollars or even to an infinite amount of money. We suspect that all would agree that with these changes in the outcomes, no rational investor would choose prospect G. Even so, F does not dominate G by FSD — a paradoxical result.

Why does the FSD fail to reveal the superiority of F over G in this example? The explanation is that the set of preference U_1 contains all monotonic non-decreasing utility functions including preferences which in practice do not fit any investor. For example, choose the utility function given in Eq. (9.5) and choose $x_0 = 2$, which is a legitimate preference belonging to the set U_1. With this utility function and the returns on prospects F and G given in Figure 9.3, we have the following expected utility difference:

$$\Delta \equiv E_F U(x) - E_G U(x) = \int_a^b [G(x) - F(x)]U'(x)dx$$

$$= \int_a^2 [G(x) - F(x)]U'(x)dx + \int_2^b [G(x) - F(x)]U'(x)dx.$$

As in the range $(a, 2)$ we have $[G(x) - F(x)] < 0$, and as $U'(x) = 1 > 0$, the first term on the right-hand side of the above equation is negative. The second term is equal to zero as in the range $x > 2$, $U'(x) = 0$ (see Figure 9.3 and the utility function given by Eq. (9.5) for the specific case where $x_0 = 2$). Thus, with this utility function, prospect G is preferred as $E_F U(x) < E_G U(x)$.

Suppose that in a very large sample of subjects facing these two prospects, all subjects choose F. This means that the utility function given in Eq. (9.5) with $x_0 = 2$ does not fit the preference of any investor. Thus, if there is a preference which technically belongs to U_1, but does not fit the preference of any investor, this preference is classified as "pathological," and we can safely eliminate it from U_1. The generality of the FSD rule allows us to establish strong results, but there are flies in the ointment such as the utility function presented in Eq. (9.5). The AFSD rule will refine the analysis by eliminating such preferences.

For establishing the AFSD rule, we construct a new set of non-decreasing monotonic preferences denoted by U_1^*, where $U_1 \supseteq U_1^*$, and the set U_1^* contains only non-pathological utility functions. This is the main idea of AFSD rules, implying that in the example given in Figure 9.3, we have AFSD of F over G for almost all utility functions because the pathological preferences, like the one given in Eq. (9.5), are eliminated from the set U_1. As, in the economy, we may have irrational investors or investors who choose according to some pathological preference (or who may even prefer a 1% to a 10% return with certainty), we call the suggested rule an almost stochastic dominance rule, as it relates to most investors, and not to irrational ones or to those with extreme changes in the marginal utility over the various ranges of return.

9.1.3. *The AFSD rule and non-pathological preferences*

With the AFSD criterion, almost all investors in practice choose the prospect which is superior by this rule; hence, a paradox which exists with FSD, like the one given previously, vanishes once the AFSD rule is employed.

To clarify the difference between the FSD and AFSD rules, suppose that, as in Figure 9.2(b), the cumulative distribution of F (stocks) is located below that of G (bonds) in most of the range of returns (a favorable property for stocks), but there is a very small range of returns, generally located with stocks and bonds on the left-hand side of the distribution of returns, where F is located above G (an unfavorable property for stocks); hence, there is no FSD. In some cases, as we shall see in what follows, the AFSD rule establishes dominance despite the fact that F and G cross.

Let us elaborate on the AFSD rule: Define by s_1 the ranges[4] of returns where $F(x) > G(x)$, that is, the ranges where the FSD of F over G are violated (see area A in Figure 9.2 for such a violation range), and by s_2, the ranges supporting the FSD of F over G, that

---

[4]With stocks and bonds, we typically have only one FSD violation area, but, generally, we may have several ranges of violation if the cumulative distributions cross several times.

is, a range where $F(x) < G(x)$ (see area B in Figure 9.2), and by $s_1 \cup s_2 = (a, b)$, where $\cup$ denotes the union sign. The expected utility difference between F and G is given by

$$\Delta \equiv E_F U(x) - E_G U(x) = \int_a^b [G(x) - F(x)]U'(x)dx$$

$$= \int_{s_1} [G(x) - F(x)]U'(x)dx + \int_{s_2} [G(x) - F(x)]U'(x)dx \quad (9.6)$$

where the first term is negative, and the second term is positive. Define by Δ^* the following equation:

$$\Delta^* \equiv Sup U'(x) \int_{s_1} [G(x) - F(x)]U'(x)dx$$

$$+ Inf U'(x) \int_{s_2} [G(x) - F(x)]U'(x)dx. \quad (9.7)$$

As the integral over the range s_1 is negative, by taking the largest U' over this range, we decrease the negative term, and as the integral over s_2 is positive, by taking the smallest U' in this range, we decrease this positive term. Therefore, $\Delta^* \leq \Delta$. In other words, if by employing Δ^* to rank prospects, we find that F has a larger expected utility than G, then this assertion is *a fortiori* intact with Δ. In brief:

$$\Delta^* > 0 \Rightarrow \Delta > 0 \text{ but not vice versa.} \quad (9.8)$$

From Eq. (9.8), we can conclude that the AFSD rule, which is defined in what follows, is a sufficient, but not a necessary, rule for dominance. This means that it is possible that, for some utility functions, F has a larger expected utility than G, yet $\Delta^* < 0$, and the AFSD rule is unable to reveal this preference.

With the AFSD rule, we confine ourselves to all preferences, U_1^* for which $\Delta^* > 0$. Eq. (9.7) is positive, that is, $\Delta^* > 0$, if the following holds:

$$Sup U'(x) \int_{s_1} [G(x) - F(x)]U'(x)dx >$$

$$- Inf U'(x) \int_{s_2} [G(x) - F(x)]U'(x)dx,$$

or

$$SupU'(x) < -InfU'(x) \int_{s_2} [G(x) - F(x)]U'(x)dx/$$

$$\int_{s_1} [G(x) - F(x)]U'(x)dx \qquad (9.9)$$

where the inequality sign is reversed as we divide both sides by a negative term (recall that the integral over s_1 is negative). As

$$\int_{s_1} [G(x) - F(x)]U'(x)dx = -\int_{s_1} [F(x) - G(x)]U'(x)dx,$$

inequality (9.9) can be rewritten as

$$SupU'(x) < InfU'(x) \int_{s_2} [G(x) - F(x)]U'(x)dx/$$

$$\int_{s_1} [F(x) - G(x)]U'(x)dx. \qquad (9.10)$$

We define, as before, the relative FSD violation area by ϵ_1, which is the ratio of the absolute value of the negative area enclosed between the CDFs of F and G, s_1 (which is the source of the no FSD situation), divided by the total absolute area enclosed between F and G:

$$\epsilon_1 = \int_{s_1} |G(x) - F(x)|dx/ \int_a^b |G(x) - F(x)|dx$$

(this is exactly the ratio $(A/A + B)$, as depicted in Figure 9.2), to obtain

$$(1/\epsilon_1 - 1) = \frac{\int_{s_1} [F(x) - G(x)]dx + \int_{s_2} [G(x) - F(x)]dx}{\int_{s_1} [F(x) - G(x)]dx} - 1$$

$$= \frac{\int_{s_2} [G(x) - F(x)]dx}{\int_{s_1} [F(x) - G(x)]dx}.$$

Hence, Eq. (9.10) can be rewritten as

$$SupU'(x) < InfU'(x) \left[\frac{1}{\epsilon_1} - 1\right]. \qquad (9.11)$$

Suppose that, in practice, indeed, all investors choose F rather than G, yet there is no FSD. In such a case, all preferences that fulfill inequality (9.11) are included in the set U_1^*, provided that $\epsilon_1 < 0.5$, and are classified as non-pathological preferences because they reveal a preference for F. The requirement that $\epsilon_1 < 0.5$, as we have seen before, implies that a necessary condition for dominance of F over G by AFSD is that the mean return of F must be larger than the mean return of G.

These utility functions are classified as non-pathological preferences because, with these utility functions, the expected utility of the prospect selected in practice by all investors is larger than that of the other prospect; hence, no paradox emerges. The AFSD rule is summarized in the following proposition:

Proposition 9.1. *Given an FSD-violation area $\epsilon_1 < 0.5$, prospect F dominates G by AFSD for all preferences for which inequality (9.11) holds, preferences which belong to the set U_1^*. This set includes only non-pathological preferences — preferences that reveal a choice that conforms with the choice of all investors, in practice.*

The interpretation of the AFSD rule and its relationship to the FSD violation area is as follows: suppose that the two distributions under consideration cross (hence, there is no FSD), and $\epsilon_1 < 0.5$ is the relative FSD violation area. Further, suppose that, in practice, all investors choose F rather than G. Thus, from the investors' choice, we can conclude that the benefits from F (mainly from the large returns located on the right-hand side of the distributions) are relatively large, such that the investors "allow" this violation area and still choose F. In sum, if all investors choose F and there is no FSD, there is AFSD for all utility functions that fulfill inequality (9.11). These utility functions are classified as non-pathological as they conform with the choice of all investors, in practice.

9.2. Determining the Allowed FSD Violation Area by Experiments

Thus, a pathological preference is one by which the expected utility of G is larger than that of prospect F, yet all investors choose prospect F. In practice, however, one cannot screen all preferences corresponding to all potential investors and their choices in order to identify all the pathological preferences. However, as a first step in the direction of identifying the pathological preferences, one can run an experiment with a large number of subjects to find a case where even though there is no FSD, all investors choose one prospect, say prospect F. By this experiment, we can find the maximum allowed FSD violation area, ϵ_1. Such an experiment was conducted by Levy et al.[5]

In this experiment (one of the several conducted), the subjects had to choose between prospects F and G with the following distributions of return:

Prospect G: The return is either \$100 or \$200, each with an equal probability of $\frac{1}{2}$.

Prospect F: The return is either \$50 or \$$Z$, each with an equal probability of $\frac{1}{2}$.

Figure 9.4 presents the cumulative distributions of the return corresponding to prospects F and G, respectively, for two possible values of Z. As F starts to the left of G, F can never dominate G by FSD. However, if Z is smaller than \$200, then G dominates F by FSD.

In this experiment, we were looking for a situation where F dominates G by AFSD even though there is no FSD dominance because regardless of the chosen Z (as long as it is larger than \$200), the two cumulative distributions intersect. Specifically, the subjects were asked:

> *"What is the minimum value required such that you would choose F rather than G?"*

Obviously, all subjects require $Z > \$200$ (as it is irrational to choose F for $Z < 200$, as in this case G dominates F by FSD), as depicted in Figure 9.4. Suppose that a subject requires \$500. Of course, he would be better off with a larger return, but recall that this

---

[5]Levy, H., M. Leshno and B. Leibovitch (2010). Economically relevant preferences for all observed epsilon. *Annals of Operations Research* 176(1), 153–178.

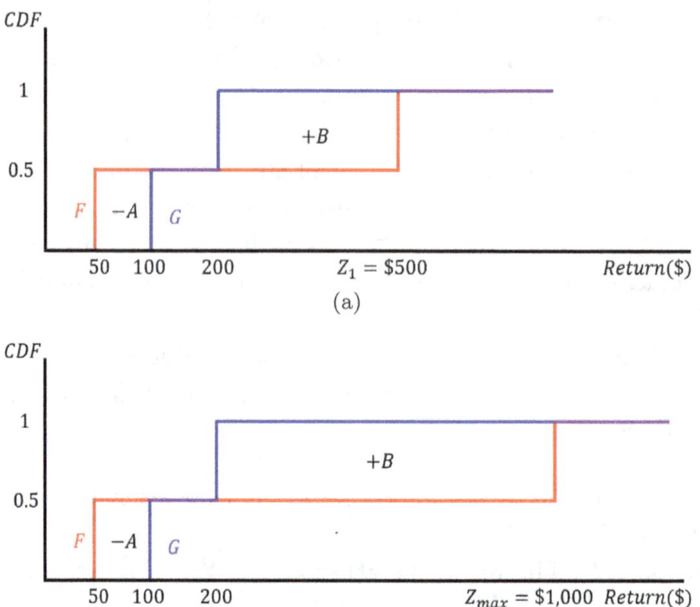

Figure 9.4: The cumulative distribution functions with two selected values, Z_1 and Z_{max}: (a) With $Z_1 = \$500$; (b) With $Z_{max} = \$1,000$.

is the *minimum* required return to convince an investor to choose F. Thus, with $Z = \$500$, the allowed FSD violation area is

$$\epsilon_1(Z_1) = \frac{|-A|}{[|-A| + B(Z_1)]} = \frac{\frac{1}{2}(50)}{\frac{1}{2}(50) + \frac{1}{2}(300)} = \frac{50}{350} \cong 0.143$$

or about 14.3% (see Figure 9.4(a)).

In the experiment conducted by Levy, Leshno, and Leibovitch, the maximum required value of Z selected in the experiment was \$1,000. For this subject, who required $Z = \$1,000$, the maximum allowed FSD violation relative area is as follows:

$$\epsilon(Z_1) = \frac{|-A|}{|-A| + B(Z_{max})} = \frac{\frac{1}{2}(50)}{\frac{1}{2}(50) + \frac{1}{2}(800)} = \frac{50}{850} \cong 0.059,$$

that is, about 5.9%.

9.2.1. *Discussion*

(1) First, note that all other subjects require a maximum value of Z less than \$1,000; therefore, by definition of the FSD violation area, all subjects agree to choose F rather than G even with less compensation, that is, they allow a larger FSD violation area, and still choose prospect F. For example, with $Z = \$50$, the allowed FSD violation area is 14.3%, while with the maximum value $Z = \$1,000$, it is only 5.9% (see Figure 9.4). Of course, an investor who agrees to a 14.3% FSD violation area would be better off with only a 5.9% FSD violation area.

(2) Thus, because the value $Z = \$1,000$ guarantees that *all* subjects will choose F over G, we can use this information to define all the non-pathological preferences. Recall that, by all the non-pathological preferences, the expected utility of F is larger than that of G, which conforms with the choices of all subjects in practice (in our case, in the experiment where the value $Z = \$1,000$). The set of the non-pathological preferences (preferences that conform with the choice of F), as derived from the experiment, is given by all utility functions which fulfill inequality (9.11) , that is, the inequality

$$SupU'(x) < infU'(x)\left[\frac{1}{\epsilon_1} - 1\right]$$

where $\epsilon_1 = 5.9\%$ is determined by $Z = \$1,000$ in the above calculation. To illustrate the determination of the set of all non-pathological preferences, let us assume myopic preferences given by

$$U(x) = x^{1-\alpha}/(1-\alpha) \quad \text{with the first derivative,}$$
$$U'(x) = x^{-\alpha} = 1/x^\alpha.$$

That is, for the sake of illustration only, we assume that all subjects have a myopic preference with different degrees of risk-aversion parameter, α. With the above example, we have

$$SupU'(x) = (1/50)^\alpha$$

as the largest first derivative is obtained with the lowest value x: and the smallest first derivative is obtained with the largest value x, and with these distributions, we have $(1/\epsilon_1 - 1) = (1/0.059 - 1) \cong 15.95$.

$$InfU'(x) = (1/1,000)^\alpha$$

Thus, all myopic preferences which fulfill the following condition (which conforms with the choice of F by all subjects) are non-pathological:

$$(1/50)^\alpha < 15.95 \times (1/1,000)^\alpha.$$

In other words, the non-pathological myopic preferences according to the choices in this experiment are given by

$$log((1/50)^\alpha) < \log(15.95) + log(1/1,000)^\alpha$$

or

$$\alpha \times (log(1/50)) < 2.77 + \alpha \times (\log(1/1,000))$$
$$\alpha \times (-3.91) < 2.77 + \alpha \times (-6.91).$$

Hence,

$$\alpha \times (3) < 2.77 \text{ and finally, } \alpha < .923.$$

Thus, if all subjects participating in the experiment have a myopic utility function, then all functions with risk-aversion parameter $\alpha < 0.923$ are classified as non-pathological, as they reveal a preference for F. Note that large α implies a relatively large marginal utility (or more risk aversion); hence, for these subjects, the value $Z = \$1,000$ constitutes sufficient compensation for the FSD violation.

Is it possible that some investors with $\alpha > 0.923$ also would choose F despite not being included in the set of non-pathological preferences? The answer is positive! Recall that the AFSD rule is a sufficient, but not necessary, rule for dominance. This is so because

$$\Delta^* > 0 \Rightarrow \Delta > 0 \text{ but } \Delta > 0 \nRightarrow \Delta^* > 0 \text{ (see Eq. (9.8)).}$$

With the value of $Z = \$1,000$ in the given example, we can safely determine that in all preferences which fulfill inequality (9.11), the expected utility of F is larger than that of G; hence, all these preferences belong to the non-pathological set, $\boldsymbol{U}_1^*$. However, because of the condition given in Eq. (9.8), it is possible that for some utility functions not included in $\boldsymbol{U}_1^*$, prospect F also provides a larger expected utility than prospect G, but the AFSD rule fails to identify these preferences; thus, they are mistakenly not included in the non-pathological set of preferences U_1^*. Therefore, while U_1^* contains only non-pathological preferences, it is possible that it does not contain all of them.

For the purposes of illustration, to figure out whether there are more non-pathological preferences, a direct expected utility calculation is needed. Specifically, in the experiment discussed previously, a myopic investor is indifferent between F (with $Z = \$1,000$) and G, if the following holds:

$$50^{(1-\alpha)}/(1-\alpha) + 1,000^{(1-\alpha)}/1 - \alpha$$
$$= 100^{(1-\alpha)}/(1-\alpha) + 200^{(1-\alpha)}/(1-\alpha).$$

The risk-aversion parameter which solves this equation is $\alpha \cong 1.46$. This implies that for all investors with $\alpha < 1.46$, obtaining the prospect with the outcomes (50,1,000) is better than obtaining the prospect with the outcomes (100,200). For more risk-averse investors, the opposite holds.

Thus, all preferences for which Eq. (9.11) holds are defined by the AFSD rule as non-pathological; that is, all myopic preferences with $\alpha < 0.923$ are defined by the AFSD rule as non-pathological. However, all preferences not fulfilling inequality (9.11) with $\alpha < 1.46$ are also non-pathological, and only preferences with $1.46 > \alpha$ are pathological (as they reveal a preference for the outcomes (100,200), in contrast to the choices in practice). Thus, as the AFSD rule is a sufficient and not necessary rule, it is able to identify only all preferences with $\alpha < 0.923$ as non-pathological.

In sum, we have the following FSD relationships:

$$\boldsymbol{U_1} = (\boldsymbol{U_1^*}) \cup (\boldsymbol{U_1^{**}}) \cup (\boldsymbol{U_1^{***}})$$

where U_1 is the set of all non-decreasing preferences (to which the FSD rule refers), U_1^* is the set of all non-pathological preferences as determined by the AFSD rule, U_1^{**} is all the non-pathological preferences that the AFSD rule is unable to discover (because it is only a sufficient rule, these functions can be discovered by a direct expected utility calculation), and U_1^{***} is the set of pathological preferences, revealing a preference for the outcome (100,200) over the outcomes (50,1,000), which does not fit the preference of any investor.

Finally, recall that this experiment provides only a first indication of the allowed FSD violation area, and the result may be different in other experiments, as well as with empirical distributions of the return on stocks and bonds to which we devote great attention in this book.

9.3. Comparing Stocks and Bonds by AFSD for Various Horizons, N

We turn now to the ongoing debate of the relative attractiveness of stocks and bonds for the long run. As the horizon increases, as shown previously, there are two opposing forces: the FSD violation area decreases and the minimum returns also decrease. These two factors simultaneously determine the change in the size and content of the set of all non-pathologic preferences. However, note that for a *given* investment horizon, we can safely determine that the smaller the FSD relative violation area, ϵ_1, the larger the set of non-pathological preferences, that is, the larger the proportion of investors for which the choice by expected utility and by the AFSD rule coincide. For example, in the experiment described in Figure 9.4, because there is no horizon effect, as we increase value Z, the FSD violation area decreases and, as a result, the set of all non-pathological preferences increases.

This result is not intact when changing horizons. With stocks and bonds, the FSD violation area decreases with the horizon, but this does not necessarily imply that the set of non-pathological preferences increases with the horizon. With a varying horizon, we cannot safely determine what will be the change in the size of the non-pathological preferences. As we shall see in what follows, the set of the non-pathological preferences for various horizons depends on the utility functions and the distributions of returns under consideration. Specifically, for some utility functions, the non-pathological preferences may decrease rather than increase with the horizon.

In the following, we first provide a hypothetical example of the return on stocks and bonds and calculate the changes in the FSD relative violation area with the horizon, and then calculate this violation term with actual empirical returns on stocks and bonds. In the second step, we evaluate the two opposing forces affecting the size of the non-pathological preference set.

Table 9.1 provides a hypothetical example of the return on two prospects. Note that the probability of a relatively low return and a relatively large one is greater with stocks than with bonds, as characterized by these two assets in practice.

Figure 9.5 provides the cumulative distributions of these two hypothetical investments, showing that there is no FSD as the two cumulative distributions cross.

Assuming identical independent distribution (*i.i.d.*), we derive by simulation the multi-period distributions F^n and G^n, and with these multi-period distributions, we can then calculate the violation area ϵ_1^N. Table 9.2 reports the change in the relative violation area with the horizon.

As Table 9.2 reveals, the relative FSD violation area decreases sharply from about 9.5% for an $N = 1$-year horizon to 2% for an $N = 5$-year horizon, and it is almost zero for an $N = 50$-year horizon (see footnote 2). These results conform with the theoretical argument that asserts that the prospect with the larger geometric mean

Table 9.1: The distributions of returns of F and G.

Rate of Return X	5%	7%	9%	12%
$\Pr(X = x)$ (Stocks): F	0.1	0	0	0.9
$\Pr(X = x)$ (Bonds): G	0	0.4	0.6	0

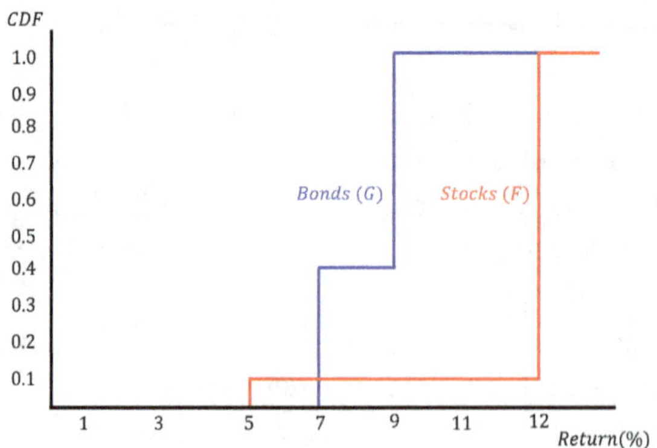

Figure 9.5: The cumulative distributions of F and G.

Table 9.2: The FSD violation area as a function of the horizon, N.

N	ϵ^N
1	0.095
2	0.063
5	0.020
10	0.005
50	5.4×10^{-7}

(in our example, stocks) almost surely will end up with larger terminal wealth than the one with the lower geometric mean (in our example, bonds).[6] One thing is clear: as the FSD violation area decreases with the horizon, the probability of stocks ending up with larger terminal wealth than bonds increases with the horizon. However, this fact is insufficient for claiming that the attractiveness of stocks relative to bonds increases with the horizon.

We turn now to analyze the FSD violation term with actual empirical distributions of stocks (the S&P 500 stock index) and

---

[6]See Latané, H. A. (1959). Criteria for choice among risky ventures. *Journal of Political Economy* 67(2), 144–155.

bonds (10-year Treasury bonds). The employed data are the annual rates of return corresponding to these two assets for the period 1928–2020.[7] The multi-period returns are derived from these annual data series by assuming *i.i.d.*, as explained in the previous chapters. For example, for an $N = 10$-year horizon, 10 observations are drawn (with repetitions) from the historical distributions, and the compounded 10-year return is calculated. We repeat this procedure 100,000 times, which is employed in calculating the 10-year horizon distribution of returns, where to each of these 100,000, we assign an equal probability. Figure 9.6 provides the cumulative distributions for various horizons. As we can see from this figure, stocks are superior to bonds in most of the range of return, but not in the whole range; hence, there is an FSD violation area for all horizons. While this area is substantial for $N = 1$ year, it decreases with the horizon and almost completely vanishes for an $N = 20$-year horizon, let alone for longer horizons.

Table 9.3 provides the violation FSD term ϵ_1^N of stocks and bonds for various horizons. It decreases from about 24% for $N = 1$ year to about 6% for $N = 5$ years, and approaches zero for $N = 30$ years.

As ϵ_1^N decreases with the horizon, by looking at inequality (9.11), one is tempted to believe that when comparing stocks and bonds, the set of non-pathological preferences increases with the horizon. This would indicate that the relative attractiveness of stocks over bonds increases with the horizon (as more investors select F by (9.11)), and supports the investment strategy "stocks for the long run." However, this is generally an incorrect conclusion because the non-pathological set of preferences, counterintuitively, may decrease rather than increase with the horizon. Specifically, for a given utility function, it is possible that for $N_2 > N_1$, the expected utility of stocks is larger than that of bonds for N_1, while the opposite holds for the longer horizon N_2. Thus, we cannot assert that the FSD rule implies that "stocks for the long run" is the optimal investment strategy for all utility functions.

---

[7]*Source*: http://people.stern.nyu.edu/adamodar/pc/datasets/histretSP.xls.

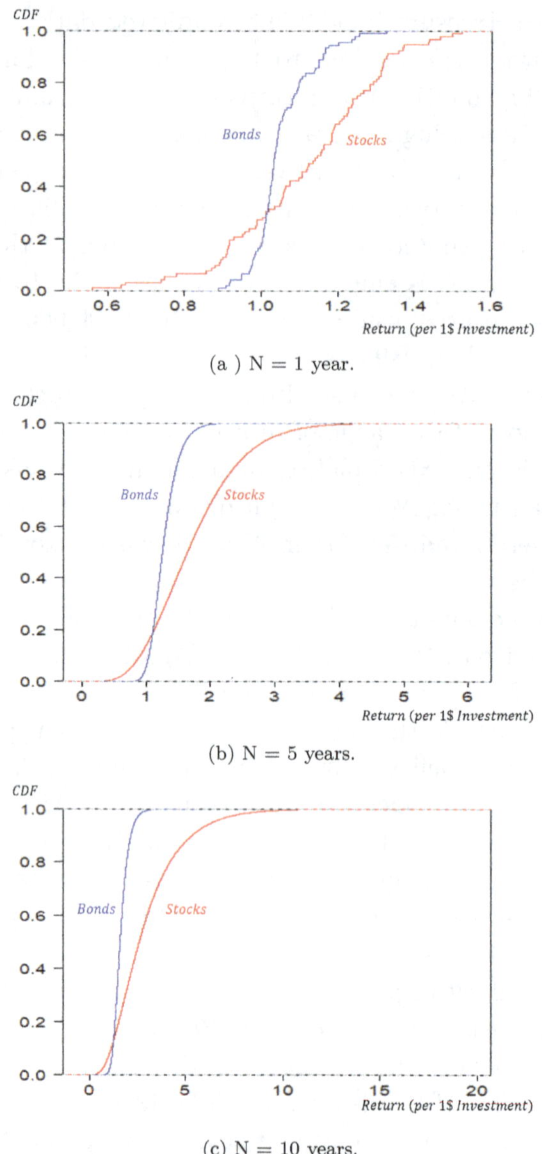

(a) N = 1 year.

(b) N = 5 years.

(c) N = 10 years.

Figure 9.6: The cumulative distributions of the returns on stocks and bonds for various horizons: (a) The returns of the S&P 500 stock index (red) and bonds (blue) for horizon $N = 1$; (b) The returns of the S&P 500 stock index (red) and bonds (blue) for horizon $N = 5$; (c) The returns of the S&P 500 stock index (red) and bonds (blue) for horizon $N = 10$; (d) The returns of the S&P 500 stock index (red) and bonds (blue) for horizon $N = 15$; (e) The returns of the S&P 500 stock index (red) and bonds (blue) for horizon $N = 20$.

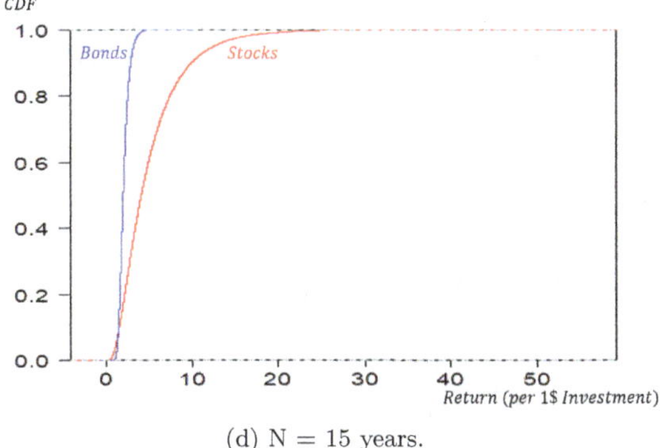

(d) N = 15 years.

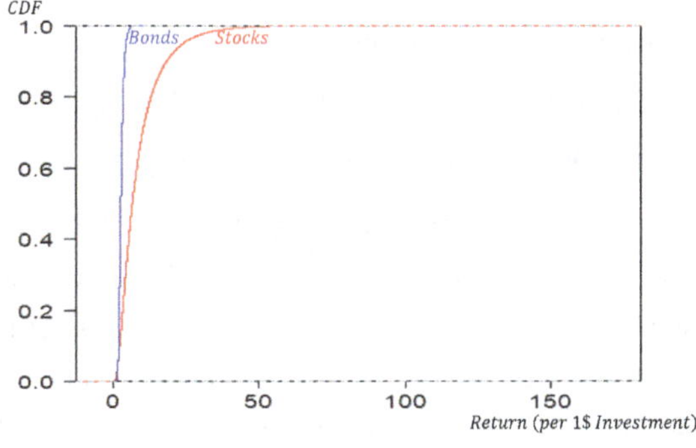

(e) N = 20 years.

Figure 9.6: (*Continued*)

Table 9.3: The FSD violation, ϵ_1^N, as a function of the horizon, N, for stocks and bonds.

Horizon, N, Years	ϵ_1^N
1	0.2410
5	0.0614
10	0.0187
15	0.0067
20	0.0027
25	0.0012
30	0.0005

In two studies, Levy[8] shows that such a situation, namely a preference for bonds rather than stocks in the long run, is indeed possible. To see the rationale for this claim, consider two prospects F and G where, as before, F (stocks) does not dominate G (bonds) by FSD due to a relatively small violation area. Inequality (9.11), which defines the set U_1^* of utility functions that are non-pathological (hence, selecting F), can be rewritten as

$$\frac{SupU'(x)}{InfU'(x)} < \left[\frac{1}{\epsilon_1}-1\right]. \tag{9.12}$$

While it is agreed that as the horizon N increases, ϵ_1 decreases, hence $\left[\frac{1}{\epsilon_1}-1\right]$ increases, Levy shows that $\frac{SupU'(x)}{InfU'(x)}$ also typically increases with the horizon (depending on the utility function and the distributions under consideration). If $\frac{SupU'(x)}{InfU'(x)}$ increases faster than $\left[\frac{1}{\epsilon_1}-1\right]$ with the horizon, we may find that for a horizon N_1, inequality (9.12) is intact and for a longer horizon N_2 such that $N_2 > N_1$, inequality (9.12) no longer holds. In this case, for the horizon N_1 the utility function under consideration is classified as non-pathological because it shows that F (stocks) has a larger expected utility than G (bonds), but for the longer horizon, N_2, inequality (9.12), for the same utility function, does not hold. Therefore, the same utility function may reveal a preference for F (stocks) over G (bonds) for a relatively short horizon, but reveal a preference for G (bonds) over F (stocks) for the longer horizon. Therefore, if indeed all investors prefer stocks to bonds for the two horizons under consideration, this preference may be pathological for long horizons, but not so for short horizons. Hence, the claim is that due to the fact that the FSD violation area decreases with the horizon, we cannot conclude that the investment strategy "stocks for the long run" is optimal, at least not for all utility functions. Let us illustrate this point numerically.

---

[8]Levy, M. (2007). Almost stochastic dominance for the long run. *European Journal of Operation Research* 194(1), 250–257; Levy, M.(2019). Comment on 'Aging population, retirement, and risk taking.' *Management Science* 66(6), 2787–2791.

Suppose that for $N = 1$ year, the lowest return of F is 0.6, and the largest return is 2. Assuming *i.i.d.* for an $N = 2$-year horizon, the lowest return on F is 0.36, and the largest return is 4. Let us consider the utility function $U(x) = x^{.5}/0.5$ with a derivative $1/x^{.5}$. Obviously, the largest derivative and the smallest derivative are obtained at these lowest and highest returns, respectively. Thus, we have

for $N = 1$:

$$SupU' = (1/.6)^{.5} \cong 1.29,$$

$$Inf\, U' = (1/2)^{.5} \cong 0.707$$

and therefore,

$$\frac{SupU'(x)}{InfU'(x)} = \frac{1.29}{0.707} = 1.82.$$

for $N = 2$:

$$SupU' = (1/.36)^{.5} \cong 1.67,$$

$$Inf\, U'(1/4)^{.5} \cong 0.50$$

and therefore,

$$\frac{SupU'(x)}{InfU'(x)} = \frac{1.67}{0.50} = 3.34.$$

Thus, the left side of inequality (9.12) increases with the horizon from 1.82 to 3.34. The decrease in ϵ_1 depends on the structure of the distributions of F and G, but with stocks and bonds, it certainly decreases with N. However, one can always construct distributions F and G, such that the increase in $\left[\frac{1}{\epsilon_1}-1\right]$ (see inequality (9.12)) will be at a slower pace than the increase in $\frac{SupU'(x)}{InfU'(x)}$, such that inequality (9.12) may hold for short horizons, but not for long ones. Therefore, we may find that for $N = 1$, this specific utility function is non-pathological, whereas for $N = 2$, it is pathological. In such a case, the non-pathological set of preferences may decrease rather than increase with the horizon.

Suppose that F stands for the distribution of the return on stocks and G stands for the distribution of the return on bonds. With this specific utility function, we may find for $N = 1$ that the expected utility of stocks is larger than that of bonds, but for $N = 2$, as this preference is no longer non-pathological, we may find that the expected utility of bonds is larger than that of stocks. In such a scenario, one cannot draw the conclusion of "stocks for the long run." Obviously, such a conclusion depends on the utility function and the distribution functions under consideration, which, in turn, determine the pace of the increases on the two sides of inequality (9.12).

Note that we have the empirical distributions of stocks and bonds, but we lack information on all investors' preferences. Although the AFSD rule assumes that there is no full information on the utility functions, in the following we examine the commonly employed preferences in the literature for various degrees of risk aversion. We estimate the break-even risk-aversion parameter for various horizons such that, for a larger risk-aversion parameter, bonds are preferred to stocks. Thus, for these specific preferences, we test if the assertion "stocks for the long run" is indeed supported by the AFSD rule. Note that even if for one utility function, stocks are better than bonds for the short run and the opposite holds for the long run, we cannot support the investment strategy "stocks for the long run."

9.4. Stocks, Bonds, and the Horizon: The Set of Non-Pathological Preferences

By the AFSD rule, we divide all preferences into two sets: the non-pathological set and the complement set that includes both pathological and non-pathological preferences (because the AFSD rule is a sufficient but not necessary rule for dominance, it can't detect all non-pathological preferences). Suppose that we compare stocks (F) and bonds (G) for various horizons by the AFSD rule and assume, for simplicity only, that all investors have a myopic preference with various degrees of risk aversion.

As stocks have a higher mean than bonds, bonds cannot dominate stocks either by FSD or by AFSD (a dominance of bonds also does not exist by other commonly employed rules), as the condition on the means is a necessary condition for dominance. Do stocks dominate bonds by the AFSD rule? Is the dominance relationship affected by the assumed horizon. Is it possible that stocks dominate bonds for relatively short horizons, but for some legitimate utility function, the expected utility of bonds is larger for a relatively long horizon? If this is the case, the AFSD rule does not support the "stocks for the long run" investment strategy because for relatively long horizons, bonds have a larger expected utility than stocks for some legitimate preferences. We devote this section to these issues.

To illustrate the various scenarios, we assume myopic preferences. For the myopic preference, it is estimated empirically that $\alpha \cong 2$. However, as this is the average parameter across investors, it is also obvious that there are investors with a larger risk-aversion parameter. For illustrative purposes only, suppose that for all investors we have an upper bound on the risk-aversion parameter, say $\alpha < 10$, with an average across all investors of $\alpha = 2$. Thus, we assume that there is no investor with $\alpha > 10$. Therefore, if for $\alpha = 10$, we have AFSD of stocks over bonds, we have a dominance for all investors, although there is no FSD because the cumulative distributions cross.

Suppose that for relatively short horizons, say $N < N_1$, the FSD violation area is relatively large, and we find that the set of non-pathological preferences includes only the myopic functions with $\alpha < 1$. Thus, there is no AFSD for all relevant investors because for many of them, $\alpha > 1$; therefore, in such a scenario, we cannot support the "stocks for the long run" assertion because there are investors with "reasonable" α who prefer G (bonds) to F (stocks). Furthermore, suppose that for horizons $N_2 > N > N_1$ the non-pathological set of preferences includes all relevant myopic functions with $\alpha < 10$. In this case, although there is no FSD, there is AFSD for all relevant myopic preferences, and we conclude in this situation that "stocks for the long run" is the best investment strategy. But is this also a valid recommendation for horizons longer than N_2? The answer depends on whether the AFSD non-pathological set of preferences increases or decreases with the horizon. To explain this issue in a more transparent way, suppose that in the market there are investors with a horizon longer than N_2: is it possible that for a horizon N, where $N_2 < N$, the set of non-pathological preferences decreases rather than increases? Hence, for some relevant investor with $\alpha < 10$, we find that bonds are preferred to stocks for such very long horizons. If this is indeed the case, we cannot assert that stocks dominate bonds in the long run.

If the AFSD rule was determined solely by the relative FSD violation area, such a situation where bonds would become preferred to stocks by some legitimate utility function would be impossible, as the FSD violation area decreases with the horizon (see Table 9.3 for an empirical illustration); hence, the set of non-pathological preferences would increase with the horizon. In such a scenario, if for a given utility function stocks have a larger expected utility than bonds for a given horizon, stocks would definitely have a larger expected utility than bonds for longer horizons. However, we have seen that the AFSD rule and the size of the non-pathological preferences also depend on the term $\frac{SupU'(x)}{InfU'(x)}$, which increases with the horizon (see Eq. (9.12)). Hence, in principle, it is possible that as we further increase the horizon N, the set of non-pathological preferences decreases rather than increases, and for some utility function for which the expected utility of stocks is larger than that of bonds for some relatively short horizon, the opposite may hold for longer horizons. For example, the utility function, with, say, $\alpha = 2$, which is included in the non-pathological set of preferences for short horizons, may be eliminated from the non-pathological set of preferences with relatively large horizons, N.

Figure 9.7(b) illustrates a hypothetical case where the set of non-pathological preferences decreases with the horizon due to the term $\frac{SupU'(x)}{InfU'(x)}$ increasing at a faster pace than the term $\left[\frac{1}{\epsilon_1}-1\right]$. Figure 9.7(a) relates to the case where the size of the non-pathological preferences expands with the horizon; hence, if stocks dominate bonds by the AFSD rule, for all relevant risk-aversion parameters for a short horizon of, say, $N = 5$ years, such dominance is also intact for longer horizons of, say, $N = 10$ years. In our specific example, if stocks dominate bonds by the AFSD rule for all myopic investors with $\alpha < 10$ for $N = 5$ years, then *a fortiori*, such dominance is intact for $N = 10$ years, and we can safely assert with this utility function,

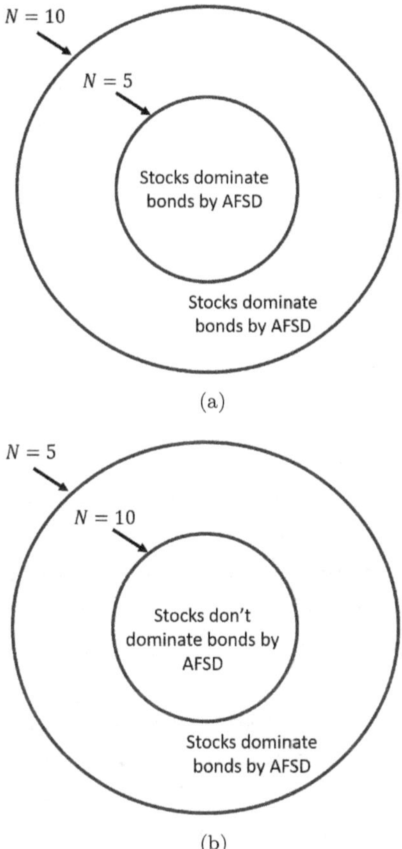

Figure 9.7: The non-pathological sets for $N = 5$ and $N = 10$: (a) The non-pathological set increases with N; (b) The non-pathological set decreases with N.

that the AFSD rule supports the "stocks for the long run" investment strategy despite the absence of dominance by the FSD rule. However, the case also illustrated in Figure 9.7(b) is possible, namely that the set of non-pathological preferences may decrease with the horizon. In this case, we may have that stocks dominate bonds by the AFSD rule, and a given utility is included in the non-pathological preferences for, say, $N = 5$ years, but not for $N = 10$ years.

In sum, with cumulative distributions of stocks and bonds that cross for all horizons, we do not have FSD. However, we may have, as in our example, that for myopic preferences with $\alpha < 10$, all investors with a horizon of $N = 5$ years or less prefer stocks to bonds, but some investors, albeit not all, with $\alpha < 10$ and a 10-year horizon may prefer bonds to stocks. Hence, if such a situation occurs, the AFSD rule does not support the "stocks for the long run" investment strategy.

To analyze whether the example in Figure 9.7 is relevant in practice or merely depicts a hypothetical case, we need to screen all possible non-decreasing monotonic preferences to examine whether for some preferences the attractiveness of bonds increases with the horizon. This, of course, is an impossible mission. However, we can directly calculate the expected utility of stocks and bonds corresponding to various horizons and for various risk-aversion parameters. We focus on two commonly employed preferences: the negative exponential function and the myopic preference. We investigate the change in the expected utility difference of stocks and bonds with the horizon. If this difference is positive for short horizons and becomes negative for long horizons, this phenomenon refutes the assertion of "stocks for the long run," as the same investor prefers stocks to bonds for relatively short horizons, and bonds to stocks for relatively long horizons.

Note that by this methodology, we do not analyze the changes in the non-pathological set of preferences with the horizon, but rather conduct a direct expected utility calculation. To see this, recall that by the AFSD rule, we divide all preferences into three sets:

$$U_1 = (U_1^*) \cup (U_1^{**}) \cup (U_1^{***})$$

(see the discussion of these sets earlier in this chapter). The AFSD rule relates only to the set which is definitely non-pathological (U_1^*), and the purpose of the direct expected utility calculation is to also identify the non-pathological preferences included in the set U_1^{**}, namely the non-pathological preferences which the AFSD rule cannot detect.

9.4.1. *The negative exponential utility function*

The utility function is given by $U(x) = -e^{-\alpha x}$, where α is the risk-aversion parameter. This function has a positive first derivative and a negative second derivative, and it is bounded from above at zero.

As this preference is widely employed, presumably because of its mathematical convenience in research, we analyze the implication of this preference on choices for various risk-aversion parameters and various horizons. However, because of one of its drawbacks, best known as "the value of a blank check," we take the mathematical results corresponding to this function with a grain of salt. Specifically, the fact that the utility function is bounded from above makes the investor indifferent about receiving a relatively low certain return and a 50–50 chance of zero gain or infinite wealth (a blank check). This absurd situation indicates that the exponential preference is inappropriate for characterizing investors' preferences, particularly for a relatively large risk-aversion parameter.[9] Keeping this reservation in mind, we technically analyze the effect on the AFSD and "stocks for the long run" issue with exponential preferences.

Employing the annual stocks' rate of return on the S&P 500 stock index and the annual rates of return on bonds for the period 1928–2020 (see footnote 8), the distributions of returns are derived for various horizons. As mentioned before, for example, for an $N = 10$-year horizon, we draw 10 observations, and calculate the compounded returns on stocks and on bonds. Repeating this procedure 100,000 times, we derive the distribution of rates of return for $N = 10$ years. By a similar procedure, we derive the distribution for N-year horizons where $1 \leq N \leq 30$. Having the distributions of the returns on stocks and bonds for various horizons, we can calculate the expected utility with the exponential utility function.

Figure 9.8 presents the expected utility difference of stocks and bonds, Δ for various horizons as a function of the risk-aversion parameter, α.

As expected, for all horizons, we obtain that Δ is positive for relatively small values of the risk-aversion parameter, α and it is negative for relatively large α. For very large and unrealistic values of α, we have that $\Delta \cong 0$. These results can be explained as follows: For relatively low risk aversion, stocks are better than bonds, and the opposite holds for relatively large risk aversion. Recall that the

---

[9]For more details, see Markowitz, H. M., D. W. Reid and B. V. Tew (1994). The value of a blank check. *The Journal of Portfolio Management* 20(4), 82–91.

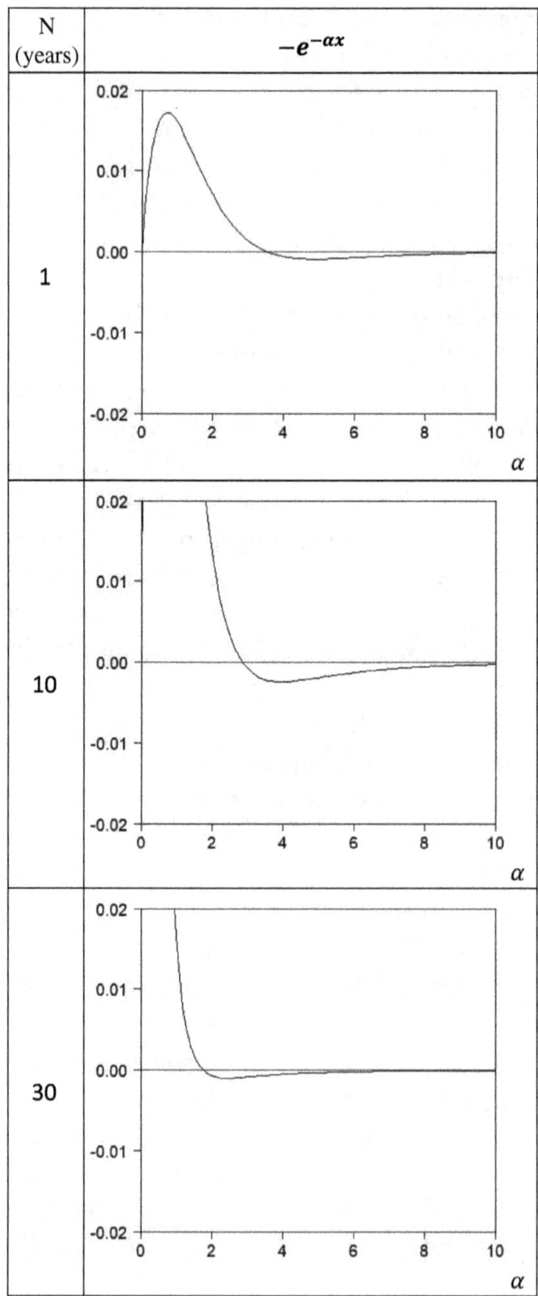

Figure 9.8: The expected utility difference $\Delta = E[U(Stocks)] - E[U(Bonds)]$.

advantage of stocks over bonds is due to their relatively large rates of return (the right tail of the distribution). With a relatively low risk-aversion parameter, this advantage is translated into a larger expected utility of stocks than bonds. However, the utility value of these large returns sharply diminishes when α increases, as the utility is $U(x) = -e^{-\alpha x}$; hence, for large values of α, the expected utility of bonds is larger than that of stocks. Finally, as the utility function is bounded from above, for a very large α, both expected utilities of stocks and bonds approach zero and, therefore, $\Delta \cong 0$, (see Figure 9.8).

Suppose that all investors have exponential utility functions with different risk-aversion parameters. Thus, there is no FSD of stocks and bonds because the cumulative distributions cross for all horizons. In this case, will the set of investors with exponential preferences who prefer stocks over bonds increase or decrease with the horizon? Recall that if the set of investors with this preference class decreases with the horizon, it is possible that for some investors, stocks are better than bonds for short horizons, but bonds are better than stocks for long horizons. Thus, we do not support the assertion "stocks for the long run."

To see this possibility, recall that with prospect F (stocks) and prospect G (bonds), there is no FSD as the two cumulative distributions intersect. However, it is possible that for relatively short horizons, say $N = 5$ years, all investors (with all relevant values of α) prefer F over G, but for longer horizons, it is possible that some investors may prefer G to F. In such a case, the assertion "stocks for the long run" is invalid.

Table 9.4 provides the risk-aversion parameter α for which the expected utility on these two assets is equal for various horizons. For example, for $N = 10$ years, we have $\alpha = 2.87$. This implies that for $\alpha > 2.87$, bonds have a larger expected utility than stocks, and for $\alpha < 2.87$, just the opposite holds. As we can see from Table 9.4, this critical value decreases with the horizon, implying that the set of the exponential preferences for which stocks have a larger exacted utility than bonds decreases with the horizon. Recall that bonds, with their lower mean, can never dominate stocks by AFSD, but for some specific preferences, bonds may have a larger expected utility than

Table 9.4: Values of α for which the expected utility for bonds is equal to the expected investment in stocks.

Horizon, N	Mean Equating Parameter
1	3.5762
5	3.2548
10	2.8734
15	2.5573
20	2.2391
25	1.9554
30	1.7670

stocks. Also, there is no FSD because the cumulative distributions of stocks and bonds cross. As we can see from this table, for $N = 10$ years, stocks have a larger expected utility than bonds for all values of $\alpha < 2.87$, and for $N = 30$ years, stocks have larger expected utility than bonds only for all investors with $\alpha < 1.77$. Hence, with the horizon, the set of investors for which stocks are better than bonds decreases. If an investor with, say, $\alpha = 2$ invests for 5 years, stocks are better than bonds. Furthermore, suppose that this investor decides to switch from a 5-year horizon to a 30-year horizon investment. Then bonds become better than stocks (see Table 9.4). Even if there is one investor like the one described in this example, the assertion "stocks for the long run" is still not valid.

Finally, recall that this technical result may be economically irrelevant as the exponential preferences have drawbacks. Nonetheless, we analyze the result corresponding to this utility function in this chapter as it is widely employed in research.

9.4.2. *The myopic preferences*

We employ the myopic preference:

$$U(x) = U(A + x)^{1-\alpha}/(1 - \alpha) \quad \text{for } A = 0, \ A = 1, \text{ and } A = 5.$$

First, note that with myopic preferences, the risk-aversion parameter is estimated to typically be $\alpha \cong 2$, and some researchers advocate that it is even much smaller. Secondly, with a myopic preference with $A = 0$ and with annual revisions, the horizon does not affect the expected utility ranking. In other words, if stocks have a higher expected utility than bonds for short horizons, this result is also intact for long horizons as long as *i.i.d.* prevails. In Table 9.5, we calculate the expected utility of stocks and bonds, and the difference between them without revisions for $A = 0$, 1, and 5.

Table 9.5: The value of the risk-aversion parameter, α, for which there is indifference between stocks and bonds, as a function of the horizon N with myopic preferences.

Horizon, N, Years	$\frac{x^{1-\alpha}}{1-\alpha}$	$\frac{(x+1)^{1-\alpha}}{1-\alpha}$	$\frac{(x+5)^{1-\alpha}}{1-\alpha}$
1	3.41	7.04	21.37
2	3.46	7.07	21.20
3	3.40	6.89	20.41
4	3.44	6.92	20.30
5	3.44	6.89	19.99
6	3.43	6.78	19.44
7	3.47	6.77	19.22
8	3.42	6.66	18.73
9	3.45	6.66	18.53
10	3.34	6.61	18.22
11	3.47	6.56	17.89
12	3.45	6.49	17.54
13	3.50	6.51	17.43
14	3.44	6.44	17.07
15	3.46	6.35	16.73
16	3.42	6.27	16.32
17	3.50	6.34	16.38
18	3.49	6.29	16.06
19	3.38	6.13	15.50
20	3.36	6.03	15.16
21	3.33	6.06	15.09
22	3.48	6.01	14.78
23	3.44	5.99	14.63
24	3.51	5.97	14.36
25	3.39	5.77	13.78
26	3.50	5.91	14.00
27	3.56	5.91	13.89
28	3.37	5.78	13.43
29	3.48	5.71	13.12
30	3.46	5.70	12.96

First, for $A = 0$, the risk-aversion parameter which equates the expected utility of stocks and bonds is almost constant for all horizons, about $\alpha_0 \cong 3.44$. Therefore, for all myopic risk averters with $\alpha < \alpha_0$, stocks provide a larger expected utility than bonds. As in practice α is estimated to be about 2, we advocate that for almost all investors with myopic preferences that stocks provide a larger expected utility. In any case, we cannot claim that one asset becomes more attractive than the other with the horizon, as the critical value does not change with the horizon. For $A = 1$ and particularly $A = 5$, stocks become less attractive with the horizon. For example, with $A = 5$ and $N = 1$, stocks have larger expected utility than bonds for all investors with $\alpha < 21.37$, but for $N = 30$, this preference is only for investors with $\alpha < 12.96$. Thus, although it seems that the set of investors who prefer stocks over bonds decreases with the horizon, it is meaningless if, indeed, in practice, the risk-aversion parameter is about 2, implying that all investors prefer stocks to bonds. It is interesting to note that Levy also found for the general myopic preference that bonds have a larger expected utility than stocks for relatively large risk-aversion parameters of $\alpha > 10$.[10]

9.5. Summary

It is well known that in the comparison of stocks and bonds, there is no FSD as the two empirical cumulative distributions of stocks and bonds typically intersect regardless of the assumed investment horizon. In this chapter, we introduced the almost FSD (AFSD) rule, where stocks "almost" dominate bonds, despite the FSD-violation area occurring in the left tails of the distributions under consideration — a range of returns where stocks have a lower rate of return than bonds. Note that bonds can never dominate stocks (by any rule employed, including the FSD and the AFSD), as bonds have a lower mean return than stocks.

---

[10]Levy M. (2019). Comment on 'Aging population, retirement and risk taking.' *Management Science* 66(6), 2787–2791.

As the investment horizon increases, the FSD violation area shrinks; hence, one is tempted to believe that for long horizons, stocks dominate bonds for almost all investors, or for all non-pathological preferences, where a pathological preference is defined as a preference that does not fit any investor.

If the set of non-pathological preferences increases with the horizon, the dominance relates to a larger set of investors. Specifically, in a comparison of the change in the relative attractiveness of stocks and bonds, if the set of non-pathological preferences revealing a preference for stocks increases with the horizon, it indicates that the set of investors who prefers stocks to bonds increases with the horizon, a fact that supports the "stocks for the long run" investment strategy. Notwithstanding, because the negative return on stocks also decreases with the horizon, it is ambiguous whether stocks dominate bonds in the long run. In other words, the set of non-pathological preferences may increase or decrease with the horizon.

To figure out the effect of the horizon on the set of non-pathological preferences is not an easy task, as one has to screen all possible utility functions, where most are unknown. To partially analyze the change in the size of the non-pathological preferences with the horizon, we confined ourselves to two utility functions that are widely employed in the literature: the negative exponential utility function and the general myopic preferences. With the negative exponential utility function, we find that the group of investors who prefer bonds to stocks increases with the horizon, allegedly revealing that the assertion "stocks for the long run" is erroneous. However, as this utility function is bounded from above and leads to some paradoxes (e.g., the blank check paradox), we are skeptical of the economic meanings of these results. The more interesting preference is the general myopic utility function $U(A + x)$. With this function, with $A = 0$, the attractiveness of stocks and bonds is unaffected by the horizon, and with a risk-aversion parameter smaller than about 3.4, stocks are preferred to bonds for all horizons. As the average risk-aversion parameter is estimated to be about 2, we conclude that for most, albeit not all, investors, stocks provide a larger expected utility than bonds for short and long horizons alike. As we may have some investors with a relatively larger risk-aversion parameter who prefer bonds to stocks, we emphasize that the preference for stocks is for most, but all, investors. With $A > 0$, the attractiveness of stocks relative to bonds diminishes somewhat with the horizon, yet for a risk-aversion parameter of $\alpha < 12$, stocks are still preferred to bonds.

In sum, with the AFSD rule, we cannot unequivocally assert that the set of non-pathological preferences increases with the horizon; hence, we cannot safely support the assertion of "stocks for the long run." Moreover, recall that we analyzed only two types of preferences, and presumably there are many other unknown preferences for which the non-pathological set of preferences decreases with the horizon. Hence, by the AFSD rule, we cannot safely advocate that "stocks for the long run" is the optimal investment strategy.

Finally, the AFSD rule has been developed in the expected utility framework. There is experimental evidence that subjects choose between prospects by the probability to end up with large wealth, called "probability dominance," a goal which does not necessarily conform with the expected utility framework.[11] Such a goal supports the assertion of "stocks for the long run," as the probability of stocks outperforming bonds increases with the horizon. Those investors who advocate stocks for the long run either have a utility function that supports this claim, or believe in a probability dominance paradigm.

---

[11]Diecidue, E., H. Levy and M. Levy (2020). Probability dominance. *The Review of Economics and Statistics* 102(5), 1006–1020.

Chapter 10

Prospect Theory and the Horizon

There are several theoretical decision-making models under uncertainty, but the two that are probably most important are the von-Neumann and Morgenstern[1] expected utility paradigm and the prospect theory of Kahneman and Tversky.[2] This chapter examines the effect of the investment horizon on choices, particularly between the investment in stocks and bonds in the prospect theory framework. This is an interesting horizon issue for two reasons: (1) with prospect theory, we have a reference point that generally changes location with the investment horizon; and (2) the location of the distributions of return on stocks and bonds also change with the horizon. The interaction between these two shifts with the horizon, that is, the reference point and the location of the distributions may affect choices in a peculiar way. The location of the reference point in prospect theory is important because it proposes that to the left of the reference point, risk-seeking prevails, whereas to its right, risk aversion prevails.

Prospect theory value function is different from the traditional utility function. By the expected utility paradigm, in the discrete case, the investor's goal is to maximize the expected utility given

---

[1]von Neumann, J. and O. Morgenstern (1953). *Theory of Games and Economic Behavior,* 3rd ed., Princeton University Press, New Jersey.

[2]Kahneman, D., and A. Tversky (1979). Prospect theory: An analysis of decision under risk. *Econometrica* 47(2), 263–292.

429

by $EU(X) = \sum_{i=1}^{n} p_i U(X_i)$, where X_i is the terminal wealth (total wealth and not change in wealth) of the investment, and p_i is the probability to obtain X_i. The utility function, U, can be concave, convex, or have both types of segments. Prospect theory differs from expected utility in several respects, and the three main differences are as follows:

(a) With prospect theory, the investor is concerned with the *change* in wealth and not with terminal wealth.

(b) The value function, $V(x)$, which substitutes for the utility function, is a function of the change in wealth — where in this chapter, this change is denoted by a lowercase x to distinguish it from the total wealth denoted by an uppercase X. Preference is given by a value function, V, which has an S-shape with an inflection point at the reference point. In the original prospect theory study, the reference point is represented by the point $x_i \equiv \Delta X_i = 0$, where ΔX_i stands for the change in wealth induced due to the investment. In subsequent studies, other reference points are suggested.

(c) Instead of using the probabilities p_i, in prospect theory, decision-makers employ subjective decision weights DW_i.

In this chapter, we analyze the effect of the horizon on choices with prospect theory focusing on the first two components of the theory: the change in wealth and the S-shaped value function.

10.1. The Basic Ingredients of Prospect Theory

Instead of the utility function, U, in prospect theory, it is assumed that the preference is represented by a value function V of the form:

$$V(x) = \begin{cases} -\lambda(-x)^{\beta} & \text{for } x \leq 0 \\ x^{a} & \text{for } x > 0 \end{cases} \tag{10.1}$$

where x is the change in wealth relative to the reference point (with a reference point $x = 0$ in the above formula), the exponents α and β are positive constants, and the constant $\lambda > 1$ is known as

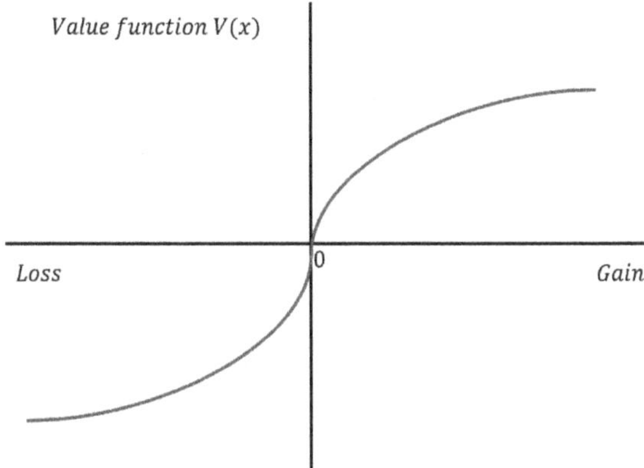

Figure 10.1: Prospect theory value function with current wealth as the reference point.

the loss-aversion parameter. Tversky and Kahneman[3] experimentally estimate these parameters to be $\alpha = \beta = 0.88$, and $\lambda = 2.25$.

Figure 10.1 illustrates the typical S-shaped value function suggested by prospect theory. The value function intersects the horizontal axis at the point $x = 0$, that is, at the point of a zero change in wealth (with respect to the reference point). To the right of this inflection point, the value function is concave, which is similar to a utility function with risk aversion (actually, it is similar to a utility function with constant relative risk aversion (CRRA), but in terms of change in wealth rather than total wealth). To the left of this inflection point, the value function drops sharply (the well-known "loss aversion" characteristic), and then becomes relatively flat. However, the important feature of the S-shaped value function is that in the positive range, we have risk aversion, while in the negative range, we have risk seeking. Around the inflection point, a loss hurts much more than the benefit from a gain of the same amount, hence the concept of loss aversion.

As the prospect theory value function has a unique S-shape, in this chapter, the analysis of choices under uncertainty is confined

---

[3] Tversky, A. and Kahneman, D (1992). Advances in prospect theory: Cumulative representation of uncertainty. *Journal of Risk and Uncertainty* 5(4), 297−323.

to this type of preference. In contrast, within the expected utility paradigm, there is no one particular shape of utility function, and a wide spectrum of preferences is accepted. Generally, with expected utility, there are two possibilities commonly employed in the literature:

(a) $U' \geq 0$ is assumed (monotonic non-decreasing utility functions, as employed by Friedman and Savage and Markowitz, as well as by first-degree stochastic dominance, FSD), and this set of preferences includes all shapes of preferences, including the possibility of an S-shaped preference; and

(b) $U' \geq 0$ and $U'' \leq 0$ is assumed (monotonic non-decreasing functions, in other words risk aversion), where in most economic equilibrium models, risk aversion is assumed.

Also, the utility is defined on total wealth $(w + x)$, whereas the value function is defined on the change in wealth, x.

There is experimental support for the assertion that investors (or more precisely, the participants in the various experiments), make choices based on change in wealth rather than total wealth, in contrast to what is advocated by the expected utility paradigm, and there is more sensitivity to losses than to gains around the inflection point of the value function, i.e., loss aversion prevails. It is interesting to note that the loss aversion property was first documented by Markowitz[4] in as early as 1952. A utility function with risk-seeking and risk-aversion segments aiming to explain the purchase of an insurance policy and lottery tickets simultaneously was suggested by Friedman and Savage[5] in 1948.

In their first prospect theory paper, Kahneman and Tversky[6] suggested that the reference point is the current wealth, and as x

---

[4] Markowitz, H. (1952). The utility of wealth. *Journal of Political Economy* 60(2), 151–158.

[5] Friedman, M. and Savage, L. J. (1948). The utility analysis of choices involving risk. *Journal of Political Economy* 56(4), 279–304.

[6] See footnote 2.

measures the changes in wealth, the reference point of the value function is at $x = 0$, that is, the current wealth. Therefore, it is common to refer to the current wealth or to the change in return, $x = 0$, interchangeably as the reference point. Thus, the change in wealth due to the investment $x = 0$ implies that the rate of return on the investment is $R = 0$, and this is also identical to the reference point. In sum, current wealth, as suggested by the original prospect theory, is identical to $x = 0$ or $R = 0$; therefore, both are different ways of stating the same reference point. Let us elaborate on the selection of the reference point and discuss other suggested reference points.

The value function, $V(x)$, is determined by the change in wealth given by $x = w_0(1 + R) - w_0 = w_0 R$, where w_0 is the current wealth, and R is the rate of return on the investment. If, for example, \$100 is invested and if $R = -10\%$, then the change in wealth is $x = -\$10$. If $R = +5\%$, then the change in wealth is \$5. When the return on the investment is $R = 0$, then $x = 0$ is the inflection point of the value function (see Figure 10.1). Another suggested reference point is the expected value $w_0(1 + ER)$ where ER is the expected rate of return.

Following the breakthrough of the original prospect theory paper, several researchers suggested other various reference points. For example, if r stands for the interest rate, a plausible reference point is $w_0(1 + r)$ since the counterfactual to not investing in the risky asset would be investing in the riskless asset, rather than avoiding investment altogether. Hence, in such a case, x is defined as $x = w_0(1 + R) - w_0(1 + r) = w_0(R - r)$, the excess return over the risk-free rate. This implies that any rate of return on the risky investment that falls below the riskless interest rate (which is the certain alternative rate of return) is considered to be a loss. For example, if the riskless interest rate is $r = 3\%$, then the reference point in our example is \$110$-$\$107 = \$3. Hence, \$3 is located at $x = 0$ in the value function, $V(x)$. Any return on the investment below \$3 falls into the loss region of returns, which is also the risk-seeking

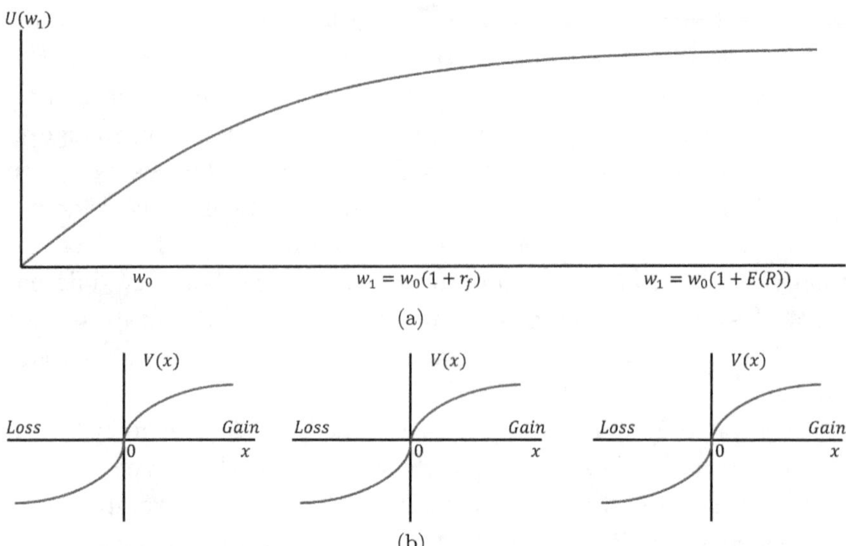

Figure 10.2: The utility function and three value functions with reference points: (a) The utility function; (b) The three prospect theory value functions.

range of returns. Thus, in this case, the inflection point is located on the horizontal axis at $x = \$3$. Any outcome below this reference point is considered to be a loss, and any outcome above it is considered to be a gain. Thus, if the reference point is $w_0(1+r)$, it is translated into the value function as $x = w_0(1 + R) - w_0(1 + r)$. With this reference point, any rate of return, R, lower than the riskless interest rate, r, is considered to be a loss. Another suggested reference point is the expected value $w_0(1 + ER)$ where ER is the expected rate of return.

Figure 10.2 provides a hypothetical utility function with three points marked on the horizontal axis corresponding to three reference points of prospect theory value functions. The three alternative reference points depicted in the utility function are w_0, $w_0(1+r)$, and $w_0(1 + ER)$, where ER is the expected rate of return on the risky investment. These three points imply three value functions with a reference point of $x = 0$, located just below the reference points depicted on the utility function.

As commonly perceived in economics, the first reference point implies that any reduction in the current wealth is considered to be a loss; hence, this point is located in the loss range of returns. By the second reference point, a loss is considered whenever the rate of return on the investment is below the interest rate. Finally, the third reference point implies that any outcome below the expected return on the risky investment, ER, is considered to be a loss. As can be seen from Figure 10.2, the larger the reference point, the larger the proportion of outcomes that are considered as losses by the prospect theory's investor. As we shall see in this chapter, the selected reference point has a direct implication for the comparison of investments in stocks and bonds for various horizons.

10.2. The Reference Point, the Distributions of Return, and the Horizon

In order to understand the implications of the shift in the reference points with the horizon on choices, we investigate the cumulative distributions of the annual rates of return on stocks and bonds for various horizons, covering the period from 1928 to 2020.[7] As before, for an N-year investment horizon, we draw N years from the historical rates of return, calculate the compounded return for these N years, and subtract 1 to get the N-year rate of return. We repeat this procedure 100,000 times, and with these 100,000 observations, we draw the cumulative distribution of the rate of return on stocks for investors with N-years horizons. By this procedure, we draw the cumulative distributions of stocks (the S&P 500 stock index) and risky bonds (10-year Treasury bonds) for various horizons, N. For this period, the annual riskless interest rate, which serves as one of the reference points, was about $r = 3.4\%$.

Figure 10.3 provides the cumulative distributions of the rates of return on stocks for three alternative investment horizons of $N = 1$ year, $N = 5$ years, and $N = 10$ years.

First, note that, as expected, the cumulative distribution (CDF) shifts to the right with the horizon as the returns typically increase

---

[7]http://www.stern.nyu.edu/~adamodar/pc/datasets/histretSP.xls.

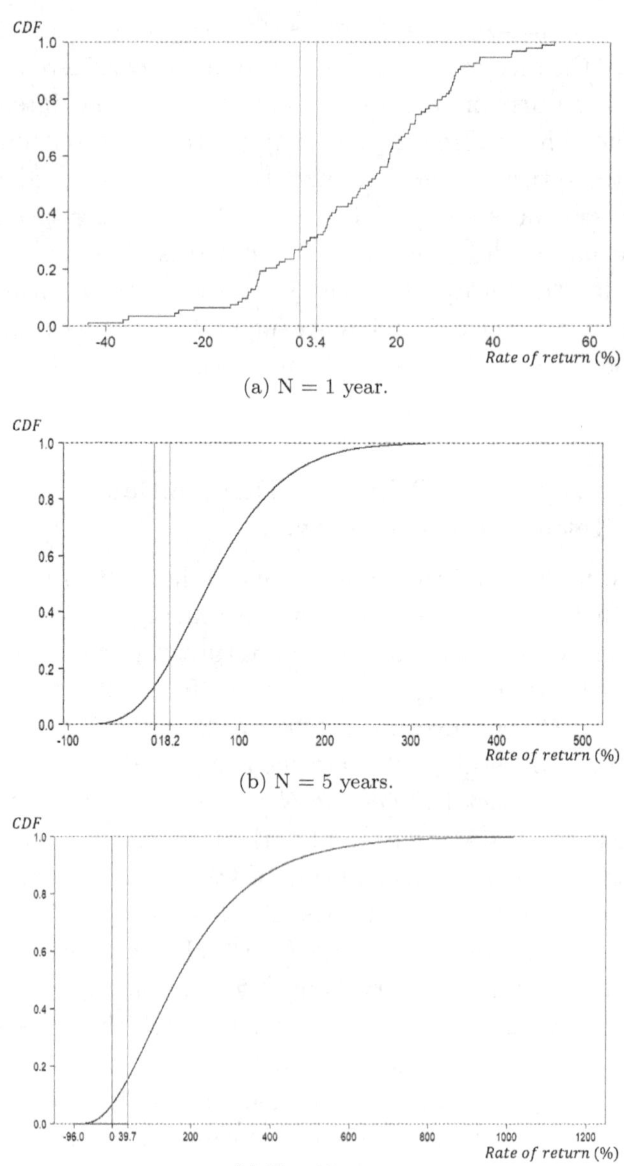

(a) N = 1 year.

(b) N = 5 years.

(c) N = 10 years.

Figure 10.3: The cumulative distributions of the rate of return on stocks (S&P 500 stock index) for various horizons with two reference points: $x = 0$, and $x = (1 + r_f)^N - 1$ (a) $N = 1$ year; (b) $N = 5$ years; (c) $N = 10$ years.

Note: *The left reference point is the zero change in wealth, $R = 0$. The second reference point is $R = (1 + r_f)^n - 1$, where the change in wealth is relative to the riskless annual interest rate of $r = 3.4\%$.

with it. This is demonstrated by the increasing scale of the return with the horizon — compare the horizontal axis of the figure corresponding to the various horizons.

For these three figures, we assume two alternative reference points. The first one, as suggested by Kahneman and Tversky, is the current wealth, that is, the rate of return, R, which is equal to zero. This reference point is invariant to the assumed horizon. The other reference point is the riskless annual interest rate, which was about 3.4% a year. Unlike the first reference point, here, the reference point increases with the horizon. It is 3.4% for $N = 1$, and it increases to $(1 + 0.034)^5 - 1 = 0.182$ or 18.2% for $N = 5$ years, and to $(1 + 0.034)^{10} - 1 = 0.397$ or 39.7% for $N = 10$ years (see the location of these points in Figure 10.3).

There are three important effects to the change in the horizon on the prospect theory expected value function, $EV(x)$:

(a) The minimal return of the investment under consideration typically decreases with the horizon. The reason for this is very simple: if there is even one annual rate of return of, say, -30% in a given year, with a 5-year investment horizon, there is a probability, albeit a very small one, that this negative return will be repeated in all five years (or in some of those years). This factor decreases the expected value function, $EV(x)$, with the horizon. Note that the same effect also exists with the utility function; however, due to the loss aversion characteristic, we suspect that this effect will be more intensive with prospect theory than in the expected utility paradigm.

(b) Because most of the distribution of the return shifts to the right with the horizon, the probability of being in the "gain" range of the value function increases with the horizon. This factor increases the expected value function, $EV(x)$, with the horizon.

(c) For any positive annual reference point, such as the riskless interest rate, the reference point shifts to the right with the horizon (see Figure 10.3, and note the different scales). Thus, the range of returns falling in the negative region of the value function (to the left of the reference point) increases with the horizon. This factor decreases the expected value function, $EV(x)$, with the horizon.

As we observe opposing effects of the horizon on the expected value function, later in the chapter, we will quantify these three factors simultaneously for stocks and separately for bonds, as they may affect the change in the attractiveness of stocks and bonds with the horizon within the prospect theory paradigm. Thus, we will investigate the change in the optimal stock–bond diversification with the horizon with the prospect theory value function for two possible reference points.

In Figure 10.3, we have two vertical lines standing for two reference points: one for zero return, R, (that is, the initial wealth is the reference point), and the other vertical line stands for $(1 + r_f)^N - 1$ as a reference point. Therefore, with this reference point, any N-period rate of return on the investment below the riskless interest rate falls in the loss region of the value function. Two interesting features emerge from Figure 10.3. First, the minimum value of the return on stocks, as expected, decreases with the horizon. As mentioned before, this factor decreases the expected value function with the horizon. The other factor is that the probability of a return falling left of the reference point decreases with the horizon (as the distribution of returns shifts to the right), a factor which increases the expected value function.

Figure 10.4 is very similar to Figure 10.3, but it relates to 10-year Treasury bonds. In a comparison of Figures 10.3 and 10.4, note that, as expected, the returns, on average, are smaller with bonds, and the minimum value is also larger, as bonds are typically less volatile than stocks. However, the two reference points are identical with both.

Table 10.1 summarizes the main results corresponding to the distributions of the return of stocks and bonds. As we can see from this table, the probability of being in the loss region of the value function typically decreases with the horizon. For stocks, it is 26.7% (or probability of 0.267) for $N = 1$ year, decreasing to 13.4% for $N = 5$ years, and further decreasing to 6.8% for $N = 10$ years. This factor by itself induces an increase in the expected value function

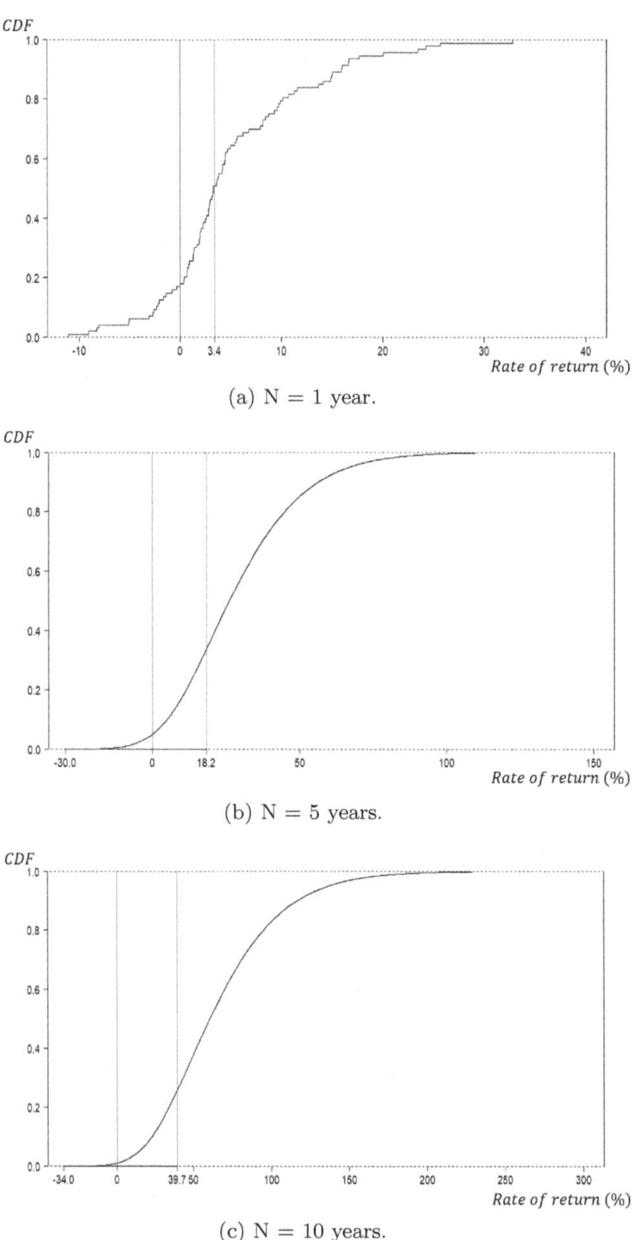

(a) N = 1 year.

(b) N = 5 years.

(c) N = 10 years.

Figure 10.4: The cumulative distributions of the rate of return on bonds for various horizons with two reference points: $x = 0$, and $x = (1 + r_f)^N - 1$ (a) $N = 1$ year ; (b) $N = 5$ years; (c) $N = 10$ years.

Table 10.1: The probability of returns falling in the loss region of the value functions for stocks and bonds with various horizons.

Horizon	S&P 500 Stock Index	10-year Treasury Bonds
Probability of being smaller than $R = 0$ (in %)		
1	26.7	18.1
5	13.4	5.1
10	6.8	1.0
Probability of being smaller than reference point $R = (1 + r_f)^N - 1$ (in %)		
1	31.1	50.7
5	22.4	33.5
10	15.6	25.8
Minimal values		
1	−43.8	−11.1
5	−83.1	−28.6
10	−96.2	−31.1

with the horizon. However, the minimum return on stocks decreases from -43.8% for $N = 1$ year to -83.1% for $N = 5$ years, and further to -96.2% for $N = 10$ years, and this factor by itself induces a decrease in the expected value function. The results with bonds are very similar.

Figure 10.5 superimposes the density distribution $f(R)$ of the excess rates of return on stocks on prospect value function $V(x)$ for $N = 1$ and $N = 5$ years, with the reference point corresponding to the annual riskless interest rate of 3.4%. For $N = 5$ years, the change in wealth, $x = 0$, corresponds to the return on stocks of $R = 18.2\%$. In drawing the density, $f(r)$, from the return on stocks, we subtract the reference point, which is 3.4% for $N = 1$ and 18.2% for $N = 5$. In a transparent way, these two figures show the two impacts of the increase in the horizon on the expected value function: most of the distribution of the return shifts to the right with the horizon,

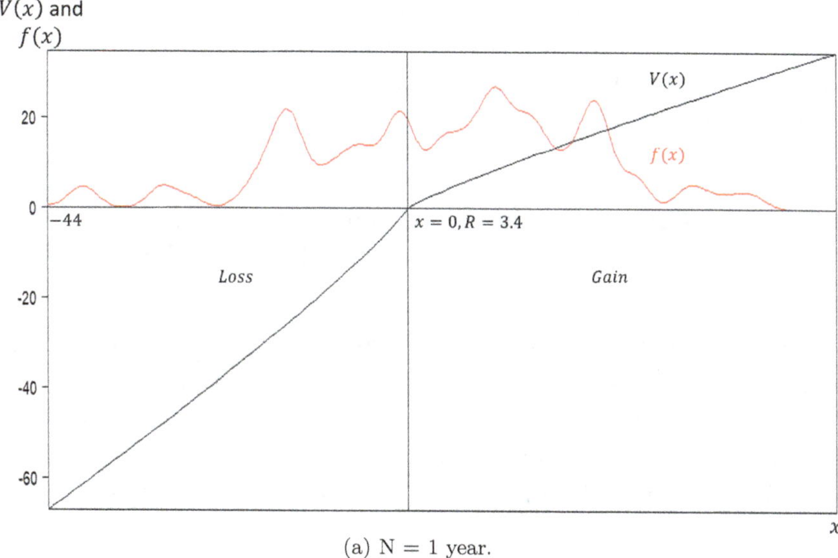

(a) N = 1 year.

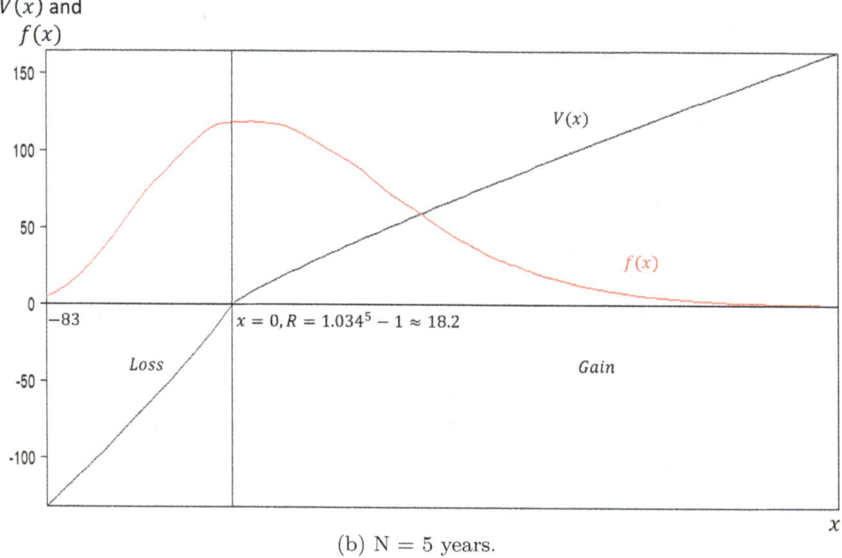

(b) N = 5 years.

Figure 10.5: The value function and the distributions of excess returns on stocks $(R - r_f)$ for $N = 1$ and $N = 5$ years with annual reference point $r_f = (1 + 3.4\%)^N - 1$: (a) $N = 1$ year; (b) $N = 5$ years.

but there is a nagging left tail with an extreme negative value that decreases with the horizon. In our specific case, the decrease is from about -44% for $N = 1$ year to about -83% for $N = 5$ years (see Figure 10.5).

10.3. The Change in the Expected Value Function of Stocks and Bonds with the Horizon with Two Reference Points

As the increase in the horizon induces two opposing forces on the expected value function, we next examine the change in this function of stocks with the horizon with two alternative reference points, $R = x = 0$ and $R = 3.4\%$, but the reference point, $R = 3.4\%$, increases with the horizon by the formula $R = (1.034)^N - 1$, where N stands for the horizon in years. To calculate $EV(x)$, we employ Eq. (10.1). For example, for a horizon of N years, we draw N observations from the return series and calculate the compounded return for these N years. Then, by subtracting 1, we obtain the N-year rate of return. Next, we calculate x by subtracting from the rate of return the reference point, which is either zero or $R = (1.034)^N - 1$, depending on the selected reference point. Thus, for each compounded rate of return, we have one value x and one value $V(x)$. We repeat this procedure 100,000 times (for each horizon, N), and then calculate the expected value $EV(x)$, by assigning to each of the 100,000 observations an equal probability. We first conduct this procedure for stocks and for bonds separately and then examine optimal diversification for various horizons. Figure 10.6 provides the results. As we can see, the expected value function increases with the horizon. However, the increase is much faster for stocks than for bonds.

10.4. Stock–Bond Diversification with Prospect Theory

Finally, the most interesting issue is the change in the optimal prospect diversification between stocks and bonds with the horizon. This time, we draw 50,000 observations of annual returns (obviously

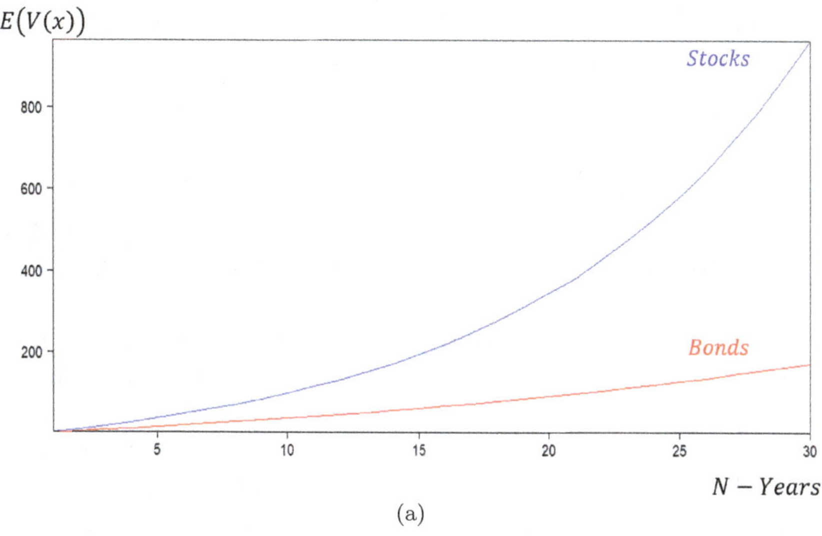

(a)

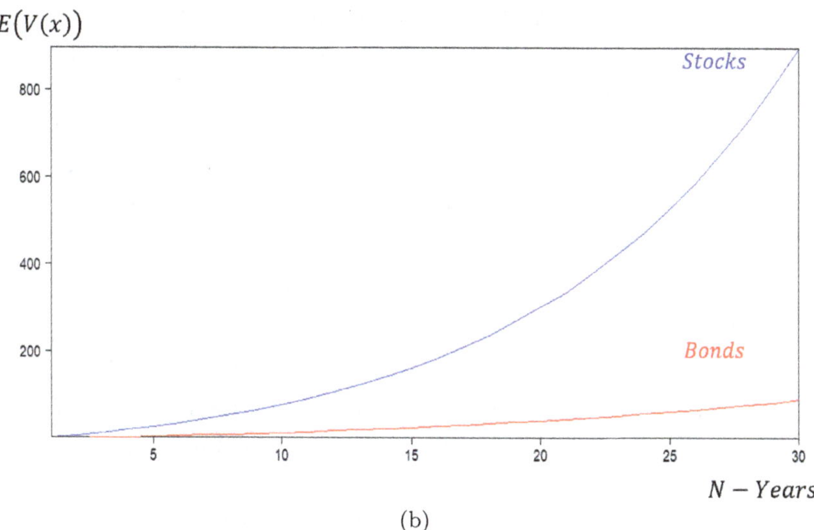

(b)

Figure 10.6: The expected value function, $E(V(x))$, of stocks and bonds for various horizons, N, with two alternative reference points: $x = 0$ and $x = (1.034)^N - 1$: (a) Reference point $x = 0$ (namely, $R = 0$); (b) Reference point $x = (1.034)^N - 1$ (namely $R = (1 + r_f)^N - 1$).

with repetitions), which provide 50,000 pairs of annual returns on stocks and bonds. We have the following steps:

1. First, we calculate the diversified portfolio annual return,

$$(1 + R_w) = w(1 + R_S) + (1 - w)(1 + R_B),$$

   where w is the arbitrary proportion invested in stocks, $(1 - w)$ is the proportion invested in bonds, and R_S and R_B are the rates of return on stocks and bonds.

2. Drawing 50,000 observations, for each year, we have the diversified portfolio return; hence, we can calculate the N-year compounded return. Thus, by this procedure, it is assumed that the investor revises their portfolio every year such that w is kept constant. Finally, we subtract 1 from the compounded return, obtaining the N-period rate of return on the selected diversified portfolio.

3. For each horizon, N, we calculate the prospect theory change in wealth by subtracting the N-year reference point from the portfolio rate of return.

4. Having the prospect theory change in wealth x, we employ Eq. (10.1) to calculate $V(x)$ for each value x, and then calculate the expected value $EV(x)$ by assigning, as before, an equal probability to each of the 50,000 values of $EV(x)$.

Because for each w and for each horizon, N, we have the expected value of the portfolio under consideration, we can figure out the optimal prospect theory diversification between stocks and bonds for each horizon N. In other words, we figure out which diversification policy, w, maximizes the prospect theory expected value function. Figure 10.7 provides the change in the expected value as a function of the investment proportion, w, for three horizons $N = 1$, $N = 5$, and $N = 10$ with the reference point $R = 0$ and with the reference point $R = (1.034)^N - 1$.

From Figure 10.7, we observe two main results: First, there is a strong preference for stocks in the stock–bond portfolio with prospect theory (note that the graphs increase with w), and the other obvious result is that the expected value function decreases with the reference point.

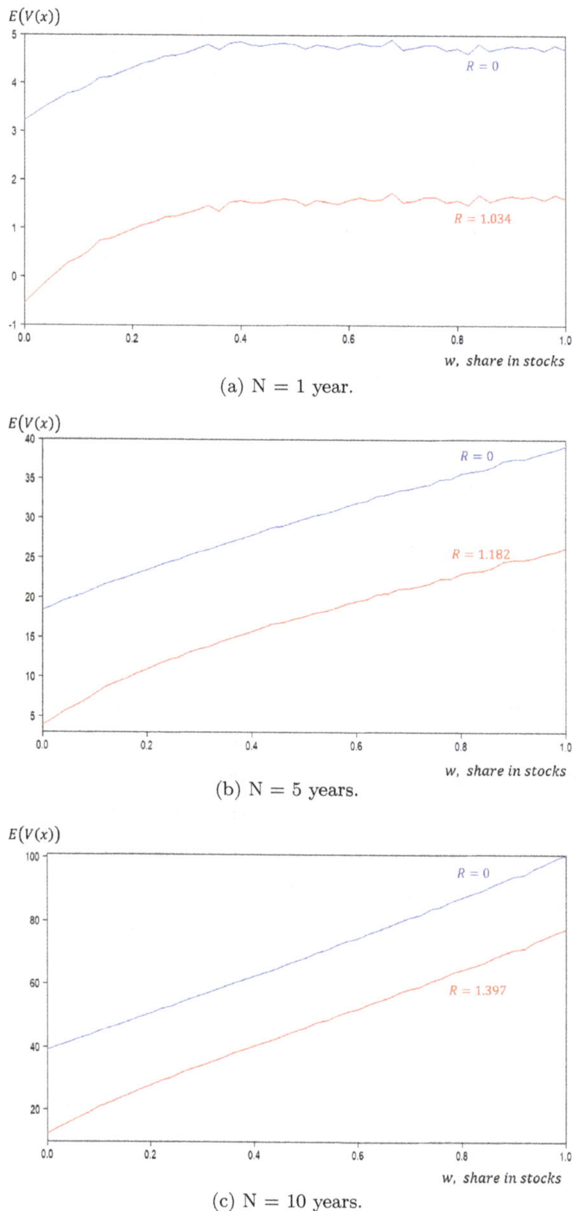

(a) N = 1 year.

(b) N = 5 years.

(c) N = 10 years.

Figure 10.7: The $E(V(x))$ as a function of the investment proportion in stocks, w, for various horizons with reference points $R = 0$ and $R = (1.034)^N - 1$: (a) $N = 1$; (b) $N = 5$; (c) $N = 10$.

Table 10.2: The optimal investment in stocks, w, with prospect theory value functions in the stock–bond portfolio for various horizons and two alternative reference points.

	Reference Point	
N	$R = 0$	$R = 1.034^N - 1$
1	0.6	0.6
2	0.9	0.9
3	1	1
4	1	1
5	1	1
10	1	1
15	1	1
20	1	1
30	1	1

Table 10.2 provides the optimal investment in stocks with prospect theory.

For a horizon of 2 years or less, some diversification is optimal. However, for horizons of 3 years or longer, a 100% investment in stocks is optimal. Thus, despite the decreasing minimal return with the horizon, and despite the loss aversion, the gap between the return on stocks and bonds is still very large in favor of stocks, and this gap increases with the horizon, leading to the superiority of stocks over bonds in the diversified portfolio with the prospect theory paradigm as well.

10.5. Summary

Prospect theory and expected utility are the two main paradigms employed in decision-making models under uncertainty. This chapter focused on prospect theory, which differs from expected utility in several respects. In this chapter, we examined the following characteristics of this theory: the S-shaped value function with loss aversion for negative change in wealth, the argument for the value function that is the change in wealth and not total wealth, and the selected reference point, which is the inflection point of the S-shaped value function.

As the investment horizon increases, a few changes occur that are similar to those obtained in expected utility analysis: the minimum return decreases with the horizon, which decreases the expected value function, and most of the distribution shifts to the right, which increases the expected value function. Also, if the reference point is positive (e.g., the riskless interest rate), this point shifts to the right with the horizon, which decreases the expected value function. Unlike expected utility analysis, with prospect theory, we have loss aversion, implying a possible intensive reduction in expected value function with the horizon, as the minimum return (which is negative) decreases with the horizon.

Taking all of these conflicting factors into account, we find that for both reference points, zero and the riskless interest rate, stocks dominate bonds in the stock–bond diversified portfolio, and for a horizon of three years or longer, allocating 100% to stocks, by prospect theory, is optimal. Thus, the investment strategy "stocks for the long run" is also supported by prospect theory, as long as we rely on the stock risk reflected by about 100 years of history. Any unforeseen future risk, not reflected in the historical distribution of returns on stocks, may change this conclusion.

Chapter 11

The Change in the Relative Attractiveness of Stocks and Bonds with the Horizon with a Riskless Asset

We have seen in the previous chapters that regardless of the length of the assumed investment horizon, the cumulative distributions of the returns on stocks and bonds intersect; hence, neither asset dominates the other by first-degree stochastic dominance (FSD).[1] Consequently, based solely on the FSD rule, we cannot support the common idiom "stocks for the long run" for all investors. While it is true that the range of return where bonds outperform stocks shrinks with the horizon, which is a favorable phenomenon for investors in stocks, the extreme negative return, particularly on stocks, also decreases with the horizon, which is an unfavorable phenomenon for these same investors. Therefore, there may be investors for a relatively long horizon with a legitimate utility function assigning a relatively large utility weight to the range where bonds outperform stocks (typically the left tails of the distributions of returns). Thus, for these long-horizon investors, the expected utility of bonds may be larger than that of stocks, which avoids the FSD of stocks over bonds, namely the preference of stocks over bonds for all investors. Hence, considering

---

[1]This one intersection of the cumulative distributions of stocks and bonds is also documented in other studies, e.g., see Bali, T. G., K. O. Demirtas, H. Levy, and A. Wolf (2009). Bonds versus stocks: Investors' age and risk taking. *Journal of Monetary Economics* 56(6), 817–830.

449

these two opposing forces, it is not clear whether the attractiveness of stocks relative to bonds increases or decreases with the horizon.

Notwithstanding, practitioners and life cycle fund managers typically believe that stocks become more attractive than bonds with the horizon. Moreover, there is empirical evidence that practitioners also act according to this belief as, in practice, the management of life cycle mutual funds declares an investment strategy that conforms with the "stocks for the long run" investment strategy.

Given this investment policy in practice, we are looking for other factors that may rationalize the "stocks for the long run" strategy, as the FSD rule fails to rationalize it. In Chapter 9, we examined whether stocks dominate bonds for long horizons by the almost FSD rule (AFSD) for most utility functions, albeit not all. Thus, by employing the AFSD rule, we compare the expected utility of stocks and bonds only for non-pathological preferences. By this rule, it is assumed that pathological preferences assign an unrealistically large marginal utility to the range of returns where bonds outperform stocks, and a relatively low marginal utility is assigned to the range of returns where stocks outperform bonds. As it is suspected that there is no FSD of stocks over bonds due to these pathological preferences that do not fit the preference of any investor, these utility functions are eliminated by the AFSD rule in the comparison of stocks and bonds for various horizons.

Suppose that we focus only on the non-pathological preferences. Does the attractiveness of stocks relative to bonds by the AFSD rule increase with the horizon? In Chapter 9, we showed empirically that in employing this rule, we also cannot unequivocally support the assertion "stocks for the long run," as the attractiveness of stocks over bonds generally does not increase with the horizon. Technically, we found that the set of non-pathological preferences does not increase with the horizon. Therefore, according to the AFSD rule, we cannot rationalize the observed preference of practitioners for stocks in the long run. Specifically, if we find that stocks do not dominate bonds for short horizons, but find that such dominance does exist for long horizons, we would have support, at least by this rule, for "stocks for the long run." As this is not the case, the AFSD rule cannot rationalize the practitioners' investment strategy.

Thus, we have no FSD and no AFSD of stocks over bonds even for long horizons; hence, the behavior of investors, in practice, needs another explanation. What is the rationale for this investment strategy of life cycle mutual funds, as well as for other practitioners in light of the fact that stocks do not dominate bonds for long horizons by either FSD or AFSD? It is worth mentioning that adding the risk-aversion assumption also does not help, as no rationalization of stocks for the long run emerges with investment rules that assume risk aversion.

In Chapter 9, we suggest the "probability dominance" (PD) rule as an explanation for the tendency to allocate a larger weight in stocks with the horizon, which conforms with the statistical fact that the probability of stocks ending up with a larger wealth than bonds indeed increases with the horizon (actually it approaches 1, as the horizon increases indefinitely). While experimentally the PD rule has been found to be a criterion that subjects employ in making choices among uncertain prospects, which can hence explain the "stocks for the long run" strategy, this rule does not always conform with expected utility maximization. Thus, we still have no rationalization for the "stocks for the long run" investment strategy, which conforms with expected utility theory.

In this chapter, we try another avenue in the expected utility framework to find whether there is theoretical (and empirical) justification for the "stocks for the long run" investment strategy. In a nutshell, like with the extension of the mean–variance (M–V) rule of Markowitz,[2] by adding the riskless asset to the Sharpe ratio criterion,[3] we conduct a parallel extension of the FSD to the FSDR rule by adding the riskless asset, where we add the letter R for the riskless asset to the FSD notation. Thus, in this chapter, we examine

---

[2] Markowitz, H. (1952). Portfolio selection. *The Journal of Finance* 7(1), 77–91.
[3] Sharpe, W. F. (1966). Mutual fund performance. *The Journal of Business* 39(1), 119–138.

whether combinations of stocks and the riskless asset become more attractive than combinations of bonds and the riskless asset with the horizon. Then we study portfolios of stocks and bonds with the riskless asset, and examine whether the weight of stocks in the portfolio increases or decreases with the horizon.

11.1. The Return on a Portfolio of Stocks and the Riskless Asset

Denote by R_S the rate of return on stocks, by r_f the riskless interest rate, which is assumed for simplicity only to be identical for borrowers and lenders, and by R_α the rate of return on a portfolio of stocks and the riskless asset. Thus, we have:

$$R_\alpha = (1 - \alpha)r_f + \alpha R_S \tag{11.1}$$

where $1 - \alpha$ is the proportion of the riskless asset in the portfolio whose rate of return is R_α. If $0 < \alpha < 1$, some positive investment weight is allocated to both the riskless asset and stocks. This is a defensive portfolio. If $\alpha > 1$, it implies that the investor borrows money and invests more than 100% in stocks, that is, they are leveraging their portfolio, and this is an aggressive portfolio. In this chapter, we do not discuss the case $\alpha < 0$, implying we avoid analyses of short-selling of stocks and investing more than 100% in the riskless asset.

Let us first illustrate the effect of the introduction of the riskless asset on the cumulative distributions of the induced portfolios, relative to the cumulative distribution of stocks. For simplicity only, let us assume first that stocks can achieve three values -4%, 2%, and $+12\%$ with an equal probability of $1/3$, and the riskless interest rate is 2%. Table 11.1 provides the rates of return on three alternative portfolios with $\alpha = 1$, $\alpha = 1/2$, and $\alpha = 2$.

As we can see from this table, if the return on stocks is 2%, the return on the portfolio remains 2% for all values α. This result follows directly from Eq. (11.1). As we can see from Table 11.1, for defensive portfolio ($\alpha = 1/2$), the mean return and variance of the portfolio decrease relative to a portfolio with 100% in stocks ($\alpha = 1$), while the opposite occurs for an aggressive portfolio ($\alpha = 2$).

Table 11.1: Rates of return on three portfolios $R_\alpha{}^*$.

Return of Stocks, R_S	Portfolios		
	$\alpha = 1/2$	$\alpha = 1$	$\alpha = 2$
-4%	-1%	-4%	-10%
2%	2%	2%	2%
12%	7%	12%	22%

Note: $^*R_\alpha = (1 - \alpha)r_f + \alpha R_S$ when $r_f = 2\%$.

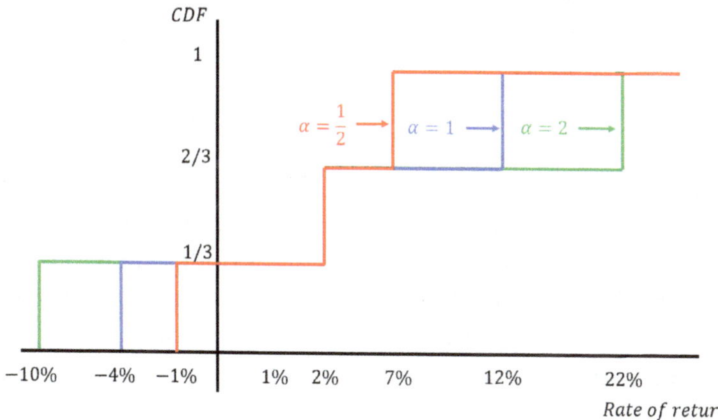

Figure 11.1: The cumulative distribution of R_α for $\alpha = 1/2$, $\alpha = 1$, and $\alpha = 2$.

Figure 11.1 demonstrates the change in the shape of the cumulative distribution of the return on stocks induced by the introduction of the riskless asset. Introducing the riskless asset induces a shrinkage in the cumulative distribution toward the point $r_f = 2\%$ in the case of a defensive portfolio, where $\alpha < 1$ (in our example, $\alpha = 1/2$): note that the red line, the CDF of the portfolio which is divided equally between stocks and the riskless asset, "shrinks" relative to the blue line, which is the CDF of a portfolio fully invested in stocks — the smallest possible values become larger and the largest possible values become smaller. On the other hand, there is an expansion in the cumulative distribution toward the point $r_f = 2\%$, in the case of an aggressive portfolio, where $\alpha > 1$ (in our example, $\alpha = 2$): note the green line, the CDF of a portfolio which borrows at the risk-free rate in order to leverage the investment in stocks, is an expansion of the blue line — the smallest possible values become smaller and the largest possible values become larger. Obviously, all cumulative distributions intersect at the rate of return on stocks, $R_S = r_f = 2\%$, because, with this return on stocks, mixing the stocks with the riskless asset creates a portfolio with exactly a 2% rate of return (see Eq. (11.1)).

In Figure 11.1, we have a discrete random variable; hence, the cumulative distribution is a step function. With a continuous random variable, we have only one critical point — the point where $R_S = r_f$, where all distributions intersect. This is the rate of return at which we have a shrinkage or expansion of the CDFs of the portfolios created by combinations of stocks and the riskless asset.

Figure 11.2 demonstrates the effect of adding the riskless asset to the actual stock rates of return. For this purpose, we employ actual stock return data covering the period 1928–2020. The rates of return correspond to the S&P 500 stock index, and the riskless interest rate is the rate of return on T-bills which in this period averaged about 3.4%.[4] As we have many observations, the cumulative distribution functions are almost continuous. As in the example given

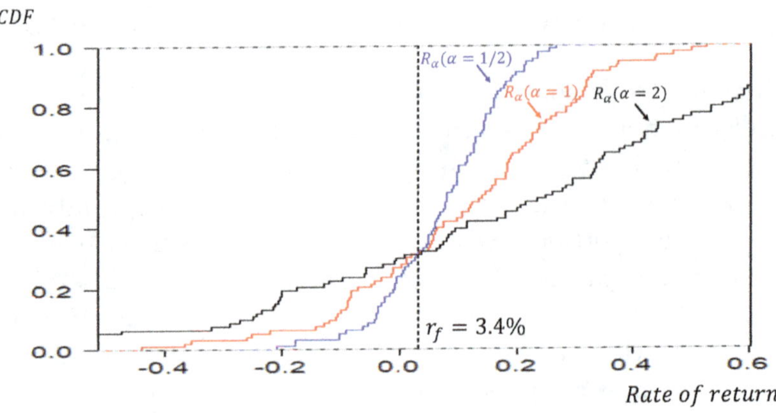

Figure 11.2: The CDF of portfolios of a combination of stocks with the riskless asset for $\alpha = 1/2$, $\alpha = 1$, and $\alpha = 2$ for the horizon $N = 1$ year.

---

[4] http://www.stern.nyu.edu/~adamodar/pc/datasets/histretSP.xls.

in Figure 11.1, we draw the cumulative distribution function of the return on three portfolios: $\alpha = 0$, $\alpha = 1/2$, and $\alpha = 2$.

As we can see, the cumulative distributions (CDFs) of the stocks shrink and expand toward the pivot point $(r_f, F(r_f))$, which also can be envisioned as rotations of the cumulative distributions toward this point. The CDF of the portfolio with $\alpha = 1/2$ becomes steeper than the CDF of stocks (shrinks), and the CDF of the return on the portfolio with $\alpha = 2$ becomes flatter than that of stocks (expands).

This rotation of the distribution of stocks with the riskless asset may create a situation where a portfolio of stocks and the riskless asset dominates a portfolio of bonds with the riskless asset, although neither stocks nor bonds dominate the other by FSD. Let us first provide an intuitive explanation for such a dominance possibility induced by the introduction of the riskless asset. In principle, such situations of having FSDR but not FSD are similar to the case where we have two assets (say, with normal distributions) where there is no M–V dominance between them (hence, both are M–V efficient), and by introducing the riskless asset, we obtain the Sharpe ratio (see footnote 3), generally inducing that only one asset is M–V efficient and the other is inferior.[5] With a comparison of FSD and FSDR, we have a similar situation with two differences in comparison to the M–V case:

(a) With FSD and FSDR, we are not confined to the M–V rule, that is, no normal distribution is assumed.
(b) With the Sharpe ratio, we obtain a complete ordering, while with FSD and FSDR, we have only a partial ordering. Thus, while by the Sharpe ratio, generally a dominance of one asset over the other is obtained (the one with the largest Sharpe ratio is dominant), with the FSD and FSDR, we may have a situation where the two assets are also efficient. Hence, introducing the riskless asset does not necessarily create a complete order of dominance when using the FSDR.

---

[5] There is a rare situation where both assets are located on the same Sharpe line. In this case, the investor is indifferent about the two assets and, arbitrarily, one of these two assets can be relegated to the inefficient set.

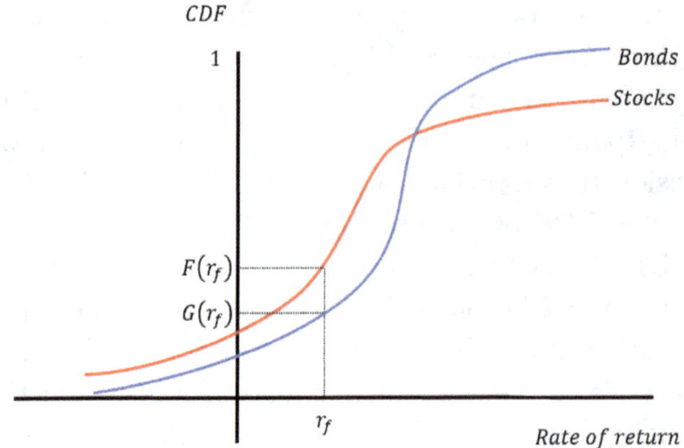

Figure 11.3: Stocks do not dominate bonds by FSDR.

Figure 11.3 illustrates a scenario where stocks do not dominate bonds either by FSD or by FSDR. There is no FSD because the two cumulative distributions, F (stocks) and G (bonds), cross. We cannot have FSDR because $F(r_f) > G(r_f)$; hence, no matter what the mix of stocks and bonds at the point $R_s = r_f$ is, we have $F(R_\alpha) = F(R_s) = F(r_f) > G(r_f)$. The fact that the cumulative distribution of R_α, which combines stocks and the riskless asset, does not change at the point $R_s = r_f$ has been demonstrated in Table 11.1 and Figures 11.1 and 11.2. Thus, in the example demonstrated in Figure 11.3, there is no portfolio of stocks and the riskless asset which dominates bonds by FSD.

From the above examples and discussion and from Eq. (11.1), we can state the following necessary condition for FSDR of F over G:

Proposition 1. *A necessary condition for dominance of F (stocks) over G (bonds) by the FSDR rule is that*

$$F(r_f) \leq G(r_f). \tag{11.2}$$

This is a necessary condition because mixing stocks with the riskless asset creates a new cumulative distribution that always passes through the point $(R_s = r_f, F(r_f))$. Hence, if (11.2) does not hold,

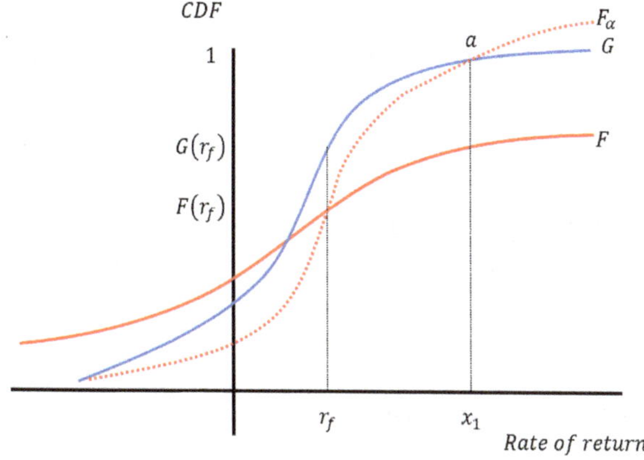

Figure 11.4: F does not dominate G by FSDR even though $F(r_F) \leq G(r_f)$.

F_α will be above G at this point for all possible created portfolios; therefore, F cannot dominate G by FSDR.[6]

Finally, note that Eq. (11.2) provides a necessary but not sufficient rule for FSDR of prospect F over prospect G. Thus, even if Eq. (11.2) holds, we may have no FSDR of prospect F over prospect G. To illustrate this claim, consider the case given in Figure 11.4. In this figure, the necessary condition is fulfilled; however, with any mix of stocks and the riskless asset, we may obtain that the stock portfolios F_α cross the CDF of bonds. Note that we mix F with the riskless asset such that F_α becomes lower than G on the left-hand side of the distribution. However, as a result of this necessary shrinkage (or rotation of the CDF) toward the point $(r_f, F(r_f))$ of F, F_α may cross G on the right-hand side (see point a in Figure 11.4).

Note that Figure 11.4 provides a hypothetical case where any rotation of F toward the point $(r_f, F(r_f))$ crosses G. Hence, with this specific case, for any rotation α, there is no FSD dominance of F_α over G and, hence, no FSDR dominance of F over G. But, if for one rotation α, there is no FSD dominance of F_α over G, is it possible to find another mix of stocks and the riskless asset, α',

---

[6]Generally, if $F(r_f) > G(r_f)$, one needs to check whether G dominates F by FSDR.

which creates FSD of $F_{\alpha'}$ over G? Thus, the challenge is to examine whether there is a mix α such that F_α is located, in the weak sense, entirely below G. If we can shrink or expand F toward the point $(r_f, F(r_f))$ such that F_α is entirely located below G, we can safely assert that F dominates G by the FSDR rule, despite not having FSD. The technique for finding whether such a mix of F and the riskless asset which dominates G exists is provided by the FSDR criterion that we discuss as follows.

11.2. The FSDR Criterion

Because there are an infinite number of combinations of the riskless asset and stocks, all possible mixes cannot be examined. Fortunately, we do have a technique that allows us to determine whether there is FSDR of one risky asset over the other with only one examination. To state the condition for the existence of FSDR, we need to employ the quantile approach for stochastic dominance. Let us elaborate:

Denote the quantile of order p of the distribution F by $Q_F(p)$ (such that $Pr(x \leq Q_F(p)) = p$). Then F dominates G by FSDR if the condition given in the following (11.3) is intact.

Theorem 1. *Prospect F dominates prospect G by FSDR if and only if*

$$\underset{F(r_f)<p\leq 1}{Sup}\ \frac{Q_G(p) - r_f}{Q_F(p) - r_f} \leq \underset{0\leq p\leq F(r_f)}{Inf}\ \frac{Q_G(p) - r_f}{Q_F(p) - r_f}. \tag{11.3}$$

This theorem has been proven by Levy and Kroll[7] (for more details, see also Levy[8]). If the above condition holds, it guarantees that at least one value of α can be found such that the portfolio $F_\alpha = (1 - \alpha)r_f + \alpha F$ dominates G by FSD (i.e., such that the return

---

[7]Levy, H. and Y. Kroll (1978). Ordering uncertain options with borrowing and lending. *The Journal of Finance* 33(2), 553–574.

[8]Levy, H. (2016). *Stochastic Dominance: Investment Decision Making Under Uncertainty*. Springer, New York.

CDF of portfolio F_α is located entirely below the return CDF of G).[9] The FSDR condition (11.3) is equivalent to the statement that at least one "shrinkage" or "expansion" of the CDF F toward r_f exists such that the new CDF, F_α, dominates G by the FSD rule.[10] Thus, having the returns on stocks (F) and bonds (G) and the riskless asset, one can employ (11.3) to figure out whether stocks dominate bonds by the FSDR. Moreover, more relevant to our analysis is that one can employ the multi-period distributions to examine whether the FSDR of stocks over bonds exists for long horizons but not for short horizons. If this is indeed the case, we can use FSDR to justify the assertion of stocks for the long run as long as the riskless asset is available.

Looking deeply at the FSDR procedure discussed previously, one may correctly raise the following objection: why not also allow portfolios of G with the riskless asset? Is it a fair comparison to allow mixing F with the riskless asset and comparing it to G rather than to a portfolio of G with the riskless asset? This issue is not overlooked and is handled carefully by Levy and Kroll (see footnote 7). Specifically, they proved that if (11.3) holds, then for any combination of G with the risk-free asset, there exists another combination of F with the risk-free asset that dominates it by FSD. To illustrate, suppose that we find one combination F_α which dominates G, namely

$$F_\alpha = (1 - \alpha)r_f + \alpha R_s \text{ dominates } G \text{ by } FSD.$$

Now suppose that we mix G also with the riskless asset, that is, we create the function G_β:

$$G_\beta = (1 - \beta)r_f + \beta R_b, \text{ where } R_b \text{ is the return on bonds.}$$

Does the fact that F_α dominates G by FSD imply that it also dominates G_β by FSD? Not necessarily. However, although it is

---

[9] F_α is the standard notation in the FSDR literature to denote the CDF of a return of a portfolio with an investment proportion α in asset F and an investment proportion $1-\alpha$ in the risk-free asset.

[10] Note that while borrowing at the risk-free rate is allowed, short-selling of prospect F or prospect G is not allowed. For more details, see Levy and Kroll (footnote 8).

possible that F_α does not dominate G_β by FSD, if F_α dominates G by FSD, one can establish another combination of F and the riskless asset, say F_γ, such that F_γ dominates G_β by FSD. Thus, Levy and Kroll first prove that if the condition of Theorem 1 holds, then there is a mixture, F_α, which dominates G by FSD. Next they prove that if such dominance exists, then for any portfolio G_β, there is another portfolio F_γ which dominates it by FSD. In a nutshell, we have the relationships as summarized in Theorem 2:

Theorem 2. *If there is α such that F_α dominates G by FSD, then $\{F_\alpha\}$ dominates $\{G_\beta\}$ by FSDR, where $\{F_\alpha\}$ and $\{G_\beta\}$ are the sets of all combinations of F with the riskless asset and G with the riskless asset, respectively. This is a "set dominance," as for each element in the set $\{G_\beta\}$, there is at least one element included in the set $\{F_\alpha\}$ which dominates it by FSD.*

As with set dominance, if we allow mixing both F and G with the riskless asset, both distributions can shrink or expand toward r_f. Recall, however, that by mixing F (or G) with the riskless asset, the shrinkage (or expansion) does not change the CDF at the point where the return is equal to r_f, and both $F(r_f)$ and $G(r_f)$ are invariant to mixtures with the risk-free asset, namely $F_\alpha(r_f) = F(r_f)$ and $G_\beta(r_f) = G(r_f)$ for any arbitrarily selected α and β. Thus, if F is above G at r_f, this will not change by mixtures of both F and G with the risk-free asset. This property conforms with the fact that a necessary condition for dominance of F over G by FSDR is that $F(r_f) \leq G(r_f)$.

In the comparison of the empirical CDFs of stocks (F) and bonds (G), which will be presented later in the chapter, we empirically find that indeed $F(r_f) < G(r_f)$, and this is true for all investment horizons N. Thus, bonds cannot dominate stocks by FSDR, but stocks may dominate bonds, as the necessary condition for dominance holds for all investment horizons. Whether stocks dominate bonds by FSDR, and for which investment horizons, are the empirical questions that we address in this chapter. That is, we examine whether the condition given in Eq. (11.3) holds for various investment horizons in which F stands for stocks and G for bonds.

11.3. Numerical Illustration of the FSDR Rule

We turn now to a numerical example to demonstrate a case where F does not dominate G by FSD; however, there is α such that F_α dominates G by FSD. In the second step, we show that there is β such that F_α does not dominate G_β by FSD, but for each selected β, there is a value $\gamma = \alpha\beta$ such that F_γ dominates G_β by FSD. In short, if there is one value α such that F_α dominates G by FSD, we have dominance of the set $\{F_\alpha\}$ over the set $\{G_\beta\}$.

Table 11.2a and Figure 11.5a present the return on two prospects F and G such that neither F nor G dominates the other by FSD. Note that F is riskier than G, with a larger expected return than G; hence, in this example, F stands for stocks and G stands for bonds.

Table 11.2b and Figure 11.5b reveal that despite not having FSD, there is FSDR of F over G with selected $\alpha = 1/2$. Note that it is

Table 11.2: There is FSDR set dominance.

Table 11.2a: The returns on F and G: No FSD.

F		G	
Probability	**Rate of Return**	**Probability**	**Rate of Return**
1/4	-8%	1/4	-4%
3/4	30%	3/4	14%

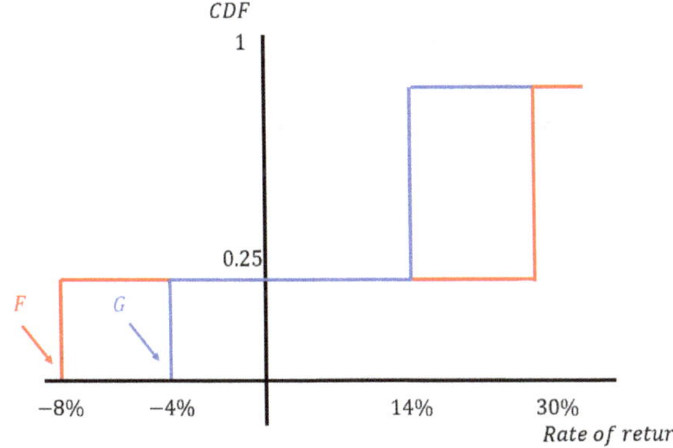

Figure 11.5a: The cumulative distributions of F and G cross.

Table 11.2b: The return on F_α and G with $r_f = 2\%$ and $\alpha = 1/2$: F_α dominates G by FSD.

F_α		G	
Probability	**Rate of Return**	**Probability**	**Rate of Return**
1/4	$1/2 \times 2 + 1/2 \times (-8) = -3\%$	1/4	-4%
3/4	$1/2 \times 2 + 1/2 \times 30 = 16\%$	3/4	14%

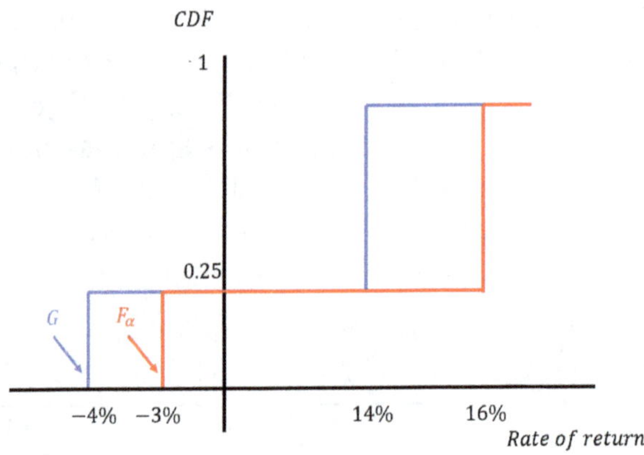

Figure 11.5b: The cumulative distribution of F_α and G: F_α dominates G by FSD.

enough to find one value α such that F_α dominates G to guarantee FSDR of F over G, but in practice, one may find many different values of α such that such dominance is achieved.

We next allow mixing also G with the riskless asset. For example, we choose also $\beta = 1/2$ and create a portfolio mixed from bonds and the riskless asset. The return on this portfolio is given by

$$R_b(\beta) = (1 - \beta)r_f + \beta R_b$$

where R_b stands for the rate of return on bonds. Table 11.2c and Figure 11.5c reveal that neither F_α nor G_β dominates the other by FSD.

However, by selecting $\gamma = \alpha\beta$, we obtain that F_γ dominates G_β by FSD; hence, we have "set dominance." Table 11.2d and

Table 11.2c: The distribution of F_α and G_β when $\alpha = 1/2$ and $\beta = 1/2$: neither F_α or G_β dominates the other.

F_α		G_β	
Probability	**Rate of Return**	**Probability**	**Rate of Return**
1/4	−3%	1/4	−1%
3/4	16%	3/4	5%

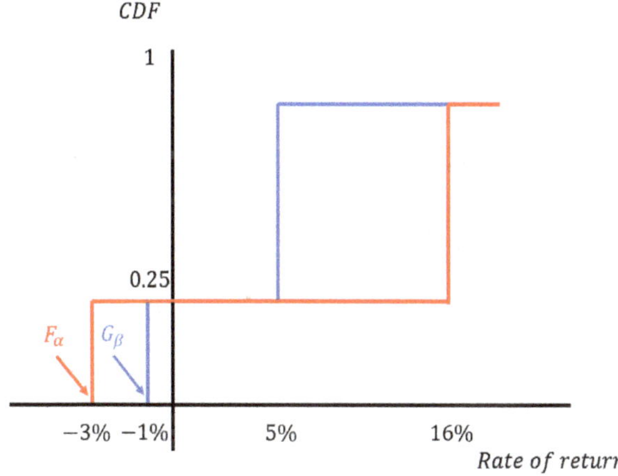

Figure 11.5c: The cumulative distributions of F_α and G_β: There is no FSD.

Table 11.2d: The distributions of F_γ and G_β when $\beta = 1/2$ and $\gamma = \alpha \times \beta = 1/4$: F_γ dominates G_β by FSD.

F_γ		G_β	
Probability	**Rate of Return**	**Probability**	**Rate of Return**
1/4	−1/2%	1/4	−1%
3/4	9%	3/4	5%

Figure 11.5d reveal that indeed for a selected β, one can always select $\gamma = \alpha\beta$ to obtain a dominance of stocks over bonds.

Figure 11.6 provides the intuition behind the claim that it is enough to find one combination of F and the riskless asset which dominates G by FSD to have set dominance.

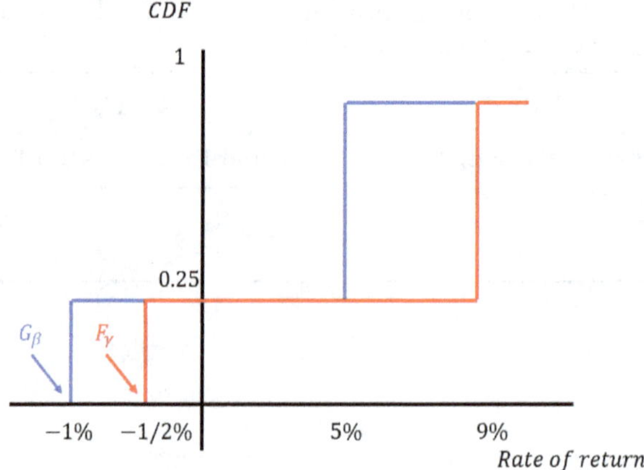

Figure 11.5d: The cumulative distributions of F_γ and G_β.

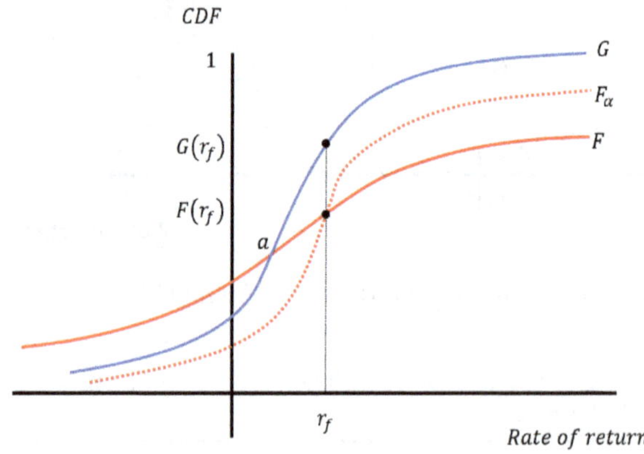

Figure 11.6: The set dominance of $\{F_\alpha\}$ over $\{G_\beta\}$ by FSD[*].

Note: [*]Any rotation of G toward $(r_f, G(r_f))$ is followed by a parallel rotation of F_α toward $(r_f, F(r_f))$.

First, note that F and G cross at point a; hence, there is no FSD. Suppose that there is at least one portfolio such that F_α dominates G by FSD, as shown in Figure 11.6 (note that F_α is located entirely below G). Now, let us mix also G with the riskless asset creating G_β; hence, we have a rotation of G toward the pivot point $(r_f, G(r_f))$ and, as a result, F_α and G_β cross. By the set dominance argument, simply rotate F_α toward $(r_f, F(r_f))$, which is parallel to the rotation of G, and we obtain F_γ such that F_γ is located entirely below G_β. To avoid a complex figure with many crossing curves, G_β and F_γ are not drawn in Figure 11.6.

11.4. Stocks versus Bonds and the Horizon: The FSDR Empirical Evidence

So far, we have presented the FSDR rule, showing that we may have two assets with no FSD, yet by adding the riskless asset, such dominance emerges. In this section, we examine empirically whether stocks dominate bonds by the FSDR criterion, and particularly, whether there is no FSDR for relatively short horizons, but there is FSDR for relatively long horizons. If this is the case, we have empirical support for the "stocks for the long run" investment strategy.

We report in this subsection the main FSDR empirical results of Levy and Levy's[11] study. They employ the historical annual returns on the S&P 500 stock index (including dividends), and the annual returns on 10-year United States (US) government bonds (risky bonds) over the 1928–2018 sample period (91 annual returns).[12] As inflation risk may be substantial in the long run, they employ Treasury Inflation-Protected Securities (TIPS) as the riskless asset. The yields on TIPS with horizons from 1 to 30 years are provided by the US Department of the Treasury. Accordingly, they investigate investment horizons of 1 to 30 years. They conducted the entire analysis in real terms; that is, they employ the inflation-adjusted real returns on stocks and bonds. Annual inflation rates for the 1928–2018 period are published by the US Bureau of Labor and Statistics. As the current forward-looking TIPS rates for horizons of 1–30 years are reported, they used these rates directly, with no need to estimate the real riskless interest rate.

They generate the N-period return distributions (with $N =$ 1, 2, 3, 5, 10, 15, 20, and 30-year horizons). They randomly draw

---

[11]Levy, H. and M. Levy (2021). Stocks versus bonds for the long run when a riskless asset is available. *Journal of Banking and Finance* 133.

[12] http://www.stern.nyu.edu/~adamodar/pc/datasets/histretSP.xls.

annual returns from the historical return distributions (with replacements), and calculate the N-period returns as $1+R_N = \prod_{i=1}^{N}(1+r_i)$, where the r_is are the randomly drawn annual rates of return. This approach assumes that the annual returns are independent and identically distributed (*i.i.d.*), and it has the advantage that it yields a very large number of N-period return observations. The following results are for 100,000 such observations.

They found that the two CDFs cross for all horizons; hence, neither stocks nor bonds dominate by FSD (or vice versa). Stocks also do not dominate bonds by SSD because the minimal return on stocks is always lower than that on bonds. We can also safely conclude that bonds do not dominate stocks by SSD because the mean return on bonds is smaller than that on stocks. Thus, neither stocks nor bonds dominate the other by FSD nor by SSD (and of course, there is no dominance by the M–V rule), and this assertion is intact for all horizons. Hence, in comparing stocks to bonds without the riskless asset, they found that there is no empirical support for the "stocks for the long run" assertion.

For the 1-year horizon and the empirical return distributions, FSDR dominance does not hold. If we "shrink" the stock CDF toward r_f so that it is below the bond CDF on the left side, then this shrinkage will cause the stock CDF to be above the bond CDF on the right side.

However, as the horizon increases, FSDR dominance of stocks over bonds is obtained, and it becomes even more pronounced as the horizon increases. Table 11.3 shows that stocks do not dominate bonds by FSDR for $N = 1$. This is also true for $N = 2$. However, for all horizons of $N \geq 3$ years or more, stocks indeed dominate bonds by FSDR.

Table 11.3 also reveals that the skewness of the stock return distribution increases dramatically with the investment horizon, consistent with the findings of Fama and French[13] and Bessembinder.[14]

---

[13]Fama, F. F. and K. R. French (2018). Long-horizon return. *The Review of Asset Pricing Studies* 8(2), 232–252.
[14]Bessembinder, H. (2018). Do stocks outperform treasury bills? *Journal of Financial Economics* 129(3), 440–457.

Table 11.3: Return parameters and dominance between stocks and bonds for different horizons.

Horizon, N (Years)	Stocks				Bonds				TIPS Annual Rate (%)	TIPS N-Period Rate[b] (%)	Inf	Sup	FSDR of Stocks Over Bonds
	Mean (%)	Median (%)	Std. (%)	Skewness	Mean (%)	Median (%)	Std. (%)	Skewness					
1	8.1	10.4	19.5	−0.13	2.2	1.0	8.1	0.52	0.78	0.78	0.30	0.49	No
2	17.1	15.8	30.1	0.26	4.3	3.3	11.8	0.55	0.42	0.84	0.38	0.42	No
3	26.6	23.2	40.1	0.54	6.5	5.1	14.6	0.60	0.29	0.87	0.43	0.36	Yes
5	48.4	39.5	61.6	0.94	11.0	8.8	19.8	0.68	0.21	1.05	0.48	0.29	Yes
10	119.4	89.1	134.6	1.67	23.2	19.0	31.4	0.87	0.20	2.02	0.55	0.22	Yes
15	226.0	157.5	254.5	2.39	37.0	30.3	43.2	1.06	0.32[a]	4.91	0.60	0.18	Yes
20	382.6	247.8	455.2	3.18	51.5	41.9	55.4	1.26	0.44	9.18	0.65	0.14	Yes
30	958.5	546.5	1320.5	5.15	86.7	69.1	85.2	1.55	0.71	23.65	0.75	0.09	Yes

Note:

[a]Extrapolation between the published 10-year and 20-year rates.

[b]Calculated by compounding the one-year yield for N years.

The mean, median, standard deviation, and skewness of real N-period returns for stocks (S&P 500 including dividends) and 10-year government bonds are shown in the first columns. The risk-free rate is taken as the TIPS yield for the relevant horizon, as reported by the US Department of the Treasury in August 2019. Inf and Sup stand for the values of $Inf_{0 \leq F(r_f)} \frac{Q_G(p) - r_f}{Q_F(p) - r_f}$ and $Sup_{F(r_f) < p \leq 1} \frac{Q_G(p) - r_f}{Q_F(p) - r_f}$ employed in the FSDR condition in Eq. (11.3), where F stands for the stock CDF and G stands for the bond CDF. When $Inf > Sup$, stocks dominate bonds by FSDR, as indicated by the far-right column of the table.

Source: Levy and Levy (see footnote 11).

The skewness of the bond return distribution also increases with the horizon, but this effect is much larger for stocks.

11.5. Stock–Bond Portfolios with the Riskless Asset

The analysis up to this point follows the traditional "stocks versus bonds" literature, where the pure-stock portfolio is compared with the pure-bond portfolio. But, of course, portfolios of both stocks *and* bonds (and TIPS) are possible, and the finding that stocks dominate bonds reported in Table 11.3 does not imply that the pure-stock portfolio dominates stock–bond combinations. In order to examine the efficiency of stock–bond portfolios, Levy and Levy consider 11 portfolios: a pure-stock portfolio, a portfolio with 90% in stocks and 10% in bonds, a portfolio with 80% in stocks and 20% in bonds, ... and a pure-bond portfolio. The portfolio weights are rebalanced annually, and they examine FSDR dominance relations among these portfolios at various investment horizons (recall that each of the 11 portfolios can be "mixed" with TIPS). In this analysis, we employ the basic bootstrap methodology.

A portfolio is included in the FSDR efficient set if and only if none of the other portfolios dominates it by FSDR — it is enough that one other portfolio dominates a given portfolio to imply that no investor with non-decreasing preferences will select the dominated portfolio, deeming it inefficient. Table 11.4 reports the FSDR efficient sets for various investment horizons. A shaded "Yes" cell implies that the portfolio is included in the FSDR efficient set, and "No" implies that it is not.

For a horizon of one year, all portfolios are included in the efficient set. This implies that no FSDR dominance relations exist among the 11 portfolios (recall that we previously saw that the pure-stock portfolio does not dominate the pure-bond portfolio for the 1-year horizon). As the investment horizon increases, the efficient set shrinks toward the stock portfolios. For a horizon of 15 years or more, portfolios with less than 60% in stocks are FSDR inefficient. The economic interpretation of this result is that if an investor's horizon is 15 years or more, the investor should invest at least 60%

Table 11.4: Stock–bond portfolios with the riskless asset.

Horizon, N (Years)	100% Stocks 0% Bonds	90% Stocks 10% Bonds	80% Stocks 20% Bonds	70% Stocks 30% Bonds	60% Stocks 40% Bonds	50% Stocks 50% Bonds	40% Stocks 60% Bonds	30% Stocks 70% Bonds	20% Stocks 80% Bonds	10% Stocks 90% Bonds	0% Stocks 100% Bonds
1	Yes	Yes	Yes	Yes	Yes	Yes	Yes	Yes	Yes	Yes	Yes
2	Yes	Yes	Yes	Yes	Yes	Yes	Yes	Yes	Yes	Yes	Yes
3	Yes	Yes	Yes	Yes	Yes	Yes	Yes	Yes	Yes	No	No
5	Yes	Yes	Yes	Yes	Yes	Yes	Yes	Yes	No	No	No
10	Yes	Yes	Yes	Yes	Yes	Yes	No	No	No	No	No
15	Yes	Yes	Yes	Yes	Yes	No	No	No	No	No	No
20	Yes	Yes	Yes	Yes	Yes	No	No	No	No	No	No
30	Yes	Yes	Yes	Yes	Yes	No	No	No	No	No	No

Note: The table reports the FSDR efficient set for different investment horizons. A shaded "Yes" cell indicates that the portfolio is included in the efficient set, while "No" indicates that it is not. For a 1-year horizon, all portfolios are included in the FSDR efficient set. For horizons of 15 years or more, portfolios with less than 60% in stocks are FSDR inefficient.

in stocks. Finally, recall that these weights refer to the stock–bond mix, and do not include the weights in TIPS; thus, a portfolio with 30% in stocks, 20% in bonds, and 50% in TIPS — a portfolio for which stocks make up 60% of the risky part — is also efficient.[15] These results rationalize the practice of most target-date funds to invest heavily in stocks when the horizon is long.

Finally, note that "stocks" in our empirical analysis refer to the S&P 500 stock index, that is, to a portfolio which includes 500 stocks. Bessembinder[16] argues that such broad diversification reduces the multi-period skewness which is disadvantageous from the expected utility maximizers. Thus, future research on multi-period FSDR preferences with a smaller number of assets in the portfolio is called for.

11.6. Summary

A "stocks for the long run" investment strategy is employed in practice, but cannot be rationalized in an expected utility framework either by FSD or by SSD, as both stocks and bonds are included in the efficient sets. Thus, the nagging question remains: Why do practitioners adopt this stock for the long-run investment policy when there is no theoretical justification for this policy?

In Chapter 9, we discussed two possible rationalizations for the "stocks for the long run" investment strategy. The first one is that investors base their investment decisions on the probability dominance (PD) rule. Indeed, the probability of stocks ending up with larger terminal wealth than bonds increases with the horizon, approaching 1 as the horizon increases indefinitely. This PD rule has experimental support, but does not necessarily conform with the expected utility paradigm. The other potential explanation is by the AFSD rule. However, employing

---

[15]In other words, there is no combination of any of the other 10 stock–bond portfolios with TIPS that dominates this portfolio.

[16]Bessembinder, H. (2021). Extending portfolio theory to compound returns. Available on SSRN 3875870.

the AFSD rule, which also conforms with the expected utility paradigm, also does not rationalize this investment policy. Specifically, the AFSD rule does not reveal empirically that the longer the horizon, the more attractive stocks become relative to bonds. In this chapter, we introduced the availability of the riskless asset as a possible explanation for this investment strategy in practice. We obtain that a portfolio of stocks and the riskless asset FSDR dominates (meaning in the framework where borrowing and lending is allowed) the portfolio of bonds and the riskless asset. While this dominance does not prevail for one- and two-year investment horizons, for longer horizons, for any portfolio of bonds with the riskless asset, there is a portfolio of stocks and the riskless asset which dominate it by FSD. Thus, the availability of the riskless asset rationalizes the assertion of "stocks for the long run," which according to the empirical results implies that the long run is defined as three years or more.

Allowing investment in a portfolio that includes stocks, bonds, and the riskless asset, the obtained results are in the spirit of the previous results: as the horizon increases, portfolios with a relatively large investment weight in bonds become FSD inefficient. Thus, these portfolio results rationalize the investment strategy of life cycle mutual funds. Finally, note that a life cycle mutual fund does not need to invest directly in the riskless asset as part of the offered portfolio, as each investor who purchases these funds can choose the desired weight of the riskless asset, $1 - \alpha$, by borrowing and lending at the risk-free rate in combination with investing in the fund. Thus, each investor needs to first decide on the selected investment horizon, to then choose an efficient portfolio of stocks and bonds, and finally, to decide to diversify (borrow or lend) between the selected portfolio and the riskless asset. This is very similar to the M–V analysis (when normality is assumed) in which every investor diversifies between the M–V risky efficient portfolio and the riskless asset.

efficient frontier (EF), 30, 101, 157,
158, 176, 178, 231, 247, 249,
251–253, 256–258, 260, 262, 335,
337
efficient set (ES), 1, 2, 10, 35, 99, 100,
108, 116–119, 122, 126–128, 133,
134, 136, 137, 139–149, 152, 154,
158, 160, 161, 166, 172, 282,
376–379, 382, 383, 385, 387,
468–470
exchange-traded fund (ETF), 175,
180, 182–184
exponential utility, 265, 268, 270, 271,
281, 420, 421, 423, 424, 427

feasible set, 126, 147
first-degree stochastic dominance
(FSD), 10, 13, 107, 118–129,
133–138, 145–148, 152, 172, 304,
305, 339, 342, 348, 351, 375–379,
387, 389–391, 393–399, 401–411,
413, 414, 416–419, 423, 424, 426,
427, 432, 449–451, 455–466, 470,
471
FSDR criterion, 13, 14, 451, 455–462,
465–471

gross domestic product (GDP), 235,
236, 283, 331

independent, 1, 21, 30, 70, 74, 75, 81,
92, 101, 103, 104, 107, 110–117,
119, 120, 122, 126, 127, 133, 134,
138, 139, 187, 205, 214, 219, 220,
222, 224–227, 229, 233, 236, 237,
241–243, 246, 251, 253, 255–257,
290, 291, 296–298, 313, 314, 346,
409, 411, 415, 425, 466
inefficient set, 116, 117, 158–160, 375,
382, 387, 455
investment horizon, 1–3, 7, 15–21, 23,
27, 29–33, 37–42, 45–47, 49–55,
59–61, 63, 64, 66, 67, 80–82,
99–109, 111, 116, 117, 126, 128,
134, 136, 146–148, 154, 155, 162,

166, 170–172, 176, 179, 182,
185–187, 190, 194, 197, 200, 203,
209, 211, 213, 215, 217, 224, 226,
228–230, 232–234, 236, 247, 248,
251–253, 263, 266, 269, 270, 282,
286, 288, 291, 294, 323, 328, 329,
332–335, 339, 346, 353, 356, 359,
361, 362, 366, 368–370, 383, 386,
387, 390, 408, 426, 427, 429, 435,
437, 447, 449, 465, 466, 468, 469,
471

Jensen's alpha (JA), 10, 175–177,
179, 180, 183, 204, 206, 211–213,
217, 218, 226, 228, 229

Lagrange multiplier, 248, 249
long term capital management
(LTCM), 330

market portfolio, 82, 85, 86, 91–97,
175, 177, 178, 180, 190, 192,
204–207, 218, 220, 249, 250, 282,
371
mean-variance (M–V), 1, 2, 8, 10–13,
30, 35, 63–66, 67, 69, 70, 81, 86, 87,
91, 92, 96, 97, 101, 105–107,
108–110, 112–122, 127, 133–152,
158–161, 166–169, 171–173,
176–178, 180, 181, 203, 230–235,
242, 243, 245–253, 254–266, 269,
281–283, 286, 302, 303, 327,
334–339, 344, 347–351, 356, 389,
391, 393, 397, 451, 455, 466, 471
multi-period correlation, 11, 233,
235–246, 248, 253, 254, 282
multi-period skewness, 70–72, 74, 75,
77–80, 470
multi-period SSD, 127, 128, 133, 144,
160
multi-period variance, 71, 103, 107,
110–112, 114–116, 139, 144, 159,
161–166, 233, 294, 348, 351

CPSIA information can be obtained
at www.ICGtesting.com
Printed in the USA
JSHW021431200522
25858JS00001B/89